ADVANCED UNIX™
A Programmer's Guide

Stephen Prata

D1604658

Howard W. Sams & Co.
A Division of Macmillan, Inc.
4300 West 62nd Street, Indianapolis, IN 46268 USA

To my sister,
Georgiana

Acknowledgments

Thanks to Michael Lindbeck and to Dan Putterman for UNIX discussions and technical assistance. And to Robert Lafore and Mitchell Waite, thanks for editorial guidance that did much to shape the tone and scope of this book.

Contents

Preface

Advanced UNIX™ encompasses a wide range of topics. This book concentrates on problem solving; it is primarily a book on UNIX™ programming. Since UNIX is an operating system (a very powerful, elegant, comprehensive, and popular operating system), the phrase "UNIX programming" may seem a bit odd. But, unlike most operating systems, UNIX is highly programable. Programming is providing a sequence of instructions to accomplish a given task, and UNIX offers several ways to do that. First, through pipes and redirection, UNIX lets you combine simple UNIX commands into more complex ones. Second, the UNIX shell, a program that acts as an interface between the user and the operating system proper, is programmable. It offers the basic features of most conventional computer languages (variables, loops, decision making), using UNIX commands as its basic building blocks. Third, because UNIX itself is written largely in the C programming language, there is a very extensive interface between the UNIX system and C programs, making C the language of choice for UNIX programming projects.

This book develops these programming strengths of the UNIX system. It takes you from the simple use of single UNIX commands through complex commands to *shell script* programs. It shows you how to write C programs that fit UNIX practice and philosophy and that make full use of the C-UNIX interface. It demonstrates how to integrate the system resources, combining C programs with UNIX commands and shell scripts.

There is a strong emphasis on examples, so that you can see how various programming mechanisms work and try your hand at tinkering with them. Most of the chapters also have questions (with answers at the end of the chapter) so that you can test your understanding as you progress. Additional exercises at the ends of chapters extend the learning process.

The goal of this book is to provide the understanding, skills, and methods you need to make active use of the UNIX system and to find the best solutions to the problems you wish to solve. We of the Waite Group hope the book meets your needs. If you are a relative novice, we hope to make a programmer of you. And if you are a programmer, we hope to make a UNIX programmer of you.

1

INTRODUCTION

In this chapter you will find:

- The Reader
- The Book
- Which UNIX?
- Conventions
- A Last Word

1

Introduction

The goals of this book are to expand your knowledge of the UNIX system, to help you achieve greater mastery of the system, and to illustrate typical UNIX approaches to problem solving. UNIX is an operating system of immense power, and this power can be used in many ways, not all of them obvious. We hope to make you familiar with those abilities of UNIX that go beyond the needs of the occasional user, to the needs of someone who works with UNIX regularly.

In this chapter we will outline the course we will take to reach those goals, and we will discuss some of the assumptions we've made. Let's begin by looking at how we picture you.

THE READER

We think of you as someone who already has been introduced to UNIX, perhaps by *UNIX Primer Plus* by Waite, Martin, and Prata (Indianapolis: Howard W. Sams & Co., 1984) or other introductory text, and who wishes to know more. You know how to log in, how to use at least a few UNIX commands, how to use an editor, how to poke around the directory system, and how to log off. But you wonder about what goes on behind the scenes. What really happens when you type a command name? How does UNIX keep track of its files? What exactly are the *kernel* and *shell*, two terms that always seem to pop up in UNIX discussions?

On a more practical level, you may want to go beyond merely typing single commands. Perhaps you want to learn more about the process of linking commands together in order to accomplish specific tasks. Or perhaps you want to develop your own programs, and you want them to take advantage of the UNIX system.

In short, we assume you are curious about UNIX and want to learn more about it. We don't assume a particularly extensive background in UNIX or in programming in general. However, Chapters 7 through 10 do require that you know the C language to some extent, since those chapters are about writing C programs in the UNIX environment. If your experience in UNIX exceeds what we have described, you still may find much of interest in this book, for it covers a great range of material. We show, for example, how to create an interactive shell script to check spelling and how to create C programs that conform to UNIX practices and philosophy.

What do you need to do to use this book? For one thing, the book is full of examples, and you will help yourself learn by trying them out. Also, there are questions and exercises. Take the time to do them. Experience is a great teacher, so we encourage you to alter the examples and see what happens. If you are as curious about UNIX as we have assumed you are, then we really don't have to tell you that; but there is always the possibility that you are being forced to read this book. So even if you aren't curious, act as if you were, and you will find that you learn better and faster.

Of course, we assume you have access to a UNIX system. There are several versions of UNIX, and we will return to that topic soon. Also, we refer to the UNIX manual every now and then, and you will probably find it useful to have access to a copy. Many UNIX implementations have the manual "online", so you can summon up manual entries at the terminal by using the UNIX *man* command followed by the name of the particular command you wish to study. In addition, many installations have a printed, loose-leaf version available for reference and perhaps for sale. Finally, the manual has been published in book form as *UNIX Programmer's Manual* (2 vols. New York: Holt, Rinehart, & Winston, 1983).

Now let's take a quick look at what this book covers.

THE BOOK

Chapter 2 presents background material about the UNIX system. It discusses the roles of the kernel and of the shell, and it looks into the UNIX treatment of files and of I/O (input/output) devices. This chapter provides a conceptual framework for the more practically oriented chapters that follow it.

Chapter 3 discusses the shell more extensively, reviewing command line structure, shell metacharacters, shell redirection, and other special shell abilities.

Chapters 4 through 6 deal with "shell scripts," which are files consisting of UNIX commands. These scripts let us use UNIX almost like a programming language, complete with I/O control, variables, and control flow structures, such as *if* statements and *for* loops. These chapters show you how to use the Bourne shell to program with UNIX.

Chapters 7 through 10 cover programming in C, tapping into the power of the system by using *system calls* and *library functions*. They show how to make effective use of the C-UNIX interface and how to integrate C programming with shell programming.

Appendix A discusses four UNIX commands (*grep*, *sed*, *tr*, and *awk*) that are particularly useful tools. We use these commands elsewhere in the book, and if you find those uses obscure, you can skip ahead to this chapter.

Appendix B outlines some of the major features of the C shell, an alternative shell developed at the University of California, Berkeley.

Finally, additional appendices supplement the material in the chapters.

WHICH UNIX?

You may be aware that UNIX comes in different flavors. UNIX was developed by Bell Labs of AT&T, and AT&T versions include Version 7 (vanilla), System III, and System V (French vanilla). Then there are versions licensed by AT&T to other vendors. Among the most widespread (and the most altered) of these are the University of California at Berkeley's BSD4.1 and BSD4.2 (chocolate chip) versions. Then there are "look-alikes," operating systems that behave like UNIX but which have independently developed code.

What sort of differences are there among these versions? The more obvious differences include added commands, deleted commands, and changes in the shell. More hidden are differences in internal file management and in hardware control. Most of these differences don't affect the examples we develop in this book. The one major difference we need address is that between the Bourne (or *sh*) shell used by the majority of systems and the *csh* shell used in the BSD releases. These two shells do not work quite the same and do not use the same shell script programming commands. We don't have room to cover both, so we took the simple way out, which is to stick to the Bourne shell. Our main reason for this choice is that BSD versions give the user the option of using the Bourne shell, while the standard AT&T versions do not give the option of using the *csh* shell. Thus Bourne shell scripts can be run on all UNIX systems, while *csh* scripts cannot. We do, however, as we mentioned earlier, provide a brief rundown of the *csh* shell in Appendix B.

There still remain minor differences among systems. For example, the System V *ps* is the same as Version 7's *ps x*. We will try to point out such differences as they arise. Since we can't hope to cover all variations of all versions of UNIX, we will stick to Version 7 and to System V as standards and point out differences between them. If your system seems to respond differently from either, consult the manual for your system. However, this should not happen too often, if at all.

CONVENTIONS

This book uses a special typeface with a computer look for programs. In addition, program lines you must type are printed in black, while green print indicates computer output. For example, an exchange with UNIX could look like this:

```
$ cat file23
The ballooner distrusted the harpooner.
$
```

Within the text, references to commands and filenames look like this: *cat* and *file23*.

A LAST WORD

Don't forget to do the examples. Reading about ideas is no substitute for using them.

2

UNIX OVERVIEW

In this chapter you will find:

2

UNIX Overview

What is UNIX really like? What are the shell and the kernel? How does the system keep track of your files? What actually happens when you type a command name? If you are like most UNIX users, you began your association with UNIX by using some of its basic commands and learning about the UNIX system of files and directories. Most likely, however, you didn't learn too much about what goes on behind the scenes. But now you are a student of advanced UNIX, and to get the most out of UNIX, you need to know more than just how to use commands. In this chapter we will examine how UNIX is put together, and we will meet with concepts and terminology that we will need for the deeper exploration of UNIX that follows in later chapters. In particular, we will look at four main topics: the kernel, the shell, the file system, and input/output.

Although most of this book is of a how-to nature, this chapter is an exception. Instead of telling you how to do things, this chapter tells you how the UNIX system does things. This provides a valuable background, but it makes the chapter lean toward the conceptual and the abstract. If you lean the other direction and are not especially interested in, say, the UNIX file system, you may wish to skim over those parts, coming back to them when you later find you need them. At the minimum, however, you should absorb some idea of the kernel and the shell from this chapter.

Let's take a quick look, then, at the roles of the kernel and the shell before we go into more detail. The kernel is the UNIX operating system. It is the master program that controls the computer's resources, allotting them to different users and to different tasks. However, the kernel doesn't deal directly with a user. Instead, it starts up a separate, interactive program, called a shell, for each user when he or she logs on. The shell then acts as an interface between the user and the system. In its role as command interpreter, the shell takes your commands and sets them up for execution. But it is the kernel that sorts through the clamoring demands of the shells of different users and decides exactly when each requested program runs. Thus, the kernel and your shell collaborate to provide you with UNIX service.

Why is there just one kernel but several shells? The reason for multiple shells is that UNIX can handle more than one user or task at a time. Actually, only one computer "process" goes on at any one moment, but UNIX can switch rapidly from one process (such as your shell) to another (such as someone else's *sort* command), giving the illusion of simultaneous action. The different shells provide a way to separate one user or task from another, while the kernel maintains unified overall control.

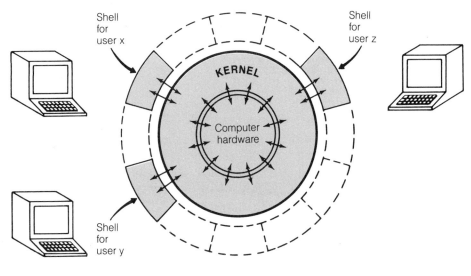

Figure 2.1
The Kernel and the Shells

Now let's move on to a closer look at the kernel.

THE KERNEL

The kernel controls the computer's resources. (That sounds familiar.) When you log in, it is the kernel that runs *init* and *getty* to check to see if you are an authorized user and have the correct password. The kernel keeps track of all the various programs being run, allotting time to each, deciding when one stops and another starts. The kernel assigns storage for your files. The kernel runs the shell programs. The kernel handles the transfer of information between the computer and terminals, tape drives, and printers. In other words, the kernel is what we call an *operating system*. It's the heart of the UNIX system, which is why it is called the kernel.

We will look at some of these kernel duties more closely now.

Time-Sharing and Processes

One of the most important kernel duties is to run the *time-sharing* system. UNIX is a *multiuser*, *multitask* system. Multiuser means that more than one person (or other sentient being) can use the computer at the same time. Multitask means that even a single user can have the computer work on more than one task or program at the same time. In UNIX, each particular task or program that the computer is undertaking is called a *process*. For example, when you run the *date* command, that's one process. If you run it again, then that's a new process.

Question 2.1

When is the *cat* command a process? (The answers to this and to subsequent questions will be found at the end of the chapter. That gives you a chance to think about the question first.)

Normally, a UNIX system has several processes to handle at the same time. However, the computers that use UNIX still have single-track minds; they can only do one thing at a time. This is because they have a single central processing unit. One of the next big advances in computers will be machines with *parallel processing*, that is, machines that can do several tasks simultaneously. However, this is not yet part of the UNIX world.

UNIX uses time-sharing to solve the problem of multiple demands upon a single-track mind. Time-sharing means what it sounds like: the kernel maintains a list of current tasks (or processes) and allots a bit of time to one process, then to the next, and so on, sharing the available time sequentially among the waiting processes. Typically, the kernel switches from one process to the next before the first finishes, so that a process will experience several cycles of time-sharing before completing.

Normally, the kernel switches from process to process so rapidly that each user has the impression that he has the undivided attention of the computer. But should the work load get too heavy, you may find yourself waiting for an eternity (that is, several seconds) between hitting a key and seeing the corresponding letter appear on the screen.

At any one time on a UNIX system, several processes generally are active. The one process that is actually running at a given moment is said to have *run* status. The ones that are waiting their turn usually have *sleeping* status. (There are other gradations of status that we won't go into.) If you want to investigate processes on a UNIX system, you can use the *ps* (*process status*) command. Let's see what that shows us about processes.

The *ps* Command

Try typing *ps* (or *ps x* on some UNIX versions). You should get output that looks something like this:

```
PID TTY TIME COMMAND
2345  12 0:12 sh
2387  12 0:01 ps
```

The *ps* command makes a process status report. The first column is the *PID*, or process identification number. Each time a process is initiated, the kernel assigns to it a unique *PID*. That is how the kernel keeps track of the different processes. (The numbering system starts over after 30000.) In our example, the only two processes are the user's shell itself (*sh*) and the *ps* command. Each, as promised, has its own *PID*. (Looking at the *PID*s, we see that some 41 other processes were created between these two, probably by other users.) Note that from the standpoint of the kernel, your shell is just another process.

If you type the same command again, you get output like this:

```
PID TTY TIME COMMAND
2345  12 0:12 sh
2399  12 0:01 ps
```

Note that the shell has the same *PID* that it did the last time, but that now there is a new *PID* for the *ps* command. The shell *PID* is the same because the same shell process is still handling your interaction with the system. It idled while the previous *ps* was run, then resumed again. However, the *ps PID* is different because the first process expired after producing the first printout. When you repeat the *ps* command, the shell starts a new process with a new *PID* to do the task.

In the computer science world, the *sh* process in this example is called the *parent*, and the two *ps* processes spawned by the shell are the *children*. In a rather macabre vein, the parent is said to wait until the child dies before resuming running status. (Aside from the aspect of creation, the analogy doesn't seem very sound biologically. Also, the usage does give the parental admonition, ''Don't stay out late!'' a chilling connotation.)

Question 2.2

You can start up a new shell by typing *sh*. Then when you give a command, like *date*, it is executed by the new shell. Is that shell a parent or a child?

What about the other headings in our example? The *TTY* column identifies the terminal or other input device that you are using. The *TIME* column tells how much computer time the process has used so far. The *COMMAND* column gives the name of the command corresponding to the process.

So far we have just looked at your processes, but *ps* has options to give fuller listings. The *-l* option provides more information about each process, and the *-e*

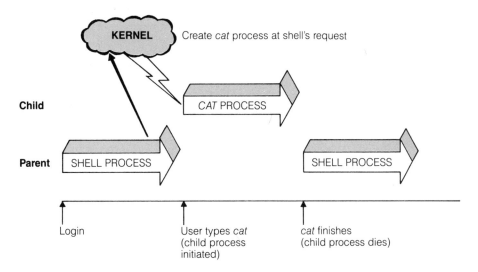

Figure 2.2
Parent and Child

(System V) or *-ax* (Version 7) options tell you about all the processes. The actual format varies from UNIX system to UNIX system. Here is a sample, heavily edited for brevity (several columns and many lines were removed):

UID	PID	PPID ...	STAT	TTY	TIME	COMMAND
0	1	0 ...	I	?	5:59	init
0	55	1 ...	S	?	15:22	/etc/update
0	58	1 ...	I	?	9:08	/etc/cron
0	86	1 ...	I	co	0:00	- 4 (getty)
205	11995	1 ...	S	11	0:07	-sh
205	12127	11995 ...	R	11	0:03	ps axl
0	23051	1 ...	I	18	0:00	- 2 (getty)
207	10927	1 ...	I	19	0:08	-sh
207	12115	10927 ...	S	19	0:11	vi april2

We've omitted much in order to concentrate on just a few points. One point is that the long listing includes status information (*STAT*). The only process running (*R*) is, naturally enough, the *ps* command itself, for it had to be running to produce the report. My shell is sleeping (*S*), waiting for the *ps* to finish. (The *I* status shown by many processes stands for *intermediate*; things can change while the *ps* command is operating.)

The *PPID* column gives the *PID* of the parent process. Thus the *PPID* of the *ps* is 11995, which is just the *PID* of my shell process.

> **Question 2.3**
>
> Which process is parent to the *vi april2* process in the last line of the example?

Next, note that the system is running some processes independently of any user or terminal. These are the ones with a *TTY* value of *?* (no terminal number). The *init* program is part of the system startup, and the other two (*/etc/update* and */etc/cron*) represent tasks that the kernel runs on a continuing basis.

The *getty* command monitors a terminal, waiting for someone to log on.

Although this is a very abbreviated list, it illustrates the process-scheduling aspect of the kernel's duties.

The Kernel and System Calls

Another important aspect of the kernel's duties is that it serves as an interface between the shell and the UNIX commands on the one hand and the system hardware on the other. When you type something at the keyboard, the kernel collects your input and delivers it to the shell. When you use the *cp* command to copy a file, the kernel finds space on the disk (if your system uses a disk for memory storage) for the new file and keeps track of the relevant information, such as the location and size of the file.

The kernel is the part of UNIX that directly communicates with the hardware. Process scheduling and the examples we just mentioned illustrate that. When UNIX is adapted to a new kind of computer, it is the kernel that has to be modified in order to make communication possible. But kernel modification is not something the typical user need worry about, for the kernel insulates the user from direct contact with the hardware. For example, we don't need to know what goes on inside the machine in order to use the UNIX *cp* command. We can even write a new *cp* program without knowing about the innermost secrets of the hardware, for UNIX lets us tap the kernel's power and knowledge through the use of *system calls*.

In UNIX, system calls are basic routines used in the kernel and which you can use in a C program. When you make a system call, the portion of the kernel with the relevent programming is run. If you use a system call to open a file, then the part of the kernel that opens files is invoked in your behalf. Each system call accomplishes a specific basic task. One system call opens a file, another lets you read a file, another closes a file, another launches a new process, and so on. The system calls are part of the kernel and are used to do its work.

The system calls are also the basic building blocks upon which UNIX commands (like *cp*) are based. The programming for a command may use system calls directly by name, or indirectly, by using UNIX library functions that in turn use system calls. As we will discuss in Chapter 7, we too can use system calls in C programs. The important point is that regardless of what computer we use, we can use the same system calls. That is, the hardware instructions for opening a file on a Cray computer may be different from those for opening a file on a Vax or an IBM PC, but for all three (if we use UNIX) we can use the *open( )* system call to do the job. The system call approach helps make UNIX so portable. Reprogram the system calls for a new computer, and they will support the entire UNIX superstructure.

Although the kernel is really the head honcho, you normally deal with its emissary, the shell. It is the interface between you and the computer. To see how the shell works, let's start by examining what happens when you type a command.

RUNNING A COMMAND: THE SHELL

What happens when you type a command such as *date*? The easy answer is that the current time and date appear on your terminal screen, but our real interest is in what goes on behind the screen.

Let's begin at the beginning (a reasonable choice). When you log in, the kernel starts up a program (the shell) that handles your interaction with the system. The shell sends a prompt symbol (typically a *$* for Bell releases or a *%* for BSD releases) to the screen, then waits for input from you. When you type a command, (*date*, for example) and hit the ⌐Return⌐ key, the shell obtains your command, executes it if possible, and returns a prompt to you when it is done and ready for your next command. (The kernel does the actual fetching and returning of data at the request of the shell.) Because the shell translates your typed commands to actions, it is termed a *command interpreter*. (The UNIX shell also is a programming language, as we shall see in later chapters.)

How does the shell go about its task of translating commands? There are a few built-in commands that are part of the shell, but the vast majority of commands are separate programs stored elsewhere in the system. When given, say, the command *date*, the shell searches for a file named *date*. If it finds such a file and if the file contains an executable program, the shell starts the program running and goes into a waiting mode. When the program finishes, the shell resumes. (To accomplish this waiting and resuming, the shell uses the fork-and-wait approach discussed in Chapter 8.)

In looking for the command file, the shell searches through a predefined list of directories given by the *PATH* shell variable. (That will be explained in Chapter 4). Typically this list includes your current working directory and system directories devoted to storing files of commands. The usual directories for this purpose are /*bin* and /*usr*/*bin*. To see what directories are in your search path, just type

echo $PATH

The response will be something like this:

```
.:/bin:/usr/bin
```

Here the colon is used to separate directories, and the period stands for your current working directory. Thus this example instructs the shell to look for a command first in your current directory, then in the */bin* directory, and finally in the */usr/bin* directory. If it doesn't find the command in one of these directories, the shell reports back that the command was not found. Thus for the *date* command, for example, to be recognized, it must be stored in one of the directories in this list.

Question 2.4

What would be the effect of changing the value of *PATH* to

```
.:/usr/della/bin:/bin:/usr/bin
```

Most UNIX commands themselves are compiled C programs, and the remaining few are *shell scripts*, which are files containing other UNIX commands. (In Chapters 4 and 5, we show how to create your own shell scripts, and in Chapter 7 we show how to create C programs.)

A Program Hierarchy

The UNIX system includes a vast number of programs that you can use. We can view them as being arranged in a hierarchy of dependence. The most basic programs are the system calls, which form part of the kernel program. Typically, the programming of a call varies from one hardware system to another, but the name and the function of a system call is the same for all computers running UNIX.

Next, there is a library of programs in the C programming language. (We discuss them along with system calls in Chapter 7.) These C library programs use the system calls to handle the interface between the programs and the hardware. Since different systems have the same system calls, the library, in principle, is portable. That is, once you write a program based on library functions, you can transport it from one UNIX-based machine to another.

Then there are the UNIX commands. They represent the level at which most users deal with UNIX. The commands are programs like *who* and *cat* and *ls* and so on. These commands, for the most part, are written in the C language and use system calls and/or C library programs.

Figure 2.3
The Shell Fetches a Command

Finally, some commands are shell scripts. That is, they are files that contain a list of other UNIX commands. When the shell script command is run, what actually happens is that the list of commands in the file gets run. We will examine shell scripts in the next chapters.

A Brief Synopsis of the Shell Process

In summary, when you log in, the kernel starts a shell process for you. When you type a command, the shell process uses the kernel to start up a process for the corresponding command. Then the shell waits for this new child process to complete and die. Then the shell process resumes running. Each process is assigned its own *PID*. This lets the kernel know which process is which. (Also, we need to know the *PID* in order to use some commands; see *kill* in Chapter 3 for an example.)

The shell has many talents we have not yet discussed. We are saving them for Chapters 3 through 5. There is one more point we would like to emphasize about the shell now, however. The point is this: a separate shell procedure is started up for each user. Your shell doesn't pay attention to Sal's commands, and Sal's shell is unaware of your commands. The time-sharing system makes this possible. If you refer back to the long *ps* listing we showed, you can see that each of the two users shown has his own shell with its own *PID*.

Shell, kernel, system calls, commands — the code for all these programs is stored in files on a UNIX system. Let's take a closer look at the file system now.

FILES AND DIRECTORIES

You are probably familiar with the tree structure of the UNIX file and directory system, but no UNIX book would be complete without a diagram and explanation of it. So we present to you our current version.

In this scheme, every file is assigned to a *directory*. A directory is a specialized form of file that maintains a list of all the files in it. What makes this organizational scheme powerful is that a file in a directory can be a directory itself; it would be called a subdirectory of the original. This capability makes it possible to develop a tree-like structure of directories and files. You can visualize the directories as being the various limbs, branches, and trees, with the files as the leaves attached to them. Each user has a home directory and is free to create her own subdirectories, sub-subdirectories, and so on. There is however an inherent limit on the number of subdirectories — approximately 35; *ls* and other utilities start breaking down at this point; *rm* also chokes, which makes removing such directories difficult. The *root* directory, which is named /, is the prime directory. All other directories are subdirectories. In the UNIX tradition (and in our figure), / is often portrayed as the trunk of a tree — so much for biological verisimilitude.

The tree scheme makes it easy to organize files. You can create one subdirectory for C programs, one for correspondence, one for your research project, etc. These you can further subdivide if necessary. The UNIX *cd* command lets you change from one directory to another. For example, the command

    cd /

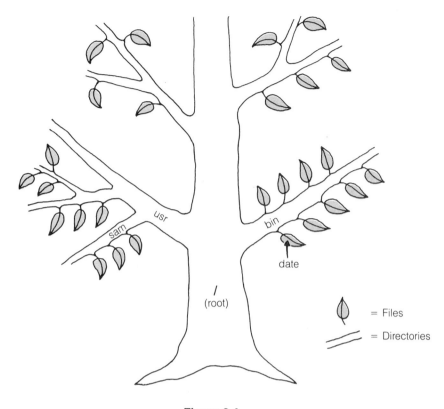

Figure 2.4
The UNIX Directory System

places you in the root directory /, which then becomes your *current working directory*. Another UNIX command, *pwd*, prints out the name of your current working directory in case you forget where you are.

However, the tree scheme does pose a difficulty in identifying files. How do you distinguish, say, between a file called *fig* in your directory and one by the same name in another directory? First, if you just give a simple filename, the shell assumes that you mean a file in your current working directory. But you always have the choice of giving the full *pathname* of the file. This means to precede the name of the file with a list of all the directories leading to it. For example, consider the file *fido* in Figure 2.5.

The full pathname for the file is */usr/nemo/pets/fido*. Here, the first slash (/) stands for *root*, the great trunk of the whole directory system. (All pathnames lead from *root*.) The other slashes serve to separate each directory name from the next, so the pathname leads us from the *root* directory to the *usr* directory to the *nemo* directory to the *pets* directory and finally to the *fido* file.

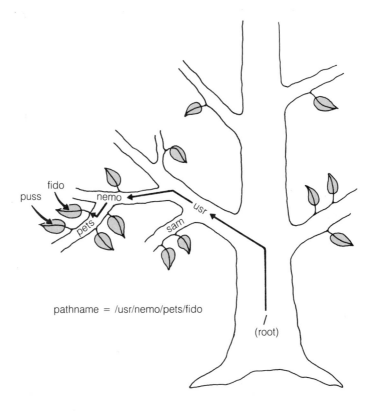

pathname = /usr/nemo/pets/fido

Figure 2.5
Finding *fido*

The tree image provides a helpful way to visualize the file and directory system, but it doesn't reveal what actually goes on when you create a file. (No, UNIX does not scratch out directory drawings on the hard disk.) Let's look at the inside story.

File Creation

Suppose you use an editor to create a file called *oddword* containing the following text.

```
kalakagathia -- a combination of the good and the beautiful in a
person.
```

Several things happen when you create this file in UNIX.

First, the kernel allots space in the computer's memory storage (typically a disk, so we will assume a disk henceforth) to hold the file. There the text is stored one character per byte of memory. (A byte is a unit of memory size. It is a convenient

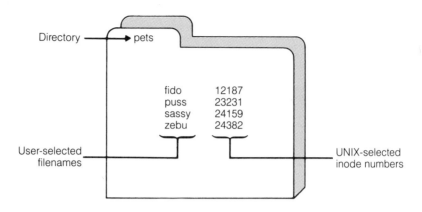

Figure 2.6
Directory Entries for the *pets* Directory

size for storing the code to represent a single letter, digit, or other character.) The file holds these characters (including special characters to represent the spaces and the startings of new lines) and nothing more. The file contains nothing special to mark its beginning or its end or to indicate its name.

This makes for a very simple file structure, but something more is needed to keep track of the file and its properties. That's where the second and third points come in.

Second, an *inode* entry is created on a section of the disk set aside for that purpose. The inode contains nearly all there is to know about the file. This information includes the location on the disk where the file starts, the size of the file, when the file was last used, when the file was last changed, what the various read, write, and execute "permissions" are (that is, permissions detailing who can make what use of the file), who owns the file, and other administrative information. (The inode is where the *ls –l* command gets all that information it prints out about files.) One particularly important item there is the inode number. Each file has its own unique inode number, and it is by this number that the system refers to the file. The only things missing from the inode are the contents of the file and its name.

Third, a directory entry is created. A directory is just a file itself, and each directory entry consists of just two items: the inode number of a file and the user-selected name of that file. When you type something like

```
cat fido
```

in order to display the *fido* file on the screen, the system uses the directory entry to find what inode number corresponds to *fido*. Then the system uses that inode number to locate the file.

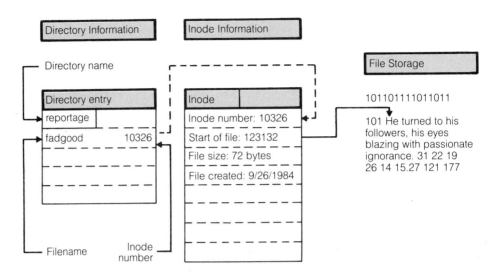

Figure 2.7
Directory Entry, Inode Entry, and File Contents

In short, in this idealized view of the UNIX file system, the contents of a file are stored in one place, most of the relevant information in a second location, and the name in a third. (The reality often is more complex, with a file scattered over several locations, but since the operating system is willing to attend to the grungy details, we'll stick to the idealized view.)

Question 2.5

You create a file called *tonky* in the directory *honky*.

a. What information is stored about *honky* in *tonky*?
b. Later, you add new material to *tonky*. What changes take place in the directory, inode, and file?

Inodes in Action

Let's see how this system works. Suppose you give the command

```
cat oddword
```

The kernel collects this command and passes it to the shell. The shell then starts a *cat* command process. This process causes the kernel to check the directory to find the inode number for the *oddword* file. Next, checking the appropriate inode, the kernel locates the starting point of the file, and the kernel's input/output functions begin transmitting the contents of *oddword* to your terminal. This continues until the number of characters given by the inode's size description has been transmitted. (UNIX uses the size of file to figure out where it ends.) The *cat* process terminates, and the shell uses the kernel to send the prompt back to your terminal.

Why do you need to know about the inodes? If you are just going to use the standard UNIX commands and not create your own programs, you don't need to know about inodes. The system uses the inodes as it processes your demands, but you need never mention them. But if you write C programs that create and manipulate files (as we will do in later chapters), then you may use system calls that deal directly with inodes. At that point, an understanding of inodes is pretty useful. But even if you never deal with inodes, knowing about them will give you the satisfaction of understanding the UNIX system better.

Inode Numbers and Filenames

Let's look more closely at the relationship between inode numbers and filenames.

If you are curious about the inode numbers of your files, you can use the *-i* option of *ls* to display them:

```
$ ls -i oddword
24677 oddword
```

Here the name of the file is preceded by the inode number.

Changing a file or moving it does not change the inode number:

```
$ mkdir newdr
$ mv oddword newdr/kword
$ ls -i newdr/kword
24677 newdr/kword
```

Here we have created a new directory and moved our file to it while changing the filename. As you can see, the inode number is unchanged. However, the original directory will have a new directory entry describing the new *newdr* directory, giving its name and its inode number. And the *newdr* directory will have an entry giving the name and inode number for the *kword* file. (An exception occurs if the file is moved to a different *file system*. A new file system represents a different hardware storage area, as described later. In that case a new file and a new inode number result.)

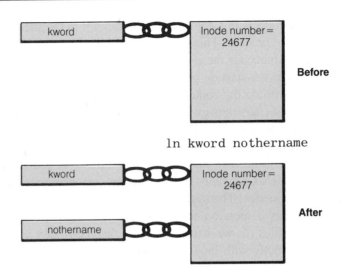

Figure 2.8
In **Assigns Additional Names to a File**

We can think of the filename as providing the user with a link to the true name of the file — the inode number. Indeed that is all the *ln* (link) command does:

```
$ cd newdr
$ ln kword nothername
$ ls -i
24677 kword
24677 nothername
```

Here no new file has been created, and no new inode has been created; *kword* and *nothername* have the same inode number. However, the inode contains one particular entry that lists the number of links, so that particular entry is increased by one. The only other change is that the *newdir* directory now links the name *nothername* with the inode number 24677. Thus the *ln* command allows several different names to indicate the same file and the same inode. If you wish to read or modify the file, you can use any of the names linked to it.

Similarly, the command

```
rm kword
```

serves only to remove that name-number linkage from the directory and to decrease the inode link-count by one. Only when all name links to a file are removed is the storage space in memory freed up and the inode entry removed.

Inside a UNIX File

The file itself, as we have said, is just a series of bytes. Let's examine this idea further.

What's in a file? Text, perhaps, or binary data, or even machine language instructions might be found in a file. Does this mean, then, that a text file is completely different from, say, a binary data file? Not on a UNIX system; there, all files consist of a stream of bytes. When we say that UNIX files consist of a stream of bytes, this means that even if the file consists of, say, 32-bit instructions, the file still can be read 1 byte (8 bits) at a time, breaking the instruction into 4 parts. However, it doesn't have to be read that way. The difference lies not in the file's format, but in the way a program interprets it. A brief discussion of how computers store information will make this clear.

Bits, Bytes, and Words

The fundamental unit of storage in a computer is called a *bit*. We can think of a bit as being able to store just one item, and that item can be either a 0 or a 1. Another basic storage unit is the *byte*, which on nearly all systems consists of 8 bits. Thus a byte can store some combination of eight 0s and 1s; for example, a byte could hold the combination 00100101.

The next storage size is the *word*. It is the natural storage size for a particular machine. For example, a VAX computer has a 32-bit (or 4-byte) word; this is the size of storage unit it is set up to manipulate.

Anything stored in the computer, whether it be numbers, text, or instructions, is stored as a combination of 0s and 1s. A number, for example, can be represented as a binary number, for the binary number system conveniently just uses 0s and 1s. (See Appendix C.) To represent a character (such as the letter ''S'') the computer has to use a code in which a byte-sized binary number is used to represent the letter. The most prevalent code is the ASCII code shown in Appendix D. Machine language instructions, too, are represented by a binary code.

Since numbers, characters, and instructions are all represented by binary numbers, a program that reads a particular part of memory has to know in advance what kind of information is stored there. The same combination of 0s and 1s will have widely different meanings if interpreted as computer instructions instead of as, say, text. Fortunately, the system normally keeps track of these matters for us.

The *cat* program, for example, assumes that a file contains text and treats it accordingly. It looks at the first byte and finds an eight-bit binary number stored there. Then *cat* uses the ASCII code to convert that binary number to a text character. If, for example, the byte contains an 83 (in binary form), then that becomes the character ''S''.

Suppose, instead, that a file contains numerical data stored in pure binary form. Typical UNIX systems use a two-byte (16-bit) or even a four-byte (32-bit) word as a basic storage unit for integers. For example, suppose the number 3115 is stored in a two-byte word in a file. In binary form, the number looks like this:

0000 1100 0010 1011

If we used *cat* to look at this file, *cat* would interpret this single data item as *two* separate character bytes: 000 1100 and 0010 1011. In decimal these correspond to 10 and 43, the ASCII code for a linefeed and the + character, so *cat* would start a new line and print a +. (On most systems, the *low byte*, or last 8 bits of a word, get read first. In that case, the sequence would be printing a + sign and then starting a new line.) On the other hand, a program that is expecting to read a file of two-byte integers will interpret the same two bytes as representing the number 3115.

Since all files are just strings of bytes, the *cat* program has no way of knowing how the contents of a file are meant to be interpreted. So if you *cat* a nontext file, such as a directory or a machine-language program, expect to get a lot of nonsense on the screen display. (This can be a real problem for some graphics terminals that interpret some nontext characters as graphing instructions!)

Inspecting File Contents

Luckily, if you are curious, there is a UNIX command that lets you look into nontext files. It is called *od* (for *octal dump*), and its options let you specify how it should try to interpret file contents. For example, the *-c* option of *od* interprets the file byte-by-byte in ASCII code, using the notation of the C language to represent certain nonprinting characters such as tabs and newlines. The *-b* option also interprets the file byte-by-byte, but as octal (base eight) numbers. The *-d* option, on the other hand, interprets the file word by word, printing the results as decimal numbers. Other options provide further choices. Let's try a few options on a text file containing the hearty phrase "What ho!":

```
$ od -cbd whatho
0000000    W   h   a   t       h   o   !  \n
        127 150 141 164 040 150 157 041 012
            26711   29793   26656   08559   00010
0000011
$
```

The \n is a symbol (borrowed from the C language) for *newline*; it appears at the end of each line in a text file. It causes the cursor to move to the beginning of the next line when the file is printed on the screen, and for paper printers it causes the printing mechanism to begin a new line. The big numbers on the left (0000000 and 0000011) count, in octal, the cumulative number of bytes. Thus the 0000011 is 9 in decimal, and equals the number of characters in the file. (Spaces and newline characters are counted, too.) Under each character is the corresponding octal ASCII code; thus the space character is 040 in octal, or 032 in decimal. The next line contains a decimal number corresponding to two-byte words. For example, 26711 represents the W and the h above it. (If you are a stickler for detail, you may notice that this machine uses the low-byte first system we mentioned earlier. Thus ''26711'' actually corresponds to the sequence ''hW'', and the ''W'' gets read first.)

File Security — Read, Write, and Execute Permissions

We have just seen a couple of ways you can inspect your files. Suppose someone else on your UNIX system wants to investigate your files. Can they? That is up to you, for UNIX allows you to specify who can and who cannot use your files.

UNIX divides the universe of users into three categories: the user (you), members of your group, and others. This choice reflects the research environment in which UNIX developed. There, those working on a common project could be assigned to the same group and share access to each other's files. More generally, the system administrator decides who goes into which group.

For each of these three divisions, the system keeps track of three sorts of *permissions*: read, write, and execute. If you possess read permission for a file, you can read it. You can, for example, use commands that read a file without altering it, such as *cat* or *cp*. Write permission allows you to alter a file. For example, it allows you to edit or delete a file. Execute permission lets you run a file containing a program.

All told, then, there are nine permissions, three each for three categories of users. To find what they are for a file, list the file using the *-l* option of *ls*. Typically, the results look something like this:

```
$ ls -l purfekt
-rw-r--r-- 1 glibomen            28939 Jan 16 12:32 purfekt
$
```

Information about permissions is contained in the ten-character string beginning the output. The first character (a hyphen here) specifies the type of file; we'll return to that topic later in the chapter. The next three characters (here *rw-*) tell us what permissions are *set* for the user. In this case the user has read (*r*) and write (*w*) permissions, but no execute permission. The hyphen marks the place the *x* would appear if execute permission were set. The next group of three characters (*r--*) indicates the permission that other members of the user's group have, and the final set of three (also *r--*) indicates permissions for everyone else. Here both of these groups can read the *purfekt* file, but cannot alter it.

This combination (*rw-r--r--*) is the one that most UNIX systems provide by default. The system administrator, however, can alter that file-creation default and, as we will describe in Chapter 8, you can override that default. In the meantime, let's see how you can change the permissions for existing files.

UNIX lets you set each permission of a file individually. The tool is the *chmod* (*ch*ange *mode*) command. This command actually offers two ways to change permission. One is the *symbolic* mode, which lets you add or delete permissions. To use it, you follow the *chmod* command with an instruction string followed by the filenames to be affected. The basic instruction string has three parts. The first part consists of one or more letters indicating the groups affected; *u* is *user*, *g* is *group*, and *o* is *other*. Next, a + or - sign indicates whether permissions are to be set to *yes* or to *no*. Finally, a string of one or more characters indicates the permissions that are affected: *r* is *read*, *w* is *write*, and *x* is *execute*. For example, to give members of your group write permission for the *oddities* file, you can give this instruction:

```
chmod g+w oddities
```

If you later decide you don't want anyone else to read or write on your file, you can give this command:

```
chmod go-rw oddities
```

Note that this is a valid command even if *others* never had write permission to begin with. And if you want to protect yourself from accidentally erasing this file, you can give this command:

```
chmod u-w oddities
```

Question 2.6

How could you restore write permission for yourself and for other group members for the file *oddities*?

The second way to use *chmod* is the *absolute* mode. Instead of telling *chmod* which permission you wish added or deleted, you simply specify what the permissions should be. This is done by providing *chmod* with a three-digit octal number.

The first digit sets the user permissions, the second digit sets the group permissions, and the final digit sets the permission for others. A command could look like this:

```
chmod 640 eggman
```

In this method, a *4* means read permission, a *2* means write permission, and a *1* means execute permission. To indicate multiple permissions, just add the permission numbers together. Thus, in the example above, the user has read and write (*4 + 2 = 6*) permissions, the group has read permission (4), and others have no permissions (0).

Question 2.7

What command would give you read, write, and execute permissions, give group members read and execute permissions, and give others just read permission for the file *foop*?

We'll look at *chmod* again in Chapter 8. Meanwhile, let's turn from file permissions to file systems.

File Systems — What Are They?

The UNIX manual tells us that *ln* (link) cannot link across file systems. That's nice to know, but it would be even nicer if we knew what the phrase *file system* meant in this context. The answer has to do with how files and inodes are stored on a system. What happens is that a disk or portion of a disk is set aside to store files and the inode entries. The entire functional unit is termed a *file system*. This chunk of disk memory is divided into *blocks* typically 512 bytes in size. (System V uses 1024-byte blocks, and BSD4.2 uses 4096-byte and 8192-byte blocks.) These blocks are organized into three groupings. The first group consists of block 1 and is called the *super block*. It contains information about that particular file system. For example, it tells how many blocks are in the entire system, how many blocks are devoted to inodes, and how many blocks are free. The second group consists of the blocks devoted to inodes, and the third and final portion of the file system consists of blocks for storing the files themselves. If you want a complete discussion of this file system structure, you can read the *FS* entry in Section 4, Volume 1 of the UNIX manual (System V) or the *FILSYS* entry in Section 5 (Version 7).

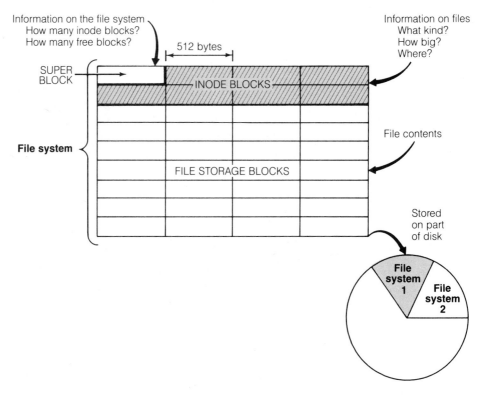

Figure 2.9
A File System

Multiple File Systems

Usually the entire UNIX set of files and directories uses more than one such file system unit. Even a single-disk system may have the disk partitioned into subsections, with one file system per subsection. The root directory and the essential system files are kept together in one file system, but the rest may be spread over several other file systems. When a UNIX system is started up (*booted*), the root file system is automatically included. The other file systems, however, need to be *mounted* to the root system. In effect, the chief directory of the mounted system becomes a subdirectory of root; it's like grafting a many-limbed branch to a tree trunk. To the user, the joins are nearly invisible. When you use *cd* or *cp*, it makes no difference what particular file system contains the files and directories you name. However, it does make a difference to the *ln* command. Since a directory is a file in a particular file system, any links in that directory can only be to inodes in the same system. And that is the meaning of the caution from the UNIX manual with which we opened this section: you cannot link across file systems.

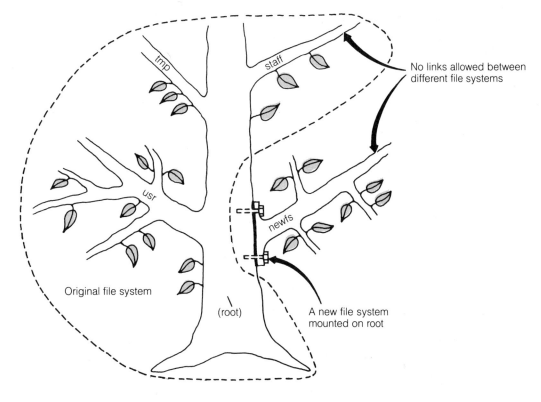

tmp

staff

No links allowed between
different file systems

usr

newfs

Original file system

(root)

A new file system
mounted on root

Figure 2.10
A Mounted File System

Checking File Systems

You can use the *df* (disk free) command to see what file systems your system has. (In System V documentation, the description of this command and the following *mount* command are in the Administrator's Manual. The Version 7 documentation describes them in Volume 1, Section 1, the usual section for commands.) The *mount* command not only lists all the file systems, it also tells you how much space is available in each:

```
$ df
/dev/hp0a 1820
/dev/hp0b 12321
/dev/hp1a 24129
/dev/hp1b 6578
```

Here we find four file systems. The first has 1820 free blocks of memory. At 512 bytes per block, this means the first file system has about 900 kilobytes free. The *hp* indicates a particular kind of disk drive; your system may use *rp* or some other notation. Typically, the root system would be listed first.

Question 2.8

How many file systems does your UNIX installation have?

The */dev* in the name tells us we are dealing with a device. The *hp* indicates a certain kind of disk drive. The digit (0) tells us this is the first disk drive (the numbering starts with "0"), and the following letter (a) tells us we are dealing with the first file system on the disk. Similarly, */dev/hp0b* refers to the second file system on the first disk drive; and */dev/hp1a* is the first file system on the second disk drive. Some systems use a second digit instead of a letter to label the different partitions of a disk. And a different labeling scheme may be used for the disk drives themselves.

To find what directory names are associated with the other file systems, use the command */etc/mount*. (The */etc* directory is not part of the usual command search path that we mentioned earlier, so we have to use the the full pathname of the command file.) This command lists each mounted file system and its main directory name:

```
$ /etc/mount
hp0b on /usr
hp1a on /staff
hp1b on /newsys
```

This means, for example, that all the subdirectories and files stemming from */usr* are stored physically on the second partition of the first disk drive.

Let's alter course a bit and note that the name */dev/hp0a* seems to suggest two separate ideas. First, the name format is just that of any file pathname, suggesting that */dev/hp0a* is a file. But the actual words (*dev* and *hp*) suggest that we are dealing with a device. Both of these implications are true, for UNIX treats devices as files. We will explore this concept next.

PERIPHERAL DEVICES AND UNIX: SPECIAL FILES

Each device connected to a UNIX system is represented by a file in the */dev* directory. To get an idea of the contents of that file, we can use the *-l* option of *ls*. To refresh your memory about this option, let's use it first on a regular directory

```
$ ls -l
-rw-r--r--        2 francine      2439 Jun 18 12:53 canoe
-rw-r--r--        1 francine      8732 May 22 14:11 fido
drwxr-xr-x        2 francine       512 May 29 09:42 Funding
-rwxr-xr-x        1 francine      7820 Jun 14 10:35 mpgave
```
    Mode   Number File owner   File size Date last altered   Filename
           of links   in bytes

Figure 2.11
ls –l

containing a subdirectory and some ordinary files. In this case we get results like those shown in Figure 2.11.

The output begins with a 10-character string of dashes and letters called the *mode*. If the first character is a ''d'', then the file is a directory. If the first character is a ''-'', then the file is an ordinary file. The next 9 characters in the string describe the file permissions we discussed earlier. The first set of three characters, recall, refers to the user, the second set to other members of the user's group, and the third set to everyone else. An ''r'' in the first position within each set indicates permission to read the file, a ''w'' in the second position indicates permission to write in the file, and an ''x'' in the third position indicates permission to execute the file. (In this case, the file should be a program of some sort or else a directory. Execute permission for a directory allows one to search it.) A ''-'' in any of these locations indicates nonpermission. For example, everyone is allowed to read the *fido* file, since an ''r'' appears in all three groupings. However, only *francine* can write in it, since only the user group has the ''w'' set.

Question 2.9

Who can run the *mpgave* program in Figure 2.11?

Next in the listing comes a number showing the number of links to the file. The *canoe* file, for instance, has two links. (The other link is in a different directory). This is followed by the name of the owner of the file. Then comes the size of the file in bytes, the date the file was last modified, and finally the name of the file. (The *ls –l* command searched the inode entries to get much of this information.)

Now let's apply the same *ls –l* command to the */dev* directory; Figure 2.13 shows the result. (We've edited the output considerably in order to reduce repetition of devices.)

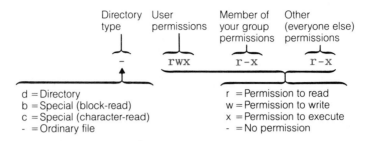

Figure 2.12
The Mode

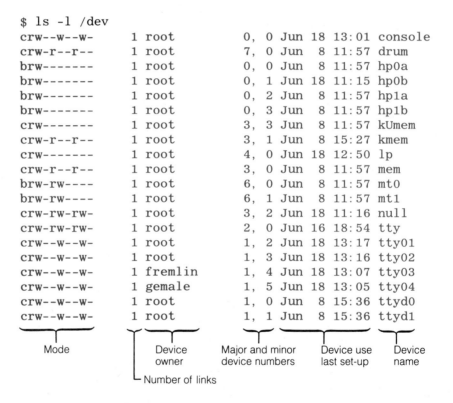

Figure 2.13
ls –l /dev

We have a variety of devices listed. The most numerous devices are the terminals; they are *tty0*, *tty1*, and so on. The *hp* entries are disk drives, *mt* indicates a tape drive, and *lp* is a printer. (Your system will probably have different devices and labels but the idea will be the same.)

The *ls –l* output for */dev* is slightly different from the one for regular files. First, the first character of the mode string is a *c* or a *b* rather than a - (hyphen) or a *d*. These label the devices as *character-devices* (*c*), like the terminals, and *block-devices* (*b*), like the tape drives. The distinction is between devices that transmit data character by character (*c*) and those that use blocks of data (*b*), typically 512- or 1024-byte chunks. The presence of either of these labels alerts UNIX that the file is a ''special file,'' one associated with a device.

The second new point is that the size parameter in the listing is replaced by a pair of numbers separated by a comma. The two numbers are, respectively, the *major* and the *minor* device numbers. The major number identifies the type of device, and the minor number labels the individual specimens of that type.

This new information (file-type and device numbers) is stored in the inodes for these special files. Thus when the kernel inspects the inode, it learns that it is dealing with a device, and it sees what kind of device it is.

We see, then, that devices are indeed represented as files. But calling a device a file doesn't make it one. How can a terminal actually be treated the same as a file? We will look at that question next.

The Device as a File

To see the similarity between how ordinary files and devices are handled, let's compare the following two commands:

```
cat justafile
cat /dev/tty5
```

The first command looks at an ordinary file, and the second command looks at the file representing our terminal, *tty5*. (How do we know that's our terminal? We use the *tty* command, which reports back which terminal we are on.)

In the first example, as we saw earlier, the kernel uses the current working directory to find the inode number of the file *justafile*. It looks in the corresponding inode, checks the mode entry, and learns that *justafile* is just an ordinary file. It finds where the beginning of the file is and what its size is. Then kernel I/O subroutines ''open'' the file and pass its contents to the *cat* function. When all the bytes are passed and processed, the program ties up loose ends (such as ''closing'' the file) and terminates.

In the second example, the kernel uses the */dev* directory to find the inode number of the file *tty5*. It looks at the corresponding inode and learns that *tty5* is a terminal. The kernel then makes the appropriate I/O connections with the terminal, and kernel I/O subroutines transmit keyboard-generated bytes (that is, the characters you type) to the *cat* function. Finally, when you type a Control D at the beginning of a line, the program finishes up its work and terminates.

As you can see, the two cases are very similar. The chief difference is in how the system decides when *cat* is finished. With the ordinary file, the method is very simple. The kernel knows from the inode how many bytes are in the file, so the process ends when exactly that many bytes have been transmitted to *cat*. But in the second case, using the keyboard, the computer doesn't know in advance how many characters you will type, so keeping track of the total number of characters will not suffice. Instead, the Control D at the beginning of the line acts as a stop signal, but how does that work? To answer that, we need to see how keyboard input works.

Buffered Keyboard Input

Normally, UNIX systems use what is known as *buffered* keyboard input. This means that the characters you type are saved in a temporary storage area (a buffer) until you hit the Return key. This gives you a chance to correct typing errors before transmitting. When you do hit the Return key, the input you typed is collected by *read*, one of the system calls we will discuss in Chapter 7. The important point here is that *read* tells the system how many characters it has read. For example, the line

$ troll Return

results in *read* reporting that it has read six characters, the five letters in *troll* and a *newline* character produced by the Return.

The Control D key also causes the buffer contents to be transmitted, but Control D produces no transmitted character of its own. Thus the sequence

$ troll Control D

causes *read* to report that it read just 5 characters, not 6. And the sequence

$ Control D

causes *read* to report that it has read no characters. This (''no characters read'') is the signal to the kernel that it is finished reading the special file, in this case, the keyboard.

We should note that it is the kernel that sees to getting a series of bytes to the *cat* program. All *cat* sees is the series of bytes being fed to it. It neither knows nor cares whether those bytes come from a file, a terminal, or some other source.

Special File Permissions and Ownership

If you refer back to the *ls –l* listing of */dev* (Figure 2.12), you will note that each device has read, write, and execute permissions, just as files do. (However, one can't execute a device, no matter how objectionable its behavior may be, so the execute permissions are set to –.) Each device also has an owner, usually *root*. But when you use a terminal, you become the owner of that terminal. Note that mode string for a terminal is

```
crw--w--w-
```

This usually means that only the owner can read a terminal. Thus you don't normally have to worry about someone stealing the contents off your screen. (Some terminals have *block mode* and represent a classic security hole, first discovered at UCB in 1981.) However, you do have to worry about someone adding to your screen, since everyone has write permission for your terminal! Actually, this permission is needed so that others can use the *write* command to communicate with you. Of course, they can also do things like

```
cat bigjunkfile > /dev/tty5
```

and flood your screen with garbage (or computer art). You can always use the *chmod* or the *mesg n* command to turn off write permissions for others, thus protecting yourself from these outside interruptions. If you don't do this before someone starts to communicate with you, you have to wait until the damage has been done. While it's taking place, there isn't much that you can do.

There are a couple of device files in */dev* that merit special mention; we turn to them now.

Two Special Devices: */dev/tty* and */dev/null*

These two device files share the peculiar property that they don't correspond to a definite physical device. The first one, */dev/tty*, serves as a synonym for the terminal that you are using. That is, if you are on *tty5*, then the following two commands have the same effect:

```
ls > /dev/tty5
ls > /dev/tty
```

The main use of the synonym comes when you write a program. If, for example, you use redirection to */dev/tty* in a program, then that program can be used on any terminal, since it interprets *dev/tty* to be whatever terminal is actually being used. For instance, a shell script could contain the following line:

```
echo You cannot do that > /dev/tty
```

Then whoever used that shell script would get the message "You cannot do that" sent to his or her terminal. We'll see the importance of this technique later, when we get into shell scripts.

The second device, */dev/null*, is not much. Everyone has permission to read it and to write to it. Its chief use is as a place to dump unwanted output. A typical example is when you want to time a command and aren't concerned with the exact output. For example, you wish to compare the sorting speed of two different programs without going through the time-consuming process of sending the output to your screen:

```
$ time sort1 bigfile > /dev/null

real            2.9
user            1.4
system          0.9
$ time sort2 bigfile > /dev/null

real            10.2
user            6.4
system          1.4
$
```

(The results of the *time* command still come to the screen, for this command uses the standard error instead of the standard output to express its results. We'll discuss the standard error and the standard output in Chapter 4.)

In summary, UNIX treats devices as files. Each device has a corresponding file in the */dev* directory. The inodes for these files control the identification and the use of the devices. Use of devices is controlled by the same permission scheme used for regular files.

CONCLUSION

We have looked at the UNIX system in order to acquire a general idea of how it functions. In particular we have looked at the roles of the shell and of the kernel, we have looked at how files and directories are put together, and we have viewed UNIX I/O. Let's summarize the main points.

The shell is an interactive program that acts as an interface between you and the UNIX system. In its role as a command interpreter, it takes your commands and launches their execution by initiating the appropriate processes (running programs). Once your request is finished, the shell comes back for your next command.

The kernel is the master program that controls the computer's resources. It shares time among the various processes (including user shells) clamoring for attention. It maintains the file system, allots storage, and controls I/O.

Files themselves are simple streams of bytes. The file system contains file information in three places. The file itself contains just the data placed into it. The corresponding inode contains most of the relevant information about the file (location, size, number of links, dates of use, and so on). A directory links the user-selected name for the file with the internal name, the inode number.

I/O devices are associated with special files in the /dev directory. Programs can use files and I/O devices interchangeably for input and output; for either case, the program just sees the stream of bytes flowing into or out of it, neither knowing nor caring about the source or destination.

Now that we have some idea about how UNIX is put together, let's look at strategies for using what is there. That will be the next chapter's topic.

ANSWERS TO QUESTIONS IN CHAPTER 2

2.1 The *cat* command is a process when it is being used as a command, as in *cat me*. The file storing the *cat* program is not a process.

2.2 It is both. It is parent to *date* and child to the original shell.

2.3 The shell with the *PID* of 10927 is the parent.

2.4 This would cause the shell to look in the */usr/della/bin* directory after looking in the current directory and before looking in the */bin* directory when searching for a command file.

2.5 **a.** Just the name of the file (*tonky*) and the inode number for the file.

    b. The directory entry is unchanged, since the name and inode number remain unchanged. In the inode file, the file size, time of last access, and time of last modification are updated. In the file itself, the new material is added.

2.6 chmod ug+w

2.7 chmod 754 foop

2.8 You'll have to find out yourself; type *df* and see.

2.9 Everyone

3

PROBLEM-SOLVING APPROACHES IN UNIX

In this chapter you will find:

3

Problem-Solving Approaches in UNIX

When you use a computer, you usually have a goal or two in mind. You may wish to learn more about the system, play a game, write a program to calculate cometary orbits, edit a letter, write a business report, prepare a spreadsheet, do some file housekeeping, communicate with electronic mail, work on a group project, analyze an opinion poll, or do all of the above. An operating system offers you a work environment for satisfying your goals.

UNIX offers a superior environment for you to use. It has the usual file-handling commands found in most operating systems, and it has dozens of commands that are not standard equipment on most operating systems. For instance, there are commands that count words, search for strings, time programs, check spelling, format text and equations for typesetting, and convert EBCDIC files to ASCII files. Then UNIX provides ways to use its many commands as building blocks from which to construct new commands. The UNIX shell even lets you program, using the basic UNIX commands as elements of high-level programming language.

With all this versatility, the UNIX system offers several approaches to problem-solving. They range from the very simple to the complex, and the approach you use will depend on the problem and on your own knowledge. In this chapter we will outline the main approaches to forming UNIX solutions.

The simplest approach is to find a UNIX command that directly solves a problem. If, for example, you have a list of names to sort alphabetically, you don't have to develop a sorting program. Just use the UNIX *sort* command. Or if you want to check the spelling in a report, just use the UNIX *spell* command.

If you can't find a UNIX command that solves the problem directly, look for an appropriate combination of commands. If, for example, you wish to extract from the file *greatfood* those lines containing ''Fresno'' and have those lines arranged alphabetically, you can use the UNIX command *grep* to do the first part and *sort* to do the second. By using the UNIX pipe facility, you can even combine these two into one command:

```
grep Fresno greatfood | sort
```

This really is a form of programming, using UNIX commands as the basic programming elements to construct a compound command that does something that neither command can do alone. Ordinary programming languages manipulate variables and operators (like addition and multiplication operators); the UNIX shell manipulates files and commands.

A more complex problem may require that you carry the UNIX programming concept a step further and develop a *shell script* (or *shell procedure*). This is a file of UNIX commands that is used as a program to tell the shell what to do. UNIX allows you to use standard programming structures like loops and branching in shell scripts, so this approach is a powerful, flexible one. A shell script also gives you a simple way to save and use a frequent combination of commands.

Sometimes a shell script won't solve a problem or else will solve it too slowly. In that event, you can use a standard programming language. The obvious choice on a UNIX system is the C language, since UNIX is written in C and the UNIX system calls and library functions are available to C programs as ordinary C functions, easily accessed.

These, then, are the four approaches to problem solving that we will outline in this chapter: single command solutions, combined command solutions, shell script solutions, and C program solutions.

In solving a problem, your usual plan of attack should be to try the first approach first, and then the second, and so on, using the simplest technique that suffices. (We won't always follow that advice in this book. The basic UNIX commands accomplish so much that strict adherence to our advice would cut into the stock of simple examples we use to illustrate the other approaches.)

We can wrap up the first two approaches to problem solving rather quickly. It will take most of the remaining chapters, however, to explore the final two approaches. We begin with the single-command approach.

USING SINGLE UNIX COMMANDS TO SOLVE PROBLEMS

This seems to be a simple enough method: find a command that solves your problem and use it. There are a couple of sticking points, however. First, there are hundreds of UNIX commands, and most of these commands have options available, yielding thousands of possibilities. Thus it is quite possible that there may be a UNIX command tailor-made for what you wish to do, and you may not know about it! Second, you have to know how to use the command correctly. One solution to these problems is to browse through the UNIX manual, scanning the command descriptions and reading in depth about the ones that interest you. Because the manual is rather concise and abstruse, reading it with understanding is an acquired ability. Therefore we will take a look at the science of UNIX manual reading. The manual assumes you are familiar with the general procedures for using a command, so let's begin by reviewing the structure of a UNIX command line.

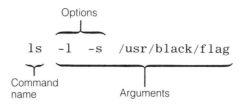

Figure 3.1
A Command Line

The UNIX Command Line

The simplest command lines consist just of a single command name, such as *date* or *who*. Usually, however, you will follow the command name with one or more *arguments*. These arguments provide additional information for the command. Often, these arguments are filenames or directory names:

```
mv thurst thrust
cd /usr/include
```

Here we provided the *mv* command with the filenames it needs, and we gave the *cd* command a directory name to use.

Another type of argument is the ''option,'' which modifies the behavior of a command, telling, for instance, the *sort* command to sort in reverse order. The UNIX tradition (not always upheld) is that options are marked with a leading hyphen. This makes it simple to tell an option from a filename:

```
sort -r giftlist
```

Here *giftlist* is a filename argument, and the *-r* is the reverse-order option for sort. (Try not to use filenames beginning with hyphens; a file called *-r* could sorely confuse *sort*.)

A command may have several arguments; they should be separated from one another by spaces or tabs:

```
ls -l -s   /usr/black/flag
```

When you use both option arguments and file or directory arguments in the same command, the usual rule is that the options should come first. There are exceptions, however, for UNIX is no slave to petty consistency. The command description in the manual, of course, is your guide in such matters.

When several options are used, they can often be strung together on one hyphen:

```
ls -lsa
```

However, this is not always the case. This is another matter you can glean from the manual on a command-by-command basis.

The command line normally ends (where else?) at the end of the line. When you hit the ⎡Return⎤ key, everything up to that point is taken to be the command line. If you want to extend the command to the next line, precede the ⎡Return⎤ key with a backslash:

```
$ ls -i good better \ Return
> best Return
12341 good
34212 better
24215 best
$
```

The secondary prompt (>) indicates that the command is being continued to the next line. (We show the ⎡Return⎤ key explicitly so that you can see exactly when to hit it.)

Question 3.1

What, if anything, is wrong with each of the following commands?

a. ls -l-s
b. cat file1, file2
c. ls - s Factdir

We'll have more to say about command lines when we discuss multiple commands, but let's turn now to advice on reading the UNIX manual.

Exploring The UNIX Manual

The UNIX manual provides the final word on what each command does and on how to use the command; the manual is a major resource, and understanding the manual is a major asset. The UNIX manual comes in two forms: the printed manual and, stored on the system, the "on-line" manual. The precise contents of either form, of course, vary from one version of UNIX to another, but the various versions share the same general form. The regular commands are found in Volume 1, Section 1 of the UNIX manual written by Bell Lab's staff. The manual is usually supplied in loose-leaf form to the purchasers of a UNIX system, and is also available

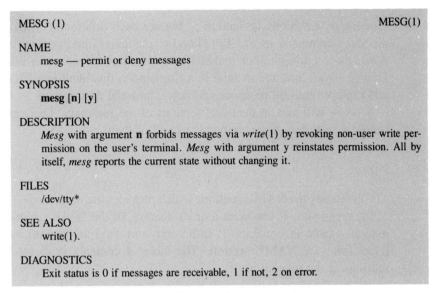

Figure 3.2
UNIX Manual Entry for *mesg*

in book form (*UNIX Programmer's Manual,* 2 vols. New York: Holt, Rinehart, & Winston, 1983). We will take our excerpts from the System V version, but all share the same format.

To use the online form, type *man* and the name of the command you wish to study. For example, to learn about *cat*, type the following command:

```
man cat
```

The online form is useful for checking on commands you already know, but it is ill-suited for browsing, since you have to know the name of the command you want to see. For browsing, you can use the printed manual.

To use the printed manual, seat yourself comfortably, resting the manual in your lap, on a table, or on a desk. (You may wish to develop your own style in this matter. Or your style may be dictated by a manual chained in place.) Now turn through the pages. You will note that the commands are arranged alphabetically, with numbers preceding letters. (Thus, *f77* is listed before *factor.*) You will also notice that the various entries share identical formats. Figure 3.2 shows a typical entry. Let's examine the format.

The Heading

At the top of the page we see MESG(1). The ''MESG'' is obviously the capitalized name of the command. The ''(1)'' indicates the entry is from Section 1 of the manual. Some commands have the same name as system calls in Section

2 or library functions in Section 3, but are used differently. Thus we can refer to the *sleep* command as *SLEEP(1)* and to the *sleep* library function as *SLEEP(3)*. Also, the section number makes it easy to refer to entries in different sections. Finally, if you have the manual in a ring binder, this identification of section helps you replace removed pages or add new command descriptions.

Now we will look at the titled sections of the summary. There are nine possible headings, but very few commands use all of them.

Name

First comes the NAME section, which provides the name and a brief description of the command. If you want a quick scan of all the UNIX commands, check the manual's table of contents. It lists each command along with its description as taken from the NAME section. The table of contents is divided into the same sections as the manual itself.

Synopsis

Next comes the SYNOPSIS section, which shows exactly how the command is used. This is the most concise portion of the manual format, and it requires the most explanation. The manual has several conventions for this section. Here they are:

- Material in boldface is to be typed literally, just as it appears in the manual. If an argument is not in boldface, you substitute the particular value, filename, etc., that you wish to use. For instance, the entry for *what* says

what files

When using this command, you type *what* literally, but you substitute for "files" the actual filenames you use:

```
what foogel.c  a.out
```

- Square brackets indicate optional arguments. Thus *mesg* can have *y* as an argument, *n* as an argument, or no argument at all. On the other hand, *what* as shown above must have at least one argument, since "files" is *not* enclosed in brackets.
- Ellipses (. . .) indicate that the previous argument can be repeated. For instance, *cat* has this synopsis:

cat [**-u**] [**-s**] file . . .

This means that one *or more* files can be concatenated with one command. (The usages "files" and "file . . ." have the same meaning.) Note that **-u** and **-s** are in boldface, meaning that they are to be typed literally if they are used.

- The word *name* is understood to denote a filename:

diffmk name1 name2 name3

There are refinements to these basic rules. Often several options will be lumped together within one bracket pair:

ls [**-logtasdrucifp**] name . . .

This means that any number of these option letters can be strung after the same hyphen:

```
ls -lasr backup
```

Bracketing options separately suggests that they cannot be strung together. This may be because they are mutually exclusive, as in

cmp [**-l**] [**-s**] file1 file2

where one option gives an extended output, and the other suppresses the output altogether. Or it may be that the options themselves require additional data, as in

eqn [**-d**xy] [**-p**n] [**-s**n] [**-f**n] [files]

Here the **-d** is to be typed literally, but you will need to read the manual entry for *eqn* further to find what the "xy" after the **-d** represents.

You can have "nested" brackets. For example, the synopsis for *sort* includes this combination:

[**+***pos1* [-*pos2*]] . . .

(In the description section for *sort* we learn that "pos1" and "pos2" are numbers identifying fields.) The nested brackets mean that the option, if present, can be something like *+3*, which is just the outer bracket, or else *+3 –5*, which includes the inner bracket. The ellipses indicate that the entire pattern of plus and minus numbers can be repeated, as in

```
+3 -5 +1 -3
```

Here, $+3 -5$ describes the first sorting field, and $+1 -3$ describes the second sorting field.

Sometimes, when the quantity or variety of options gets out of hand, you will see a SYNOPSIS entry like this:

cc [options] . . . files . . .

In this case the DESCRIPTION section of the manual will detail the options and their effects.

Question 3.2

An as yet hypothetical UNIX command has this synopsis:

klutz [**-qms**] [**-x**] file1 file2

Which ones of the following uses are invalid? Why?

a. `klutz drumpy`
b. `klutz -qm tom tap`
c. `klutz -qx drin krin`
d. `klutz -s-x ace two`

Description

Because many people have contributed to the ranks of UNIX commands and because these commands have such a varied range of applications, some commands are not easily accommodated by the synopsis format. So be prepared to read through the DESCRIPTION section.

The DESCRIPTION follows the SYNOPSIS. Here the command is described tersely and its options outlined. On first reading, you may not always find the descriptions entirely intelligible. But you have another resource at your behest: the experimental method. Put together a small test file or two (if required), and try out the command and its options. Using the command is the real thing; descriptions are abstractions.

Example(s)

Some (all too few) entries include an EXAMPLE(S) segment. When an example is given, it usually tends to provide a rather complex application of the command.

In some cases, such as the following two, the examples may require careful thought to decipher fully:

find / \(-name a.out −o −name *.o\) −atime +7 −exec rm {}\;
sort −u +0f +0 list

But trying the example out, perhaps selectively varying it, can teach you much about a command.

Files

Some commands have a FILES section. This section lists system files used by the command. For instance, the *mesg* command of our example uses the various */dev/tty* files since it controls the *write* permission in the file governing your terminal.

See Also

The SEE ALSO section found with some commands points out related commands and information. Note how our *mesg* example refers to *write(1)*, not just *write*, thus indicating the proper section to read.

Diagnostics

The next potential heading is DIAGNOSTICS. This section is intended to help you unravel problems using the command. Sometimes potential error messages are explained. In our *mesg* example, the ''exit status'' of the command is discussed. This is a matter we will discuss further in Chapter 5.

Warnings

Then the command summary may continue with WARNINGS to point out potential pitfalls. For example, the entry for *cat* warns you against such constructions as

cat file1 file2 > file1

pointing out that this destroys the contents of *file1* before concatenating *file1* and *file2*.

Bugs

Finally, the *man* entry may conclude with a BUGS section which points out known failings or restrictions of the command. For instance, the entry for *sleep*

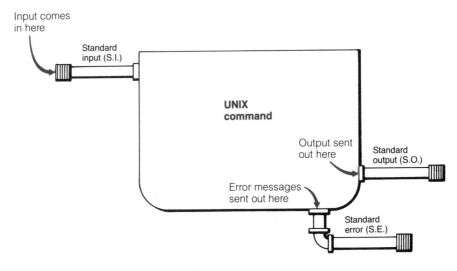

Figure 3.3
Standard Input, Standard Output, and Standard Error

points out that the time argument for the command must be less than 65536 seconds. (The actual numerical value for this bug will depend on the installation.)

Standard Input, Standard Output, and Standard Error

Now that we have discussed the organization of the manual entries, we should look at some of the terminology. Two of the most recurrent phrases are *standard input* and *standard output*. Trailing behind in popularity is *standard error*. In a UNIX system, a program, including many UNIX commands, is normally connected automatically to three files called the standard input, the standard output, and the standard error. If the program does not explicitly request other files, it gets its input from the standard input, sends its output to the standard output, and sends any error messages to the standard error. Unless otherwise specified, all three files default to your terminal. (Remember that devices are treated as files.) So when a command is described as reading from the standard input and writing to the standard output, that means it takes input from your keyboard and sends output to your screen.

Why not just use the terms *keyboard* and *screen* for the standard input, output, and error? First, you may be using some other type of device, perhaps a teletype. More importantly, UNIX allows you to *change* the standard input and output temporarily by using pipes and redirection. This facility is of enormous importance to our next major topic, *combining* UNIX commands and operations.

COMPOUND UNIX COMMANDS

When a single UNIX command does not suffice to solve a problem or do a task, try joining commands together. The chief tools for this are redirection and the pipe. As a student of advanced UNIX, you probably know about these facilities, but it will do no harm to review them in the context of standard input and output.

Redirection

Redirection changes the *assignments* for standard input and standard output. The > operator makes the filename following the operator become the new standard output, and the < operator makes the filename following it the new standard input. For example, *cat* writes to the standard output. Consider this command:

```
cat part1 part2 > wholething
```

The redirection operator declares *wholething* to be the standard output, ousting the terminal screen from that role. Thus the string of bytes produced by *cat* is sent to that file (*wholething*) and not to the screen. (If the file does not exist, it is created. If it does exist, it is wiped clean and refilled with the new data.) Redirection, then, reassigns which files are used for standard input and standard output. (Remember that a device, such a terminal, is treated as just another file by the UNIX operating system.)

Note that this change in standard output is temporary. When the command ends, your terminal once again becomes the standard output.

Now let's look at input redirection. The UNIX manual says that *cat* reads from the standard input *if no input file is given*. This allows us to do the following:

```
$ cat
We have all passed a lot of water since then -- Samuel Goldwyn
Control D
We have all passed a lot of water since then -- Samuel Goldwyn
$
```

First we typed *cat* and then hit the Return key. Thus we provided no input filename. Then, what we typed next was gathered as standard input, and *cat* passed it on to the standard output, the terminal screen. (Recall that a Control D at the beginning of the line acts to mark the end of keyboard input; it simulates reaching the end of an ordinary file.)

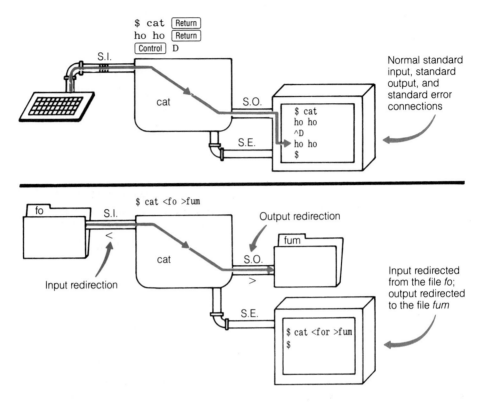

Figure 3.4
Redirecting Standard Input and Standard Output

Well, any command that accepts standard input also accepts input redirection. So let's try that out as a way to feed a file to *cat*:

```
$ cat < samwyn5
It's more than magnificent -- it's mediocre.
$
```

Now the *samwyn5* file became the standard input, and *cat* reports its contents to us.

Incidentally, how is this last example different from the following?

```
$ cat samwyn5
It's more than magnificent -- it's mediocre.
$
```

Both produce the same final result. The difference is that in the latter example, *samwyn5* was *not* the standard input. Instead, the standard input remained the

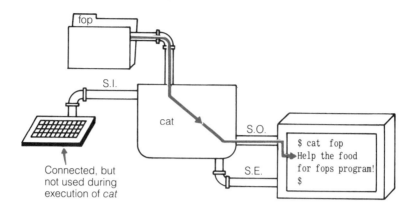

Figure 3.5
Combined Keyboard and File Input

terminal, and the internal programming of *cat* caused the *samwyn5* file to be opened in *addition* to the standard input.

Indeed, *cat*, like many file-reading programs, can read the standard input *and* a file input during the execution of the command. The standard method (and the one used by *cat*) is to use a hyphen instead of a filename to stand for standard input. Here is an example that uses the file *samwyn5* as the first input and the standard input (here the keyboard) as a second input:

```
$ cat samwyn5 -
Include me out -- Samuel Goldwyn
Control D
It's more than magnificent -- it's mediocre.   .
Include me out -- Samuel Goldwyn
$
```

As you can see, *cat* concatenated the two inputs. Since the filename came first, it was printed first. Then the keyboard input, represented by the hyphen, was printed.

Question 3.3

How can you use *cat* to create a file *tale* consisting of keyboard input sandwiched between the contents of two files *start* and *end*?

Another redirection operator is the *append* operator, $>>$. It is similar to $>$, except if the target file already exists, the new output is appended to its end:

```
date >> daterec
```

This command appends the current time and date to the end of the file *daterec*.

Redirection is a very useful tool. If you wish to add several files to the end of an existing file, give a command like

```
cat par.3 par.4 par.5 >> report
```

Or suppose you have an old FORTRAN program (*oldftr*) written in the days when standard input was data on a deck of do-not-spindle cards. Now that data has been transcribed to a file called *oldftr.data*. You can process that data and collect the output in a new file with a command like

```
oldftr < oldftr.data > oldftr.output
```

The first bit of redirection (< *oldftr.data*) establishes that input is to be taken from the *oldftr.data* file, and the second bit of redirection (> *oldftr.output*) establishes that output is to be routed to the *oldftr.output* file. The order of the redirection instructions doesn't matter; we could just as well use this command:

```
oldftr > oldftr.output < oldftr.data
```

There are more redirection operators, but they are used chiefly in shell scripts, so we will postpone their discussion to later.

Pipes

UNIX redirection lets us connect programs to files. The UNIX pipe facility lets us connect programs to other programs.

The fact that many UNIX commands accept input from the standard input and send output to the standard output lets us link such commands together with a *pipeline* or *pipe*. A pipe (represented by |) makes the output of one program the input of another. In a command like

```
grep Fresno billsdue | sort
```

the output of *grep* (lines in the file *billsdue* containing *Fresno*) becomes the input to *sort*, and we wind up with lines containing *Fresno* (these are the output of *grep*) sorted according to the first character on each line (this is the output of *sort*).

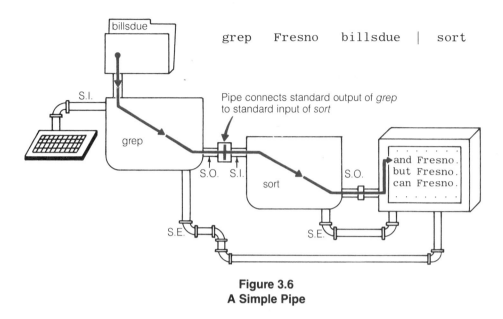

Figure 3.6
A Simple Pipe

(Appendix A discusses the uses of *grep*.) We can visualize the data flowing through the pipe from one program to the next.

Question 3.4

Design a pipe that sorts by login name the list of people currently using the system.

In many cases, input from a pipe can be combined with input from files. The trick, as in combining redirection with files, is to use the special symbol - (a hyphen) for those commands that recognize that as meaning standard input. For instance, consider this command:

```
grep Fresno billsdue | sort - olddue > newdue
```

The output from *grep* becomes the standard input to *sort*. Meanwhile, *sort* opens the file *olddue*. The contents of this file are sorted together with the the *grep* output (represented by the hyphen), and the *sort* output is redirected to the file *newdue*.

So redirection routes output to files while pipes route output to other programs. What if you want to do both? UNIX offers the *tee* command.

The TEE

The *tee* command reads the standard input and sends it on to the standard output. It also redirects a copy of what it has read into the file of your choice. The form is this:

```
cat part1 part2 | tee total | lpr
```

The output of *cat* becomes the standard input of *tee*. It is sent on through another pipe to the *lpr* line printer command. Meanwhile, a copy is stored in the file *total*. The net effect is the same as with this sequence:

```
cat part1 part2 > total
lpr total
```

If you wish to append to a file using *tee*, just use its *-a* option:

```
cat part3 part4 | tee -a total | lpr
```

Filters

The UNIX system of pipes and redirection makes for marvelous flexibility. Its success depends on two factors. The first is the UNIX treatment of devices as files. This allows the same commands to work equally well with files and with terminals, tape drives, and other I/O devices. The second factor is that many UNIX commands are designed as *filters*. A filter is a program that can take a flow of data from standard input, process (or *filter*) it, and send the result on to standard output. This design philosophy makes connecting UNIX commands a very natural process. The fact that *cat*, *sort*, and *grep* are all filters is what lets us link them together with pipes in our examples. How can you tell if a command is a filter? Read its description. If it can take input from the standard input and if it sends its output to the standard output, then it is a filter.

When you develop a program of your own, you should seriously consider whether or not it, too, would benefit from being designed as a filter. Many of the examples you will encounter later in this book illustrate how to create filters.

SHELL SCRIPTS

Once you have found a sequence of commands you use often, you can commit them permanently to a file. You can then have the shell read the file and follow the script of commands in it. Such a file is called a shell script. Here is a rather simple example to illustrate the basic principle. Suppose we place the following lines in the file *example*:

```
echo Here is the date and time:
date
```

(The *echo* command prints out its arguments.) To run this script, we can give the file name as an argument to the *sh* (for shell) command:

```
$ sh example
Here is the date and time:
Tue Jun 12 16:43:02 PST 1984
$
```

What happens here is that the *sh* command creates a new child shell process. This new shell reads the file *example*, executes the commands it finds there, and dies, returning control to the original shell.

Why can't we simply type

```
example
```

and have it work? The reason we can't is that when we create a new file, it is normally created with read and write permissions turned on, and execute permission turned off. We can get around that by using the *chmod* (change mode) to make the *example* file executable. Giving the file *x* (executable) permission results in your being able to run the shell script from that moment on by typing the filename:

```
$ chmod u+x example
$ example
Here is the date and time:
Tue Jun 12 16:44:52 PST 1984
$ example
Here is the date and time:
Tue Jun 12 16:45:23 PST 1984
$
```

Here, too, a new shell process is created just to run the script. (We typed *example* twice to show that the *chmod* change is not a one-shot deal.)

Question 3.5

Write a shell script that salutes the user and tells who's on the system.

This kind of shell script is pretty tame. Shell scripts have several features to elevate their powers. We will explore those features in the next three chapters, but here are some of the main points now:

- Shell scripts can take arguments, just like most commands. These arguments (or *parameters*) can be symbolically represented within the script. Thus you can pass on values, filenames, and the like to be used as arguments for commands inside the script.
- The shell allows you to create *shell variables* and to assign values to them. These can be used by shell scripts for many purposes.
- The shell has a collection of predefined *metacharacters*, characters assigned special meanings that greatly expand the applicability of shell scripts.
- The shell provides control structures such as *if...else* constructs and *for* loops that let you implement programming language approaches.

Clearly we have much to look forward to in the coming chapters!

The shell script approach is a powerful one. Indeed, several of the standard UNIX commands are actually shell scripts. A script built upon standard UNIX commands is highly portable from one UNIX system to another, for the workings of a UNIX command are further removed from the idiosyncracies of a particular machine than are, say, the workings of a standard programming language. Thus shell scripts often require less tinkering when moved from one machine to another than do other forms of programs. Another advantage of shell scripts is that they take up little storage, for most of the work is done by programs that are already part of the system.

Probably the chief drawback to the shell script is that it is relatively slow. Often, ''relatively slow'' is still fast enough. If it isn't, we may choose to turn to C programming.

C PROGRAMS FOR SOLVING PROBLEMS

Why C? Because it is the language that most (90%) of UNIX is written in. Thus the interface between C and UNIX is straightforward and natural. Do you want to use system calls, the subroutines used by the kernel? They are C functions. UNIX has about 60 such system C functions, and they can be used in C programs just like any other C functions. An even greater number of C functions is available in various C libraries in the system. And if you want a C program to use one of the regular UNIX commands, that, too, is possible. Thus there are enormous capabilities at the disposal of a C program, and in Chapters 7 through 10, we will explore them.

Beyond this on-hand power, there are the innate advantages of the language itself. But that is another topic. (See, for example, *C Primer Plus* by Waite, Prata, and Martin [Indianapolis: Howard W. Sams & Co., 1984].) Here let's talk about the mechanics of producing a C program.

C is a compiled language. This means you use one of the system editors to write a program. Then you submit the program to the C compiler, which converts it to an executable program in machine language. Then you can run the program. Note that writing a program is not the interactive process that it is with BASIC or LOGO. The actual procedure goes as follows:

1. Use an editor, such as *vi*, *ex*, or *ed*, to write the program. The name of the file containing the program must end in *.c* in order to identify it as a C program to the compiler. For example, we could place the following program in *howdy.c*:

```
main()
{
printf("Howdy, howdy, howdy!\n");
}
```

   The \n is C notation for the newline character. It causes the screen cursor or the printer head to go to the beginning of the next line.

2. Submit the file to *cc*, the C compiler:

```
cc howdy.c
```

   If your program is okay, the compiled version is placed in a file called (by default) *a.out*. (If the program is not okay, you will get a list of complaints from the compiler.)

3. To run the program, type *a.out*:

```
$ a.out
Howdy, howdy, howdy!
$
```

4. If you like the program and want to keep it, change the name of the *a.out* file; otherwise your next compilation will wipe out the previous one:

```
mv a.out howdy
```

   Now you just type *howdy* to run the program.

Question 3.6

Which of the following are acceptable filenames for C-code programs?

a. `osaycanu.c`

b. `findsumc`

c. `23.c`

d. `rag_mop.c.c.c`

Those are the basic steps. We will discuss some of the *cc* options when we return to C programs later in the book.

BUILDING YOUR OWN COMMAND LIBRARY OF PROGRAMS

By the time you have finished this book, you most likely will have developed a set of programs (executable shell scripts, C programs, or both) that you use regularly. Part of the problem-solving process is to make it easy to use the solutions, so we will look at a method to make your programs easily accessible.

As long as you are in the same directory in which the program is stored, there is no problem. You can run the program just by typing its filename. But often it would be nice if you could run the program in any directory without having to type the full pathname of the command. This is easily accomplished.

First, create a subdirectory in which to keep your program files, and move your programs to it. Since most of the regular UNIX commands are stored in */bin* and */usr/bin*, a common practice is to name the subdirectory *bin*. Thus the user *furdly* might store his programs in */usr/furdly/bin*. Of course, you can choose a different name for the subdirectory. (The use of *bin* for a name is a mild pun. It is a shortened form of *binary*, indicating files of binary code, and, of course, *bin* also suggests a place to store stuff.) Now we have gathered all the executable programs in one place, and that is a worthwhile organizational step by itself.

The next step is get your shell to search through that directory of programs automatically whenever you type a command. To do that, look in the *.profile* file in your home directory. Normally, this file is created for you when your UNIX account is set up. When you log in, UNIX scans this file for instructions on how to handle your account. (BSD versions use *.login* for a similar purpose.) Typically, one of the lines in the file will look like this:

```
PATH=.:/bin:/usr/bin
```

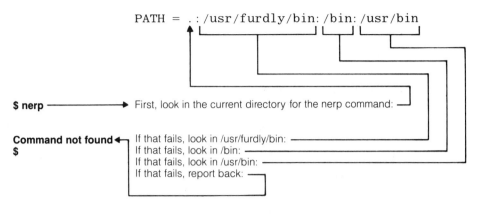

Figure 3.7
PATHways

Here *PATH* is one of the built-in shell variables that we will discuss in the next chapter. It provides the list of directories the shell uses to find command names; a colon is used to separate one directory name from the next. Suppose you type a command line. Then the shell begins looking for the file that stores that command. For this particular value of *PATH*, the shell first looks in . (your current working directory), then in */bin*, then in */usr/bin*.

Use an editor to insert your chosen directory into the *PATH* definition. Remember to use a colon to separate entries. The new *PATH* may look like this:

```
PATH=.:/usr/furdly/bin:/bin:/usr/bin
```

Now, if the shell fails to find the command in *furdly*'s current directory, it will search */usr/furdly/bin* for it. If it still hasn't found it, the shell moves on to where the regular UNIX commands are stored. Where you place the new entry makes a difference. If, for instance, you place it as we did here, and if you have a command called *cp*, then your version of *cp* will be run instead of the system version. That is because the shell searches the directories in the order they appear in *PATH*, and as soon as it finds a command by the requested name, it searches no further.

Once you have created this setup, you can use your commands the same as you use UNIX commands. They can even appear in other shell scripts and C programs. Note, however, that any changes you make to *.profile* do not go into effect until the system reads that file again. Normally, the *.profile* file is read at login time, but you can use the dot command (see Chapter 4) to get it read immediately.

CONCLUSION

In many cases a single UNIX command is all you need to accomplish a given task. But because UNIX has so many commands and options, you need to acquire familiarity with the UNIX manual.

When one command won't do, the UNIX philosophy of filters, pipes, and redirection makes it a simple matter to blend several commands and files together into more complex instruments of your will.

For more elaborate tasks, you can use shell scripts to create full-blown UNIX programs. And if that isn't sufficient, you can write C programs that tap into the full power of the UNIX system.

Once you create your own library of commands, you can place them in a directory and redefine your *PATH* so that you can use your commands in the same fashion as you use UNIX commands.

ANSWERS TO QUESTIONS IN CHAPTER 3

3.1 a. Should be a space between the two options: *ls –l –s*
b. Don't use commas to separate arguments: *cat file1 file2*
c. Should be no space between hyphen and option label:
```
ls -s Factdir
```
3.2 a. Need two files
b. Okay
c. q,x require separate hyphens
d. Need a space between the two options
3.3 cat start - end > tale (Use Control D to terminate keyboard input.)
3.4 who | sort
3.5 echo Hail to thee!
echo Here is who is on the system:
who
3.6 All but b.

EXERCISE

1. Create your own *bin* subdirectory in your home directory and make it part of the search *PATH*.

4

WORKING WITH THE BOURNE SHELL

In this chapter you will find:

4

Working with the Bourne Shell

The shell is the interface between you and the system. As we saw in Chapter 2, it acts as a command interpreter, but its capabilities go far beyond that. In this chapter we will look at additional shell abilities and see how they can be used to construct useful shell scripts. In UNIX, shell scripts can perform many tasks often relegated to standard programming languages. The shell-script approach is usually more portable and simpler to implement, making shell scripts an important UNIX tool. We will examine the shell's filename expansion system, shell variables, various special shell mechanisms, and some of the shell options. We will see how to incorporate these features into the UNIX programs known as shell scripts or shell procedures.

First, however, we should note that "the shell" is a bit of a simplification. There are, in fact, two shell programs in widespread use. The most widespread shell program is the Bourne Shell, the standard shell developed by Stephen Bourne of Bell Labs for Bell Lab releases of UNIX. The BSD versions of UNIX, developed at Berkeley, use another shell, called *csh*, which, in some ways, emulates aspects of the C language. However, the Bourne shell can be evoked on BSD UNIX systems by typing *sh*. Because applications developed using the Bourne shell can be used on all UNIX systems, we will concentrate on it. There are also minor differences in the Bourne shell from system to system. We will stick to the System V version, but most of what we say is generally applicable.

Let's turn now to studying the shell's features. We will take a look at its filename-expansion powers, at shell variables, positional parameters, command substitution, more command line properties, built-in shell commands, and other shell features relating to shell scripts. A great number of these features, we will see, are invoked through using special characters and notations. We'll begin with an example which is probably familiar to you, the shell's filename expansion capabilities.

FILENAME EXPANSION: SHELL METACHARACTERS

Filename expansion is the ability to expand a shorthand notation for a group of filenames to a complete set of explicit filenames. We humans use a similar system when we expand "Mr." to "Mister" when reading aloud. The shell uses a set of special symbols called *metacharacters* to let you produce patterns or templates to match various classes of filenames. Here is the system:

1. The *?* metacharacter stands for any single character. For example, the pattern *d?g* would match any three-character filename starting with *d* and ending with *g*. Possible matches include *dog*, *dig*, *d4g*, and even *d_g*. Note that the concept of characters is not limited to just letters of the alphabet. A second important point is that only existing matches are found. That is, if you give a command like *ls d?g* , you only get *dog* as part of the output if you already have a file called *dog* in the directory.

2. The * metacharacter stands for any combination of zero or more characters. (There is an exception; it will not match a period at the beginning of a filename). For example, the pattern *s*n* matches any filename, regardless of length, that starts with *s* and ends with *n*. Possible matches include *sn*, *sun*, *soon*, *sudden*, *s747n*, and *s-1.bin*. Similarly, the pattern * used by itself, as in *ls * * or *rm * *, matches every filename in the directory except those beginning with a period. This restriction is to protect you from accidentally removing files like *.profile*.

3. The *[]* metacharacter notation lets you represent a *restricted* range of single characters enclosed within the brackets. For example, you can provide a list of characters, as in *[acdfACDF]*, or indicate a range by using a hyphen, as in *[a-m]*. For example, the pattern *d[io]g* matches *dig* and *dog* and nothing else, not even *diog*. Each bracket pair represents just one character place in a name.

These metacharacters can be used in conjunction with one another to create more involved patterns. For instance, the pattern *[A-Z]*[0-9]* matches any filename starting with a capital letter and ending with a digit. Possible matches include *B2*, *Questions8*, and *AVARICE24*.

Here is a similar example. The pattern *[0-9][0-9]* matches any filename ending with two digits. Note that you can't use *[10-99]*, for a single bracket pair matches only one character. The construction *[10-99]* would be interpreted to mean the character "1", the characters "0" through "9", and the character "9"; in other words it is a redundant form of *[0-9]*.

The two main uses of filename expansion are to save typing of long names and to make it convenient to use a systematic nomenclature. For example, you could collect a series of dog descriptions in files called *dog0*, *dog1*, etc. Then you could print them all with the single command

```
lpr dog*
```

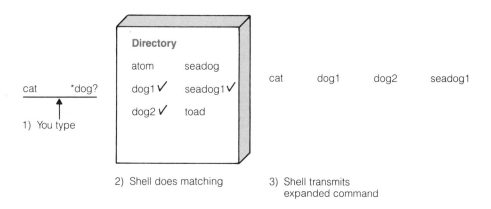

Figure 4.1
Filename Expansion in the Shell

When you give a command like this, the shell does the work of compiling the list of files that match this pattern. Then the actual list of matching files, not the pattern, is passed on to the *lpr* command.

Question 4.1

Devise a pattern using metacharacters to match each of the following situations:

a. All two-character filenames
b. All filenames consisting of two lowercase letters
c. All filenames ending in .c
d. All filenames beginning with *c* and ending in a digit
e. All filenames beginning with *p* and having a *t* somewhere

---

Even casual users of UNIX systems often make use of the filename expansion system. Our next topic, however, takes us to the province of the more advanced user.

SHELL VARIABLES

In computer programming, a variable is a name associated with a value. It offers a symbolic way to represent and manipulate data. Most computer languages have variables, and so does the shell. Shell variables come in two varieties: those created and maintained by the UNIX system itself, and those created by the user. To see how shell variables work, let's start by creating our own.

User-Created Shell Variables

To create a shell variable, simply type something of the form

```
name=value
```

and a shell variable is created bearing the left-hand name and having the right-hand value. This can be done interactively (for your immediate gratification) or within a shell script file.

For example,

```
pet=bulldog
```

creates a shell variable having the name *pet*; its value is the ''string'' *bulldog*. A string is just a series of characters. Shell variables are *string variables*, that is, variables whose values are strings. For example, consider the following:

```
weight=156
```

Here, the value of *weight* is a three-character string consisting of the digit characters ''1'', ''5'', and ''6''. The value of *weight* is not the number *156*. However, the shell can, if necessary, interpret a digit-string numerically, as we will see when we discuss the *test* and *expr* commands in Chapters 5 and 6. Meanwhile, we will stick to strings.

There is one special string of some importance, and that is the null string. It is a string consisting of no characters. Any of the following equate a variable to the null string:

```
vacuous=''
notmuch=
idea=""
```

Note that no spaces are used when we assign a value to a variable. For instance,

```
pet = bulldog
```

typically will not be accepted, for it has spaces on either side of the equals sign. (Some versions are a little more forgiving and will ignore the spaces, but it is best not to rely upon the forgivingness of machines.)

You can use letters, digits, and the underscore character in variable names; *figaro*, *HO*, *name2*, and *go_where* all qualify. Other characters are illegal for use in the name of a variable, but they can be used in the strings that form the value of a variable. Thus

```
big-foot=squasher
```

is illegal because it has a hyphen in the variable name, but

```
squasher=big-foot
```

is okay.

To find out the value of a shell variable, you can use the *echo* command. Ordinarily, *echo* merely echoes its arguments to the screen:

```
$ echo pet
pet
$
```

But if we use a variable name preceded by a *$* as an argument to *echo*, the value of the variable is echoed:

```
$ echo $pet
bulldog
$
```

Here *pet* is the variable's name, and *$pet* is the variable's value. You can use both in the same *echo* statement:

```
$ echo The value of pet is $pet
The value of pet is bulldog
$
```

An attempt to echo a null string or an undefined variable produces a blank line.

System Shell Variables

The shell, we have said, maintains its own set of shell variables. The box describes some of the common ones, but to see what your system is using, just type *set*. Here is a typical response, one that corresponds to what the user *fafner* might find:

```
$ set
EXINIT='set ai nu'
HOME=/usr/fafner
IFS=
```

```
MAIL=/usr/mail/fafner
PATH=.:/bin:/usr/bin
PS1=$
PS2=>
TERM=adm5
$
```

The *set* command makes the shell print out the variables it knows. If you had already defined a variable yourself, it, too, would appear in the list. The name to the left of each equals sign is the name of a variable, and the stuff to the right is the value of the variable. Thus the variable *TERM* has the value *adm5*, and *MAIL* has a pathname for a value. It is a UNIX tradition (but not a requirement) that built-in variable names are in upper case. You may not have the exact set of variables we have here, but this collection is typical. The box provides a fuller description of these and other common shell variables.

Some Standard Shell Variables

Here are some standard shell variables found on many systems. Your own system may add to or subtract from this list. Some of the descriptions refer to shell variable values given in the example in the text.

EXINIT: Initialization instructions for the *ex* and *vi* editors.

HOME: This is set to the pathname of your home directory.

IFS (Internal Field Separator): This is set to a list of the characters that are used to separate words in a command line. Normally this list consists of the space character, the tab character (produced by the tab key), and the newline character (produced by hitting the ⌷Return⌷ key). They are ''invisible'' characters, so you don't see them in the output. But you can see, for example, that the newline character has produced a blank line following *IFS*.

LOGNAME: The user's log-in name.

MAIL: This variable's value is the name of the directory in which electronic mail addressed to you is placed. The shell checks the contents of this directory every so often, and when something new shows up, you are notified that mail has arrived for you.

PATH: This names the directories which the shell will search to find commands that you use. A colon is used to separate the directory names; there are no spaces. The directories are searched in the order given. For example, if you give the command *cat*, the shell first searches your current directory (.) for an executable file by that name (*cat*). If it doesn't find one there, then it looks in

/bin. If it still hasn't found *cat*, it looks in */usr/bin*. And if it still hasn't found a *cat* program, the shell reports back that it can't find that command. Note that this particular sequence of directories in *PATH* means that if you have an executable file called *cat* in your current working directory, that *cat* is executed rather than the standard system *cat*, which would be in one of the subsequent directories. (Note: if the very first character in the string is a colon (:), the shell interprets that as .:, that is, as if the current directory is first on the list. Similarly, a final colon is interpreted as :., that is, as if the current directory is last on the list.)

PS1 (Prompt String 1): This is the symbol used as your prompt. Normally (as in this example) it is set to *$*, but you can redefine it merely by assigning a new value. For example, the command *PS1 = #* resets the prompt to a *#* symbol.

PS2 (Prompt String 2): This prompt is used when UNIX thinks you have started a new line without finishing a command. You can continue a line, for example, by using a backslash (\) before hitting the [Return] key:

```
$ echo O give me a ho\
> me where the buffalo roam
O give me a home where the buffalo roam
$
```

We discuss \ and other special characters later in this chapter.
TERM: This identifies the kind of terminal you habitually use. Knowing this, the shell knows what to interpret as a backspace key, etc.

Some of these variables, such as *PS1*, are defined by default. Others, such as *PATH*, are defined in your *.profile* file. See the section further on in this chapter describing *.profile* for more on this.

Many UNIX commands use the built-in shell variables. For example, the *cd* command without an argument is interpreted to mean *cd $HOME*. This enables the *cd* command to take each user to his or her own home directory, since *HOME* is defined differently for each user.

Similarly, you can use the system shell variables and shell variables of your own devising in your programs.

Question 4.2

What command will change your prompt to *Proceed:*?

Local and Global Shell Variables: *export*

Ordinarily a shell variable is a *local* variable. That is, it is known only to the shell that created it. When you start a new shell, however, (by running a shell script, say, or by typing *sh*), that shell is born ignorant of the old shell's variables. You can create a new variable in the new shell using one of the old names, but it will be a distinct variable, and the old shell won't know it. In short, each shell's variables are private (*local*) to itself. This exchange illustrates the point:

```
$ CAT=kate              ← First CAT gets its value
$ echo $CAT
kate
$ sh                    ← Create new shell
$ echo $CAT
                        ← Echo response to undefined variable
$ CAT=munchkin
$ echo $CAT             ← A second CAT gets its value
munchkin
$ [Control] D$echo $CAT ← Return to old shell
kate                    ← Doesn't know about new shell's CAT
$
```

Sometimes we want the new shell to know the old shell's variables. Then we use the *export* command. Any shell variable used as an argument for this command will have copies of the variable and its value presented to all shells descending from it. This kind of variable is termed *global*. (However, even exported variables are not completely global, for they are only exported to child processes, not back to a parent process.) Let's repeat the preceding exercise, but this time using *export*.

```
$ export CAT
$ CAT=kate                  ← First CAT gets its value
$ echo $CAT
kate
$ sh                        ← Create new shell
$ echo $CAT
kate                        ← The new shell has a copy of the 1st CAT
$ CAT=munchkin              ← The copy gets a new value
$ echo $CAT
munchkin
$ [Control] D $ echo $CAT   ← Return to old shell
kate                        ← Original CAT has original value
$
```

As you can see, variables can be exported down to subshells, but they cannot be exported back up to parent shells. The reason for this is that the *export* command causes a new shell to be given a *copy* of the original variable. This copy has the same name and value as the original. Subsequently, the value of the copy can be changed, but when the subshell dies, so does the copy. Meanwhile, the original variable has been left untouched.

To find out what variables are already exported, just type *export* without any arguments.

Understanding the *.profile* File

When you log in to a UNIX system, the system looks into your directory for a file called *.profile*. This file contains *startup* instructions for your account. For example, *fafner* might have a *.profile* file that looks like this:

```
$ cat profile
HOME=/usr/fafner
MAIL=/usr/mail/fafner
PATH=.:/bin:/bin:/usr/bin
TERM=adm5
export HOME MAIL PATH TERM
$
```

This file contains definitions for several shell variables, and it exports them to make them global.

Since your *.profile* file belongs to you, you can modify it. For instance, Fafner can revise the preceding file to this version:

```
YES? cat profile
HOME=/usr/fafner
MAIL=/usr/mail/fafner
PATH=.:$HOME/bin:/bin:/bin:/usr/bin
TERM=adm5
PS1='YES? '
export HOME MAIL PATH TERM PS1
date
echo Welcome back, Fafner.
YES?
```

Why does this sample start with a *YES?* instead of with a *$*? This happens because *fafner* has redefined the regular prompt to be *YES?* instead of *$*. Using the single quotes allows him to include a space in the definition of the prompt string.

Note, too, that he has redefined *PATH* to include a *bin* subdirectory in his home directory. He could have done this by using

```
PATH=.:/usr/fafner/bin:/bin:/bin:/usr/bin
```

However, he used the equivalent *$HOME/bin* instead of */usr/fafner/bin*; this saved him a little typing.

You can include regular UNIX commands in *.profile*; *fafner*, for example, used *date* and *echo*. Commands placed in *.profile* execute when you log in. Indeed, the *.profile* file is nothing more than a form of shell script that is enacted when you log in. By adding to and altering the contents of this file, you can customize your UNIX environment.

SHELL SCRIPTS

In Chapter 3 we discussed how to create and use a shell script. To review, you create a shell script by placing UNIX commands into a text bfile. You run the shell script by typing *sh* followed by the filename, or else you use the *chmod* command to make the file directly executable by typing its name. The simple example we gave then used fixed commands with no arguments, producing a clear but unimaginative script. One way to enliven a script is to design it so that it can accept additional information at *run time*, information such as what files or what options to use. Run time means at the time you actually run a program or script.

There are two main approaches to this end. The first is to write an *interactive* script that requests the information it needs from the user. An interactive program usually prompts the user for input, perhaps by asking a question, and then reads the user's answer. (The shell is an interactive program; it prompts with *$* and reads the commands you type.) The second approach is to have the script accept arguments from the command line; these arguments come directly after the command name. (Most UNIX commands work this way; in *cat flopsie*, *flopsie* is a command-line argument telling *cat* which file to process.) The first approach is useful in creating programs to be used by the occasional or inexperienced user. The second approach allows you to construct programs based on the filter philosophy we discussed in Chapter 3. The command-line approach is, perhaps, the more powerful and flexible of the two, but it is not exactly the epitome of user-friendliness.

Interactive Shell Scripts

Interactive scripts are based on using UNIX shell commands *read* and *echo*, and on using shell variables. This simple example shows the basics:

```
echo Dear User, what is your name\?
read name
echo Glad to meet you, $name.
```

Here we use the backslash to remove the special pattern-matching property of the question mark character. (This is called *escaping* or *quoting* the character. The method can be used with other metacharacters, too, and we will discuss it further later in this chapter.) The *read* statement assigns your typed input as the value of the variable *name*. In the following *echo* statement, the *$name* causes this value to be printed out. If this program is placed in the file *gladto*, and if we use *chmod* to make the file executable, it can be used like this:

```
$ gladto
Dear User, what is your name?
Benito Fudd
Glad to meet you, Benito Fudd.
$
```

Question 4.3

What's wrong with this interactive shell script?

```
echo What month is this?
read $month
echo $month is as good a month as any.
```

The *read* command is more flexible than the last example shows. For instance, you can follow *read* with a list of variable names. If you respond by typing several words on your response line, the first variable gets the first word you type, the second variable the second word, and so on. If there are more words than variables, all the left-over words get assigned to the last variable. If there are more variables than words, the unused variables are not assigned values. Incidentally, *read* is a built-in shell command, that is, it is part of the *sh* program. It is described in the *sh* section of the manual and does not have its own separate entry. Let's modify the file *gladto* to illustrate this feature *read*:

```
echo Dear User, what is your name\?
read first rest
echo Glad to meet you, $first.
echo Do you know Leonardo $rest\?
```

Here is a sample run:

```
$ gladto
Dear User, what is your name?
```

```
Bobby Joe Gripspoon
Glad to meet you, Bobby.
Do you know Leonardo Joe Gripspoon?
$
```

Here, *first* becomes *Bobby*, and the second and final variable (*rest*) gets assigned the rest of the input.

In a more practical vein, here is a simple interactive program to copy files:

```
echo This program copies a file.
echo What file do you wish to copy\?
read original
echo What name do you desire for the copy\?
read copy
cp $original $copy
echo $original has been copied into $copy
```

Place it in an executable file called *copy*. Then running it could look like this:

```
$ copy
This program copies a file.
What file do you wish to copy?
blackmoor
What name do you desire for the copy?
greyfen
blackmoor has been copied into greyfen
$
```

This is fairly primitive, since it doesn't check, for example, to see if the requested original file exists. In the next chapter we will discuss error checking methods.

Question 4.4

Write a shell script that requests the user's age and then echoes it, along with some suitable comment.

Now that we see how to feed information to an interactive shell program, let's see how we deal with a noninteractive script using command-line arguments.

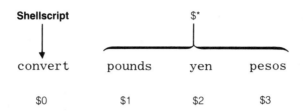

Figure 4.2
Positional Parameters: Shell Script with Arguments

Shell Script Arguments: Positional Parameters

Most UNIX commands accept arguments in the command line. For example, the command

```
mv fish ghoti
```

uses the arguments *fish* and *ghoti* to tell the *mv* command the original and the desired filenames. We can use the same approach in a shell script. The trick is that, within the script, we refer to the first argument as *$1*, the second argument as *$2*, and so on. In addition, the special symbol *$0* stands for the name of the command itself, and *$** stands for all the arguments from *$1* on up. These numbered arguments are referred to as *positional parameters*. One more special notation is *$#*, which represents the number of arguments.

Again, let's use a simple example to show the mechanism at work. Suppose we place the following text in the file *show*:

```
echo I am the powerful $0 command.
echo These are my arguments: $*
echo I now shall determine the first of these $# arguments!
echo It is -- $1!
```

Here is a sample run:

```
$ sh show me the way
I am the powerful show command.
These are my arguments: me the way
I now shall determine the first of these 3 arguments!
It is -- me!
```

Here is a somewhat less frivolous example:

```
cp $1 $HOME/storage/$1.sv
```

Suppose we place it in the executable file *save*. Now suppose we have a file called *snap*. Can you see what the following command does?

```
save snap
```

If the user's home directory is */usr/fafner*, then this command translates to

```
cp snap /usr/fafner/storage/snap.sv
```

Thus it places a copy of the *snap* file in the user's subdirectory *storage*, adding the suffix *.sv*. *$HOME* is replaced by its value, and *$1* is replaced by its value. Note that we can use *$1* more than once. Note, too, that positional parameters and shell variables can be used as part of longer strings; the second appearance of *$1* is embedded in a long pathname. Finally, note that using *$HOME* instead of */usr/ fafner* makes the script more general. Sue can use the same script to copy files to her */usr/sue/storage* directory.

Question 4.5

Write a shell script that takes 3 command line arguments. The first argument is the name of a destination file, and the other two arguments are names of files to be placed in the destination file.

Here is one more example, one that lets you make a shell script into an executable command:

```
chmod u+x $1
```

Place this in a file *es* (for execute script). First we can make *es* itself executable by typing

```
sh es es
```

Then, whenever we call for an executable script, we can use *es* on the script to do the job. For example,

```
es show
```

would make the *show* script executable.

If you frequently make new shell scripts, this *es* command makes a useful addition to the personal command directory we described in Chapter 3.

There is another way to give positional parameters values, and that is to use the built-in shell command *set*.

Positional Parameters and *set*

The *set* command is part of the shell and is described in the *sh(1)* section of the manual. Recall that typing *set* alone produces a list of all current shell variables and their values. We can also use *set* to assign values to positional parameters. First, we will see how this feature works, then we will see how to make it useful. Consider this interchange, for example:

```
$ set seven swans aswimming
$ echo $2 $1
swans seven
$
```

Here *$1* was set to the first argument following *set*, and so on.

This particular example isn't extraordinarily useful; to print *swans seven*, we could have more easily used this:

```
$ echo swans seven
```

Nonetheless, this use of *set* can be rendered quite useful when it is used in conjuction with *command substitution*. Let's see what that is.

Command Substitution

What makes the *set* command useful in assigning positional parameter values is that its arguments need not be fixed in advance. Often *set* is used in conjunction with the metacharacter ` (the backquote, or accent grave). When a command is enclosed in backquotes, the command is replaced by the output it produces. The process is called *command substitution*, and here is an example:

```
$ echo date          ← No backquotes, echo literally
date
$ echo `date`        ← Backquotes, echo command's output
Tue Jun 19 11:47:31 PDT 1984
$
```

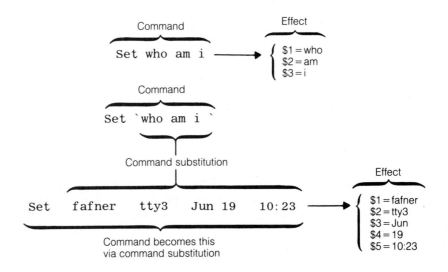

Figure 4.3
Using *set* and Command Substitution

The construction `date` was replaced by the output of the `date` command, so that the second *echo* command is translated to

```
echo Tue Jun  19  11:47:31 PDT 1984
```

Tue becomes the first argument of *echo*, *Jun* becomes the second argument, and so on.

Here is how we can use *set* with the backquote feature. Suppose we want a script to print out the user's name. The *who am i* command comes close, for it prints that information out along with other data:

```
$ who am i
fafner     tty3       Jun 19  10:23
$
```

We can extract just the *fafner* part with a script segment like this:

```
set `who am i`
echo $1
```

Here, *who am i* is replaced by its output string (*fafner*, etc.), and *fafner* is assigned to *$1*, *tty3* to *$2*, and so on. Then the *echo $1* command echoes just the *fafner*.

Of course, if we use this in a script, it will erase previously assigned values for the positional parameters. Here is a simple example illustrating how to get around that problem; it alters a filename by tagging a period and the user's login name to its end.

```
filename=$1              ← Save original $1
set `who am i`           ← Assign new value to $1
mv $filename $filename.$1
```

In this script, *$1* initially is the first argument of the shell script. In the second line, *$1* is redefined as the user's login name. Fortunately, the shell variable *filename* has been used to store the original value, so we can use both values in the final line. Put these three lines in a file called *possess* and let Fafner check it out:

```
$ ls
hoard
$ possess hoard
$ ls
hoard.fafner
$
```

This script enables *fafner* to place his imprint upon filenames.

In summary, we can use positional parameters to pass information to a script. This can be done directly, with the parameters representing command-line arguments to a script, or indirectly, using *set* and command substitution, letting the parameters represent the output line of a command.

Question 4.6

Write a shell script that prints out *date* information in this order: time, day of week, day number, month, year — that is, like this:

```
13:44:42 PDT Sun 16 Sept 1984
```

Let's look at one more script. See if it is clear to you what the script will do.

```
echo Do not panic!  All is well.
set `who am i`
name=$1
```

```
echo You know, $name, that you are one of my favorite users.
set `date`
echo It is $1, $2 $3, $6 -- quite a nice day.
echo So relax, $name, and do not fret about the time ... even
echo if it is already $4 $5.
```

But the subject of information flow doesn't end with shell variables and positional parameters. There is also the flow of information from file to program, from program to file, and from program to program. Let's see, then, how pipes and redirection relate to shell scripts.

Scripts, Pipes, and Redirection

A script can use pipes and redirection both internally and externally. That is, pipes and redirection can be part of the commands within a script, and the script as a whole can use pipes and redirection to control its input and output. Let's look at a case using pipes first. Suppose we want a command that concatenates (joins) a list of files, passes the resulting file through *pr* to format the file, and sends that output to *lpr*. We can use this script:

```
cat $* | pr | lpr
```

The *$** gathers all the command-line arguments (presumably filenames) and passes them to *cat*. The *cat* command concatenates the files and sends the combined output to the *pr* formatter. It, in turn, sends its output to the *lpr* line-printer command.

This illustrates that we can use pipes in a shell script just as we would in a regular command line.

Suppose this command is in the executable file *prnt*. Can it be used in a pipeline? Sure. Since the initial command within *prnt* is *cat*, *prnt* can be used the same way as *cat* is to collect input:

```
sort newstuff | prnt
```

passes the sorted material to *prnt*, which does the formatting and printing. Similarly,

```
sort newstuff | prnt oldstuff -
```

concatenates *oldstuff* and the new sorted material arriving from the *sort newstuff* command. That is, this command becomes

```
sort newstuff | cat oldstuff - | pr | lpr
```

Once again, as we discussed in Chapter 3, the hyphen represents the standard input, which in this case is connected by a pipe to the standard output of the *sort* command.

Similarly, we can use redirection within a script. A common type of script is one that searches a certain file for information. For instance, an agent might have a file of authors and specialties:

```
$ cat /usr/frebish/data/authors
James Bennlark     historical romance (civil war, naval)
Vanetta Fullips    gothic romance
Mike Graken        cats, computers
Lelia McNee        science fiction, naval cats, fantasy
$
```

Here's a script to search this file for a string given in the command line:

```
grep $1 < /usr/frebish/data/authors
```

It instructs *grep* to search through the */usr/frebish/data/authors* file for the string represented by *$1*. Place it in a file called *auth_does* and make it executable. Then you can use it as follows:

```
$ auth_does romance
James Bennlark     historical romance (civil war, naval)
Vanetta Fullips    gothic romance
$
```

Thus we find only those authors engaged in romance. Of course, *grep* doesn't really need redirection to open a file, but it can use it.

Redirection, pipes, backquotes, filename expansion — the shell seems to use quite a few special characters. Indeed, its repertoire exceeds what we have revealed so far, so perhaps it's time to summarize what's available.

MORE SHELL FACILITIES AND SHELL METACHARACTERS

As we know, the shell recognizes several characters (*metacharacters*) and combinations as having special meaning. In fact, it has many more special characters than we have yet discussed and the shell also has ways to remove these special meanings. Many potential applications require using these metacharacters, so they deserve our attention. We'll summarize the more common metacharacters now and then show how to neutralize them. Below we have summarized the characters and combinations we have mentioned so far. When we complete our survey of metacharacters, we'll present a fuller, more detailed list.

Wildcard substitution: * ? [ ]
Redirection: > >> <
Piping: |
Continue command on next line: \
Value of a variable named *var*: $var
Value of the nth positional parameter: $n
List of all the positional parameters: $*
Name of the command using positional parameters: $0
Total number of positional parameters: $#
Command substitution: `. . .`

To this list we will now add several more special characters and character combinations. We will group them into three classes: more command-line metacharacters, some special shell variables, and characters for demetafying metacharacters.

Because there are so many special symbols, we will keep the examples short and simple, showing how they work. In the following two chapters, we will show what all these special characters can do for you in real-life applications.

Special Command-Line Characters

Here we discuss the characters used in constructing a command line. The >, <, >>, |, and \ characters fall in this category, and we will now examine some more:

Word Separators

One set of special characters consists of those characters used to separate one word from the next. These are termed *internal field separators* in UNIX, and they are defined by the shell variable *IFS*. Normally, these characters are the space character (produced by the space bar), the tab character (produced by the tab key), and the newline character (produced by the return key). Spaces and tabs are known collectively as *blanks*.

To see how this works, try redefining *IFS*. For example, you can type

```
IFS=Q
```

Then you will have to type commands this way:

```
cpQdefoeQdefriend
```

Remarkably, most users leave this variable alone.

Sequential Commands: ; (Semicolon)

You can put several commands on the same line by separating them with a semicolon:

```
$ ls -i flank; mv flank right; ls -i right
 3910 flank
 3910 right
$
```

Only after you hit the [Return] key is the sequence of commands executed.

You might do this, for example, to make sure that related commands in a shell script are kept together during subsequent editing:

```
PS1='YOUR WISH? '; export PS1
```

Or you might use this feature to keep the code more compact.

Background Process: & (Ampersand)

Terminating a command with an ampersand (&) causes it to run in background mode. Normally, as we discussed in Chapter 2, the shell *waits* until the child process produced by a command dies. Thus you can't issue a new command until the preceding one finishes. When a job is run in background, however, the process is launched, and control returns to your shell immediately. Your background job becomes one of the many processes sitting around waiting for its portion of time-sharing. Meanwhile, you can use your terminal to start other activities. Typically, you would use a background process for a longer task, such as sorting a large file or compiling a huge program. For example, you might wish to check the spelling in a big file:

```
$ spell warandpeace > wap.spell &
4562
$
```

The number reported back on the next line is the *PID* for the background process. This is the same identification number that *ps*, as discussed in Chapter 2, would provide. Note that we have used redirection to collect the output. Otherwise the list of misspelled words would be sent on to the terminal, perhaps in the midst of some editing work. Running a job in background doesn't change the standard input or output, so you have to take care of such matters yourself.

Question 4.7

Write a shell script that takes a filename as a command line argument, and in background uses *spell* to check the spelling in the file, and that places the output of *spell* in a file whose name is the original filename prefixed with *sp..*.

Command Grouping: *()* (Parentheses)

We can use parentheses to *group* commands. Suppose, for example, we wish to send the current date and time along with the contents of a file called *results* to a second file, *datres*. Then we can do this:

```
(date; cat results) > datres
```

This sends the output of *date* followed by the output of *cat* to the file *datres*. If we had used

```
date; cat results > datres
```

the result would have been the same as using

```
date
cat results datres
```

That is, the output of *date* goes to the screen, and the output of *cat* goes to the file. Try out some combinations yourself to see how this feature works.

More Redirection: Standard Error, *2>*, and *>&*

The redirection examples we've seen so far deal with the standard input and the standard output. The shell also provides for redirecting the standard error, letting you control where error messages are sent. (In Chapter 3 we identified the standard error as the file to which error messages are sent.) Normally, the standard error, like the standard output, is your terminal. The > redirects the standard output to another file, but doesn't affect the standard error; error messages are still sent to the terminal. After all, normally you want to collect good data and not error messages in a file. However, you can redirect the standard error, too, if you want. The operator is *2>*, and it is followed by the name of the destination file. This sequence shows the mechanics:

```
$ cp nome rome
cp: cannot open nome        ← Error sent to screen
$ cp nome rome 2> ermsg     ← Error sent to ermsg file
$ cat ermsg
cp: cannot open nome        ← Show contents of ermsg file
$
```

The second *cp* command resulted in the error message being placed in the file *ermsg*. Only when we used *cat* to see the contents of that file did we get to see the message.

The *2* in this command is a *file descriptor*. The UNIX system assigns a file descriptor integer to each open file. The numbers 0, 1, and 2 are assigned to the standard input, the standard output, and the standard error respectively. So the notation

```
2> ermsg
```

indicates that the standard error (file descriptor 2) is redirected to the file *ermsg*. Indeed, this usage is just a special case of

```
n> file
```

which redirects the file with file descriptor *n* to *file*. There must be no space between the digit and the > symbol.

Question 4.8

What does the command

```
cat food 1> kitty
```

do?

One common use for standard-error redirection is for background jobs. You can collect the regular output in one file and the error messages, if any, in a second:

```
sort chicago > chicago.sort  2> sorterr &
```

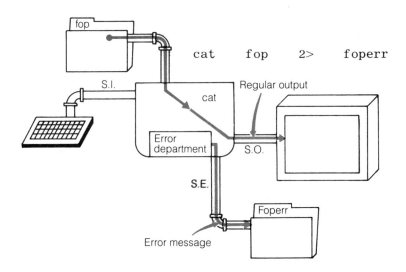

cat   fop   2>   foperr

Figure 4.4
Redirection of the Standard Error

Here the sorted output is placed in the *chicago.sort* file. Any error messages are routed to *sorterr*.

Suppose you want both standard output and standard error to be redirected to the same file. Perhaps you want to time a command in background, collecting both the command output (which normally goes to the standard output) and the *time* command output, which goes to the standard error. The shell has a mechanism for combining two such *streams*. Here we use the $>\&$ operator. For example, to merge the standard error into the standard output, use

```
2>&1
```

To merge the standard output into the standard error, use

```
1>&2
```

When would you use this capability? A common use of the second form is to ensure that messages in a shell file reach the user. For example, you may create a shell script that sends an error message if things go wrong:

```
echo There is no file $filename
```

Suppose this is part of a shell script called *fileclerk* and that you give a command like

```
fileclerk nuclier > newsys
```

This redirects the output of the *fileclerk* command to the *newsys* file. But what if something goes wrong and there is no *nuclier* file? Then the error message, being part of *fileclerk*, also gets redirected to *newsys*. That doesn't alert you immediately that something has gone wrong. It would be much better if the error message went to the screen. That is exactly what our next version will do. It uses *1>&2* to redirect the output of the line to the standard error, your terminal:

```
echo There is no file $filename 1>&2
```

Note that this redirection applies only to the one line. Other standard output from the file goes to wherever the output of the shell script as a whole is directed; for our example, that would be the file *newsys*.

But how does your script find out in the first place that there is no file by the given name? That's a task for the *test* command, and we discuss it in Chapter 5.

And More Redirection: Standard Input and <<

We've seen (in our *auth_does* example) how a shell script can use redirection to take input from another file. There is also a facility that allows a shell script to get its input from the *same* file that holds the script. Data used this way is said to be in a *here document*. To create a here document, we use the << operator. Here is how *auth_does* would be rewritten to use this feature:

```
grep $1 <<tohere          ← Read for input up to tohere
James Bennlar             historical romance (civil war, naval)
Vanetta Fullips           gothic romance
Mike Grak                 cats, computers
Lelia McNee               science fiction, naval cats, fantasy
tohere                    ← Marker for end of data input
```

When confronted with <<*tohere*, the shell then takes as input the file contents up to where the word *tohere* appears at the beginning of a line. If there is no such *tohere* marker, the shell reads to the end of the file. The word *tohere* was an arbitrary choice on our part. We could have chosen *stop* or *marker* or any other name or symbol. Of course, we wouldn't want to use an author's name:

```
grep $1 <<Mike
James Bennlark            historical romance (civil war, naval)
Vanetta Fullips           gothic romance
Mike Graken               cats, computers
Lelia McNee               science fiction, naval cats, fantasy
tohere
```

This example would stop searching when it reached the word *Mike*. By the way, what do you suppose would happen if you gave this command?

```
auth_does 'gothic romance'
```

You may as well try it out and see, for we won't discuss the answer and what to do about it for a while. (We don't want you to get too lazy; learning works better as an active rather than a passive process.)

Conditional Execution: && and ‖

We continue this survey of special characters by looking at the two *conditional* operators. They provide for the execution of a command on the condition that some other command has succeeded or failed. For instance, sometimes we want the second part of a sequence of commands done *only if* the first part is *successful*. Other times we may want a program to do something *only if* an initial command *fails*. The shell supplies the && (double ampersand) and the ‖ (double pipe) operators to meet these desires.

Suppose you use *grep* to search a file for a word. Then *grep* reports back to the shell on whether it was successful or not in finding that word. Like other UNIX commands, it does this by providing an *exit status*. If a command goes off without a hitch, this status value is 0. If something goes wrong, the status is nonzero; the actual value may depend upon what exactly went wrong. The *grep* command, for example, returns an exit status of 1 if it fails to find the pattern, and a value of 2 if something worse (such as a garbled pattern) turns up. In a command like

```
grep Aida slaves && echo Save Aida!
```

the command following the && is performed only if the exit status is 0, that is, only if the string *Aida* were found in the file *slaves*. Similarly, in a command like

```
grep Aida slaves || echo No Aida!
```

the command following the ‖ is performed only if the initial command fails, that is, has a nonzero exit status.

You can use a conditional operator to make a simple compile-and-run script:

```
cc $* && a.out
```

This says, "Compile the list of files given as command-line arguments. If the compilation of the C program succeeds, run the compiled version (*a.out* by default)."

Or suppose you want a script that *cat*s a program only if it contains the desired word. You can create a file (call it *grat*, for example) and place the following script in it:

```
grep $1 $2 > /dev/null && cat $2
```

Let's make the file executable and try it out.

```
$ grat Fertie ami
$
```

The string *Fertie* was not found in the file *ami*, so nothing was printed. Now try again:

```
$ grat Lara ami
Sandy  McTavish
Lara Felimar
Tug Uniflare
Ben Gong
Teresa Tigora
$
```

Now, because Lara is in the *ami* file, the entire file was shown. Incidently, we used redirection to the file */dev/null* (as discussed in Chapter 2) to discard the output of a successful *grep*. Otherwise the matching line would have been printed twice: once by *grep* and once by *cat*.

In the next chapter we will discuss the *if* statement; it represents an extension of the powers of these conditional statements.

Command Terminators: *newline, ;, and &*

How does the computer know where one command ends and another begins? Normally, the *newline* character, generated by the ⌷Return⌷ key, acts as the signpost. But the semicolon and the ampersand also serve as command terminators. We've already seen that a command line like

```
cd plonk; ls -l
```

causes *cd plonk* to be treated as one command and *ls –l* as the next. Similarly, the command

```
spell epic > epic.sp & ed opera
```

is interpreted the same as

```
spell epic > epic.sp &
ed opera
```

Since the & is a command terminator, the

```
spell epic > epic.sp
```

is regarded as one command, while the edit command is treated as a second, subsequent command.

Special Shell Variables

We've seen that the shell keeps track of special shell variables such as *PATH*. There is another set of special shell variables (or parameters) that are set automatically by the shell. We've seen one of these already: *$#*, the parameter that keeps track of the number of positional parameters (*$1*, *$2*, etc.) that have been set. Here is the complete set:

$#	The number of positional parameters
$-	Shell options
$?	The exit status of the last executed command
$$	The process number *(PID)* of the current shell
$!	The process number of the last background command
$0	The name of the command being executed
$*	The list of positional parameters (shell arguments)
$@	Same as *$**, except when enclosed in double quotes

Here are some annotated examples:

```
$ date >> datelog
$ echo $?          ← What was status of last command?
0                  ← It was 0 (success)
$ date >> datelog &
4321
$ echo $!          ← What was the PID of the last background job?
4321               ← It was 4321
$ echo $$          ← What is the PID of the current shell?
3865               ← It is 3865
$
```

The response to *echo $?* tells us that the first command was successful. The response to *echo $!* tells us that the *PID* for the background command is 4321, and the response to *echo $$* tells us that the *PID* for the current shell is 3865.

The *$$* notation is convenient for producing unique names for temporary files. For instance, in a script you might have a line like

```
sort $1 >$1.$$
```

This would create a new, most likely unique, filename, such as *fardles.6854*, if *fardles* were the file being processed and if *6854* were the current *PID*. Later on, when the script cleans up its workspace, you could have a line like

```
rm $1.$$
```

to remove that file. This approach minimizes the chances of your accidentally wiping out some preexisting file unfortunate enough to have the same name as the temporary file produced by the script.

Question 4.9

Write a shell script that tells you its name and its *PID*.

We will discuss *$-* and *$@* later. Now let's move on to another special notation concerning shell variables.

Conditional Parameter Substitution: { } (Braces)

The braces are used for several constructions in which the value of the expression depends on whether or not a variable has been defined. More exactly, these constructions test for the variable to be defined and to not be the null string.

Let's look at the first form. It looks like this:

```
${variable-word}
```

If the variable exists, then this expression has the value of the variable. If the variable doesn't exist (or is the null string), then the expression has the value *word*.

For example, let's suppose that there is no variable called *fruit*. Look at the following exchange:

```
$ vege=potato
$ echo ${vege-radish}
potato
$ echo $fruit

$ echo ${fruit-peach}
peach
$ echo $fruit

$
```

First, we define the *vege* variable to be *potato*. Then, when we *echo* the expression *${vege-radish}*, we get *potato*, the value of *vege*. If *vege* had not been defined, the word *radish* would have been echoed. We see that sort of behavior for *echo ${fruit-peach}*. Here *${fruit-peach}* has the value *peach*, since *fruit* was undefined. The value of *fruit* is left undefined.

What would be a practical use for this construction? One example would be a script that works one way if the user does nothing and another way if the user creates a particular exported variable. For instance, suppose a script includes an *ls* command somewhere. By default, the command will be used with, for example, the *-s* and the *-a* options. But the user can create an exported variable (perhaps by defining and exporting it in the *.profile* file) to override the default options. We can set up this script fragment this way:

```
opts=${LOPTS-'-as'}
ls $opts
```

Then, if the variable *LOPTS* is undefined, *opts* is set to '*-as*', and the command is run this way:

```
ls -as
```

Suppose, however, the user has placed this line in her *.profile* file:

```
LOPTS='-lr' ; export LOPTS
```

Then, when the script is run, *opts* is set to *LOPTS*, and the command is run this way:

```
ls -lr
```

This creates a new default option selection for the user, and she can always change the option selection again just by redefining *LOPTS* before running the script.

There are three more conditional expressions that use braces; instead of -, they use =, +, and *?*.

The *${variable = word}* is a bit stronger than the - form. It works like the last expression except if the variable is undefined, in which case it goes a step further and assigns *word* as the variable's value:

```
$ echo ${fruit=peach}
peach
$ echo $fruit
peach
$
```

If the variable already is defined, it is left unchanged. Of the four forms, this is the only one that doesn't work with positional parameters:

```
${2-fig}          ← Ok (permits positional parameters)
${2=fig}          ← Not valid (can't use positional parameters)
```

A third variation is the expression *${variable + word}*. It has the value *word* if the variable *is* defined, and otherwise has no value:

```
$ echo ${vege+defined}
defined
$ echo ${florp+defined}

$
```

The fourth variation is *${variable?message}*. If the variable is defined, it works like the + form; that is, the whole expression has the same value as the variable. But if the variable is not defined, then *message* is printed, and the shell is exited. For example, suppose this script is in the file *catplus*:

```
cat ${plus?I am nonplussed}
echo Done!
```

Let's run this first with *plus* undefined.

```
$ sh catplus
I am nonplussed
$
```

Since *plus* was undefined, the message was printed, and the script was exited. (We can tell that the script was exited because the *echo Done!* command was never executed.)

Now let's define *plus*, setting it equal to the filename *plusfile*. (This is a file containing repetitions of the word *plus*.)

```
$ plus=plusfile; export plus
$ sh catplus
plus plus plus plus plus plus plus
plus plus plus plus plus plus plus
Done!
$
```

Now that *plus* was defined, the contents of *plusfile* (lots of *pluses*) were printed, along with the *echo* message. This form of conditional expression is useful when you put error checking into a script. It lets you halt execution of a script if things start to go wrong, as when we ran *catplus* with *plus* undefined.

Question 4.10

Suppose the only variables (other than the standard shell variables) defined in a shell are as follows:

```
goldfish=eric
halfbee=erik
```

What, then do the following commands produce?

a. echo My pet is ${goldfish-tuna}
b. echo Your pet is ${silverfish-tuna}
c. echo Her pet is ${halfbee+sidney}
d. echo His pet is ${wholebee+sidney}

Here's an example that quits execution if you forget to provide a command-line argument. Let the following be the contents of the file *checkarg*:

```
echo ${1?You forgot the argument} is the first argument
```

Now run it as a script with and without an argument:

```
$ sh checkarg flotilla
flotilla is the first argument
$ sh checkarg
You forgot the argument
$
```

If you omit the message after the question mark, the system will print a default message and terminate the script. Try it to find your system's default message.

The braces can also be used simply to enclose the variable name. That is, *${name}* is the same as *$name*. However, the enclosed form lets you combine the variable value with other characters. This lets you construct strings containing one or more variable values.

```
$ fat=lard
$ echo $fatso        ←Thinks fatso is an undefined variable

$ echo ${fat}so      ←Recognizes embedded variable
lardso
$
```

The shell thought the second line referred to a variable called *fatso*. Finding no such variable, it considered it undefined and printed the blank line. With the braces, we were able to construct a new word using the variable's value.

Note that you don't have to use this form for constructions like

```
$ echo $fat.so
lard.so
$
```

The reason is that the period is not a legal character for variable names, so the shell knows that the variable name must end before the period.

Neutralizing Metacharacters: Escapes and Quotes

Suppose you want to use some of the symbols we've seen literally, perhaps in a command like

```
echo Type a * if you are happy
```

Try it. You'll find that the * is replaced by a list of all your files! After all, that is what * means to the shell. To get around this difficulty, UNIX offers metacharacters that neutralize metacharacters. For this purpose it uses the backslash (\), which we have already met informally, single quotes ('), and double quotes (''). Let's see what each does. Characters given this negating treatment are said to be *escaped* or *quoted*.

The backslash negates the special qualities of whatever character immediately follows it. Unspecial characters are left that way. Here is an example:

```
$ echo \? \S \ \\ \[
? S \ [
$
```

Note that we need to use a \\ if we want \ printed. The single \ followed by a space is read as \space and is printed as a space, just as \S is printed as S.

Now suppose you wished to print the sequence *?*. You could use

```
echo \*\?\*
```

or you could type

```
echo '*?*'
```

The single quotes turn off the special meaning of every character between them:

```
$ echo 'Send $100 to whom?'
Send $100 to whom?
$
```

The double quotes are slightly less restrictive. They turn off all the metacharacters *except $, `, and *. We say they permit parameter expansion (recognizing the $ forms) and command substitution (recognizing the backquote form). Suppose we have a command *myname* that outputs the user's name. One possible version is this:

```
set `who am i`
echo $1
```

Now here is an example illustrating what the double quotes do:

```
$ echo `myname`
babar
$ echo '`myname` is big & smart'
`myname` is big & smart
$ echo "`myname` is big & smart"
babar is big & smart
$
```

Table 4.1 Escape Mechanisms

Escape Mechanism	Effect
\ (Backslash)	Negates special properties of the single character following it: * is a literal asterisk.
' ' (Pair of single quotes)	Negates special properties of all enclosed characters: 'Take this *$?# sentence literally.'
" " (Pair of double quotes)	Negates special properties of all enclosed characters *except* $, ` , and \: "The value of rent is $rent."

The single quotes cause the backquotes and the & to be printed literally. The double quotes also cause the & to be printed literally, but the `myname` is replaced by its output, *babar*.

Once you use an opening single or double quote, the shell expects you to provide a closing quote, too. If you hit Return before doing so, the shell shifts to its second prompt, telling you it expects more to the command:

```
$ echo 'The evening fog
> flowed through the
> low mountain passes.'
The evening fog
flowed through the
low mountain passes.
$
```

This gives you a means to print several lines with a single *echo*.

Question 4.11

How could you use *echo* to produce this output?

```
"Captain, where is the $978 screwdriver?"
```

Another use for quotes is to combine several words into one argument. Suppose we begin with the following executable shell script in the file *repeat*:

```
echo $1
```

Note the effect of using quotes now:

```
$ repeat five golden rings
five
$ repeat 'five golden rings'
five golden rings
$
```

When we omitted the quotes, *$1* is just the word *five*. When we use quotes, the entire phrase becomes *$1*. Double quotes have the same effect; of course they also allow command substitution and parameter expansion.

''$*'' and ''$@''

Earlier we mentioned that the notation *$@* meant the same as *$** unless enclosed in double quotes. Let's run a test comparing these two notations: ''$*'' and ''$@''. We place the following lines in the executable file *quotes*:

```
cat "$*"
cat "$@"
```

Now try the script out:

```
$ quotes no.1 no.2
cat: can't open no.1 no.2
This is the no.1 file.
And this is the no.2 file.
$
```

What's happening? First we're told the files can't be opened, then the file contents are printed anyway! The answer lies in how the two expressions in the script were expanded:

```
"$*"    expands to  "no.1  no.2"
"$@"    expands to  "no.1"  "no.2"
```

In other words, ''$*'' was expanded to a *single* argument, a *single* filename with a space in it. So *cat* was not complaining that it couldn't find the files *no.1* and *no.2*; instead, it complained it could not find the one file with the odd name ''*no.1 no.2*''. But ''$@'' was expanded to *two* separate filenames, so *cat* was able to work successfully. In general, we have these relationships:

```
"$*" expands to "$1 $2 $3 ... "
"$@" expands to "$1" "$2" "$3" ...
```

The first construction yields *one* argument; the second yields the same number of arguments as in the command line. Note that the ''$*'' notation follows the general pattern discussed in the preceding section, namely that material between quotes is recognized as a single argument. The *$@* provides a useful exception to the general rule.

Inserting Comments:

There is another metacharacter useful in shell scripts. It is the # symbol, and it tells the shell to ignore what follows. You don't even need a script to use it. For instance,

```
$ # this computer is not playing with a full stack
$
```

See? No reaction. The value of this metacharacter is that it lets you place explanatory comments in a shell script. Actually, not all UNIX systems recognize this meta-character. To find out if yours does, try issuing the above command and seeing whether your system complains or not.

We've gone through quite a few special shell notations, perhaps too many to easily keep in mind. The notations we've studied (along with two more that we will see in the next section) are summarized here.

SPECIAL SHELL CHARACTERS AND SYMBOLISMS

Wild-card substitution (filenames)

?	Any one character
*	Any combination of characters (including the null character) excluding an initial period
[*list*]	Any one character from the contained list
[^ *list*]	Any one character not in the contained list

Redirection and pipes

> *file*	Make *file* the standard output
< *file*	Make *file* the standard input
>> *file*	Make *file* the standard output, appending to it if it already exists
<< *word*	Take shell input up to the first line containing *word* or up to end of file
n> *file*	Make *file* the output for file descriptor *n*, where standard input is 0, standard output 1, and standard error 2

1>&2   Redirect standard output to standard error *command1* | *command2* make standard output of *command1* the standard input of *command2*

Other command line notations

\	Continue command on next line
&	Run preceding command in background
;	Command separator
spaces, tabs, and newlines	Word separators
()	Command grouping
command1 && *command2*	Run *command2* if *command1* succeeds
command1 || *command2*	Run *command2* if *command1* fails

Special shell variables

$#	The number of positional parameters
$-	Shell options
$?	The exit status of the last executed command
$$	The process number *(PID)* of the current shell
$!	The process number of the last background command
$0	The name of the command being executed
$*	The list of positional parameters (shell arguments)
$@	Same as *$**, except when enclosed in double quotes

Quoting

\	Interpret the following character literally
' '	Interpret the enclosed characters literally
" "	Interpret the enclosed characters literally except for *$* combinations and ***, which will be expanded into the corresponding parameter and filename values

Command substitution

`command`	Substitute the output of *command* for the expression inside the backquotes
#	Interpret the rest of the line as a comment

Parameter substitution

${*parameter-word*}   Has *parameter*'s value if any; otherwise has the value *word*
${*parameter=word*}   Has *parameter*'s value if any, otherwise has the value *word* and sets *parameter* to *word*

${*parameter + word*} If *parameter* is set, substitutes *word*, otherwise substitutes nothing

${*parameter?mesg*} Has *parameter*'s value if any, otherwise substitues *mesg* and exits from shell

Shell commands

:   The null command; does nothing but can have arguments

. file   Run commands in *file* without creating new shell

SHELL COMMANDS

Most UNIX commands are separate programs run by the shell, but a few commands are part of the shell program (*sh*) itself. Since no new processes need be started up to run these built-in commands, they use less time than the regular commands. Of course, their presence makes the *sh* program itself bulkier and slower, so the list of built-in commands is restricted to ones particularly useful to the shell. One example, which we have already discussed, is the *read* command for letting a shell script interactively read the value of a shell variable. There are approximately 20 shell commands described in the *sh* entry in the manual. We will look just at these: *set*, : (colon), . (dot), *export*, and *shift*.

We start with one we have used several times, *set*.

The Multipurpose *set* Command

So far we have seen two uses of *set*. The first is to produce a list of currently defined shell variables. To do that, just type the command *set* as described earlier in this chapter.

The second use is to assign values to the positional parameters *$1*, *$2*, etc. Recall, for example, that

```
set duckless fairbanks
```

sets the positional parameter *$1* equal to *duckless* and *$2* to *fairbanks*.

The third use, which we haven't yet seen, is to set options for the shell. Yes, the *sh* program, like many UNIX programs, has options. They can be specified when you explicitly create a shell:

```
sh -v
```

They can also be specified from within a shell by using the *set* command. Let's look at two options often used in debugging.

The *-v* option of *sh* causes the shell to echo each command before it is executed:

```
$ set -v
$ who am i
who am i
fafner     tty4  Jun 24 13:13
$ echo $-
echo $-
v
$
```

Now that we have set some shell options, we can try out the *$-* notation we mentioned earlier. It is supposed to provide a list of current shell options, and so it did.

The *-v* option becomes more useful when running and debugging a shell script, for we can use it to echo the commands within the strip. One way is to insert the *set -v* command in the script, but it is more convenient to invoke it as an option to the parent shell. Let's use the *possess* script we developed earlier in the chapter:

```
$ sh -v possess gold     ← We type this
filename=$1              ← Shell echoes commands in possess
set `who am i`
who am i
mv $filename $filename.$1
$
```

See how the shell echoed the commands within the script. Notice how the *set `who am i`* line is broken into two parts. First, the set command and its argument is printed. But the argument demands that the *who am i* command be run, so that command gets printed next.

The *-x* option for *sh* is similar, except that it shows the substitutions the shell makes; that is, it shows the value of expressions such as *$1* or filename expansions. It is instructive to use both options simultaneously, so that we can see the expressions before substitution (the *-v* option) and after substitution (the *-x* option). A plus sign at the beginning of a line marks the *-x* printout. Let's continue our example:

```
$ sh -vx possess gems
possess gems
+ possess gems
filename=$1              ← -v shows command from script
+ filename=gems          ← -x shows command after substitution
```

```
set `who am i`
who am i
+    fafner     tty3  Jun 24 13:18
mv $filename $filename.$1
+ mv gems gems.fafner
$
```

When a shell script misbehaves, these options let you check to see what is actually going on in the script. They are helpful debugging tools.

Question 4.12

What is the chief difference between the *-v* and the *-x* options to *set*?

The method of turning these options off depends on your version of UNIX. In System V you can turn the options off by using *set* and the option letter with a plus sign instead of a minus:

set +vx   ← Turns off v and x options (System V)

In UNIX Version 7 a lone - option turns off both the *x* and *v* options:

set -   ← Turns off v and x options (Version 7)

From the multitalented *set* let us move on to the feeble colon command.

The Do-Nothing Command: *:*

The colon is the shell's do-nothing command. That is, the following command has no effect:

```
$ :
$
```

Actually, this is a little unfair to the colon command, for it manages to be useful even when doing nothing. When a program has to select from several alternatives, doing nothing may be a valid choice for some circumstances. Or it may be used in setting up an indefinite loop, as we will see in the following chapter.

More practically, the colon command can have arguments. It doesn't do anything about them, but the arguments themselves can do something. For example, suppose you have written a script that assumes the variable *acctno* has been defined. Then you could put a line like this at the beginning of the script:

```
: ${acctno?'No acctno variable! I can\'t go on.'}
```

This will cause the script to halt if *acctno* hasn't been defined. Recall that the *${* variable *?* message *}* construction causes the procedure to terminate and the message to be printed if the concerned variable is not defined. So although the colon itself does nothing, the evaluation of its argument can stop the shell script before it makes a fool of itself.

Finally, even nonfunctioning arguments of the do-nothing colon command can be useful. Since the # symbol is not universally recognized as a comment marker, some programmers use the colon to indicate a comment. For example, you can place the following line in a script:

```
: this program cuts your taxes in half
```

Since the colon is the null command, this line has no effect on the running of the program, but someone reading the program code might find the comment useful. (In Chapter 6 we will see a possible implementation of this program.)

The shell has another command represented by a punctuation mark: the dot (.) command. Let's see what it does.

Executing Commands from a File: . (dot)

Suppose you have a list of UNIX commands in a file *comlist*. Then the following command reads and executes those commands: *.comlist*.

This sounds suspiciously like a shell script, but there are two important differences. First, standard shell scripts cause a new subshell to be created to run the script. The dot command, on the other hand, uses the same shell. It just uses redirection to take the commands from the file instead of from the keyboard. Secondly, the dot command does not allow you to use command line arguments. Obviously, this second difference makes the dot command less powerful than the standard shell script. But what are the implications of the first difference?

The most important implication is that a script executed via the dot command *can* change the value of a shell variable in the current shell. Recall that normally shell variables are local to a particular shell. The *export* command lets you pass a variable's value from parent shell to child shell, but there is no comparable mechanism for passing a value from child to parent. The *dot* command, however, creates no child process, so any changes it produces apply to the original shell. Let's look at an example. First, put the following lines into a file called *tryit*:

```
echo $tenor
tenor=bjoerling
echo $tenor
```

Make the file executable; then we can do the following:

```
$ tenor=pavarotti; export tenor
$ tryit
pavarotti
bjoerling
$ echo $tenor
pavarotti
$
```

Our *export* command passed the value *pavarotti* on to *tryit*'s subshell. There, *tryit* changed the value of its *tenor* variable, but this change had no effect upon the *tenor* variable of the original shell.

Now let's try the same sequence, but using the dot command:

```
$   tryit
pavarotti
bjoerling
$ echo tenor
bjoerling
$
```

This time the change stuck, because it took place in the same shell.

Here is a related example. This time, let the text of *cdcave* be this:

```
cd /usr/fafner/housing/cave
pwd
```

Again, make the file executable and use it as follows:

```
$ pwd
/usr/fafner
$ cdcave
/usr/fafner/housing/cave
$ pwd
/usr/fafner
$
```

What's happened here? The script took us to the new directory, but then we were returned to the original directory without asking. The point is that each shell keeps its own record of its current working directory. The script created a subshell, and the subshell changed its directory. But when the subshell died and control returned to the original shell, we also returned to the current working directory of the original shell. The dot command, on the other hand, doesn't change shells, so any directory changes made under its auspices should hold. Do they? Try it and see.

One important use for the dot command occurs when you modify your *.profile* file. Normally, the changes you make there are not effective until the next time you log in, for that is when the system normally reads *.profile*. But you can use this command to put the current commands in *.profile* into effect:

```
. profile
```

The *export* command is another built-in shell command, one that we have mentioned several times already; let's review it now.

The *export* Command

The *export* command can be used in two ways. First, as we just saw, it can be used to export the value of a variable to a subshell. Secondly, *export* without arguments results in a printout of those variables that are already exported.

The *export* command is closely related to the concept of *environment*. We'll discuss that topic after looking at one more shell command.

Shifting Positional Parameters: *shift*

Before explaining this command, let's develop a need for it. In Chapter 3 we presented a simple pipe that searched a file for lines containing *Fresno* and then sorted the output:

```
grep Fresno billsdue | sort
```

It is a simple matter to generalize this to a shell script:

```
grep $1 $2 | sort
```

Here the first command-line argument (*$1*) will represent the string to be sought, and the second command-line argument (*$2*) will specify the file to be searched. But what if we were to alter this script so that it would read several files, not just

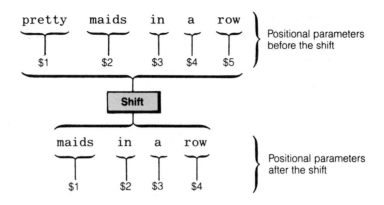

Figure 4.5
***Shift*ing Parameters**

one. That is, suppose we want it to read the files indicated by *$2*, *$3*, *$4*, and so on. We can't do this:

```
grep $1 $* | sort
```

The *$** means *$1 $2* ..., but we want *$2 $3* ... for the filename list. Otherwise *$1* will be used as the search word *and* as the name of the first file to be searched. Here's where *shift* comes in. It shifts *$2* to *$1*, *$3* to *$2*, and so on. This lets us write the script this way:

```
word=$1
shift
grep word $* | sort
```

Now *$** represents the new *$1 $2* ..., which is the same as the preshift values *$2 $3* ..., that is, the list of files to be searched.

What happens to the old *$1*? It's lost, which is why we saved its value in *word* before using *shift*.

Question 4.13

Write a script similar to that of Question 4.5, but let it take an indefinite number of files to be placed in the destination file.

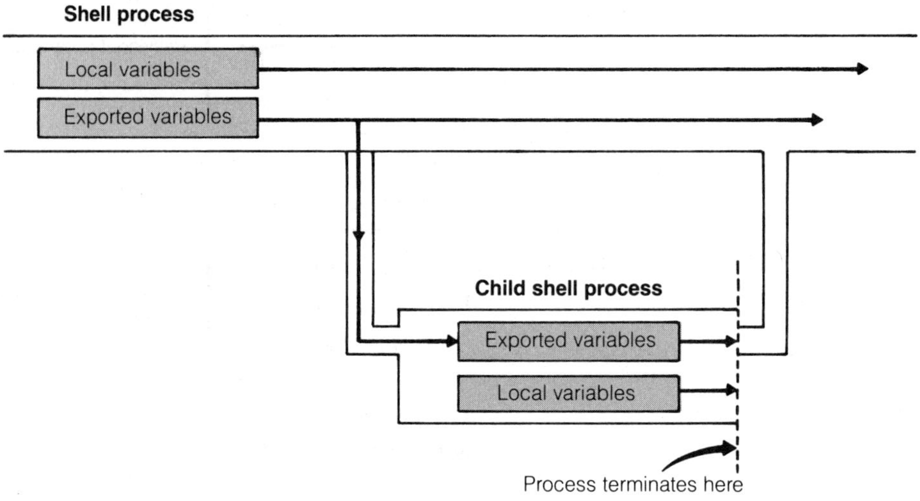

Shell process

Figure 4.6
Exported Variables Go to Child Shells

Well, those are enough shell commands for the while. We'll meet some more in the next chapter. Meanwhile, let's look at the concept of environment.

THE ENVIRONMENT

When a shell variable is exported, it is added to the *environment*. The environment is the set of all exported variables. (Typing *export* by itself, recall, causes the system to list the exported variables.) The importance of the environment is that a process can access and use any of the variables in its environment. This is true even if the process is a C program rather than a shell script. C programs, as we will see in later chapters, use the *getenv()* function to obtain those values.

The basic environment of your login shell is determined when you log in, typically by *export* commands placed in your *.profile* file. Usually, this basic environment consists of *HOME*, *PATH*, *TERM*, and perhaps one or two more variables. You can augment this basic environment with any variables that you define and export in *.profile*.

Any programs you launch, whether system programs or your own, can then use the information stored by these environment variables. One way to influence a process, then, is to alter its environment. Here are some ways to do that:

• Use the *export* command to add a new variable to the list. For example, type

```
name=wotan
export wotan
```

This variable will then become part of the environment of the current shell and of all processes (including shell scripts) descending from it. This modification of the environment lasts *only* for the duration of the shell in which the *export* command was given. If, for instance, you export a variable while in a subshell, that variable will be part of the environment only while that shell survives. When you return to the parent shell, that variable will no longer be part of the environment, unless, of course, it had also been exported in that shell. Thus, to make a variable accessible to all subshells, you should define and export it in your login shell.

- Modify the value of an exported variable before running a program by typing in the new definition first:

```
$ PATH=/usr/friplo/oddbin
$ reducto
```

Since the value of *PATH* is exported, the *reducto* program will search only the */usr/friplo/oddbin* directory for commands.

- Modify an exported variable within a shell script. For example, you may wish to have a line like

```
PATH=/bin: /bin/usr
```

in the script to make sure that the commands used in the script are the system commands and not commands of the same name in the user's directory.

- Make a temporary addition to or modification of the environment with the following construction:

```
name=value command
```

This causes the variable definition to hold only for the duration of the command. For example, the command

```
$ PATH=/usr/friplo/oddbin reducto
```

will cause *PATH* to be defined as shown only while the *reducto* command is run. Afterwards, *PATH* assumes its original value. For a longer look at this approach, suppose that the command is a shell script like this:

```
echo $utensil
```

Place it in the executable file *flatware*; then we can do the following:

```
$ utensil=fork; export utensil    ← Define and export utensil
$ flatware                        ← Run script
```

113

```
fork                              ← Output of script
$ utensil=spoon flatware          ← Run script with altered environment
spoon                             ← Altered output
$ echo $utensil                   ← Check variable's value
fork                              ← Original value
$
```

This approach of preceding the command with a variable definition on the same line changes the environment only for the command that was run. In contrast, the *export* approach changes the environment for all subsequent commands (unless overridden, as in this example). The one-command-line approach can be used to alter the value of an exported variable, but it can also be used to provide a new variable to a command's environment.

- System V provides a similar facility that also lets you temporarily replace the entire environment for a command. See the *env* entry in the manual.

The important points are that the environment is available to your programs and that you have control over the environment. Think of it as a shared pool of information for your programs.

CONCLUSION

In this chapter we have looked into many of the important features of the shell. We have seen how the shell expands patterns to match filenames. We have seen how shell variables, positional parameters, redirection of various sorts, and pipes can be used to get information into and out of shell scripts. We've seen how meta-characters and special notations unlock several special shell features, including command substitution and conditional variable evaluation. And we've looked at some of the built-in shell commands. In short, we've seen enough to reveal that the shell is a formidable, but not intractable topic.

As much as we have covered, we are not done with the shell. In the next chapter, we will take up the special programming structures that give shell programs the ability to make choices and do repetitive tasks. This makes efficient and powerful shell programs possible.

ANSWERS TO QUESTIONS IN CHAPTER 4

4.1   **a.** ??
      b. [a-z][a-z]
      c. *.c
      d. c*[0-9]
      e. p*t*

4.2   *PS1 = proceed:* or, better, *PS1 = 'proceed:'*

4.3 First, the question mark should be escaped (\?) so that it is not interpreted as a shell metacharacter. Second, it should be *read month*, not *read $month*.

4.4
```
echo Hi there!  What\'s your age\?
read age
echo $age! I\'ll be obsolete by the time I\'m that old!
```

4.5
```
cat $2 $3 > $1
```

4.6
```
set `date`
echo $4 $5 $1 $3 $2 $6
```

4.7
```
spell $1 > sp.$1 &
```

4.8 It redirects the output of *cat food* into the file *kitty*; the command is the same as
```
cat food > kitty
```
since the file descriptor 1 refers to the standard output.

4.9
```
echo My name is $0; my PID is $$
```

4.10 **a.** *eric*
   b. *tuna*
   c. *sidney*
   d. (null line)

4.11
```
echo '"Captain, where is the $978 screwdriver?"'
```

4.12 The *-v* option echoes each command before arguments and variables have been substituted for; the *-x* option echoes the commands after substitution has taken place.

4.13
```
DESTIN=$1
shift
cat $* > DESTIN
```

EXERCISES

1. Redo Question 6 as an interactive script.
2. Determine what the built-in shell variables are for your account. Which ones are exported?
3. Write a script that addresses you by your login name unless there is an exported variable called *NAME* set to (possibly) another choice, in which case that choice is used.

SHELL SCRIPTS: LOOPING AND MAKING CHOICES

In this chapter you will find:

- The *for* Loop
  - Using *for* Directly from the Shell
  - Using *for* with Command-line Arguments
  - Generating Values for a *for* Loop
  - Using a Loop
- Choice-Making: The *case* Statement
  - Setting Up Choices: | for *or*
- Conditional Looping: *while* and *until*
  - The *until* Loop
- The *if* Statement
  - The *if...then...else* Structure
  - Adding an *else if* to *if*: *if then...elif then...else*
- The *test* Command
  - File Checking
  - String Checking
  - Numerical Comparisons
  - Logical Operations
- Error Checking
  - The *exit* Command
  - Error Messages
- Cleaning Up Afterwards: *trap*
  - Signals
- Which Control Structure
- Conclusion
- Answers to Questions in Chapter 5
- Exercises

5

Shell Scripts: Looping and Making Choices

The shell, as we have just seen, has a dazzling array of capabilities. But what truly makes it into a programming language is its ability to control the flow of a program. The shell can loop through a script of similar operations, and it can choose among alternatives, taking actions that depend on the current conditions.

In this chapter we will look at the shell's mechanisms for control flow. We will begin with the *for* loop, which lets you program repetitive operations. Then we'll investigate the *case* statement, which lets you select from alternatives. From there we will move on to the *while*, *until*, and *if* constructions. As we study them, we will bring up useful related commands such as *test*. Finally, we will look into the process of making programs more robust by including error checking.

THE *for* LOOP

A *loop* is a programming device that lets you cycle through the same steps several times. Of the three UNIX shell loop forms, the *for* loop is the most used. It lets you apply the same sequence of operations to a series of subjects. Here is a simple example, a condensed and edited folk song.

```
for i in fly spider frog
do
    echo I know an old lady who swallowed a $i.
    echo Swallowed a $i\?
    echo Swallowed a $i!
done
```

Before explaining this script, let's see what it does when it is run. Assume it is in the executable file *ives*.

```
$ ives
I know an old lady who swallowed a fly.
Swallowed a fly?
```

Variable name   List of successive values for dear

```
for    dear  in  tammy dana linda hope
do
       mail $dear lvltr        ⎫  Commands to be executed for
       echo $dear >> lvlog     ⎭  each dear value in turn
done
```

Figure 5.1
A Typical *for* Loop

```
Swallowed a fly!
I know an old lady who swallowed a spider.
Swallowed a spider?
Swallowed a spider!
I know an old lady who swallowed a frog.
Swallowed a frog?
Swallowed a frog!
$
```

Now the intent should be clear. The *i* in the first line is a shell variable. The list of animals are values the variable assumes in succession as the shell executes the *for* loop. The instructions between *do* and *done* are executed with *i* set to the first value (*fly*) from the list. Then *i* is set to the next value (*spider*), and the instructions between *do* and *done* are executed again. Each time the *$i* represents the current value of the variable *i*. This continues until all values have been used.

You can use any name you like for the variable. We could replace *i* with *intake* and *$i* with *$intake*, and the program would work the same. However, *i* is a name often used, perhaps stemming from the FORTRAN tradition of using *i* as an index for a DO loop. The general form of the Bourne shell *for* loop is

```
for   variable-name in value1 value2 ...
do
    commands
done
```

The indentation is not necessary, but it makes it easier to see where loops start and stop. What is necessary is that the control words *for*, *do*, and *done* come at the beginning of a command line or else just after a semicolon or &. (The newline, semicolon, and & are the command separators we mentioned in Chapter 4. So we can restate the rule this way: the control words must follow a command separator. It is okay to have space between a separator and a control word, so a control word can be indented.) Here is an example using semicolons to produce a one-line *for* loop:

```
for i in 1 2 3;  do echo $i;  done
```

Question 5.1

Write a script that has this output:

```
Give me a U!
U!
Give me a N!
N!
Give me a I!
I!
Give me a X!
X!
```

Using *for* Directly from the Shell

We have run the *for* loop as a script in a file, but it (and the other structures we will discuss in this chapter) can be run directly from the shell, too. Here is a simple example to show you how running a loop directly from the shell works:

```
$ for i in see spot run     ← Start off with keyword ''for''
> do                        ← Shell responds to incomplete ''for'' with secondary
>     echo $i                 prompt
>done                       ← Keyword ''done'' tells shell loop structure is finished
see                         ← Now loop gets run, starting with first cycle
spot
run
$
```

Upon seeing the *for*, the shell knows the command is not complete until a *done* shows up. So it supplies the secondary prompt (the >) until it encounters *done*, then runs the script.

Using *for* with Command-line Arguments

A *for* loop also can get variable values from outside the shell instead of from an explicit list after the *in*. Here is a modified *ives* that uses command-line arguments to provide values for *i*. Recall that $* stands for all the command-line arguments following the script name:

```
for i in $*
do
    echo I know an old lady who swallowed a $i.
    echo Swallowed a $i\?
    echo Swallowed a $i!
done
```

Our new version works like this:

```
$ ives cat dog goat
I know an old lady who swallowed a cat.
Swallowed a cat?
Swallowed a cat!
I know an old lady who swallowed a dog.
Swallowed a dog?
Swallowed a dog!
I know an old lady who swallowed a goat.
Swallowed a goat?
Swallowed a goat!
$
```

Now the variable *i* takes in turn each of the three arguments as its value.
The combination

```
for i in $*
```

occurs so frequently that UNIX accepts the abbreviation

```
for i
```

for it. More precisely, this is the same as

```
for i in "$@"
```

(See Chapter 4 for more on this distinction.) This means we could rewrite the last version of *ives* as

```
for i
do
    echo I know an old lady who swallowed a $i.
    echo Swallowed a $i\?
    echo Swallowed a $i!
done
```

This version would work the same, cycling through each argument given to the script.

Here is one more example of a *for* loop. It sends a file via *mail* to several users and keeps a record (in another file) of which file was sent to whom. It is set up so that the file to be sent is the first command-line argument and the intended recipients form the remaining arguments. We have used the # symbol to introduce a few comments. If your UNIX version doesn't support this use of #, you can use the null command (*:*) instead, as discussed in Chapter 4.

```
# mailem -- sends mail and keeps a record
# Usage: mailem filename loginname(s)
letter=$1
shift
for person in
do
    mail $person <$letter
    echo $letter file sent to $person on `date` >> $HOME/letlog
done
```

The *shift* command, recall, moves the *$2* argument to the *$1* position, and so on. Thus the list of names for the *for* loop skips the original first command-line argument (the name of the file to be sent) and starts with the original arguments from number 2 on out. For example, the command

```
mailem query fonzy sheena hulk
```

would send the contents of the *query* file to *fonzy*, *sheena*, and *hulk*. Meanwhile, the *echo* command appends lines such as

```
query file sent to fonzy on Sun Jun 24 21:38:11 1984 PDT
```

to the *letlog* file in the user's home directory. Remember that backquotes substitute the output of a command for the backquoted command.

Question 5.2

Rewrite Question 5.1 so that it uses command-line input to provide the spell-out letters.

We've seen two ways to provide a list of values for a *for* loop: an explicit list after the *in*, and using command-line arguments. Now let's take a longer look at ways to do this.

Generating Values for a *for* Loop

There are many ways to get values to a *for* loop variable. Here are five:

1. List the values explicitly after *in*, as in

   ```
   for name in kinnison worsel tregonsee nadreck
   ```

2. Take the values from shell script arguments, as in

   ```
   for i in $*
   ```

   or the equivalent

   ```
   for i
   ```

   In either case, when using the program, you follow the command name with the desired list:

   ```
   mailem do.it.now  dagwood cathy beetle
   ```

3. Take filenames from a directory as values. The shell expands combinations (other than the built-in shell variables *$** and *$?*) involving * and *?* into filenames. Thus

   ```
   for file in *
   do
      cat $file
   done
   ```

   would cat in succession each file in the current working directory, and

   ```
   for file in FORT/*.f
   do
      mv $file old$file
   done
   ```

adds the prefix *old* to all the FORTRAN files in the *FORT* directory. We could use any name for the loop variable, including the venerable *i*, but we prefer to use the more descriptive *file*.

Note the difference between

```
for name in $*
```

and

```
for name in *
```

The first uses the command-line arguments as the value list for the variable *name*, while the second uses the filenames in the current working directory as the value list.

4. Take values from a shell variable. Here is an interactive program that reads and responds to a user's name:

```
echo Hi there!  What\'s your name\?
read NAME
for N in $NAME
do
     echo $N
done
echo is quite a name.
```

Putting it in the file *hi* and running it, we get

```
$ sh hi
Hi there! What's your name?
Desdemona Juliet Lear
Desdemona
Juliet
Lear
is quite a name.
$
```

The *read* command gave the value *Desdemona Juliet Lear* to *NAME*. Thus the *for* line became, in effect,

```
for N in Desdemona Juliet Lear
```

Then *N* was assigned each name from this list, one at a time. Thus each cycle through the loop printed just one name. Notice that a *for* loop can have other commands before and after it.

5. Take values from the output of a command. Recall that the backquotes allow us to obtain the output of a command. Using this, we can rework *ives* to take names from a file called *animals*:

```
for i in `cat animals`
do
    echo I know an old lady who swallowed a $i.
    echo Swallowed a $i\?
    echo Swallowed a $i!
done
```

Then the words in the file *animals* are used as successive values for *i*. With this method, you can easily extend the song to hundreds of verses.

Of these possibilities, the most common uses are choices 2 and 3, taking values from the command arguments or from the directory of filenames.

Using a Loop

The *for* loop is invaluable when you want to process several files in some manner. Many UNIX commands, of course, can already handle several files. For example, to do a word count on several files, you can just type

```
wc phys chem biol astr
```

and the word count for each file (plus the total count) are printed out. The *wc* command has a loop mechanism built in, so you don't have to make a loop to use it. But some commands don't work that way. For instance, we used a loop earlier with the *mv* command in order to change the names of several files. Or if you wanted to sort several files individually, returning each sorted output to the corresponding original file, you could use this loop:

```
for file in $*
do
    sort -o $file $file
done
```

Here, the list of files is taken from the command-line argument list. (Using * instead of *$*ch* would have sorted every file in the directory!)

Similarly, you often need a loop to apply two or more processes or operations in turn on a set of files:

```
for file in $*
do
    spell $file > sp.$file
done
```

Here each file in turn is checked for spelling, with the misspelled words redirected to an appropriately named new file. For instance, the potential misspelling from a *rattail* file would be placed in the file *sp.rattail*.

A Word-Seeking Program

Let's undertake a slightly more complicated problem. Suppose we have a file full of words, and we wish to search through several other files for each of these words. The separate file of words, for instance, could contain a list of historical names, and the other files could be chapters in a history. The *grep* command, of course, is designed to search through a file for a word. It even accepts multiple files as arguments. But it only accepts one word (or, more generally, one search pattern) at a time. So to process several words with *grep*, we need to use a loop.

Actually, we could use UNIX's *fgrep* or *egrep* to solve the problem, since these variations of *grep* do accept a list of search words; see Appendix A. But doing it that way won't teach us anything about loops, so we will stick to using *grep*. Also, your system may not have *grep's* fancier relatives.

Let's create an executable shell script called *wordseek*. The arguments to this script will be the name of the word file (the file containing the words for which we will search) and the names of the files to be searched. Here is one approach:

```
# wordseek -- searches files for words in a source file
# first argument is the source file
# subsequent arguments are the files to be searched
source=$1
shift
for i in `cat $source`    ← Get words from source file
do
    grep $i $*    ← $i is the word, $* are the filenames
done
```

Note that we have used the # symbol to include a few comments. The variable *source* is set to the first command-line argument, and the *shift* command drops the original *$1* from the argument list, leaving *$* equal to the rest of the arguments, the files to be searched. Suppose we create a source file *musicians* containing these names:

```
Wagner Haydn Mozart Beethoven Brahms Chopin Bruckner Bach
Shubert Zappa Mahler Verdi Moussorgsky Berlioz Bizet
```

We want to search the files *ch1*, *ch2*, and so on, up through *ch9*, for these names. (Perhaps we wish to prepare an index.) Using the *wordseek* script can produce results like these:

```
$ wordseek musicians ch.[1-9]
ch1: but Aunt Hildy.  Then Wagner, my dachshund, decided to
ch8: "Wagner!" I cried, "you are back!" But then I saw it was
ch1: with some early Mozart playing in the background. Ethan
ch5: the Cafe Chopin -- or was it the Cafe Shogun?  Anyway, we
ch3: when Fred Bach, the grocer, danced with little Mindy that
ch6: To her, music meant Bach. That was it. So I had to sell the
$
```

Note that one word is taken from the source file, and all the search files are searched for that one word before the next word is taken. Apparently this particular book was not heavily into music. (The *grep* command prefixes found lines with the filename when more than one file is searched.)

Now that we've seen the basics of looping, let's try choice-making.

CHOICE-MAKING: THE *case* STATEMENT

The *case* statement lets a shell script choose from a list of alternatives. The general form of the *case* statement is

```
case value in
choice1)   commands ;;
choice2)   commands ;;
   . . .
esac
```

Here *choice1* and *choice2* are labels that identify potential choices of action. If, for example, the *value* portion has the value *choice1*, then the commands following the *choice1* label are executed. The word *esac* marks the end of the *case* statement. Let's look at an example to see how a *case* statement works and to pick up some of the details.

One use for the *case* statement is to set up *menus*. As you may know, many software packages are *menu-driven*; that is, they offer you a menu of choices and ask what you want. Here is a simple example showing how to create a menu-style shell script with a *case* statement:

```
echo Please enter the number of the program you wish to run:
echo  '1  date           2  who'
echo  '3  ls             4  pwd'
read choice
case $choice in
1) date ;;
2) who ;;
3) ls ;;
4) pwd ;;
*) echo That wasn\'t one of the choices! Bye. ;;
esac
```

We used quotes in the *echo*s of lines 2 and 3 to preserve the spacing; otherwise *echo* would print just one space between each argument, ignoring what it conceives of as surplus spaces. This *case* statement tries to match the value of *$choice* to one of the following labels; in this case, we have used *1*, *2*, *3*, and *4* for labels. The *)* (right parenthesis) is used to identify label names. The double semicolon serves to separate one choice from the next. Before going into more detail, let's see what the script does. Assume the script is in the executable file *askme*. Here are two sample runs:

```
$ askme
Please enter the number of the program you wish to run:
1  date           2  who
3  ls             4  pwd
1
Mon Jun 25 11:53:11 PDT 1984
$ askme
Please enter the number of the program you wish to run:
1  date           2  who
3  ls             4  pwd
why
That wasn't one of the choices! Bye.
$
```

When we entered a "1", the case statement caused the command with the *1)* label to be run. The command labeled *)* was executed when something other than 1, 2, 3, or 4 was entered. The double semicolon (*;;*) is used to end each choice, and the *esac* (*case* spelled backwards) marks the *end* of the *case* statement. Actually, the double semicolon is not mandatory after the final choice, but it does no harm to use it there. Like *for*, *do*, and *done*, the words *case* and *esac* must come at the beginning of a command; that is, at the beginning of a line or after a semicolon or &.

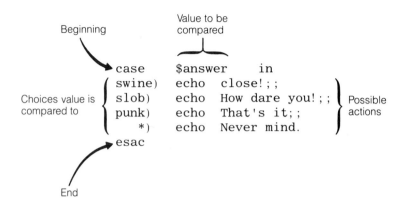

**Figure 5.2
A Typical case Statement**

There is nothing magical about using numbers to label the cases. We could just as easily use letters. Just remember to follow each choice with a) (right parenthesis) when using it as a label. Thus, instead of having

```
1) date;;
```

we could have

```
a) date;;
```

In summary, a case statement contains a list of labeled choices. The list of choices is scanned to find the first one that matches the value following the keyword *case*. The choice labeled *)* matches any value, so it is often used as the last choice to act as a catchall. (Making it the first choice would cause the first choice to match any value, and the *case* would not be searched any further.) If no choices match and if there is no *)* choice, then nothing is done, and the program moves on to whatever comes after the *case* statement. Another example of a *case* statement is shown in Figure 5.2.

Setting Up Choices: | for *or*

Let's look at a few more examples that illustrate the process of setting up and labeling choices. Instead of creating a menu, lets create a quiz format. (This one may be of some interest to Scrabble players, for all the choices are valid words.)

```
echo Which of the following is a hand spice grinder?
echo quate qursh quern quillet
```

```
read answer
case $answer in
quern) echo Correct you are! ;;
quate | qursh | quillet) echo Nope, $answer is wrong. ;;
*) echo Very wrong: $answer is not even a choice! ;;
esac
```

Aha! Something new! The bar symbol (|) here is *not* a pipe. Rather, it serves as an *or* operator. (The two are, however, the same keystroke. UNIX depends on the context to decide which meaning a | symbol has.) This *or* operator lets us attach more than one label to the same response. Notice that now the choice labels are entire words and patterns; we aren't limited to using numerals and single letters. Let's put this script in a file *quiz* and see if it works.

```
$ sh quiz
Which of the following is a hand spice grinder?
quate qursh quern quillet
qursh
Nope, qursh is wrong.
$
```

Question 5.3

Write a script that presents a multiple-choice question, gets the user's answer, and reports back whether the answer is right, wrong, or not one of the choices.

More on Choices: Command-Line Arguments

So far our examples have used a shell variable for the value part of a *case* statement. As with the *for* statement, there are other ways to feed a value to a *case* statement. For instance, the next example shows how to use a command-line argument.

```
case $1 in
dog) echo Man\'s best friend ;;
man) echo Cat\'s best friend ;;
*) echo You got me!
esac
```

131

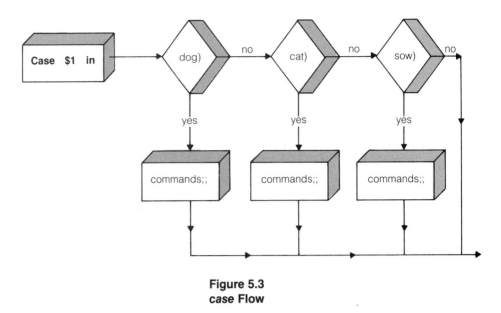

Figure 5.3
case Flow

Here we use a positional parameter instead of a regular shell variable for the *case* value. If this script were placed in the executable file *identify*, it would be used like this:

```
$ identify dog
Man's best friend
$ identify UNIX
You got me!
$
```

In each case, the command-line argument was matched to the list of choices in the script. That is, in the first run, *$1* was replaced by *dog*.

Pattern Matching

We can use the UNIX shell's pattern-matching abilities in the choice labels. We used one example already, when we used *)* to match any pattern. We can also use the *?* and *[]* metacharacters. They are used for matching patterns in the same way as they are used in matching filenames. (See Chapter 4 for a review.) For instance, consider the following example:

```
case $1 in
dog) echo Man\'s best friend ; ;
[aeiouAEIOU]*) Echo word beginning with a vowel ; ;
```

```
??) echo a two-letter word ;;
*) echo I don\'t know
esac
```

Here, for instance, the pattern *[aeiouAEIOU]** stands for any one letter from within the brackets followed by any characters whatsoever. Put the script in the file *whatisa*, make it executable, and run it a few times:

```
$ whatisa obelisk
word beginning with a vowel
$ whatisa dog
Man's best friend
$ whatisa computer
I don't know
$ whatisa oo
word beginning with a vowel
$
```

The last example (*oo*) illustrates our earlier claim that a *case* stops after the first match. That is, *oo* matches the *??* pattern, but since it also matches the preceding pattern for vowels, the *case* doesn't check any further than the first match.

Question 5.4

Write a script which accepts the word oak as an answer regardless of whether upper-case or lower-case letters are used anywhere in the word.

More on Using *case*

The *case* value portion can be a shell variable or a shell script argument or anything else that produces a value. For example

```
case `pwd` in
```

would be a valid beginning of a *case* statement. The backquotes cause the output of *pwd*, namely, the current working directory, to be the value against which the choices are compared.

What if you want more than one command to be executed for a given choice? Then just use the standard conventions for command lines. That is, you can put one command per line, or you can separate commands on one line by a semicolon. Just place the double semicolon after the final command of the series.

Let's look at another example. Here's a script that uses both a *for* loop and a *case* statement to do some housekeeping:

```
for file in *      ← Look at all files in current directory
do
    case $file in
       *.old)  rm $file ;;
       *.c)    mv  $file $HOME/cstuff ;;
       *.f)    rm -i $file ;;
    esac
done
```

The *for* line causes each file in the current directory to be examined in turn. As each filename is passed along to the *case* statement, the *case* statement decides what, if anything, is to be done with the file. Files whose names end in *.old* are removed. Files whose names end in *.c* are moved to another directory. Files whose names end in *.f* are removed using the *-i* option of *rm*, which asks the user to verify if he or she really wants the file removed. The *case* statement is processed once each cycle of the *for* loop, each time for a new filename. Note how the value used by the *case* statement (*$file*) comes from a variable that gets its value from a *for* statement.

In summary, the *case* statement is a powerful and flexible tool. It matches a value to a list of choices, and it then executes the instructions following the matching label. The value portion of the statement can come from shell variables, shell-script arguments, or command outputs. The patterns that are matched to this value can use shell metacharacters such as *, ?, and []. The patterns can also use the metacharacter | to mean *or*, so that more than one pattern can correspond to a given command. The commands themselves can use pipes and redirection, and more than one command can be attached to a given choice.

Now let's return to the subject of looping.

CONDITIONAL LOOPING: *while* AND *until*

UNIX offers three loop structures: *for*, *while*, and *until*. The *for* structure, as we have seen, takes a list of things (files, perhaps, or arguments) and runs through a set of commands on the list members until the list is exhausted. The *while* and *until* structures, on the other hand, do not use a list. Instead, they hinge their behavior upon the success or failure of a command.

The general form of the *while* loop is this:

```
while control command
do
      commands
done
```

Each cycle, the shell attempts to execute the control command. If the command returns a zero exit status (success), the commands between *do* and *done* are executed. The process continues until the control command yields a nonzero exit status.

Let's look at some samples and see how this works.

```
# grit -- grep and quit when word not found
# Usage: grep word file(s)
word=$1        ← Save word
shift          ← Move first file to $1
while grep $word $1 > /dev/null
do
   shift       ← Move next file in input to $1
done
echo First file not containing $word is \1
```

As the comments and message suggest, this script searches through a list of files and halts at the first file that does not contain the given word. Let's look at the logic of the program and at how *while* works. Suppose we give a command like

```
grit UNIX report.[1-9]
```

and that the directory contains the files *report.1* through *report.9*. First, the variable *word* gets set to *UNIX*. Then the shift command shifts *report.1* to *$1*. The *while* command now becomes

```
while grep UNIX report.1  > /dev/null
do
   shift
done
```

What happens now? First, the command *grep UNIX report.1* is run. As we discussed in Chapter 4, this command returns an *exit status* to inform the shell of its success or failure. We redirect the output to */dev/null* because we are just interested in whether or not the word is found and not in printing out the matching lines. For many UNIX versions, the *-s* option to *grep* also suppresses such output. If the *grep* command reports success, then the instructions between *do* and *done* are executed. If it reports failure (it didn't find the word), the loop is terminated.

Suppose that *UNIX* is found in *report.1*. Then *grep* reports success, and the following *shift* command is executed. This shifts *report.2* to *$1*, and the next loop becomes this:

```
while grep UNIX report.2 > /dev/null
do
```

```
        shift
done
```

Now suppose the *grep* command fails; there is no *UNIX* in *report.2*. Then the loop terminates, and the script moves to the next line, which becomes

```
echo First file not containing UNIX is report.2
```

The program does have a bug; it fails when all the files contain the sought-after word. (The program tries to shift past the end of the command-line argument list.) This bug can be eliminated using the error-checking methods that we discuss later. Meanwhile, let's concentrate on the workings of the *while* loop.

The key point here is that the *while* loop keeps recycling until the command following the *while* fails. As previously mentioned, at each cycle, the shell attempts to execute the control command. If the command returns a zero exit status (success), the commands between *do* and *done* are executed. The process continues until the control command yields a nonzero exit status.

The UNIX *while* loop is different from the more typical *while* loops of languages like C or Pascal. Those loops test to see whether a certain condition is true or not: is X greater than 6, is Y equal to Z. The UNIX *while*, on the other hand, depends on the success or failure of a command: did *grep* find the word, did *diff* find two files to be the same or not. But what if you want your UNIX script to deal with the first kind of question? For instance, suppose you want to see if a number typed by a user is greater than 6. Then you need to use the *test* command to help make the loop work. We'll come back to that topic after we look at some more control flow statements.

The *until* Loop

The *until* loop is similar to a *while* loop, except it is executed *until* the test condition succeeds. In other words, a *while* loop runs until a control command fails, and the *until* loop runs until a control command succeeds. The until structure looks like this:

```
until control command
do
      commands
done
```

Here the control command is executed. If it fails, the commands between *do* and *done* are executed, and the control command is attempted again. The process continues until the control command reports success.

Here is an example of an until loop that reports when a file is created:

```
# isdone -- report when file $1 is created
# Usage: isdone filename
until ls | grep $1 > /dev/null
do
    sleep 30
done
echo file $1 is here
```

Here the *sleep* command causes the script to rest for 30 seconds before running the control command again. The loop continues until the name given by *$1* shows up when *ls* lists files. Such a script could be used to check on the progress of a long background job, for example. The script could also be run in background, so that you could work on something else.

Question 5.5

Write a script that takes a login name as a command-line argument and reports to you when that person logs in. Have it send a greeting to that person; you can use redirection to his or her terminal. (Such a script would be run in background.)

The *while* and *until* loops are sometimes termed *indefinite loops* because often we do not know in advance how many cycles they will loop through. This is in contrast to the *for* loop, which cycles through a list of items. The number of loopings normally equals the number of items (files, arguments, etc.) in the *for* loop control list. However, the *if* statement, which we discuss next, can be used to force an early exit to a *for* loop.

Now let's look at another kind of control flow statement.

THE *if* STATEMENT

If you have worked with FORTRAN, BASIC, Pascal, C, Logo, or any other popular high-level language, you have probably used some form of *if* statement. The UNIX shell *if* statement has one noteworthy difference from the others. In conventional programming languages, *if* statements usually are concerned with the values of variables — is *x* greater than 3, is *A$* ''human'', is *response* ''y''? The UNIX *if*, like the UNIX *while* and *until*, is concerned with the status of *commands* — did the *cp* command work properly, did *find* find the file it was looking for?

The simplest form of an *if* statement is this:

```
if control command
then
      commands
fi
```

First the command following the *if* is executed. If the command is successful (exit status of 0), then the commands between the *then* and the *fi* are performed. The words *if*, *then*, and *fi* must come at the beginning of a command line or just after a semicolon.

Here is an example of the UNIX *if*; it compares two files and removes the second one if the files are identical:

```
# clean -- removes a duplicate file
#Usage:  clean file1 file2
if cmp -s $1 $2
then
    rm $2
fi
```

To use this script on the files *tato* and *tat0*, you would type the following:

```
clean tato tat0
```

(We will assume from now on that a script is contained in an executable file bearing the name given on the first comment line.) The *cmp* command compares two files to see if they are the same or not. Normally it reports back the numerical location of the first difference, but the *-s* option of *cmp* suppresses the usual output; only the status of the command (success or 0 if the files match, failure or 1 if they don't) is reported to the shell.

Note that our example can also be represented by the conditional operator notation of Chapter 4:

```
cmp -s $1 $2  && rm $2
```

The conditional operator *&&* causes the second command to be performed only if the first one is successful. That is the same result we got from the *if* statement.

The *if...then...else* Structure

Since this second form works just as well, why do we need an *if* statement? First, the *if* form allows you to place a large body of commands between the *then* and the *fi*. Second, the *if* form is easier for programmers with nonUNIX backgrounds to recognize. (That point may be a plus or a minus, depending on your attitude.) Third, the *if* statement also gives you an *else* option.

The general form of the *if...else* construction is this:

```
if control command
then
    commands
else
    commands
fi
```

Let's use this form to extend our first example by adding an else part; we also add a second statement to the first alternative:

```
# clean1 -- removes a duplicate file
# Usage:  clean1 file1 file2
if cmp -s $1 $2
then
    rm $2
    echo The $2 file was a duplicate and has been removed.
else
    echo The files $1 and $2 are not the same.
fi
```

Following the plan we announced earlier, we'll assume that this script is in the executable file *clean1*. Then a run could look like this:

```
$ clean1 letter lettera
The lettera file was a duplicate and has been removed.
$ clean1  letter letterb
The files letter and letterb are not the same.
$
```

As you can see, the response of the program depends on how the *cmp* procedure went.

If the first command executes successfully, then the commands between *then* and *else* are executed; if they are different, the commands between *else* and *fi* are executed.

139

Adding an *else if* to *if*: *if then … elif then … else*

There is one further extension of the *if* form, one that lets you string several alternatives (multiple *elses*) one after the other. The key is using the keyword *elif*, which is short for *else if*. The general form looks like this:

```
if control command1
then
    commands
elif control command2
then
    commands
else
    commands
fi
```

If the first control command (*control command1*) is successful, then the commands after the first *then* up to the *elif* are executed. Otherwise, *control command2* after the *elif* is attempted; if it is successful, then the commands after the following *then* up to the next *elif* or *else* are executed. The process continues until the closing *fi* is reached.

Here, for example, is a script that looks through a set of two files until it finds a required word, then quits.

```
# a_or_b -- finds if name is in atype or btype file
# Usage: a_or_b name
if grep $name atype > /dev/null        ← Search atype file for $name
then
    echo $name is Type A    ← If word found, echo result and quit
elif grep $name btype > /dev/null      ← Else search btype file
then
    echo $name is Type B
else                        ← Done if word not found in either file
    echo $name was not found
fi
```

Suppose you type

```
a_or_b lancelot
```

If *lancelot* is in the file *atype*, then the script prints

```
lancelot is Type A
```

and quits. Otherwise, it goes on to search *btype* for *lancelot*, and if that fails, it goes to the final else. So each alternative is explored only if all the alternatives before it have failed.

You can extend this construction to include more elifs if you like. Just remember to give each one its own control command to check.

THE *test* COMMAND

The working of a *while*, *until*, or *if* construct depends upon whether or not a command has a successful status. But the status of a command is not the only matter of interest to us or to a script. Other factors may influence which choice a script should make. Is the argument of a shell script a file or a directory? Did the user provide enough arguments? Did the user provide the correct code word? We would like to deal with these sorts of questions. UNIX obliges by providing the *test* command. This command investigates just the sort of questions we've raised, and then it translates the result into language the control statement can understand, that is, success or failure. Let's see how that works.

Suppose we want to see if a shell variable called *dog* has the value *lassie*. We test for equality by using the *test* command:

```
$ dog=lassie        ← Set dog variable to lassie
test $dog = lassie ← Test for equality
$
```

Hmm. Nothing seems to have happened. But keep in mind that a *while* or *if* test looks at the *exit status* of a command, not at the *output* of the command. The *test* command produces no output, but it does produce an exit status. In particular, it produces a 0 exit status if the test is successful, and a 1 exit status if it fails. Let's investigate this by using the *$?* notation, which provides the exit status of the preceding command:

```
$ dog=lassie            ← Set dog to lassie
$ test $dog = lassie    ← Test if $dog is lassie
$ echo $?               ← Check status of test command
0                       ← Success: $dog is lassie
$ test $dog = pluto     ← Test if $dog is pluto
$ echo $?               ← Check status of test command
1                       ← Failure: $dog is not pluto
$
```

Aha! The status of the *test* command does depend on the truth or falsity of the arguments to *test*.

Note the form for testing the equality of strings:

```
test string1 = string2
```

There should be a space on either side of the = sign. This is different from value assignment for shell variables; in that instance, there should be no spaces next to the = sign.

Let's try out this string-comparing capacity in a simple game loop:

```
# numguess -- user guesses a number
echo I\'m thinking of a number between 1 and 50.
echo Guess it and earn my approval.
read guess
until test $guess = 33
do
    echo  Nope, guess again.
    read guess
done
echo  Well done!
```

This loop keeps prompting the user for a new guess until he gets the right number. Here is a sample run:

```
$ numguess
I'm thinking of a number between 1 and 50.
Guess it and earn my approval.
5
Nope, guess again.
6
Nope, guess again.
33
Well done!
$
```

Of course, you can also use the *test* command if you wish to base an *if* decision on the existence of files, the equality of strings, or the like:

```
echo What is the best operating system\?
if test $1 = UNIX
then
    echo I agree.
else
    echo I never heard of $1.
fi
```

Place this in an executable file *modesty* and try it:

```
$ modesty
What is the best operating system?
UNOX
I never heard of UNOX
$
```

(UNOX, of course, is widely used in agrarian societies in conjunction with PLOW-based hardware.)

The *test* command has several basic modes. First, it has several options dealing with files. Second, it can check to see if a file is actually a terminal. Third, it can compare strings, as in our examples. Finally, it can check for various numerical relationships. In each case, the command returns *true* (exit status 0) if the test is passed. The *test* command can also combine basic expressions into larger logical units. Let's take a look at these capabilities, beginning with file checking.

File Checking

The *test* command has several options for checking the status of a file. Here are the main ones:

```
-r file   ← True if the file exists and is readable
-w file   ← True if the file exists and is writable
-f file   ← True if the file exists and is not a directory
-d file   ← True if the file exists and is a directory
-s file   ← True if the file exists and has a size greater than 0
```

This represents the Version 7 list. System V offers several more options, most notably a *-x* option for identifying executable files. Most of the rest are more arcane than what we have shown here.

Here is how to use options from this set. Suppose we want to know if we have permission to change the contents of a certain file; that is, is the file writable? Then we can do this:

```
$ test -w .profile ; echo $?
0
$ test -w /etc/passwd ; echo $?
1
$
```

Yes, we can write in our *.profile* file, but the */etc/passed* file is off limits.

Note the usage. We just follow the option with the name of the file we wish to test. (There is a space between the option letter and the filename.) Then we check the status of the *test* command. Here we used *$?* to do that, but more typically, the status is used to direct one of the conditional structures. For example, a shell script could contain the following fragment, which checks to see if a file is readable before copying it:

```
if test -r $1
then
    cp $1 $HOME/project_x
fi
```

Question 5.6

Write a script that takes a command-line argument and reports on whether it is a directory, a file, or something else.

There is one file-related option that does not use a filename for an argument; instead, it uses the file descriptor we discussed in Chapter 2:

```
-t [fildes]  true if the file indicated by file descriptor fildes
(1 by default) is open and a terminal
```

Recall that the system assigns each open file a small integer *file descriptor* number, with 0, 1, and 2 representing the standard input, standard output, and standard error. So

```
test -t
```

tests if the standard output is being directed to your terminal, and

```
test -t 0
```

tests if the standard input is connected to your terminal.

This *-t* option lets you (or your program) check, for example, if the standard input has been redirected:

```
$ test -t ; echo $?
0                              ← Terminal was standard output
```

```
$ test -t > save ;  echo $?   ← Redirect standard output
1                             ← Terminal was not standard output
$
```

In the first case the standard output was the terminal, so *test* returned a 0 value. For the second case, the standard output was directed to a file, so the standard output was not the terminal.

This feature would be typically used within a shell script to help a command to decide where to route output.

The next set of variations concerns character strings.

String Checking

A string is just a series of characters; it could represent a filename, a command name, or the value of a variable, for example. The first two options we will look at compare two strings, and the first one we have already used.

```
string1 = string2   ← True if the strings are the same
string1 != string2  ← True if the strings differ
```

The spaces are obligatory:

```
test $ans = hoop     ← Valid form
test $ans= hoop      ← Invalid form
```

Three more options deal with the size of a string:

```
-n string    ← True if the string has nonzero length
-z string    ← True if the string has zero length
string       ← True if the string is not the null string
```

An undefined variable, for example, appears to be a null string:

```
$ frog=bumpy
$ test $frog ;  echo $?
0
$ test $frag ;  echo $?   ← Frag not defined
1
$
```

145

Question 5.7

Write a script that asks for the capital of California and repeats the question until the user gets it right.

We can use *test* to make a *while* loop act like a *for* loop:

```
while test $1
do
    . . .
    shift
done
```

The commands in the loop are executed using *$1*. The *shift* command moves *$2* to *$1*, and the cycle is repeated. Eventually, the loop reaches the end of the argument list, and *$1* becomes undefined. Then the test fails, and the loop ends.

The string comparisons are handy for interactive scripts.

The remaining set of basic options concerns numerical relationships.

Numerical Comparisons

These options compare integers:

n1 -eq *n2*	← True if the integers are equal
n1 -ne *n2*	← True if the integers are not equal
n1 -gt *n2*	← True if *n1* is greater than *n2*
n1 -lt *n2*	← True if *n1* is less than *n2*
n1 -ge *n2*	← True if *n1* is greater than or equal to *n2*
n1 -le *n2*	← True if *n1* is less than or equal to *n2*

Suppose, for instance, that you have designed a script that requires two arguments. You could then include these lines:

```
if test $# -ne 2
then
    echo This command needs two arguments  1>&2
    exit 1
fi
```

(The *exit* command terminates the script and provides the exit status; we'll come back to this command later.)

Question 5.8

Modify the number-guessing script of a few pages ago so that it uses a numeric comparison and so that it tells whether an incorrect guess is high or low.

Note that numerical equality is not necessarily the same as string equality:

```
5 = 5       ← True, the character string "5" is the same as "5"
5 = 05      ← False, the character string "5" is different from "05"
5 -eq 05    ← True, 5 and 05 have the same numerical value
```

A string comparison, even of numbers, only checks to see if the two strings contain exactly the same typographic characters.

In addition to these basic options, *test* lets you combine separate tests. Let's see how that works.

Logical Operations

Suppose you want to test if a file is both readable and writable. Can you do this?

```
test -rw fleas
```

If you try it, you will get an error message; *test* won't let you combine options in this manner. Instead, *test* has options to indicate logical operations. Here they are:

```
!       ← Negates the following expression
-a      ← Binary and operator
-o      ← Binary or operator
```

The *!* operator is placed before the affected test expression, and the other two operators are placed between the expressions they join. Here are some annotated examples:

```
test ! -r flam          ← True if flam is not an existing, readable file
test -r flam -a -w flam ← True if flam is readable and writable
test -r flam -o -w flam ← True if flam is readable or writable
```

Note that you must allow spaces between the various options. Also note that the *and* and *or* operators are used between the tests they link, not before or after them.

Question 5.9

Write a script that accepts the user into the Extrema Club if his or her weight is less than 80 pounds or more than 250 pounds.

Using Parentheses for Grouping

Finally, you can use parentheses to form larger groupings. Since parentheses are normally shell metacharacters, you must escape them (precede them with a backslash) for this purpose. Here is an example:

```
test \( -r flam -a -w flam \) -o \( -r flim -a -w flim \)
```

This example returns a true value if *flam* is both readable and writable or if *flim* is both readable and writable. (Actually, the parentheses aren't necessary in this example, for the *-a* operator has higher priority than the *-o* operator. That is, the *-a* pairings are made before the *-o* pairings.)

Many UNIX systems accept an alternative notation for *test*; this second notation consists of replacing *test* with *[* and also adding a closing *]* at the end of the command:

```
[$ans = pickle]
```

is the same as

```
test $ans = pickle
```

Here is an example that uses this notation to choose a response based on number ranges:

```
# age -- treats user by age
echo What is your age\?
read age
if [ $age -le 6 ]
then
    echo What a nice child!
elif [ $age -gt 6 -a $age -le 9 ]
```

```
then
    echo That\'s a good age!
elif [ $age -gt 9 -a $age -le 20 ]
then
    echo Ah! In the prime of life!
elif [ $age -gt 20 -a $age -le 30 ]
then
    echo Watch out, the younger ones are gaining on you.
else
    echo Well, have fun, and don\'t look back.
fi
```

Note the usage. For example, the test

```
[ $age -gt 9 -a $age -lt 20 ]
```

tests if the value *$age* is greater than (the *-gt* operator) 9 and (the *-a* operator) less than or equal to (the *-le* operator) 20.

Using it gives results like these:

```
$ age
What is your age?
2
What a nice child!
$
```

One of the main uses of *test* is to aid in the *error-checking* process. That is our next major topic.

ERROR CHECKING

The idea behind error checking is to head off errors on the part of the user. It is all too easy to write a program that works beautifully when everything goes right, but which crashes when an error is made. The sort of error we mean is not giving a command enough arguments, giving the name of a nonexistent file, using a directory name instead of a filename, and so on.

The first step in error checking is to anticipate possible errors that a user might make. The next step is to devise a way to detect each error. Here the *test* command and the *case* matching abilities are useful. Once an error is found, the final step is to do something about the error. Here the *if* and *case* statements are useful in organizing possible actions. The actions themselves depend on the philosophy of the program. A noninteractive program typically gives an error message and quits; here the *exit* command is useful. An interactive program can do the same, but a friendlier approach is to give the user a chance to correct the error instead of having to start all over, perhaps after ruining a file.

Let's take a simple script, identify possible errors, and then provide for them. The script is a variation of the *possess* program of Chapter 4:

```
# possess
filename=$1
set `who am i`
cp $filename $HOME/$filename.$1
```

If a user by the login name of *krypto* gives the command *possess gains*, then a copy of the *gains* file is placed in the file */usr/krypto/gains.krypto*.

What are the possible errors? First, the user might use the wrong number of arguments. This command takes one command-line argument, the name of the file to be copied. Second, the argument may not represent a file. Third, it may represent a file, but the user may not have permission (read permission) to copy that file. Here is one approach to meeting all those possibilities:

```
# possess -- copies a file to home directory and tags it
#                      with the user's login name
# check for proper number of arguments
case $# in
    1)  ;;
    0) echo  Usage: $0 filename  1>&2
       exit 1 ;;
    *) echo Warning: only the first argument is used  1>&2;;
esac

# check for file existence and copy permission
if test ! -f $1
then
    echo  $0:  file $1 not found  1>&2
    exit 2
elif test ! -r $1
then
    echo $0: file $1 found but not readable  1>&2
    exit 3
else
# No errors, proceed with main task
    filename=$1
    set `who am i`
    cp $filename $HOME/$filename.$1
fi
```

The first point to notice is that including error checking makes the program much longer! Next, note the overall logic.

First, a *case* statement inspects the number of arguments. The program expects one argument, so if *$#* is 1, the *case* does nothing; control shifts ahead to the *if* statement. If the number of arguments is 0, then the user is informed of proper usage by the *echo*, and the script terminates. If the number is other than 0 or 1, then just the first argument is used. Alternatively, we could have used this as an excuse to terminate the program.

Once the *case* hurdle is cleared, the script checks to see whether or not the argument is a filename. If it isn't a filename, the script informs the user and quits. Otherwise it goes on to check the file's readability. Only if the file is readable does the program reach the final phase of actually doing its intended task.

Question 5.10

How would you modify the script so that it would quit if more than one argument were provided?

The *exit* Command

Some details deserve further attention. Most importantly, we have used the *exit* command. It does two things: it terminates the script and it gives the script an exit status. The assigned status is simply the integer argument to the command. Since a 0 exit status implies success, we have used nonzero values to signify various failings. We could have used the same value (1, for example) for all the *exit* commands. However, we chose to use different values for different errors. Of course, the error messages already tell the user what is wrong, but the numerical code can be used by other programs that use *possess*. That is, a shell script that had *possess* as one of its commands could use the exit status to decide what to do next. We didn't provide an *exit* command for the final *if* branch. In this situation, where a script finishes without encountering an *exit* command, the script winds up with the exit status of the last command run in the script. Thus, in this case, the *possess* script will wind up with the status of the *cp* command.

Question 5.11

How can you find out the exit status of a shell script using *exit*?

The error comments themselves deserve some notice. First, note that each error comment identifies the program generating it. For example, we could get this exchange:

```
$ possess spear
possess: file spear not found
$
```

If, for example, you used the *possess* command as part of a pipe or as a command in another script, this would help you pinpoint which command was producing the error message. The terse phraseology here is typical UNIX style; you can be as expressive as you like.

Error Messages

There are two more points to notice about the error statements. First, rather than use the command name (*possess*) explicitly they use the symbolic *$0* form. If you ever change the name of the file or link it to another name, you don't have to change the file contents, for *$0* will translate to whatever the current filename is. This makes the program more portable.

Secondly, we have used the *1>&2* redirection form we mentioned in Chapter 4. Ordinarily, *echo* sends its messages to the standard output (file descriptor 1), but this form redirects it to the standard error (file descriptor 2). Using the script with a pipe or redirection to the file reconnects the standard output, so an ordinary *echo* would have its message diverted elsewhere. But with the *1>&2* form, the error messages get sent (appropriately) to the standard error (typically your terminal) even if the standard output goes elsewhere.

The importance of error checking depends on how widely and how often a program is to be used. If you are putting together a script for your infrequent personal use, the added effort of including error checking is probably not worthwhile. (Of course, you may feel otherwise if your program happens to wipe out three years of data.) If, however, you view your program as a potential addition to the local system, then you should try to make the program as foolproof as possible. Indeed, not only should your program include error checking, it should also clean up after itself. Let's see what that means.

CLEANING UP AFTERWARDS: *trap*

Many programs, such as editors and compilers, create temporary files as they go along. Indeed, the UNIX system provides a directory called */tmp* just for the purpose of holding these temporary files; you can regard it as a blackboard-like workspace. The temporary files should be removed, of course, as the programs

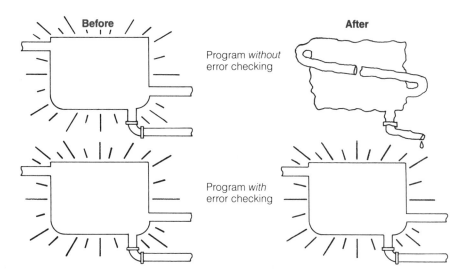

Figure 5.4
Error Checking Makes Programs More Robust

finish so as to keep free workspace available. What if you don't remove them? Eventually, the UNIX housekeeping system cleans out the older files, but a crowded system might bog down a bit until that is done.

Your own programs can use the */tmp* directory, also. In fact, it is a good idea to do so, especially if the file system containing your home directory is nearly full. But whether you use the */tmp* directory or not, your program should remove temporary files when it is done. Let's develop an example.

We have seen that *grep* will search a file for one word or phrase. Earlier in this chapter we presented a script called *wordseek* that used *grep* to search a file for several words. Now suppose we want a program that will search a file for individual lines that contain all the given search words. For instance, we could have a file of names, addresses, and automobiles, and we might wish to find all the Kaiser owners named Smith living in Chicago. We would then want a program that found all lines containing the words *Kaiser* and *Smith*, and *Chicago*. We should note in passing that a line in a file need not be restricted to the 80-character length of most terminal displays.

First, we should ask if there is a UNIX utility that would do this directly. The answer depends on how the data is stored. If it is stored systematically in predetermined fields, we can use *awk* (see Appendix A) to do the search. But then we won't have reason to develop our example. So let's assume the data is relatively unorganized; after all, some people have no cars and others have five. Now what?

One approach is to have *grep* search for the first word (*Kaiser* in our example) and to redirect its output to a new file. Every line in the new file contains the first search word, so now use *grep* again, this time to search this new file for the second

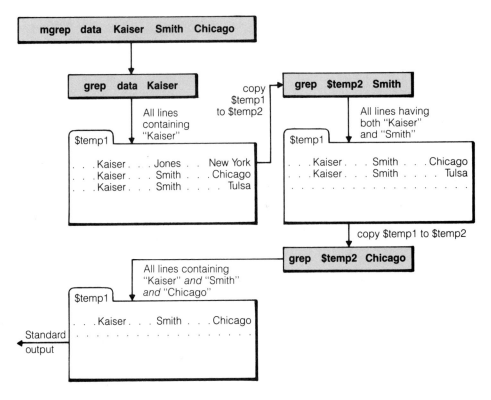

Figure 5.5
mgrep's Multiple *grep* Search

search word, and so on. By the time the last word has been sought, the final output consists of only those lines that contain all the words. In other words, the first pass eliminates all lines not containing the first word. From this new collection, the next pass eliminates all lines not containing the second word, and so on.

Here is a bare implementation of that approach (we'll leave out error checking):

```
# mgrep -- search a file for multiple words per line
# Usage: mgrep file words

file=$1
shift
temp1=/tmp/mgrep1.$$
temp2=/tmp/mgrep2.$$
for word
do
    grep $word $file > $temp1
    cp $temp1 $temp2
    file=$temp2
```

```
done
cat $temp1
rm -f $temp1 $temp2
```

First, the variable *file* is set to *$1*, the name of the file to be searched. The *shift* then makes *$** equal the remaining arguments, the list of words. That is, the first word following the filename is assigned to *$1*, and so on. The variables *temp1* and *temp2* are shorthand notation for two temporary files that are used later. The *for* loop processes each word from the argument list in turn. The first time through the loop, the original file is searched for the first word, and the output goes to file *$temp1*. This is copied to *$temp2*, and this becomes the new *file*. The next time through the loop, this file (*$temp2*) is searched, and *$temp1* is overwritten with the new output. When the word list is exhausted, the final contents of *$temp1* are output, using *cat*. Finally, the program cleans up by removing the two temporary files.

The *-f* option of *rm* removes files without asking questions. If, for example, you have a file but have removed *write* permission for yourself from it, then using a simple *rm* will produce a query asking if you wish to override the protection. With the *-f* option, the file is removed with no questions asked. However, it doesn't let you remove other users' protected files.

Well, the cleanup part seems simple enough; just use *rm –f* at the end. But there is a potential problem. Suppose part way through you decide you made an error and use the interrupt key (variously [Control] C, [Del], and [Break] on different terminals) to halt the program. Then the program will quit before reaching the final line, and the temporary files will be left sitting in */tmp*. Thus to make the cleaning-up process complete, we must somehow cause those files to be removed if the script is interrupted. We can do so by using the *trap* command.

Signals

To understand the *trap* command, we need to know a little about signals, a topic we will treat more fully in Chapter 8. A process running under UNIX is able to receive certain *signals* while running. One such signal is that generated by the interrupt key (typically [Control] C). It interrupts the process and causes it to end. Other signals include the one produced by hanging up a phone connection and the one sent by the *kill* command. The SIGNAL(2) entry of the manual lists all the signals.

The normal effect of most signals is to halt the concerned process, but UNIX lets you alter the effects of signals. In shell scripts, this is done by using *trap*. The form of the trap command is this:

```
trap    command    signal list
```

Figure 5.6
Running Processes Can Receive Signals

The *trap* function lies in wait for those signals given in the *signal list*. If such a signal shows up, then the *command* is performed instead of the usual consequence of the signal. The *command* is the first argument of *trap*, so if it contains any spaces or more than one command, it should be placed in single quotes. The *signal list* consists of code numbers for the various signals. These numbers are found in the SIGNAL(2) manual entry. In our manual, the hangup, interrupt, and terminate signals we mentioned above are denoted by 1, 2, and 15 respectively. See your own manual to find your values.

Here is how to use *trap* in our example:

```
# mgrep -- search for multiple words per line
# first argument is file to be searched
# remaining arguments are the words sought

file=$1
shift
temp1=/tmp/mgrep1.$$
temp2=/tmp/mgrep2.$$
trap 'rm-f $temp1 $temp2 ; exit 1'  1 2 15  ← The trap!
for word
do
    grep $word $file > $temp1
    cp $temp1 $temp2
    file=$temp2
done
cat $temp1
rm -f $temp1 $temp2
```

We've merely added the line

```
trap 'rm-f $temp1 $temp2 ; exit 1'  1 2 15
```

If you send an interrupt before the program reaches this line, the interrupt will act in the usual way, that is, it will terminate the program. If the interrupt is sent *after* the program has read this line, then the commands within the single quotes are executed instead. Notice that our trap-setting command explicitly includes an *exit*. Otherwise, once *trap*'s command is executed, the program resumes progress at the point the signal arrived. This fact lets you use the following form if you want a signal to be ignored:

```
trap ' ' 1
```

In this example, if a hangup signal is received, the *trap* command traps that signal, does nothing (since the single quotes contain no command), and the program resumes where it left off. This lets a command continue its execution even after you hang up on your phone connection to the computer. Otherwise, the hangup interrupt would cause the program to terminate.

WHICH CONTROL STRUCTURE

Now that we've seen UNIX's program control statements and several examples of how to use them, let's look at the more general question of when to use them. The

Bourne shell offers three looping structures (*for*, *while*, and *until*) and three choice-making structures (*case*, *if*, and the *&&-‖* pair). Which one should you use?

First, consider loops. If you have a list of items (files, arguments, etc.) to process, the *for* loop is the natural choice. (You can, of course, ape a *for* with a *while*, as we showed earlier, but why bother?) If, on the other hand, you have a loop that awaits some changing condition to halt it, then a *while* or an *until* is appropriate. The two are often interchangeable, since *while something succeeds* is the same as *until something fails*; you can base your choice on prejudice or on which test condition is more easily expressed.

Next, consider choice makers. Certainly, the *if* can do anything the other statements can. Let's illustrate that point.

First, look at the conditional operators:

1. *if com1; then com2; fi* is the same as *com1 && com2*
2. *if com1; then :; else com2; fi* is the same as *com1 ‖ com2*

(Note the use of the null command in 2; it represents the *nothing* that gets done if *com1* succeeds.) If *com2* is a single command, then the conditional operator form is more compact. If *com2* represents several commands, the *if* form is much more pleasant.

Next, look at *case*:

```
if test "$1" = -a
then
    com1
elif test "$1" = -b
then
    com2
else
    com3
fi
```

is the same as

```
case "$1" in
  -a) com1 ;;
  -b) com2 ;;
   *) com3 ;;
esac
```

Obviously, the *case* form is much more compact and easier to read. In addition, on many UNIX systems, *test* is a regular command, while *case* is a built-in shell command. This means that to run *test*, the shell program has to launch a new process and wait for it to finish. But *case* is part of the *sh* program, so no new process is needed. As a result, the *if test* form runs more slowly than the equivalent *case* statement. (In System V, *test* has been incorporated into the shell.)

Then there are many instances when only *if* will do. If you require multiple alternatives, then you have ruled out the conditional operators (unless you desire abstruse nested coding). If you are testing for anything other than equality of strings, then you have ruled out the *case* statement.

CONCLUSION

In this chapter we have outlined the shell structures used to control the flow of a program. The *for*, *while*, and *until* statements let us make loops, and the *if* and *case* statements let us incorporate decision-making into programs. We have seen how positional parameters, shell arguments, and redirection can be used to feed information to these constructs. We have seen, too, that the *test* command is invaluable to some of these structures.

Beyond seeing how these structures work, we have seen how they can be put to practical use in constructing programs that anticipate possible errors and react to them. And we have seen how to make tidy programs that clean up after themselves.

In these last two chapters we have covered most of the basics of the Bourne shell. What remains to do is to gain more familiarity with these features by using them. Here your own experience in preparing shell scripts and experimenting with them will be invaluable. To help that process along, we will devote the next chapter to developing examples and pointing out some sidelights that we missed the first time through.

ANSWERS TO QUESTIONS IN CHAPTER 5

5.1
```
for i in U N I X
do
    echo Give me a $i!
    echo $i!
done
```
5.2
```
for i
do
echo Give me a $i!
$i!
done
```
5.3
```
echo UNIX is
echo a) a Turkish Assistant Managers' club
echo b) a United Nations organization
echo c) a computer operating system
echo d) all of the above
read answer
```

```
         case $answer in
           a | b | d) echo Wrong -- the answer is c) ;;
           c) echo Right ;;
           *) echo WRONG!!
         esac
5.4   echo What kind of tree bears acorns\?
      read response
      case $response in
         [Oo][Aa][Kk] ) echo $response is correct ;;
         *) echo sorry, that is wrong
      esac
5.5   until who | grep $1 > /dev/null
      do
          sleep 300
      done
      set `who | grep $1`
      echo $1 has logged in on $2
      echo hi, $1 > /dev/$2
5.6   for name
      do
          if test -d $name
          then
               echo $name is a directory
          elif test -f $name
          then
               echo $name is a file
          else
               echo I don\'t know what $name is
          fi
      done
5.7   echo What is the capital of California\?
      read answer
      while test $answer != Sacramento
      do
            echo No, that\'s not it. Try again.
            read answer
      done
      echo That is correct.
5.8   echo I\'m thinking of a number between 1 and 50.
      echo Guess it and earn my approval.
      read guess
      until test $guess -eq 33
      do
```

```
        if test $guess -gt 33
        then
              echo Too high! Guess again.
        else
              echo Too low! Guess again.
        fi
        read guess
    done
    echo Well done!
```

5.9   `echo Greetings, and what is your weight\?`
```
read weight
if test $weight -lt 80 -o $weight -gt 250
then
      echo Welcome to the Extrema Club!
else
      echo You must work to further distinguish yourself.
fi
```

5.10 Change the *case* statement default to
```
*) echo $0 takes just one argument 1>&2
   exit 2
```

5.11 The same way you can find the exit status of any UNIX command:
```
echo $?
```

EXERCISES

1.   Alter the answer to Question 8 so that the secret number is the *PID* of the script. You should change the instructions to reflect that the mystery number is in the range 0 – 30,000.

2.   Implement the *modesty* program (the one that asks for the best operating system) using a *case* statment instead of an *if...else* statement.

3.   Write a version of our *mgrep* program that looks for exactly three words and that uses pipes instead of temporary files.

4.   Add error checking for the readability of files to the *wordseek* script in this chapter.

5.   Write an interactive file-handling program. Let it offer the user the choice of copying, removing, renaming, or linking files. Once the user has made a choice, have the program ask him or her for the necessary information, such as the filename, new name, and so on.

6.   Modify Exercise 5 so that once an operation is complete, the user is given the opportunity to continue with a new operation. (One way is to put the whole program inside an indefinite loop. You can have the loop condition check for the desire to quit, or that can be made one of the menu choices.)

6

SHELL SCRIPT EXAMPLES

In this chapter you will find:

- Lest We Forget—A Beeper Script Example
    A Reminder Loop: *true* and *false*
- Adding Arithmetic to a Shell Script: *expr*
- A Countdown Loop
- Script Example: Printing a Collection of Files
    Improvements to *cap* — Error Checking
    Adding a Shell Script Option to *cap*
- Shell Scripts with Multiple Options
- Passing Arguments to Scripts: Subtle Points
- Giving the User Another Chance
- Helping Out the *spell* Command
    The Plan for *speller*
    The Big Picture
    Redirection in *speller*
    Second Thoughts — Adding a Context Printout
- Important Shell Script Considerations
    Trouble-Shooting
    Compatibility
- Conclusion
- Answers to Questions in Chapter 6
- Exercises

6

Shell Script Examples

In Chapters 4 and 5 we have seen the main features available to shell scripts. In this chapter we will look at several examples of scripts in order to see how these features can be used in real life (or in some reasonable approximation thereof). As we do so, we will introduce additional features and supporting commands, and we will further illuminate some matters that we have already touched upon.

Here are some of the topics we will cover for shell scripts:

- Making arithmetic calculations
- Making a counting loop
- Creating *default* arguments (values used when the user omits command-line arguments)
- Giving scripts options
- Passing arguments
- More error checking
- More redirection
- Creating system-compatible programs

We'll need quite a few examples to present all these points, and we begin with a script that provides a simple reminder.

LEST WE FORGET — A BEEPER SCRIPT EXAMPLE

It is all too easy to while away unnoticed hours at the keyboard. Wouldn't it be nice to get a gentle reminder that time is slipping by? We can use the *sleep* command to get our attention. Here is simple example:

```
# beepme -- beeps user after $1 seconds
sleep $1
echo ^GTime is up!^G
```

The ˆ G is one way of representing the [Control] G character. Just hold down the control key while striking the G key, and the UNIX editors will indicate this sequence by showing a ˆ G on the screen. This two-character representation (a caret and an uppercase G) counts as the single character [Control] G. It makes most terminals emit a beep or perhaps ring a bell. The *sleep* command, recall, causes the program to wait for the specified number of seconds. You would run this program in background, using the & operator:

```
$ beepme 600 &
```

Ten minutes (600 seconds) elapse.

```
$
(beep!)Time is up! (beep!)
$
```

The *(beep!)* represents the resplendent sound produced by your terminal. (Unfortunately, reproducing the beeps aurally would add too much to the expense of this book.)

A Reminder Loop: *true* and *false*

We can spruce up this nice short script in several ways and at the same time demonstrate some generally useful techniques. First, we can make the script into a loop so that it gives periodic reminders rather than just striking once and quitting. To get a loop that runs indefinitely, we can use a while loop in conjunction with a command that always runs successfully. That is, we want to begin the loop with something of the form

```
while always-works-command
```

We could make up such a command; for example, *test 4 = 4* should have a rather high success rate. But UNIX supplies even better choices. One is the *true* command. It consists of the following script:

```
exit 0
```

All it does is produce an exit status of 0, hence it is an automatic success. *True* has a *false* sister which, in its entirety, consists of *exit 1*. This command always fails. Of course, it is meant to fail, so we could say it succeeds in what it attempts to do, but UNIX is not interested in such logic chopping. Using *true*, we can create this script:

```
# beeper1 -- periodic beeper
while true
do
    sleep $1
    echo ^G Another $1 seconds have gone by. ^G
done
```

The command

```
beeper1 600 &
```

will produce the message and beep alert every 10 minutes until you kill the program or log off.

Another possibility is to use the *:* (colon) command instead of *true*. The colon command, recall, is the null command and does nothing; it is quite successful at it. The advantage of using *:* instead of *true* is that the colon command is part of the shell, while the *true* is a separate command. That means it takes a little extra time for the shell to find and run *true*.

Adding a Default Argument

The astute reader will have guessed that the name *beeper1* implies we have other versions in mind. Our next refinement is to have the program have a default time period of 600 seconds if you fail to provide an argument:

```
#beeper2 -- improved periodic beeper with default time period
case $# in
    0)  sec=600  ;;    ← Set sec to 600 if no arguments given
    *)  sec=$1         ← Else set sec to first argument
esac
while true
do
    sleep $sec
    echo ^G Another $sec have gone by. ^G
done
```

If the number of command-line arguments (*$#*) is 0, then *sec* is set to 600 seconds by the *case* option labeled *0)*; otherwise *sec* is set to the first argument typed by the user. The *case* mechanism we have used offers a simple and effective way to set up default values. We will use this method in many of the examples to follow.

Question 6.1

Suppose you want a program that uses a directory name. Normally, it obtains this name from a command-line argument, but if no argument is given, you want the program to default to using your home directory. How would you set up the beginning of the script?

ADDING ARITHMETIC TO A SHELL SCRIPT: *expr*

Most users would find it more convenient to give a time period in minutes, but *sleep* requires seconds. Wouldn't it be nice if we had a way to do simple arithmetic? Then we could have the script make the conversion from minutes to seconds. The *expr* command gives us that power. It takes an arithmetic expression (such as a sum or a product), evaluates it, and outputs the result. Let's look at some examples using *expr*.

```
$ expr 3 + 5
8
$ expr 9 - 2
7
$ expr 4 * 3
syntax error
$ expr 4 \* 3     ← Need to escape or quote the * metacharacter
12
$ expr 12 / 3
4
$ expr 14 / 5
2
$ expr 14 % 5     ← % is the modulus operator
4
$
```

First, note that the arguments (including the arithmetic operator) must be separated by blank space from one another. Second, we must escape the * operator with a backslash or quotes; otherwise it is interpreted by the shell as a request for filename expansion. (Review Chapter 4 for more on escaping.) Third, *expr* division is *integer* division. That is, the result is truncated to the largest integer equal to or less than the result; 14/5 is 2.8, and that is truncated to 2. Note that truncation does not

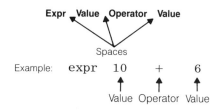

Figure 6.1
Syntax For *expr* Arithmetic

necessarily produce the nearest integer to the actual value. Finally, note that *expr* uses the % or *modulus* operator. It provides the remainder resulting when the first number is divided by the second. For example, 5 goes into 14 twice, with a remainder of 4, so 14 % 5 is 4.

How can you use the numbers produced by *expr*? One thing you can do is to assign the output of *expr* to a shell variable. The method is to use backquotes which, you should recall, result in substituting the output of a command for the command itself. Thus

```
`expr 2 + 2`
```

has the value *4*. Similarly, the command

```
cows=`expr $legs / 4`
```

would divide the value of a second variable called *$legs* by 4 and assign the answer to the *cows* variable. (This reproduces a famous cow-counting algorithm.)

Now we can modify *beeper2* to allow an argument in minutes instead of in seconds:

```
# beeper3 -- improved periodic reminder, argument now in minutes
case $# in
    0) min=10 ;;
    *) min=$1
esac
sec=`expr 60 \* $min`      ← Multiply minutes by 60 to get seconds
while true
do
    sleep $sec
    echo ^G Another $min minutes have gone by. ^G
done
```

169

Question 6.2

What happens when you type

```
beeper3 15 20
```

Let's look at an exciting example further revealing the power of *expr*. The next program actually cuts your taxes in half!

```
# taxcut -- a simple approach
echo What is the dollar amount of your taxes\?
read taxes
taxes=`expr $taxes / 2`
echo Voila! Your taxes are now \$ $taxes.
```

Does it work? You bet.

```
$ taxcut
What is the dollar amount of your taxes?
4800
Voila! Your taxes are now $ 2400.
```

Note that here we used *expr* to reassign a value to the shell variable *taxes*. The same idea can be used to develop a counting loop, as we will see next.

A COUNTDOWN LOOP

Here is a script that counts down either from 10 (the default) or from the value of its first argument. It demonstrates that we can use shell variables in an *expr* command. (The script itself is of little value, except perhaps to add youthful drama to an otherwise dull program.)

```
# countdown
case $# in
0) limit=10 ;;
*) limit=$1
esac
until test $limit -lt 1
do
```

```
    echo $limit! ...
    limit=`expr $limit - 1`
done
echo UNIX at your service!
```

The speed with which this script is executed, of course, strongly depends on the computer system, on the communication rate between computer and terminal (the *baud* rate), and, for multiuser systems, on how heavily the system is used at the moment.

The *test* command checks to see if the value of *limit* is less than (*-lt*) 1. As long as it is not, the loop is executed. Each time through the loop, the value of *limit* is echoed to the screen, then it is decreased by 1. The expression

```
limit=`expr $limit - 1`
```

is analogous to the expression

```
x = x -1
```

of many computer languages.

Question 6.3

What output is produced by this command:

```
countdown 3
```

We could have just as easily used a *while* loop instead of an *until* loop just by changing the test condition. For instance, we could have used this:

```
while test $limit -gt 0
```

The main point here, however, is that the *expr* command lets us do simple arithmetic in shell scripts. In particular, you can use it for counting. For instance, an expression like

```
count=`expr $count + 1`
```

can be used to keep track of the number of cycles a loop has gone through. But do keep in mind that the forte of shell scripts is manipulating commands, not manipulating numbers. It is actually simpler to write a script that pipes the output of *grep* to *sed* than it is to write a script that adds three numbers.

Question 6.4

a. Modify the number-guessing program of Chapter 5 (as modified by Exercise 1 in that chapter) so that it keeps track of the number of guesses and reports that result when the user finally gets the answer.

b. Our answer to Question 6.4a produces a secret number in the range 1 to 30000, since that is the range over which *PID* numbers roam. How could you modify our answer in order to restrict the range to 0 to 99?

We've used a *case* statement a couple of times to introduce a default value for a script variable. The *case* statement can also be used to introduce options into a shell script. This is one of the matters we will bring up in our next example.

SCRIPT EXAMPLE: PRINTING A COLLECTION OF FILES

Sometimes you may wish to print out several small files. A command of the ilk of

```
lpr short.c small.c tiny.c brief.c
```

does the job, but it starts a new page for each file. This is wasteful of paper if the files are just a few lines long, and makes it more awkward to look over the files with one glance. On the other hand, a command like

```
cat short.c small.c tiny.c brief.c | lpr
```

might place all the files on one page, but make it difficult to see where one ends and the next begins. We will develop a program that works something like *cat*, but prefaces each file with a blank line, then the name of the file, then a second blank line. We'll start with a bare version, then add in some error checking and the option of having the date added to the headings. We'll call the script *cap* for *caption*. Here is the first draft:

```
# cap -- cats files, adding headings
# version 1.0
```

```
# usage:  cap filenames
temp=/tmp/cap.$$                              ← File for temporary storage
trap 'rm -f $temp; exit 1' 1 2 15            ← Remove temp if interrupted
for file                                      ← Take filenames from command line
do
    echo '                                    ← Echo a blank line
'      File is $file: '                       ← Create file caption
'      | cat - $file >> $temp                 ← Add to file and save
done
cat $temp                                     ← Output collected text
rm -f $temp                                   ← Remove temporary file
```

Let's see how this works. As in the final example of Chapter 5, we use the *trap* command to clean up the temporary files in case you use a keyboard Control C, for example, to interrupt the program before completion. The body of the loop looks a little peculiar because the *echo* statement is spread over three lines. You can think of the *echo* portion as representing this single line:

```
echo '\n' File is $file '\n'
```

The \n represents the newline character. Unfortunately, the *echo* command doesn't recognize the \n notation, so we must produce the newline character by hitting the Return key. Thus typing this conceptually single line produces three actual lines, since hitting Return to produce the newline character also moves the cursor on the screen down a line. The newline character itself has to be quoted because an unadorned newline would terminate the command line.

The output of the *echo* command (two blank lines sandwiching the announcement of the filename) is piped to *cat*. There it (as represented by the standard input symbol -) is combined with the file contents (represented by *$file*) and is redirected to a temporary file, *$temp*. (We discussed a similar use of *cat* in Chapter 3.)

The *for* loop repeats this process for each file in the command-line argument list. (Opening the *temp* file every cycle is a bit inefficient; in the *speller* example later in this chapter we will show a better method.) When the loop is done, the *cat $temp* command outputs the collected contents, and then the *$temp* file is removed.

A writer surveying his character sketches might produce the following output:

```
$ cap sandy anne jim

File is sandy:

A Scot of greying hair and pale blue eyes. Likes scones. Heir to
an estate overlooking Loch Quoich. A remarkable piper.
```

```
File is anne:

Red hair, green eyes, she rides a dappled stallion by the dunes.
Likes wool, wealth.  A remarkable scone-maker.

File is jim:

Dark brown wavy hair and hazel eyes.  Fond of gems and goldwork.
Given to inscrutable smiles and standing on ridgecrests.
$
```

Improvements to *cap* — Error Checking

Next, let's make this program more suitable for the real world by putting in some error checking. First, we need to identify where errors might occur. One obvious matter to check is if each argument is, in fact, a readable file, that is, check if it exists and if the user has read permission; we can use *test −r* for that. Second, suppose none of the files turn out to be readable. Then *$temp* won't have been created, and the *cat $temp* command will run afoul! So we also have to check if *$temp* exists before trying to *cat* it. Third, it would be nice if the script sent a list of offending arguments that failed the *test −r* test to the standard error so that we will know if something has gone awry. Fourth, what if the user fails to provide any arguments? This doesn't cause any problems for the program (with no arguments, the *for* loop simply is skipped), but perhaps the user should be informed of his or her lapse. Our next draft incorporates these features:

```
# cap -- cats files, adding headings
# version 1.1 -- adds error checking
# usage:   cap filenames
case $# in                          ← Correct number of arguments?
   0) echo $0: Usage:  $0 files... 1>&2 ; exit 1 ;;
esac
temp=/tmp/cap.$$
trap 'rm -f $temp; exit 1' 1 2 15
for file
do
   if test -r $file                 ← Test if file can be read
   then
      echo '
'     File is $file: '
'     | cat - $file >> $temp
```

```
    else
        nofile=$nofile$file' '    ← Save names of test flunkers
    fi
done
if test -r $temp
then
    cat $temp
    rm -f $temp
fi
if test "$nofile"
then
    echo $0: failed to open: $nofile  1>&2   ← Report bad input
fi
```

The testing of *$file* and *$temp* is straightforward, as is the checking of *$#*. (We used the methods we developed in Chapter 5.) The handling of the shell variable *nofile* is less obvious, so let's look at that.

Handling Shell Variable Strings

First, consider this construction from *cap*:

```
nofile=$nofile$file' '
```

It simply takes the current value of the variable *nofile* and tags to its end a command-line argument that failed the *test-r* test and to the end of that tags a space. The first time through, *nofile* (like any other nondefined shell variable) starts as a null (empty) string. Any arguments failing to pass the *test –r* test are then added on; the space separates one name from the next. Thus if the first two bad arguments were *specious* and *phony*, *nofile* would go from nothing to *specious* to *specious phony*.

Question 6.5

Suppose the shell variable *name1* is set to someone's first name, and that *name2* is set to her last name. Give a command that assigns both names (with a separating space) to a single shell variable called *name*.

Next, look at following line from *cap*:

```
if test "$nofile"
```

This form of *if* (see Chapter 5) tests if *nofile* is not the null (empty) string. If no bad arguments show up, the *else* part of the loop is never entered, and *nofile* is never defined. In that case, the result of this test is negative, and the final message is skipped. Otherwise, the list of failed arguments is printed, and redirection ensures that the message goes to the standard error.

One more point needs to be made here. We had to use double quotes around *$nofile* (that is, *if test ''$nofile''*) so that *test* would see it as a single argument. Without the quotes, the spaces between names would make *test* think it had several arguments, and it would react poorly. With quotes, *test* sees a single string containing spaces. Without quotes, it sees several strings separated by spaces.

Let's try out this second version of *cap*, feeding it a mixture of valid and invalid arguments (*snady* and *robery* are nonexistent):

```
$ cap snady anne jim robery | lpr
cap: failed to open: snady robery
$
```

Have we anticipated all the potential problems? No. For one, we have relied upon the fact that *nofile* starts out as a null string. There is one circumstance that would upset this assumption, and that is if the user had defined a variable by the same name in the parent shell and had exported it. Then *nofile* would start off with the value it inherited from the parent shell. The remedy is simple; just put this line at the beginning of the shell script:

```
nofile=' '
```

Here we initialize *nofile* to the null string, overriding any exported assignments. The following commands would also assign the null string to *nofile*:

```
nofile=""
nofile=
```

The problem with the third version is that someone reading the script could not tell for sure whether *nofile* had been set to the null string or to some nonprinting character.

Let's make that addition to *cap*, and while we are at it, let's add an option.

Adding a Shell Script Option to *cap*

Let's have *cap* optionally print the current date on the same line that shows the filename. UNIX options are usually indicated by a hyphen and a letter between the command name and the other arguments, so let's stick to that convention. For example, we can use *-d* to indicate the date option:

```
cap -d anne mike flipper
```

If there is no option argument, we want the script to act as before. To accomplish this task, we use a *case* statement. It will take special action only if the option is present. Here is our third draft of *cap*:

```
# cap -- cats files, adding headings; -d option adds date
# version 1.2
# usage:  cap [-d] filenames
case $# in
    0) echo $0: Usage:  $0 [-d] files... 1>&2 ; exit 1 ;;
esac
nofile=' '                    ← Initialize the nofile variable

case $1 in                    ← Look for -d in argument list
-d) date=`date`               ← If option set, set date to current date
    shift ;;                  ← Shift $2 to $1, etc.
*) date=' ' ;;                ← Otherwise set date to null string
esac

temp=/tmp/cap.$$
trap 'rm -f $temp; exit 1' 1 2 15
for file
do
    if test -r $file
    then
        echo '
'       $date File is $file: '    ← Add date value to caption
'       | cat - $file >> $temp
    else
        nofile=$nofile$file' '
    fi
done
if test -r $temp
then
    cat $temp
    rm -f $temp
fi
if test "$nofile"
then
    echo $0: failed to open: $nofile  1>&2
fi
```

What happens now? The comments point out the new parts of the program. If the first argument (*$1*) is *-d*, then the variable *date* is set to the current output of the *date* command. (That's the *date* = `date` part.) Then the *shift* command moves *$2* to *$1*, and so on. This is so that the first argument for the *for* loop will be the first filename in the list and not *-d*. Then the value *$date* gets included in the *echo* statement. We want it in the same *echo* statement as the rest so that the whole message is piped on to *cat*. If the first argument is not a *-d*, then all is as before. Well, almost all. There is still a *$date* in the *echo* statement, but in this instance the *case* statement assigns a null string to it, so nothing gets printed.

Suppose we want to imitate big-time UNIX commands and include several options in a script. How do we go about that? Read on.

SHELL SCRIPTS WITH MULTIPLE OPTIONS

We may devise options of our own that we wish a script to have, or we may wish to pass on options to a standard UNIX command used within our script. The usual method in either case is to use hyphens to identify the options and to have the options come first in the argument list. Then use a *while* loop containing a *case* and some *shift*s to identify the options and remove them from the argument list one at a time. A new command (*break*) is used to get out of the loop when no more options are found in the argument list. To illustrate the principle, we'll prepare a script (to be called *lsp*) that sends directory listings to the printer, and we will create three "new" *ls* options by combining some existing options. For example, our new *-L* option will combine the *-l* (long) option with the *-a* (all) option.

```
# lsp --Sends directory listing to printer
# usage: lsp [-L] [-I] [-D] [directories or files]
flagL=' '      ← Initialize "flags" to null string
flagI=' '
flagD=' '
while true
do
    case $1 in
      -L) flagL='-la' ; shift ;;
      -I) flagI='-is' ; shift ;;
      -D) flagD='-dp' ; shift ;;
      *) break ;;
    esac
done
ls $flagL $flagI $flagD $* | lpr
```

Let's look at the *while* loop. If the first argument is *-L*, *-I*, or *-D*, a shell variable (*flagL* or *flagI* or *flagD*) gets set to the option combination prescribed for case. For example, if a *-I* shows up as *$1*, then *flagI* is set to *-is*. Then a shift command

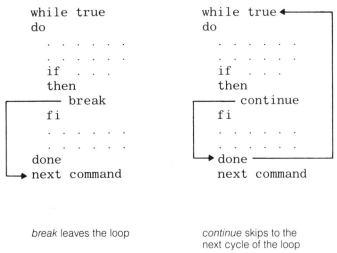

break leaves the loop

continue skips to the
next cycle of the loop

Figure 6.2
break* and *continue

moves the next argument to *$1* and the process is repeated. This goes on until an argument shows up that is not one of these three choices. Then we go to the *)* label, where we meet the new command, *break*. This is a built-in shell command that causes the *while* loop to break off its looping and causes program flow to move on to the next step. Without this *break* command in the loop, the loop would continue forever. The *break* command is a specialized version of the *goto* command of many languages.

Our *lsp* command can be used with zero, one, two, or all three options (*-L*, *-I*, and *-D*), and they can be given in any order:

```
lsp -L
lsp -L -I /usr/hilda
```

However, each option must be given separately; they cannot be strung together as they can be with *ls*:

```
ls -il      ← Okay
lsp -IL     ← No good
lsp -I -L   ← Okay
```

The *break* command can be used with any of the three UNIX shell loops: *while*, *until*, and *for*. In all cases it causes the execution of the loop to terminate and program control to pass to the next step. *Break* has a companion command called *continue*. When used in a loop, *continue* causes the program to skip the remaining steps in the loop and to start the next cycle of the loop. Users of the C language will recognize these two UNIX commands as being analogous to the C keywords of the same names. The figure below illustrates the difference between *break* and *continue*.

Question 6.6

Write a script that takes a command-line argument of miles and, by default, converts that number to feet. Also provide a *-y* option to convert miles to yards instead, and an *-r* option to convert miles to rods (320 rods to a mile).

Our *lsp* example involved passing arguments from the command line to commands within a script. The process of argument-passing involves some subtleties we haven't gone into yet, so perhaps we had best do so now.

PASSING ARGUMENTS TO SCRIPTS: SUBTLE POINTS

Often the arguments of a shell script are passed on to become arguments of commands inside the shell script. Usually this poses no difficulty, but sometimes matters may turn out differently from what you might expect. Consider this script:

```
# wordsave -- saves lines containing given word
# Usage: wordsave word file...
pattern=$1                    ← Save first argument for search pattern
shift                         ← Make remaining arguments a list of files
grep $pattern $* > $pattern   ← Save found lines in a file named after the pattern
```

The intent of this program is to search a collection of files ($*) for lines containing a given word ($pattern) and to save the results in a file named after the word. Indeed, the program actually does what it is supposed to do:

```
$ wordsave mease seatale landtale
$ cat mease
seatale: and 10 mease of herring topped off the load. Captain
seatale: tremendous blow.  A mease spilled over the deck, and
landtale: as Sarah sang softly to mease his troubled spirit.
$
```

Here *wordsave* searched for the word *mease* in the files *seatale* and *landtale* and created a file called *mease* which contained all references to the word *mease* in the files *seatale* and *landtale*.

But see what happens if we try to find a phrase:

```
$ wordsave 'top dog' seatale landtale
grep: can't open dog
$
```

Apparently the program is ignoring our expressed intent that *top dog* be considered a single argument. This may seem odd, for the command

```
grep 'top dog' seatale landtale
```

works fine. The problem must lie with the passing of *wordsave*'s arguments to *grep*. Let's see what is involved.

When we give a command with arguments, the shell *scans* the command line, using spaces and quotation marks (' or '') to decide where one argument begins and another ends. For instance, if we give the command

```
grep good one two
```

the shell senses three arguments. In this case, *grep* would be instructed to search for the word "good" in the files *one* and *two*. But if we give the command

```
grep 'good one' two
```

or the command

```
grep "good one" two
```

the shell senses two arguments. In this case, *grep* would be instructed to search for the phrase "good one" (the first argument) in the file *two* (the second argument). So far there is no problem. But now suppose that the command is a script. In fact, let's use our malfunctioning example:

```
wordsearch 'top dog' seatale landtale
```

The shell handles this correctly, so that *$1* and subsequently *$pattern* becomes the first argument, "top dog". Similarly, *$2* becomes the remaining filename.

But when these arguments are used again, this time within the script as arguments for *grep*, they are scanned again, this time by the *subshell* executing the script. At this stage, the *$pattern* variable is read as two words, "top" and "dog". In other words, the beginning of the final line in our script is reduced to

```
grep $pattern $*
```

which is replaced with

```
grep top dog seatale landtale
```

Aha! The quotes around "top dog" have disappeared, so now the meaning is misconstrued. The parent shell uses the quotes, but does not pass the quote marks down to the subshell, so *grep* sees four arguments instead of the original three.

To get the script to work, we have to get the quotes back. Since they aren't passed down to the shell, we need to put them in the shell ourselves. So we will:

```
# wordsave -- saves lines containing given word
# Usage: wordsave word file...
pattern=$1
shift
grep "$pattern" $* > $pattern
```

Now the beginning of the final line is

```
grep "$pattern" $*
```

and is rendered as

```
grep "top dog" seatale landtale
```

when executed, and all should be well. We had to use double quotes instead of single quotes, because the former allows shell variable evaluation and the latter doesn't. (See Chapter 4 if you wish to review this distinction between single quotes and double quotes.)

Now let's try this revised version:

```
$ wordsave 'top dog' seatale landtale
$ cat 'top dog'
seatale: in London, but here I am top dog!"  Grimpy recoiled
landtale: in Paris, but here I am top dog!"  Gisela recoiled
$
```

Note that we now have an unusual filename, *top dog*. We can access it with *cat* by using quotes to show that the space is part of a single filename.

1) Shell finds one argument

2) Shell hands one argument
    to script subshell

3) Script <u>without</u> double quotes
    flubs it

But

4) Script <u>with</u> double quotes
    gets it right

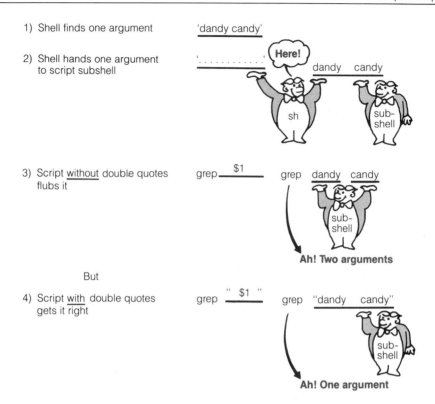

Figure 6.3
Bad and Good Argument Passing

There is another way to fix the *wordsave* script, and this is it:

```
# wordsave -- saves lines containing a word in a like-named file
pattern=$1
grep "$@" > $pattern
```

Recall that the special notation ''$@'' expands to ''$1'' ''$2'' and so on. In this particular case, the *grep* part would become

```
grep "top dog" "seatale" "landtale"
```

We began with three arguments to *wordsave* and we end up with three arguments to *grep*. Perfect! (Note that neither *$** nor ''*$**'' does the trick. The first produces four arguments, making *grep* think *dog* is a filename. The second produces one argument, making *grep* think that ''top dog seatale landtale'' is the pattern it is to look for.)

Question 6.7

Suppose we have this script:

```
#catit -- try stuff out
cat $*
cat "$*"
cat '$*'
cat "$@"
```

What will this script try to do for each of the following commands?

a. `catit one two three`
b. `catit "alpha beta" gamma`

You also may need to use double quotes in scripts using the *test* command. Consider the line

```
if test $ans = no
```

If *ans* is undefined, this line becomes

```
if test   = no
```

and the system complains of a syntax error because there is no argument to the left of the equals sign. The remedy is to use

```
if test "$ans" = no
```

for then an undefined *ans* leads to this expansion:

```
if test "" = no
```

The quotes act as a place holder, showing that there is indeed an argument before the equals sign.

In summary, it is sometimes necessary to place the values of shell variables and positional parameters within double quotes. This can be done to show how the arguments should be grouped or to act as a placeholder in the eventuality of null arguments. We'll see another instance of this in the next section.

For our next selection, we will look at error checking in an interactive shell script.

GIVING THE USER ANOTHER CHANCE

Error checking in noninteractive shell scripts normally leads to termination if an error is made. Interactive scripts, on the other hand, are often meant for the less experienced user and should be more user-friendly. Thus they may say things like "Hi!" and "Please". More important, they often give the user the opportunity to correct errors, such as typing incorrectly or entering a wrong value. Any elaborate interactive program should probably be written in a standard programming language, for shell scripts run slowly compared to compiled programs. But you may wish to develop a simple script or to test out some programming idea in shell script form before writing C code. Often too, you can use a shell script to customize a more general program. Thus there are many circumstances that can use interactive error checking. As an example, we will illustrate a basic correction loop.

Suppose we have a program that begins by asking for an item of information, for example, the user's name. We can't check if the user is telling the truth (at least not until we can hook up electrodes between the terminal and the user), but we can check to see that he or she has at least given *some* name and not just hit the Return key. Since just hitting the Return key without other input causes a program to read in the null string as input, one way to check for that is to use an *until* loop that continues until the user's answer is a non-null string:

```
echo Your name, please:
read name
until test  "$name"
do
   echo You didn\'t give a name\; please try again:
   read name
done
echo Well met, $name!
```

We placed *$name* in double quotes in case *name* includes spaces, as it would if someone replied "Babe Ruth". Note that we read in a name once before the loop starts. Then, if the loop is entered (*name* not defined), another read attempt is made. This continues until a non-null string is entered. An exchange using this fragment could look like this, assuming it is in a file called *interview*:

```
$ interview
Your name, please:
Return
You didn't give a name; please try again:
None of your business
Well met, None of your business!
$
```

(Creating a computer-friendly populace is a problem beyond the scope of this book.)

We could elaborate on this interactive script fragment. Want to reject the user if he or she persists in refusing acceptable input? We can create a shell variable (*count*, for example) that keeps track of how many cycles the loop has gone through. Then we could modify the loop so that it exits if too many attempts have been made:

```
if test $count -ge 5
then
    echo Sorry, I can\'t take this any more...bye.
    exit 1
fi
```

When the value of *count* reaches 5, the script complains and exits.

Question 6.8

Incorporate this suggestion into the name-gathering segment.

Another addition would be to show the user her response and ask if it is correct:

```
echo You typed $name.
echo If correct, hit [return], else retype your name
read check
```

This would be used with a loop that continues until *$check* is the null string:

```
echo You typed $name.
echo If correct, hit [return], else retype your name
read check
until test -z "$check"
do
  name=$check
  echo You typed $name.
  echo If correct, hit [return], else retype your name
  read check
done
```

This makes use of the fact that hitting ⌐Return⌐ with no other input causes *check* to get the null string.

Here is a more terse variation:

```
check=n
while test "$check" != y
do
    echo Please enter your name:
    read name
    echo Is this right [y/n]: $name
    read check
done
```

Now that we have examined both noninteractive and interactive shell scripts, let's look at one that combines features of both approaches.

HELPING OUT THE *spell* COMMAND

By now we have accumulated several programming tools. It's time to put them to use by creating a full-fledged script, one that serves a useful purpose beyond teaching concepts, that complements the system, and that utilizes many of the techniques we have developed. We will center this effort around the UNIX *spell* command.

One of UNIX's many aids is the *spell* command. To find potential spelling errors in the text file *salaryraise*, you would type

```
spell salaryraise
```

and the *spell* command will send a list of potential "misspelled" words to the standard output, normally the screen. Actually, *spell* can't really tell if a word is misspelled, it can only tell if a word is not in its list of acceptable words. So if you type *bare* instead of *bear*, *spell* will let it pass, since both words are on its list. On the other hand, you may use correctly spelled words unknown to the *spell* command, and they will turn up on its suspect list. Thus, the command does not answer all problems, but it certainly does help with misspellings like *occurence*, *occurrance*, and *ocurrence*.

However, all that *spell* does is provide you with the list of potentially misspelled words. It leaves to you the work of finding the words in the original file and correcting them. Thus, *spell* provides the backbone for an interactive spelling checker, but the tendons and meat are missing. If the list of suspect words is long, you may have to redirect them to a file, print up the file, and sit down at the editor, list in hand, to make the corrections. Our goal is to develop a script to help automate and add intelligence to this task. In doing so, we will encounter several interesting applications of redirection, so please take note of them.

First, we need to decide what we would like the spelling-helper script to do. Here is a reasonable list of specifications:

1. Take a file as input and run *spell* on it.
2. Collect a list of potential spelling errors.
3. Show the user each word from the list, one word at a time, letting the user correct the word or accept it.
4. Correct the original file and send the corrected version to standard output.

The final point gives us the choice of redirecting the result to a file or piping it on to some other program, perhaps UNIX's *pr* or *nroff*.

We will add more features to the program later, but this list gives us a good start.

The Plan for *speller*

How do we implement this list? Ideally, we should rely as much as possible on existing UNIX programs to do the work for us. Clearly, we can use *spell* and redirection to collect a list of suspect words. The problem is how to have our corrections to these words applied to the original file. One way involves using the *sed* stream editor. If you are unfamiliar with this tool, you may wish to read the discussion in Appendix A. In brief, *sed* takes editing commands (such as directions for deleting lines or substituting words) and applies them in succession to each line of an input file. Lines with no corrections are passed as they are. The net result is that *sed* sends an edited version of the input file to standard output. One approach to our problem, then, is to create a series of appropriate editing commands and have *sed* apply them to the original file.

What do these commands look like, and how do we get them applied?. Well, the commands are the same as those used by the *ed* editor. For instance, to change all instances of *occurrance* to *occurrence*, use this command with *sed*:

```
s/occurrance/occurrence/g
```

For our script, then, we can show the user a suspect word, get his correction, construct a similar command using those two words, and place the editing command in a file. The –f option of *sed* lets it take its editing commands from a file, so after we have gone through the whole list of suspect words, we can use *sed* and the editing file to edit the original file. The whole script will take one command-line argument, the name of the file to be checked and corrected. It will output a corrected version. That is the plan we will follow in our first draft. It may sound a little complicated, but after presenting the script, we will go through the details and present a flow chart. Here then, is the first draft:

```
# speller -- makes spelling changes interactively  Version 1.0
# Usage: speller filename
case $# in
   1)   ;;
   *) echo Usage: $0 filename 1>&2 ; exit 1 ;;
esac
missp=/tmp/sp.m.$$          ← File to store spell's output (suspects)
chsp=/tmp/sp.c.$$          ← File to store editing changes
nouse=no_use.$$            ← File to store unused words from spell
spell "$1" > $missp        ← Collect misspelled words from input file
for word in `cat $missp`  ← Process each misspelled word
do
   echo  The unidentified word is $word. > /dev/tty ← Show it
   echo Enter the correct word. To skip, hit [return] > /dev/tty
   read correct               ← Get correct spelling
   if test "$correct"         ← If correction made
   then               ← Create editing script file for sed
       echo "s/$word/$correct/g" >> $chsp
   else                ← If no correction entered
     echo $word >> $nouse      ← Save unmodified words
   fi
done
sed -f $chsp "$1"    ← Apply corrections to input file
echo Unused words are in the file $nouse > /dev/tty
rm -f $missp $chsp
```

The Big Picture

This skeletal version of *speller* is already rather long. Let's investigate its features. First, not being too ambitious, this script handles just one file, so we screen out other usages by using a *case* statement to require that there be just one command-line argument. We should also test to see if *$1* is in fact a readable file; however, we have chosen to omit most error checking in the first draft in order to make it easier to understand the structure of the program.

Next we announce three files to be used in the program; using *$missp*, *$chsp*, and *$nouse* as symbolic names for them. We placed the first two in */tmp* because they are temporary and get removed eventually. It might be useful to have a list of the suspect words we don't change (perhaps we don't yet know the correct spelling), so we set aside the third file in the current working directory to store them.

Now the real work starts. First we collect *spell*'s output in the temporary file *$missp*. Then we initiate a *for* loop that operates on each word in turn from this file. We are shown the word and asked to type a correction. If we do, an editing command is created using the original word and our correction. For instance, the script might show us a *word* value of *photun*. We can respond with *photon*. Then the line

```
echo "s/$word/$correct/g" >> $chsp
```

becomes

```
echo "s/photun/photon/g" >> /tmp/sp.c.8126
```

and the line

```
s/photun/photon/g
```

is appended to the editing file. (This assumes that *$$*, the current *PID*, is 8126). Otherwise, if we just hit ⎡Return⎤, the word is saved in the file *$nouse*, and nothing is added to the editing file.

Once all the words are processed, the collected set of editing commands is applied to the original file using the stream editor *sed*. Finally, the temporary files are cleaned up and we are told of *$nouse*'s actual name.

If that seems like a lot of programming, it is. It turns out that not all real-life tasks can be done in three-line shell scripts. For another way of looking at this script, see the visual summary offered in Figure 6.4.

Redirection in *speller*

We have some improvements in mind for *speller*, but before going on to them, let's take a breather of sorts, and look at how redirection is used in *speller*.

The first point is that some *echo* commands are followed by redirection to */dev/tty*. This, you may recall, is shorthand for the terminal being used by the user. Without this redirection, the output of these *echo* commands would go to wherever the standard output of the whole shell script was redirected. With the */dev/tty* redirection, even if we pipe the results to the printer, the interactive questions are sent to the user.

The second point is that we can improve the efficiency of the program by using a different form of redirection for creating the *$chsp* file. First, look at the original version:

```
echo "s/$word/$correct/g" >> $chsp
```

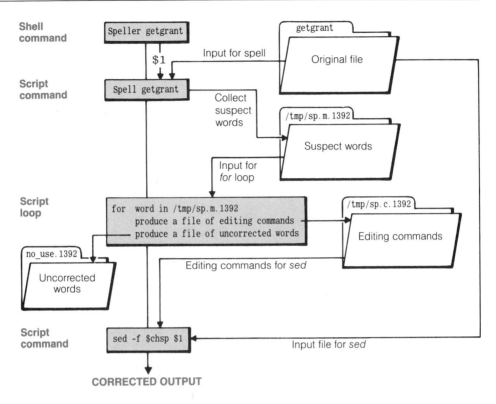

Figure 6.4
Information Flow in Speller

This is the most obvious approach to adding editing lines to the *$chsp* file. There is, in fact, a slightly better way. The first step is to replace this line with a simple

```
echo "s/$word/$correct/g"
```

So far, so bad. Now the editing command gets sent out the standard output, no help for *sed*. Now comes the neat part: we can use redirection with the *for* loop as a whole. That is, we replace

```
done
```

with

```
done > $chsp
```

This channels all the standard output produced within the loop into the *$chsp* file. (Note that the other *echo* commands in the loop have their own redirection commands, so only the output of the final *echo* actually goes to *$chsp*.) Why is this

```
for word in `cat $missp;`
do
    . . .
       Echo "s/$word/$correct/g" >> $chsp
done
```
Redirection inside of loop opens and closes the $chsp file *each* cycle

```
for word in `cat $missp`
do
    . . .
  echo "s/$word/$correct/g"
    . . .
done > $chsp
```
Redirection outside of loop opens and closes the $chsp file just *once*

Figure 6.5
Two Ways to Use Redirection

better? Because it requires opening and closing the *$chsp* file only once, while our first method required opening and closing the file every time an editing command was produced. So this second approach will run more efficiently.

Question 6.9

How would you modify the first version of the *cap* script in this chapter to use this more efficient form of redirection?

Incidentally, if the possibility existed that the whole script would have its standard input redirected, we would also put in this bit of redirection:

```
done > $chsp < /dev/tty
```

This ensures that regardless of whence the script takes its input, that the *for* loop takes its input from the terminal. Without it, the *read* statement would try to get its answers from a redirected standard input instead of from the terminal. (The *read* command itself cannot be redirected, but an enclosing *for* loop can.)

Second Thoughts — Adding a Context Printout

Are we, aside from some error checking and signal trapping, done? That depends on how comfortable we are with laxity. The program has some grave defects. The first is that it doesn't show us the context of the misspelled words. Of course, the context is hardly necessary for a word like *recieved*, but what about *themy*? Did we mean *them*, *they*, *theme*, or something else? The partial answer to this dilemma is to use *grep* to search the original file for occurrences of the word and print them out when the user is shown the suspect word. Let's revise *speller* to include this addition and the modified redirection approach. While we are at it, we will add a little more error checking:

```
# speller -- makes spelling changes interactively  Version 1.1
# Usage: speller filename
case $# in
   1)   ;;
   *) echo Usage: $0 filename 1>&2 ; exit 1 ;;
esac
if test ! -r "$1"
then                                      ← Quit if can't read file
    echo $0: cannot read $1 1>&2
    exit 1
fi
missp=/tmp/sp.m.$$
chsp=/tmp/sp.c.$$
nouse=no_use.$$
spell "$1" > $missp
if test -r $missp -a ! -s $missp   ← If error file is empty
then
    cat "$1"                              ← Pass on original file
    exit 0                                ← And quit
fi
for word in `cat $missp`
do
  echo  The unidentified word is $word. > /dev/tty
  grep "$word" "$1"  > /dev/tty     ← Show context
  echo Enter the correct word. To skip, hit [Return] > /dev/tty
  read correct
  if test "$correct"
  then
      echo "s/$word/$correct/g"
  else
    echo $word >> $nouse
  fi
done > $chsp
sed -f "$chsp" "$1"
if test -r $nouse
then
  echo Unused words are in the file $nouse > /dev/tty
fi
rm -f $missp $chsp
```

Here's what's new in error checking. First, we've tested to see if the *$1* file is readable. Second, if the *$missp* file is empty (the *-s* option of *test* checks if a file exists and has nonzero size, so our combination tests if it is readable but of 0 size), then there are no errors found, so we send the original contents on and skip the rest of the script. Third, we've tested to see if there is a *$nouse* file to print.

Can we run into problems with the *sed* command assuming that a *$chsp* and a *$1* file exist? No. First, if *$1* doesn't exist, the program quits at the initial *case* statement. Second, if no potential spelling errors occur, the program also quits without using *sed*. If there are spelling errors, then *$missp* contains words, and the *for* statement is executed, causing the *$chsp* file to be created. Possibly we may make no corrections. In this case *$chsp* is an empty file, but that is okay, for then *sed* runs the file with no changes.

Here is a sample run:

```
$ speller dearmom > lpr
The unidentified word is themy.
So I told themy they could have the old one if they wanted
Enter the correction. To skip, hit [return]
them
$
```

To show why this is but a partial fix, here is another run:

```
$ speller dearsis > saveit
The unidentified word is themy.
themy!!
Enter the correction. To skip, hit [return]
Return

Unused words are in the file no_use.3419
$ cat no_use.3419
themy
$
```

This time the context told us nothing, so we skipped making any changes. We'll have to go back and look at the original. Fortunately, we have the pesky word saved in the *no_use.3419* file. Should we try to battle the matter further, finding a way (perhaps with *awk*) of printing the preceding and following lines as well? For our own use, we feel that is too much programming for too little additional benefit.

Improving the Search Pattern

But there is yet another problem, one stemming from the fact that *sed* and *grep* recognize string patterns, not words. That means any changes you make will affect even words that contain the original string within them. For example, suppose you make the editing command

```
s/gle/gel/g
```

Then the sentence

```
I gleaned but a single fact from the color of the gle.
```

would become

```
I gelaned but a singel fact from the color of the gel.
```

This, perhaps, may not be what you had in mind.

To deal with this situation we have to draw upon the pattern-matching abilities of *grep* and *sed*. The obvious one of

```
s/ $word / $correct /g
```

is not good enough. Usually a word has a space before and after it, but it might come at the beginning or end of a line, or it might be preceded by a parenthesis or followed by a period, and so on. Here is a version that makes a more ambitious attempt at pattern matching. For *grep* we use three patterns. One attempts to find the word at the beginning of a line, the second looks in the midst of a line, and the third looks at the end of the line. The *sed* patterns are similar, but more complex, for they have to specify changing just part of the pattern. In Appendix A we develop and explain the patterns used here.

```
# speller -- makes spelling changes    Version 1.2
# Usage:  speller filename
case $# in
   1)  ;;
   *) echo Usage: $0 filename 1>&2 ; exit 1 ;;
esac
if test ! -r "$1"
then
    echo $0: cannot read $1 1>&2
    exit 1
fi
missp=/tmp/sp.m.$$
chsp=/tmp/sp.c.$$
nouse=no_use.$$
spell "$1" > $missp
if test -r $missp -a ! -s $missp
```

```
then
   cat "$1"
   exit 0
fi
for word in `cat $missp`
do
  echo  The unidentified word is $word. > /dev/tty
  grep -n '^'"$word"'[^a-zA-Z]' "$1" > /dev/tty
  grep -n   '[^A-Za-z]'"$word"'[^a-zA-Z]' "$1" > /dev/tty
  grep -n   '[^A-Za-z]'"$word"'$' "$1" > /dev/tty
  echo Enter the correct word. To skip, hit [return] > /dev/tty
  read correct
  if test "$correct"
  then
      echo 's/^'"$word"'\([^a-zA-Z]\)/'"$correct"'\1/
           s/\([^A-Za-z]\)'"$word"'\([^a-zA-Z]\)/\1'"$correct"'\2/g
           s/\([^A-Za-z]\)'"$word"'$/\1'"$correct"'/g'
  else     # save unmodified words
    echo $word >> $nouse
  fi
done > $chsp
sed -f "$chsp" "$1"
if test -r $nouse
then
   echo Unused words are in the file $nouse > /dev/tty
fi
rm -f $missp $chsp
```

We'll stop here. The program will handle most situations well enough, and if something unusual shows up, we can always skip the word and make changes later using the old-fashioned way. To help with that, we've used the *-n* option for *grep* to indicate the line number on which a pattern is found. The other main points to notice are

- Redirection using */dev/tty* lets you create scripts that can both handle interactive exchanges and work like filters. (This particular example is a half-filter; it can start pipes but not receive them.)
- A for statement as a whole can be used with redirection.
- Programming effort is often inversely proportional to the fraction of input that requires it.

Now that we have investigated several examples, let's take a more general view of the principles we should keep in mind when writing shell procedures.

IMPORTANT SHELL SCRIPT CONSIDERATIONS

The shell facilities make it possible to create flexible, powerful programs in the form of shell scripts. The mechanics of writing a script are simple; you just need to know how to use an editor. The process of designing a script, on the other hand, may involve some effort. Thus one important point about shell scripts is that you should be prepared to test them. A second important point is that it is a good idea to make your scripts compatible with the rest of the UNIX system. Third, it is important to know the strengths and weaknesses of the shell programming approach. We will take a quick look at these three matters now.

Trouble-Shooting

The most important trouble-shooting tool is your mind; if you fail to use this resource, you can get into trouble. The most important trouble-shooting tool offered by the system is the combined -*vx* option of the shell. As we discussed in Chapter 4, it lets you trace the execution of a script step by step, showing you what substitutions the program makes as it goes along.

You also have other things you can do. One is to prepare specially tailored files or arguments to test a program. See what happens, for example, if the input consists of an empty file. Another useful step during development is to place temporary files in your working directory and not to have the script remove them. Then you can check their contents and see if what you meant to go into them actually got there. Similarly, strategically placed *echo* statements can help you track down what is happening.

A very important point is that if you intend to develop a substantial program, start with a simplified version, get it working, then begin adding in other features. A basic design flaw, for example, will be much easier to detect before the program becomes encrusted in knickknackery.

And don't forget that when things go wrong for no apparent reason, there is always a reason; and it is almost always something you have done or overlooked. Thus the final tool sometimes is persistence.

Compatibility

A shell script intended for widespread use should incorporate the following features in order to be compatible with other system programs.

- Error-checking
- Error messages directed to the standard error

- Nonzero exit status for abnormally terminated programs
- Options, if any, to be indicated by hyphens, and to come between the procedure name and the other arguments
- Cleaning up after normal or abnormal termination

CONCLUSION

The shell script approach has many strengths. Shell features such as shell variables, positional parameters, command substitution, and programming control flow make it possible to achieve an enormous range of goals. Shell scripts have all the regular UNIX commands at their disposal to use as tools. A script, being a simple text file that uses other programs, takes relatively little storage space compared to that needed by compiled programs. Changing a script is just a matter of reediting the file; no recompilation is necessary. Finally, shell scripts are easily ported from one UNIX system to another.

The chief weakness of shell scripts is that they are relatively slow. Each time a UNIX command is used, the shell has to look around for the file containing the command and arrange for it to be run. This slowness usually is unimportant if the script generates just a few processes. On the other hand, a loop that generates a process or two each cycle can run quite slowly. Our *countdown* script is an example of that. A second weakness is that the shell is not well-suited to dealing with parts of strings or to looking at a text file character by character. Third, it's not an arithmetically oriented language.

When the shell script approach proves inadequate, then we can turn to writing C programs. Even here, however, you can use a shell script as a sort of first draft to test the logic of an approach. Once that is done, you can produce the equivalent C program. With the next chapter, we will begin our study of C programs.

ANSWERS TO QUESTIONS IN CHAPTER 6

6.1
```
case $# in
     0) dir=$HOME ; ;
     1) dir=$1
esac
```

6.2 The command-line argument of 15 is detected and assigned to *min*. Then the *expr* statement sets *sec* to 60 * 15, or 9000, and the reminder goes off every 9000 seconds. The command-line argument of 20 is ignored, for the program makes no use of *$2*.

6.3
```
$ countdown 3
    3! ...
    2! ...
    1! ...
    UNIX at your service!
    $
```

6.4 a. `echo I\'m thinking of a number between 1 and 30000.`
    `echo Guess it and earn my approval.`
    `answer=$$`
    `count=0`
    `read guess`
    `until test $guess -eq $answer`
    `do`
        `if test $guess -gt $answer`
        `then`
                `echo Too high! Guess again.`
        `else`
                `echo Too low! Guess again.`
        `fi`
        `read guess`
        `count=`expr $count + 1``
    `done`
    `echo Well done! You took $count guesses`

b. Replace
  `answer=$$`
  with
  `answer=`expr $$ % 100``
  If you are nice, you would also change the line that tells the user the limits.

6.5 `name=$name1' '$name2`

6.6 `case $# in`
    `0) echo Usage: $0 [-y] [-m] number_of_miles  1>&2; exit 1;;`
  `esac`
  `factor=5280`
  `unit=feet`
  `while true`
  `do`
    `case $1 in`
      `-y) factor=1760; unit=yards; shift;;`
      `-r) factor=320; unit=rods; shift;;`
      `*) break`
    `esac`
  `done`
  `answer=`expr $1 * $factor``
  `echo $1 miles are $answer $unit`

6.7 a. First line becomes
  `cat one two three`
  and the command tries to print the contents of the three files *one*, *two*, and *three*.
  Second line becomes
  `cat "one two three"`

and the command tries to print the contents of the single file whose name is "*one two three*" — one name with two spaces. Third line becomes

```
cat '$*'
```

and the command tries to print the contents of a file called *$**. Fourth line becomes

```
cat "one" "two" "three"
```

and the command tries to print the contents of the three files *one*, *two*, and *three*. In this case the first and fourth commands produce the same output.

b. First line becomes

```
cat alpha beta gamma
```

and the command tries to print the contents of the three files *alpha*, *beta*, and *gamma*. Second line becomes

```
cat "alpha beta gamma"
```

and the command tries to print the contents of the single file named "*alpha beta gamma*". Third line becomes

```
cat '$*'
```

and the command tries to print the contents of a file called *$**. Fourth line becomes

```
cat "alpha beta" "gamma"
```

and the command tries to print the contents of two files; the first called "*alpha beta*" and the second called "*gamma*".

6.8
```
echo Your name, please:
    count=0
    read name
    until test    "$name"
    do
        count=`expr $count + 1`
        if test $count -ge 5
        then
            echo Sorry, I can't take this any more...bye.
            exit 1
        fi
        echo You didn\'t give a name\; please try again:
        read name
    done
echo Well met, $name!
```

6.9 Replace
```
for file
 do
        echo '
'       File is $file: '
'           | cat - $file >> $temp
done
```

```
with
for file
do
    echo '
'       File is $file: '
'           | cat - $file
done > $temp
```

EXERCISES

1. Determine how long your system takes to run the *countdown* program in this chapter, starting with 10. If you are on a multiuser system, try it for different states of busyness.
2. Write a shell script using *date* that prints the usual *date* output as default but which has options for printing just the time, just the day-month-year, or just the day of the week.
3. Write a script that takes as command-line input a number *n* and a word. It then prints the word *n* times, one word per line.
4. Modify *speller* so that the end result is that the edit changes are placed in the original file.
5. Modify Exercise 3 so that it prints the input word *n* times on just one line.
6. Use the UNIX *time* command to determine the relative efficiencies of the *cap* script before and after the modification of Question 6.9.

7

SYSTEM CALLS AND THE
C LIBRARY

7

System Calls and the C Library

In this and in the following three chapters, we will explore programming in C on a UNIX system. C and UNIX both were created at the Bell Labs, and their developments have been intertwined. C is a powerful, efficient language in its own right, and its special relationship with UNIX enhances C's effectiveness. Most of UNIX (about 90 percent) is written in C, and, consequently, most of UNIX's powers are available to C programs in a rather natural way, through the many UNIX *system calls* and *library functions*. Understanding and using these calls and functions is the main theme of this chapter.

What are these calls and functions, and how are they used? The usual way to program in C is to break up a programming task into smaller modules and to program each module as a separate *function*. The complete program then consists of these task-oriented functions plus some programming to tie them together. In C, functions play the same role that subroutines, functions, and procedures play in languages such as FORTRAN and Pascal.

UNIX systems facilitate programming by providing a large number of built-in C functions that can be used in your own C programs. Bear in mind that these functions are used as *parts* of C programs; they are not stand-alone programs, the way the standard UNIX commands are. These functions fall into two groups: the system calls and the library functions. Both are used as C functions; the difference lies in how they are incorporated into the UNIX system. The system calls are more fundamental; they actually are part of the operating system. The library functions are add-ons. They expand the range of services offered by the system calls. Typically, they themselves use system calls.

The system calls are part of the kernel, so we can think of them as being part of the basic UNIX operating system. In principle, different versions of UNIX will share the same set of system calls. The library, on the other hand, is part of the UNIX superstructure, and it is often extended as developers come up with useful additions. The system calls and the library functions form a potent combination; for example, the standard UNIX commands (*cat*, *grep*, *wc*, *who*, and all those other commands we know and love) were created from these functions. Furthermore, one of the library functions lets you run any executable file. That allows you to incorporate the standard UNIX commands as well as your own shell scripts into C programs. Thus virtually all the powers of the UNIX system, as well as any shell scripts you have created or borrowed, are at your beck in a C program.

In this chapter we will examine the UNIX C functions. (Let's use that phrase to mean system calls and library functions collectively.) We'll look into the range of services offered by these functions and at how to interpret the UNIX manual's descriptions of them. This is an important skill, for the sheer number of UNIX C functions precludes our describing each and every one. Proper reading of the manual answers two key questions: what does a function do, and how do we use it in a C program? The chapter assumes you know C to some degree, but it will pause to review some aspects of the language. For examples of UNIX C functions, we'll look at I/O, including the important standard I/O package of functions found in the C library. These basics will prepare us for more involved examples in the following chapters. We'll start with some C review.

C LANGUAGE REVIEW

We hope you are at least somewhat familiar with the C programming language. (If you are not, this may be a good time to read one of the many fine books on the subject, such as *C Primer Plus*, by Waite, Prata, and Martin. When you finish, just resume reading here.) Here we wish to remind you of a few features that are particularly relevant to using the UNIX C functions and to interpreting the manual.

Functions

Functions are the basic programming modules of C. In general, a function has a name, a type (see below), an argument list, and a return value. The argument list consists of values provided to the function for its use. The return value allows the function to communicate a single value back to the calling program. (We'll discuss communication more fully later.) As an example, here is the definition of a function that returns the square of an integer value:

```
int sqri(n)
int n;
{
    return n*n;
}
```

Here *n* is the argument, which is declared to be of type *int*, or integer — more on types follows shortly. The function itself (*sqri()*) is also declared to be of type *int*, meaning that the return value (*n*n*), too, is of integer type.

Here are some sample function calls:

```
m = sqri(5);
q = sqri(m);
```

The first call returns a value of 25 to *m*, and the second call returns a value of 625 (25 squared) to *q*. C functions pass arguments by value. This means that in the second call, the value *25* rather than the variable *m* is passed on to the *sqri()* function. In other words, *n* in *sqri()* is a new, independent variable, not just a synonym for *m*, as it might be in some languages. Thus, any changes a function might make to an argument variable do not affect the original variable in the calling program. The arguments used in the function definitions are called *formal* arguments; here *n* is a formal argument. The arguments used in a function call are called *actual* arguments; here *5* and the value of *m* are the actual arguments.

Normally, the function type is not only part of the function definition but is also declared in the calling program or function. For instance, a program using *sqri()* could include this declaration:

```
int sqri();
```

This informs the program that *sqri* is the name of a function that returns a type *int* value. We said ''could'' because C programs assume that undeclared functions are type *int*; hence functions of that type are often not declared.

The return value feature is not always used; sometimes a function is used to perform an act without returning a value, much like a FORTRAN subroutine or a Pascal procedure. Current practice is to describe such functions as type *void*. Here is an example:

```
void sum(n,m)
int n,m;
{
    printf("The sum of %d and %d is %d\n",n,m, n+m);
}
```

Here the function performs some actions — calculating a sum and printing out the results — without returning any value to the calling program. When used this way, a function is called without assigning or using its value:

```
sum(20,m);
```

To use a C function, we need to know its name, its type, its arguments, and its return value. The manual, as we will see, provides this information for the UNIX C functions.

Types

C is a typed language. That is, each variable, constant, or function has a particular data type or category. The two basic conceptual types for storing information in a computer are integer and floating-point. In integer storage, a number is stored as a binary integer, a sequence of 0s and 1s. In floating-point storage, a number is stored in two pieces — a fractional part and an exponent. This form, too, is a sequence of 0s and 1s, but they are interpreted differently.

In C there are several varieties of integer storage. The most basic type is called *int*. The modifiers *short*, *long*, and *unsigned* can affect the amount of memory used to store an integer and whether or not negative numbers are allowed. Often a modifier is used by itself, with the *int* understood. Thus

```
short poot;
```

means that *poot* is a variable of type *short int*. One other integer type is *char*. This type allots just one byte of storage for a variable, and the integer value stored can be interpreted (typically via ASCII code) as representing a character.

The floating-point types are called *float* and *double*. On some systems the two are the same, but when there is a difference, *double* allows for greater precision.

These basic types have various extensions and elaborations, such as arrays, structures, and pointers, all of which we will use in our examples.

Arrays

An array is a series of elements of one data type. For example, the declaration

```
int buckets[10];
```

creates storage for 10 adjacent *int* variables. They are accessed by using an index, with 0 referring to the first element. Thus *buckets[9]* would be the last member of this 10-element array. Each element can be used in the same manner as an ordinary *int* variable.

One common form of array is the *string*. This is a type *char* array in which a special character (the '\0', or null character) is used to mark the end of the string.

Structures

Like the array, a structure is capable of holding more than one value. Unlike an array, a structure is not limited to values of only one type. For instance, consider this declaration:

```
struct {
        char name[40];
        int  iq;
        float assets;
        } pat;
```

This declares *pat* to be a structure with three members. The first member is a 40-element character array, the second element is type *int*, and the third element is type *float*. To access the different members, use the membership operator, which is a dot. For example, we would refer to the second member of the structure as *pat.iq*. Note that while *pat* is a structure, the element called *pat.iq* is just a simple *int*. The rightmost component of such a compound name determines the type.

Often structures are defined using a *tag* to identify the type. For instance, the preceding declaration could be broken into two parts:

```
struct sigother {
                char name[40];
                int  iq;
                float assets;
                };
        struct sigother pat;
```

Here *sigother* is the tag. This allows us to declare other structures of type *struct sigother*, if we choose.

Pointers

The pointer is more involved than the other derived types. Since many UNIX C functions use pointers, let's give that subject a quick review.

First, why bother with pointers? One very important point is that pointers are invaluable for passing information to and from functions. We can use function arguments and function returns to pass single-valued quantities between the calling and the called function. That may seem like a severe restriction, but if the single-valued quantity we pass is, say, a pointer to an array or to a third function, *then we give the called function the means of using that array or function.* Pointers also offer a means of two-way communication that is lacking when ordinary variables are used as arguments; we will return to that topic later.

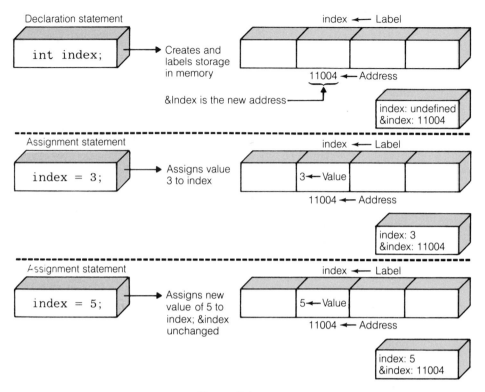

Figure 7.1
index* and *&index

A pointer, in essence, is a memory address. Giving the address of a value "points" to where it is. Just as, say, an *int* quantity can be a constant, like *3*, or a variable, like *index*, a pointer can be a constant or a variable. An example of a pointer constant would be *&index* (address of *index*); the address operator (*&*) yields the address of the following variable. For instance, consider the statements

```
int index;
index = 3;
```

First a memory location is assigned the label *index*. Then the value 3 is placed in that memory location. In this case, the value of *index* is 3, and the value of *&index* is the memory location, say 11004. If we then make the statement

```
index = 5;
```

we change the value of *index*, but that new value is still stored at the same location, memory location 11004. So *index* is a variable, but the address *&index* is a constant. Figure 7.1 shows this pictorially.

Now that we've seen a pointer *constant*, let's look at a pointer *variable*. Like any other variable, a pointer variable needs a name, so let's call it *ptr*. (It also needs to be declared, and we will return to that topic soon.) Just as an *int* variable can be assigned different integer values, *ptr* can be assigned different pointer (or address) values. That is, we can say

```
ptr = &index;
```

and later say

```
ptr = &num;
```

In each case, the *value* of *ptr* would be the *address* of the corresponding variable (*&index* and *&num*). We say that *ptr* points to *index* or that *ptr* points to *num*.

The * operator lets us *obtain* the value stored in the pointed-to variable. Suppose that *index* has the value 5 and is stored at the address 11004, and suppose we make the following assignment:

```
ptr = &index;
```

Then *ptr* has the value 11004 (the address of *index*), and **ptr* has the value of 5 (the value of *index*). In short, **ptr* yields the contents of the address pointed to by *ptr*. We can use **ptr* just as we would use *index*. For instance,

```
y = *ptr + 10;
```

assigns the value 15 (i.e., 5 + 10) to *y*, and

```
*ptr = 20;
```

assigns a value of 20 to **ptr* and hence to *index*. We can paraphrase the last statement as ''go to the location pointed to by *ptr* and place the value 20 there.''

Incidentally, we could also refer to *&ptr*, which would be the address of the *ptr* variable itself; like any other variable, a pointer has to be stored somewhere. Figure 7.2 sorts through these relationships.

We've talked of having a pointer variable, but how does one declare a pointer variable? There is no separate *pointer* type; a pointer declaration is constructed from other types. A pointer declaration should announce two facts: that the variable is a pointer, and to what type of variable it points. For instance,

```
int *ptr;
```

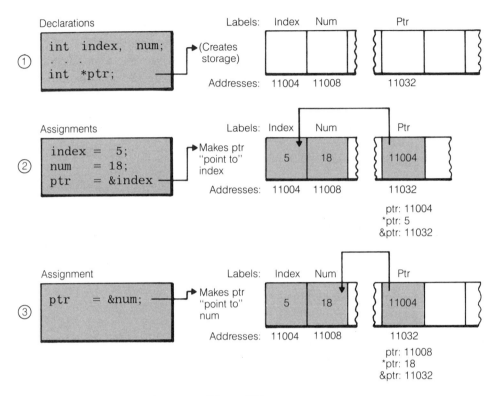

Figure 7.2
Pointers, Variables, Values, and Addresses

declares that *ptr* is a pointer to type *int*. (We would call *ptr* type "pointer-to-*int*.")
The declaration really says the quantity **ptr* is type *int*, but since the * operator is
applied to pointers, this implies that *ptr* itself is a pointer.

Similarly, the declaration

```
double *pnum;
```

declares *pnum* to be a pointer-to-double; it could be assigned the address of a type
double variable.

Is there really any difference between the address of, say, a *char* variable and a
double variable? In one sense, no. Each is the address of the *first* byte of the
corresponding variable. The address of a *char* looks no different from the address
of a *double*. Indeed, that is the very reason we have to declare different pointer
types. If we use an expression like

```
x = *pnum;
```

the computer has to know that *pnum* refers to the 8 bytes of a *double* value instead of to the single byte of a *char* value. The declaration

```
double *pnum;
```

accomplishes that.

You should be aware of three C conventions regarding pointers. The first is that the name of an array in C is a pointer to the beginning of the array. That is, if we have the declaration

```
char readin[30];
```

then *readin* is synonymous with *&readin[0]*, the address of the first element of the array. Note that an array name is a pointer *constant*; we can assign new values to array members, but we can't assign a new address to an array name. The array name convention makes it easy to pass a pointer to an array as a function argument.

The second pointer convention is that a quoted string is a pointer to the first character of the string. Consider this statement, for example:

```
printf("%u", "Hi, pal.");
```

This would print out the address where the 'H' is stored. (The *%u* format prints out an unsigned integer, which is a suitable format for printing addresses.)

Both of these conventions are quite useful for the many string-related C functions. The *puts()* function, for example, takes as an argument a pointer to a string. It then prints out characters until it reaches the null character marking the end of the string. The actual argument, then, could be a pointer variable, the name of a string array, or a quoted string.

The third convention to note is that the name of a function is a pointer to the function. These conventions make it convenient to pass pointers to functions as arguments to a function.

Incidentally, the name of a structure is *not* a pointer to a structure; don't be misled by making an analogy to array and function names.

Storage Classes

Variables in C, we have seen, are characterized by having a *type*. C variables also are characterized by having a *storage class*. The two main storage classes are *automatic* (keyword *auto*) and *external* (keyword *extern*). Variables declared inside a function belong, by default, to the automatic storage class. These variables are created automatically when the function is called and die (have their locations returned to a memory pool) when the function returns control to the calling program.

Automatic variables are *local* variables, known only to the function they are in. Because they are hidden from the calling program, we need not worry that they will produce some unexpected side effect in the calling program.

The second major C storage class, the external variable, is a global variable that can be shared by several functions. This provides a means for sharing information. Occasionally we will find reference to external variables in the descriptions of the system and library functions. These external variables can be used in our programs if we choose. You can think of them as being part of the environment of a C program (but not in the sense of belonging to the *environment* set up by the *export* command).

Less common storage classes are static and external static. The static variable is a local variable whose value persists from one function call to the next, as long as the main program continues. It is declared using the keyword *static* within the function. The external static variable is an external variable whose scope is limited to a single file of source code. It is declared using the keyword *static* outside of any function.

Information Flow Between C Functions

C programs typically consist of a *main()* function that provides the overall organization of the program and of other functions that perform the various tasks. This gives C programs a neat, easy-to-follow, modular approach. It also creates the necessity for communication between the different functions in a program. We'll look now at how that is done.

There are three channels available for communicating information between two functions in the same program. The first is one we have just discussed, the external variable. Since it is known to every function in the program, it offers two-way communication. Any function can use it, and any function can change it.

The second channel for information flow is the use of function arguments. They provide *one-way flow* of information from the calling program to the function. However, the use of pointers as arguments does provide an indirect way for the called function to alter variables in the calling function. If we pass a pointer to a variable, then the function can place a value in the pointed-to address.

To use a function, we need to know how many arguments it uses and what the types are. For example, consider this heading for a function definition:

```
double harmean(x,y)
double x, y;
```

This indicates that the *harmean()* function has two arguments (*x* and *y*), and that both are type *double*. The function itself is also type *double*, and we will see why soon.

The third channel is the *return* command; it provides a one-way flow of information from the called function to the calling function. As we mentioned earlier, the type of value returned determines the function type. This, too, we need to know. For example, let's complete the *harmean()* function:

```
double harmean(x,y)
double x, y;
{
   return ( 2.0/( 1.0/x + 1.0/y);
}
```

It calculates the harmonic mean (the inverse of the average of the sum of the inverses) of two numbers and returns the result. Since the result is also type *double*, we declare *harmean()* to be *double*. Then a calling program could use it this way:

```
. . .
double z, harmean();
   . . .
z = harmean( 3.0, 6.0 );
   . . .
```

The arguments 3.0 and 6.0 are communicated to the *harmean()* function. It calculates the answer (4.0) and uses *return* to communicate this value back to the main program, in which 4.0 then is assigned to z. This illustrates information flow to and from a called function.

Question 7.1

Here is a function definition:

```
int ispos(x)
double x;
{
return (x > 0)
}
```

a. How many arguments does it have?
b. What type is the argument?
c. What type is the return value?

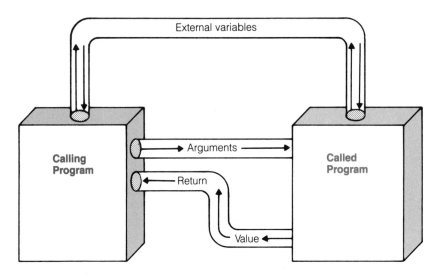

Figure 7.3
Information Flow Between Functions

Keep in mind that a C function can return but one value. This may appear to be rather limiting, but the value can be a pointer. Hence it can point to something more substantial, like a character string or a structure or a function.

Header Files

C uses a preprocessor to ease the burden of programming. The preprocessor lets one use the *#define* directive to define symbolic constants and short-hand functions known as *macros*. For instance,

```
#define YES 1
```

lets you use the symbolic constant *YES* to represent the value 1 in a program. Similarly, the definition

```
#define max(X,Y)   ( (X) > (Y) ? (X) : (Y) )
```

lets you use the macro *max(X,Y)* as maximum *function* in a program. It is not really a function. Using *max()* in a program simply results in it being replaced in the code by its definition, here a C conditional statement.

Often several functions share a batch of such definitions. For convenience, these groups of definitions can be gathered together in what is called a *header file*, so called because it comes at the head of a program. Another preprocessor directive,

#include, lets one instruct the compiler to include a header file with the rest of a program. For example, we could create a header file called *logic.h* that contains some definitions we often use in programs:

```
#define TRUE 1
#define FALSE 0
#define BOOLEAN int
```

(The suffix *.h*, like using uppercase letters in the definitions, is a convention, not a necessity). Once we have this file, we needn't type the definitions again. Instead, if we have a program in which we wish to use these definitions, we could start it like this:

```
#include "logic.h"
main()
{
   BOOLEAN inword = FALSE;
   ...
```

The preprocessor would obtain the definitions from the *logic.h* file and apply them to the program, making that first declaration into

```
int inword = 0;
```

In this case, with the name in quotes, the preprocessor would look in the current working directory for the file; we could use a full pathname to be more specific.

Several system and library functions use one or more header files. If you use these functions, you must include the appropriate header files. For example, if you use the library call *puts()*, you would place this at the beginning of your program:

```
#include <stdio.h>
```

The *stdio.h* file is one used by several functions in the C library. The angle brackets tell the system to look for the file *stdio.h* in a special directory used to hold system header files. Typically, the directory is */usr/include*.

Now that we have reviewed some aspects of C, let's turn our attention back to UNIX C functions.

SYSTEM CALLS AND LIBRARY FUNCTIONS

The system calls are the functions used in the kernel itself; they give you access to the heart of the UNIX operating system. System calls are used to create files, to provide the basic I/O services, to access the system clock, to determine file-use permissions, and to perform other such fundamental tasks.

To get an overview of what these facilities do, you should skim through Volume 1 of the UNIX manual. Section 2 lists the system calls, and Section 3 covers the library functions. These UNIX functions are also listed in Appendix E in the back of this book. To indicate the flavor of what you will find, here are a few of the system calls described in Section 2:

access()	Determine the accessibility of a file
brk() and *sbrk()*	Alter amount of memory allotted to a program
chmod()	Change mode of a file
creat(), *open()*, and *close()*	Create, open, and close files
lseek()	Find locations within a file
stat()	Get information about a file
read() and *write()*	Low-level I/O
execl()	Execute a file
signal()	Handle various ''signals'' to a program

As you can see, these functions offer some of the most basic services of an operating system: allotting memory, running processes, maintaining a file system, providing I/O, and determining access. We have included parentheses in the names to remind us that these are C functions. For instance, the function *read()* is not the same as the command *read* we used in shell scripts. These system calls provide basic building blocks for program development. For example, *access()* could be used in programming a command like the UNIX *rm* command. The system calls also are building blocks for the system library.

Now that we have seen what system calls are like, what about the UNIX library? To get a complete answer, you can skim through Section 3 of the manual or through the appendix in this book. You'll soon see that the library is full of useful programs. That's what gets them into the library. Let's summarize what you would find. First, the library contains several kinds of C programs. Many are extensions of the system calls. For instance, there is a *standard I/O package*. It includes all the standard C I/O functions (such as *getchar()*, *printf()*, *fgets()*, and the like). It also includes file-related functions such as *fopen()* and *fclose()*. Other functions relate to memory allocation (*malloc()*) and to system operations (*getpass()*, for instance, gets a password). Another major group of functions is the math library, which provides such things as trig functions, a random number function, and exponential functions.

Clearly, the math functions offer something new, but why offer functions that overlap the services offered by the system calls (such as the *standard I/O* package versus the system calls *read()* and *write()*)? The answer is that the library functions offer more convenience and versatility than do the bare-bones system calls. If you've used C, you know, for example, that sometimes it's best to use *putchar()* for output, while at other times you may want *puts()* to print a string or *printf()* to

Figure 7.4
System Calls Are at the Programmer's Disposal

print formatted information. You could use the *write()* system call plus additional programming to achieve the same results, but it is simpler to take advantage of the programming others have done in creating the library functions.

Question 7.2

What are the differences among a system call, a library function, and a UNIX command?

Each of these functions, whether a system call or a library function, is used in the same manner as a C function of your own creation. There is, however, the matter of letting your program know where to find these functions. For the system calls and some of the library functions, you don't have to worry about it; the system automatically looks for them when it puts your C program together. Other library functions require you to provide information to the compiler.

To use a UNIX C function, we need to know the function type (and hence the type of value it returns), the number of arguments used by the function, the argument types, if any external variables are involved, and if any header files are needed. Let's turn to the manual now and see how it helps us with this information.

THE UNIX MANUAL: SYSTEM CALLS AND LIBRARY FUNCTIONS

Yes, the UNIX manual does provide those facts needed to use a function. It presents the mechanical details we just described and it also explains exactly what the function accomplishes. Knowing what a function does is as important as knowing how to use it. The system calls, you may recall, are found in Section 2, Volume 1, of the UNIX manual, and the library functions are found in Section 3. The general format of these sections is much the same as that of the UNIX commands.

At the top, there is the command name, followed by a ''2'' or ''3'' to indicate the section of the manual. Next, there is a NAME section giving the function name along with a brief description. Then a SYNOPSIS section summarizes the usage for the function. Next, a DESCRIPTION section explains what the function does. Then there are a variety of other sections, such as SEE ALSO and BUGS that may or may not be present. The System V manual includes a section called RETURN VALUE for the system commands; as you might expect, it tells what values the function returns for various circumstances. Section 3 and some versions of Section 2 include this information in the DESCRIPTION portion instead.

It is time to develop a few examples. To illustrate the use of the manual, we'll look at a system call description and, later, a library description. We'll use the information there to create simple programs using the functions. As a sidelight, we'll see how to tap into the system error messages.

Once we get comfortable with the manual, we'll look at more involved examples utilizing various file I/O functions.

An Example Using a System Call

Let's look at an example and see how we can use the manual to show us how to use a function in practice. The first system call in Section 2 (at least, for most newer UNIX versions) is the *access()* function, and that is as good a place to start

ACCESS(2)   ACCESS(2)

NAME
    access — determine accessibility of a file

SYNOPSIS
    int access (path, amode)
    char *path;
    int amode;

DESCRIPTION
    Path points to a pathname naming a file. *Access* checks the named file for accessibility
    according to the bit pattern contained in *amode*, using the real user ID in place of the effective
    user ID and the real group ID in place of the effective group ID. The bit pattern contained in
    amode is constructed as follows:

        04   read
        02   write
        01   execute (search)
        00   check existence of file

    Access to the file is denied if one or more of the following are true:

        A component of the path prefix is not a directory. [ENOTDIR]

        Read, write, or execute (search) permission is requested for a null pathname. [ENOENT]

        The named file does not exist. [ENOENT]

        Search permission is denied on a component of the path prefix. [EACCES]

        Write access is requested for a file on a read-only file system. [EROFS]

        Write access is requested for a pure procedure (shared text) file that is being executed.
        [ETXTBSY]

        Permission bits of the file mode do not permit the requested access. [EACCES]

        Path points outside the process's allocated address space. [EFAULT]

    The owner of a file has permission checked with respect to the "owner" read, write, and
    execute mode bits; members of the file's group other than the owner have permissions checked
    with respect to the "group" mode bits; all others have permissions checked with respect to
    the "other" mode bits.

RETURN VALUE
    If the requested access is permitted, a value of 0 is returned. Otherwise, a value of –1 is
    returned and *errno* is set to indicate the error.

SEE ALSO
    chmod(2), stat(2).

Figure 7.5
UNIX Manual's Description of *access()*

as any. Figure 7.5, recall, reproduces the manual's description of *access()*. First,
check out the SYNOPSIS:

    int access (path, amode)
    char *path;
    int amode;

This tells us that when we use *access()*, we need to supply it with two arguments. The first argument (*path*) is a pointer to type *char*. If you have worked with C, you will recognize this as representing a character string, with *path* pointing to the first character in the string. The second argument (*amode*) is an integer. (Older manuals omit declaring *int* types.)

Next, the DESCRIPTION tells us (rather technically) that *access()* is used to determine access to a file. The *path* argument represents the name of the file to be investigated, and the *amode* is an integer code indicating the *type* of access we wish to test.

Looking down the page to RETURN VALUE, we see that *access()* returns a value of 0 if the requested access is permitted or else a value of –1 if the requested access is not permitted. There is also some remark about *errno*, which is an external variable used to indicate what error, if any, has shown up.

Question 7.3

Look up *kill(2)* in your manual or in the figure below.

a. How many arguments does *kill()* take?
b. What type is each argument?
c. What type value is returned?
d. What is the difference between *kill(2)* and *kill(1)*?

Let's use this information about *access()* to construct a program that checks to see if a file is both readable and writable. According to the code, 04 is read permission and 02 is write permission. You combine permissions by adding the corresponding permission codes; permission to read and write, then, would be represented by 06. (In C, an initial zero indicates that the number is in octal.) Here is an interactive program:

```
#define READWRITE 06
main()
{
char file[81];

printf("This program checks to see if a file is readable\n");
printf("and writable.  Please enter the filename.\n");
scanf("%80s", file);               /* read filename */
if ( access( file, READWRITE ) == 0 )  /* "file" is a pointer */
    printf("The file %s is readable and writable.\n", file );
```

KILL(2)   KILL(2)

NAME
    kill — send a signal to a process or a group of processes

SYNOPSIS
    int kill (pid, sig)
    int pid, sig;

DESCRIPTION
    Kill sends a signal to the process or group of processes specified by *pid*. The signal that is to
    be sent is specified by *sig* and is either one from the list given in *signal*(2) or 0. If *sig* is 0
    (the null signal), error checking is performed but no signal is actually sent. This can be used
    to check the validity of *pid*.

    The real or effective user ID of the sending process must match the real or effective user ID
    of the receiving process unless the effective user ID of the sending process is superuser.

    The processes with a process ID of 0 and a process ID of 1 are special processes (see *intro*(2))
    and are referenced below as *proc0* and *proc1*, respectively.

    If *pid* is greater than zero, *sig* is sent to the process whose process ID is equal to *pid*. *Pid*
    may equal 1.

    If *pid* is 0, *sig* is sent to all processes, excluding *proc0* and *proc1*, whose process group ID
    is equal to the process group ID of the sender.

    If *pid* is –1 and the effective user ID of the sender is not superuser, *sig* is sent to all processes,
    excluding *proc0* and *proc1*, whose real user ID is equal to the effective user ID of the sender.

    If *pid* is –1 and the effective user ID of the sender is superuser, *sig* is sent to all processes,
    excluding *proc0* and *proc1*.

    If *pid* is negative but not –1, *sig* is sent to all processes whose process group ID is equal to
    the absolute value of *pid*.

    Kill fails and no signal is sent if one or more of the following are true:
        Sig is not a valid signal number. [EINVAL]

        No process can be found corresponding to that specified by *pid*. [ESRCH]

        The user ID of the sending process is not superuser, and its real or effective user ID does
        not match the real or effective user ID of the receiving process. [EPERM]

RETURN VALUE
    Upon successful completion, a value of 0 is returned. Otherwise, a value of –1 is returned
    and *errno* is set to indicate the error.

SEE ALSO
    kill(1), getpid(2), setpgrp(2), signal(2).

Figure 7.6
UNIX Manual's Description of *kill(2)*

```
else
        printf("%s is not both readable and writable.\n", file );
}
```

Recall that the name of an array is a pointer to the first element of the array, so *file*
is, indeed, a pointer to *char*, as required by *access()*.

The *if* statement compares the integer value returned by *access()* with the integer
0. Thus successful access produces a true condition $(0==0)$, and the success
message is printed. Otherwise, the dismal message of failure is printed. (In C, =

is used for assigning values, and $==$ is used for comparing values.) Let's investigate failure further. In doing so, we will unearth a system feature of much greater generality than our program. This new feature will be using the external variable *errno* to obtain the system error messages.

More Error Information: *errno*

The *errno* external variable is available to any UNIX C program, not just those using the *access()* function. The simplest way to see what it does, however, is to continue with our example.

First, let's see what our program tells and fails to tell us. Suppose we compile this C program and place the executable version in the file *canrw*. Here is a sample run:

```
$ canrw
This program checks to see if a file is readable
and writable. Please enter the filename.
podge
podge is not both readable and writable.
$
```

It tells us that *podge* fails our test, but what exactly is wrong with *podge*? Does it not exist? Does it exist but is it forbidden to us? Is it readable but not writable? Several circumstances could make the *access()* test fail. Indeed, the description section for *access()* lists several possible causes for denying access. How can you find the exact reason? That is where *errno* comes in. Unfortunately, all that the *access()* entry in the manual tells us is that *errno* is set to indicate the error. The actual workings of *errno* are set forth in the manual introduction to Section 2.

Reading the introduction, we find that *errno* is an external variable of type *int*. It is availiable to any C program. When a system call goes astray, a code number is assigned to *errno* to indicate the nature of the error. Once *errno* is set, it keeps its value until you reset it or until another error occurs. The introduction lists 36 errors for System V. Figure 7.7 shows a few excerpts.

Looking at the table, we see that an error number of 2 implies that file does not exist, and an error number of 30 indicates an attempt to get write permission for a read-only file system. For each number the introduction also lists a symbolic representation. *ENOENT* stands for error 2, and *EDOM* stands for error 33. (You may have noticed that these symbolic error names were used in the description of *access()*.) The header file *<errno.h>* defines these symbolic representations in terms of the error numbers.

How do we make use of this wealth of error information? If we want to find out the value of *errno*, we should declare it as an external variable in our program. If

1   EPERM Not owner
       Typically this error indicates an attempt to modify a file in some way forbidden except
       to its owner or superuser. It is also returned for attempts by ordinary users to do things
       allowed only to the superuser.

2   ENOENT No such file or directory
       This error occurs when a filename is specified and the file should exist but doesn't, or
       when one of the directories in a pathname does not exist.

3   ESRCH No such process
       No process can be found corresponding to that specified by the process identifier (*pid*)
       in *kill*(2) or *ptrace*(2).

33 EDOM Math argument
       The argument of a function in the math package (3M) is out of the domain of the function.

34 ERANGE Result too large
       The value of a function in the math package (3M) is not representable within machine
       precision.

35 ENOMSG No message of desired type
       An attempt was made to receive a message of a type that does not exist on the specified
       message queue; see *msgop*(2).

36 EIDRM Identifier removed
       This error is returned to processes that resume execution due to the removal of an
       identifier from the file system's name space (see *msgctl*(2), *semctl*(2), and *shmctl*(2)).

Figure 7.7
Some Error Descriptions from the System Call Introduction

we want to use the symbolic representations, we can include the *errno.h* file. These
ideas apply to all the system calls, and we can incorporate them into our modest
example:

```
#define READWRITE 06
main()
{
char file[40];
extern int errno;   /* announce use of external variable */

printf("This program checks to see if a file is readable\n");
printf("and writable.  Please enter the filename.\n");
scanf("%s", file);
if ( access( file, READWRITE ) == 0 )
    printf("The file %s is readable and writable.\n", file );
else {
    printf("%s is not both readable and writable.\n", file );
    printf("The system error number is %d.\n", errno);
    }
}
```

Now run the revised version:

```
$ canrw
This program checks to see if a file is readable
and writable. Please enter the filename.
podge
podge is not both readable and writable.
The system error number is 2.
$
```

Now all you have to do is leaf through the introduction to Section 2 and find what error 2 is. There we read

```
2 ENOENT  No such file or directory
```

Or does referring to a manual seem too uncomputerlike? Perhaps we should do something along the following lines and make the program itself provide the information. First, we could preface the program with

```
#include <errno.h>
```

Then we could insert lines like the following into the program:

```
if ( errno == ENOENT )
    printf("No such file or directory\n");
```

But before we get carried away with this project, perhaps we should check to see if our desires have been anticipated by the UNIX system. Doing so leads us to Section 3 and the function *perror()*.

The *perror()* Library Function

Now we get a chance to use Section 3 of the manual, and we get to learn how to get the system error messages placed at our disposal. First, look at the entry for *perror()* (for *print error*); we show it in Figure 7.8. Note that it promises to provide error messages — exactly what we are seeking. Also note that the heading at the top says *PERROR(3C)*. We will come back to the meaning of the *3C* when we finish with the example.

The synopsis for *perror()* may seem a bit confusing at first reading:

```
SYNOPSIS
    void perror (s)
    char *s;
```

```
PERROR(3C)                                                        PERROR(3C)

NAME
     perror, errno, sys_errlist, sys_nerr — system error messages

SYNOPSIS
     void perror (s)
     char *s;
     extern int errno;
     extern char *sys_errlist[];
     extern int sys_nerr;

DESCRIPTION
     Perror produces a message on the standard error output, describing the last error encountered
     during a call to a system or library function. The argument string s is printed first, then a
     colon and a blank, then the message and a new-line. To be of most use, the argument string
     should include the name of the program that incurred the error. The error number is taken
     from the external variable errno, which is set when errors occur but not cleared when non-
     erroneous calls are made.

     To simplify variant formatting of messages, the array of message strings sys_errlist is provided;
     errno can be used as an index in this table to get the message string without the new-line.
     Sys_nerr is the largest message number provided for in the table; it should be checked because
     new error codes may be added to the system before they are added to the table.

SEE ALSO
     intro(2).
```

Figure 7.8
UNIX Manual's Description of perror()

extern int errno;
extern char *sys_errlist[];
extern int sys_nerr;

Sorting this out, we note that the NAME section lists *perror()* and all three external variables: *errno*, *sys_errlist*, and *sys_nerr*. What this implies is that these are four related functions and variables, but they need not all be used simultaneously. Indeed, we can ignore the external variables and just use *perror()*. The reason they are listed together is that they all relate to error processing. As we will see later, we can use the external variables as an alternative to *perror()*.

Second, we encounter the type *void* in the function declaration. This is a relatively new terminology in C, and it is used to identify functions that *do not return a value*. Thus you cannot have a statement like

```
x = perror ("access");      /* not valid */
```

Reading the description, we find that *perror()* prints its argument (a character string), follows it with a colon, and then prints an error message corresponding to the current value of *errno*. Let's put it into our program:

```
#define READWRITE 06
main()
```

```
{
char file[40];

printf("This program checks to see if a file is readable\n");
printf("and writable.  Please enter the filename.\n");
scanf("%s", file);
if ( access( file, READWRITE ) == 0 )
    printf("The file %s is readable and writable.\n", file );
else {
    printf("%s is not both readable and writable.\n", file );
    perror("access");
    }
}
```

We removed the *errno* declaration because our program no longer uses that variable. The *perror()* program does use *errno*, and it is declared as an external variable in that program.

Running the new version, we get

```
$ canrw
This program checks to see if a file is readable
and writable. Please enter the filename.
podge
podge is not both readable and writable
access: No such file or directory
$
```

Note that *perror()* prints the error messages that we found listed in the Section 2 introduction.

Question 7.4

What would the output have been if we had used the call *perror("oh no!")* instead of *perror("access")*? Why use the second form?

One important feature of *perror()* is that it sends the error message to the standard error, not to the standard output. So even if we redirected the output of *canrw*, the error message would still come to the terminal.

Now let's look at the external variables. The variable *sys_nerr* tells us how many error messages there are. The array *sys_errlist[]* contains pointers to the text of the various messages; thus *sys_errlist[4]* points to the text of the message that goes with an *errno* value of 4. We can use this information as an alternative to *perror()*. Here, for instance, is a short program to print out the current set of error messages; the information it provides may be more up-to-date than the manual.

```
/*  ermesg.c  -- prints out list of system error messages */
main()
{
int i;
extern int sys_nerr;
extern char *sys_errlist[];

printf("Here are the current %d error messages:\n\n", sys_nerr);
for (i = 0; i < sys_nerr ; i++)
  printf("%d: %s\n", i, sys_errlist[i] );
}
```

Compile and run it:

```
$ cc -o ermesg ermesg.c
$ ermesg
Here are the current 37 error messages:

0:
1: Not owner
2: No such file or directory
 . . .
36: Identifier Removed
$
```

Note that the error message for *errno* of 0 is blank. This is quite reasonable, since an *errno* of 0 means no errors have been detected. To find out the error messages on your system, you can run this program yourself.

Question 7.5

How could you have a program of yours use *perror()*, yet print out your version of the error messages?

The examples we've given are on the plain and simple side. However, our main intent was to show how to read and interpret the UNIX manual. Our secondary intent was to point out the existence of *errno* and *perror()*, for they are useful tools.

The *perror()* library function was used in the same manner as the *access()* system function. Some library functions, however, require additional care in their use, and the introduction to Section 3 offers some general advice in that respect. We will take that up now.

Subsections to the UNIX C Library

The library functions are divided into five groups, which are described in the introduction to Section 3 of the *UNIX Programmer's Manual*. To identify the group, a letter is appended to the 3 following the function name at the top of each summary page. Thus *perror()* belongs to the *3C* group. We'll summarize the groups now.

Functions labeled *3C* are part of the standard C library, and they are automatically loaded by the C compiler. Some require using a header file in addition; the synopsis will reveal this necessity. Older UNIX versions label these functions just with a *3*.

Functions labeled *3F* are part of the FORTRAN library; we will ignore them.

Functions labeled *3M* are part of the C math library. They are not automatically loaded; you must use the *-lm* option when compiling. If you have a mathematically oriented program called *domath.c* which uses these functions, you can compile it this way:

```
cc domath.c -lm
```

Note that the library-specification option, unlike most UNIX command options, comes after the filename. In addition, the file containing the program should have this at its beginning:

```
#include <math.h>
```

Functions labeled *3S* are part of the standard C I/O package. They are loaded automatically, but you should use

```
#include <stdio.h>
```

in the file.

Functions labeled *3X* are specialized functions that don't fit into the other categories. For instance, under *PLOT(3X)* are listed several graphics interface functions that can be used to draw lines, circles, and the like on certain graphics terminals.

Appendix E provides a list of the library functions supplied with System V. Now let's move on to the extremely important topic of file operations.

FILE OPERATIONS

Creating files, opening files, reading files, writing in files, closing files — these are essential tasks for many a program. When we use shell commands, we rely on the operating system to take care of that work for us. When we write C programs, we need to take some of the responsibility ourselves.

Suppose, having forgotten about *cat*, we wish to write a program that takes a filename as an argument and prints its contents on the terminal screen. What has to be done? First, the program has to establish a connection between itself and the file; this is called *opening* the file. Then the program has to extract information from the file; this is *reading* the file. The program also has to be connected to the terminal; this corresponds to opening the special file that describes the terminal. Then information has to be sent to the terminal; this is *writing*. Finally, the program should clean up, severing connections to the file and terminal; this is *closing* the file.

The UNIX system offers us two levels on which we can perform these tasks. On the more basic level, we can use the UNIX system calls to do the work. Or we can choose to use library functions instead. We will look at these two approaches now and see the similarities and differences.

HANDLING FILES USING SYSTEM CALLS

The fundamental UNIX system calls for using files are *creat()*, *open()*, *close()*, *read()*, and *write()*. They do what their names suggest. These functions all share the concept of the *file descriptor*. A file descriptor is an integer used within a program to identify a given file; it is a kind of *handle* to the file. The *creat()* and *open()* functions, when used, return a file descriptor value which is used by the other commands. We'll discuss the commands more fully soon, but let's take a quick look at how this system works. To open an existing file called *hoax* for reading, we would give this command:

```
fd = open("hoax",0);
```

Here *fd* is the file descriptor; it is a small integer returned by the *open()* function. The *read()* function then uses *fd* as an argument to tell it which file to read, and to close that particular file, we say this:

```
close(fd)
```

Three files are opened automatically for the use of a program. They are our old friends the standard input, the standard output, and the standard error. They are assigned file descriptors 0, 1, and 2 respectively. (Note that file descriptors, unlike the inode numbers of files, are local to a program. Other programs used by other users will also have these same three file descriptors.) The *creat()* and *open()* functions use the next available file descriptor; thus the first file you create or open will have file descriptor 3, and so on. You can have up to around 20 files open at once.

Let's run through a C example, one that opens an existing file and prints its contents.

```
/* show.c -- prints out contents of a file */
#define SIZE 10
main(argc,argv)          /* take command-line arguments */
int argc;                /* argument count */
char *argv[];            /* string arguments in an array */
{
int fd;              /* file descriptor */
char buff[SIZE];       /* temporary storage buffer */
int n;               /* number of characters read */

if (argc != 2 ) {     /* wrong number of arguments? */
    printf("Usage: %s filename\n",argv[0]);
    /* print error message */
    exit (1);          /* and quit */
    }
if ( (fd = open(argv[1], 0) ) == -1 ) /* open file; if can't */
    {
    perror(argv[0]);               /* then print error mesg */
    exit (1);                      /* and quit */
    }
while ( (n = read( fd, buff,SIZE) ) > 0 ) /* read until end */
    write( 1, buff, n);            /* write to standard output */
close(fd);
}
```

Note that *open()* assigns a value to the file descriptor *fd*, which is then used by *read()* and *close()*. The *open()* function returns a value of −1 if it can't open the file, and the program uses that fact as a check. The *write()* function is supposed to supply input to the screen, so it uses *1*, the file descriptor for standard output.

Another important point is that we've set up this program to take command-line arguments, so we've used *main()* with the standard arguments *argc* and *argv*. The argument *argc* is the number of arguments, counting the command name itself as one argument. Thus we want *argc* to be 2, to account for the command name and one filename. The argument *argv* is an array of pointers to strings. The first member of the array (*argv[0]*) points to the command name, and the second member (*argv[1]*) points to the filename. These arguments play a role similar to that of *$#*, *$0*, and *$1* in shell scripts. We will now describe these arguments in more detail.

COMMAND-LINE ARGUMENTS: *argc* and *argv*

When you give a command like

```
cat fuji kodak
```

the number of words in the command line and the words themselves are stored and made available to the command program. The number of words is made available as the first argument, usually called *argc*, of the program. In the example above, *argc* is 3, since the command name itself is included in the count. Each word is stored as a C string; that is, it is stored in a character array in which the last member is '\0', the null character, which acts to mark the end of the string. These strings are made available through the second variable, conventionally called *argv*. The declaration for *argv* is

```
char *argv[];
```

indicating that *argv* is an array of pointers to type *char*. The first member of the array is *argv[0]*, and it is a pointer to the name of the command, *cat* in this example. In particular, *argv[0]* points to the first character in the string, '*c*', in this case. Similarly, *argv[1]* points to the first character in the second string, and so on.

We can use array notation to refer to individual members of each character string. For instance, *argv[0][0]* is the first character of the first string ('*c*'), and *argv[1][2]* is the third character of the second string ('*j*'). (C arrays start numbering with 0.) Note the difference between *argv[0]* and *argv[0][0]*. The former *points* to the first character of the first string; its value is a memory address. The latter has the *value* '*c*'. It is located at the address pointed to by *argv[0]*.

Although *argv[0]* points to the first character of a string, it is also used to refer to the whole string. A statement like

```
printf("%s\n", argv[0]);
```

starts by printing the character pointed to by *argv[0]* and then keeps on printing characters until it reaches the null character marking the end of the string.

Question 7.6

Suppose we have a program called *look* and give this command:

```
look post colliers liberty
```

What would the value be of each of the following?

a. argc
b. argv[0]
c. argv[2][4]

Now let's look in detail at the UNIX system calls used in *show.c*.

The System Function *open()*

The *open()* function takes two arguments:

```
int open(filename, mode)
char *filename;
int mode;
```

The first argument is a pointer to type *char* and represents the name of the file. The second argument is an integer that indicates the desired mode for the file to be opened: 0 for read, 1 for write, and 2 for read and write. (System V has jazzed up the function a bit, but we will stick to a simpler description that is compatible with both System V and Version 7.) The *open()* function returns a file descriptor if successful and the value −1 if it fails to open the file. Thus our program assigns the file descriptor value to the variable *fd*; if this value turns out to be −1, the program bails out.

In this program, *argv[1]* points to a filename (the first command-line argument), so it is an appropriate argument for *open()*. Another possibility is to use the name of a file explicitly:

```
open("/usr/bambi/database", 0);
```

Remember, in C, a string of characters in double quotes is interpreted as a pointer to that string.

The System Functions *read()* and *write()*

The *read()* function takes three arguments:

```
int read(fildes, buffer, nbytes)
int fildes;
char *buffer;
int nbytes;
```

The first argument is a file descriptor indicating which file is to be read. In our program, this was *fd*, the value obtained from *open()*. The second argument is a pointer to a *buffer*, an area of temporary storage. The third argument is the number of characters to be read at a time. These characters are placed into the buffer. In our example, we had *read()* read 10 characters at a time, so the buffer (*buff[SIZE]*) had to have enough elements to hold the 10 characters. The *read()* function returns the numbers of characters read; a value of 0 indicates the end of file (EOF). A value of –1 indicates something went wrong. For simplicity, we didn't distinguish between the last two values; either ends the loop:

```
while ( (n = read( fd, buff, SIZE) ) > 0 )
```

Associated with the file descriptor is a file pointer which points to a location in the file. In this case, the file pointer was left pointing to the beginning of the file after the *open()* call. Then, each time *read()* finished, the pointer was advanced another 10 bytes so that the next call to *read()* would pick up there. If, eventually, there are fewer than 10 characters left to read, *read()* is intelligent enough to just read what is there. (If you wish to move through a file without reading or writing, the system call *lseek()* lets you move the file pointer to different locations within a file.)

Question 7.7

What system call will read a byte at a time from the standard input?

The *write()* function takes the same three arguments as *read()*: a file descriptor, a pointer to a buffer, and a number of characters.

```
int write(fildes, buffer, nbytes)
int fildes;
char * buffer;
int nbytes;
```

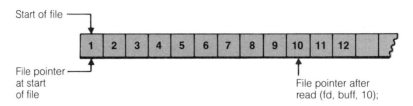

Figure 7.9
***read()* Moves a Pointer Through a File**

In this case, we used the file descriptor *1* to indicate we wanted the function to write on the standard output. The function takes characters from the indicated buffer and writes them on the indicated file; it uses the third argument to tell it how many characters to write at a time. It returns the number of characters written, and returns a −1 if there is a failure; we didn't make use of the return value.

In this example, *read()* and *write()* were teamed together to transfer 10 bytes at a time. The *while* loop continues until *read()* runs out of input and returns a value of 0 or, on mishap, a −1. More typically, *read()* and *write()* would be used to transfer one byte at a time (allowing each byte to be examined individually) or to transfer a large block (typically 512 or 1024 bytes) at a time; such blocks are efficient sizes for many devices.

The System Function *close()*

The *close()* function takes one argument, a file descriptor:

```
int close(fildes)
int fildes;
```

This function closes the file indicated by the descriptor. It returns 0 if it closes the file and −1 if it can't identify the file descriptor.

The System Function *exit()*

The *exit()* function plays the same role in C programs that *exit* does in shell scripts. It terminates the program and provides a status value.

```
int exit(status)
int status;
```

Table 7.1 System I/O Calls

Function	Action
creat( )	Create a file
open( )	Open an existing file
read( )	Read an opened file
write( )	Write to an opened file
close( )	Close an opened file

The argument you supply as the argument to *exit( )* is the value it returns to the system as the exit status. If any files are still open at the time *exit( )* is called, *exit( )* also closes the files. Many programs rely on this feature and omit using *close( )*. However, if your program uses many files, it is a good idea to close each file as you finish with it. That way you won't run into any problems with the limit for the maximum number of files that can be open, typically about 20.

The System Function *creat( )*

We didn't use this function in our example because our example opened an existing file. The *creat( )* function creates a new file or else prepares an existing file to be rewritten. It takes two arguments:

```
int creat(filename, mode)
char *filename;
int mode;
```

The first is a pointer to the name of the file, the second is an integer signifying the mode. Like *open( )*, *creat( )* returns a file descriptor if successful and a −1 if it fails. The mode description is more involved than that of *open( )*; it is described under the *chmod(2)* entry, and we will describe it briefly in Chapter 8.

Since *creat( )* creates a new file, it also takes care of creating an inode description (see Chapter 2) for it.

Table 7.1 summarizes these basic system I/O calls.

Now that we have seen the essence of the system call approach to handling files, let's look at how library functions can be used toward the same end.

LIBRARY FUNCTIONS: THE STANDARD I/0 PACKAGE

Several functions in the system library are collectively known as *the standard I/O package*. This standard I/O package is a coordinated set of functions designed to facilitate efficient and convenient transfer of information between files and programs. In the UNIX manual, package members are identified by a *3S* label and by the injunction to include the *<stdio.h>* header file. Those C mainstays *getchar()*, *putchar()*, and *printf()* are part of the package, as are several other specialized I/O functions. The family also includes *fopen()* and *fclose()* for opening and closing files. The family is bound together by a specific way of handling files and by a shared set of definitions found in the *stdio.h* file. You probably have two big questions at this point: how do we use this package, and why would we use this package? To give us a basis to answer these questions, let's see how *show.c* would be rewritten using the standard I/O library functions:

```
/* stdshow.c -- prints out contents of a file using std. I/O */
#include <stdio.h>    /* shared definitions for std.I/O package */
main(argc,argv)
int argc;
char *argv[];
{
FILE *fp;             /* pointer to type FILE */
int ch;               /* holds read-in character  */

if (argc != 2 ) {     /* stop if wrong number of arguments */
    printf("Usage: %s filename\n", argv[0]);
    exit (1);
    }
if ( (fp = fopen(argv[1],"r" ) ) == NULL )
    /* stop if can't open */
    {
    perror(argv[0]);
    exit (1);
    }
while ( (ch = getc (fp)) != EOF) /* read until end of file */
    putc(ch, stdout);            /* write to standard output */
fclose(fp);
}
```

The program very closely resembles *show.c*. Here are the main differences. First, instead of using an *int* file descriptor *fd* to identify a file, we use a pointer-to-*FILE* *fp*. *FILE* is a *structure type* defined in *stdio.h*. Second, the *fopen()* function returns a pointer-to-*FILE* instead of an *int* file descriptor. Also, while *open()* returns −1 if it fails to open a file, *fopen()* returns *NULL* in that circumstance. *NULL* also is defined in *stdio.h*. Next, instead of using *read()* and *write()*, we use *getc()* and *putc()*, two of several I/O functions that are part of the standard I/O package. These two functions get or put one character at a time into or out of the file. Both require a pointer-to-*FILE* as an argument to identify the files they are to use. Here *stdout* is a pointer-to-*FILE* defined in *stdio.h* to mean the standard output. The *getc()* function uses *EOF* (also defined in *stdio.h*) to indicate it has reached the end of file. Finally, *fclose()* uses the *fp* pointer-to-*FILE* to identify which file to close.

Question 7.8

How could you use *getc()* to read the standard input?

All in all, then, the mechanics of using the standard I/O package are much the same as the mechanics for using the system calls. Just use *#include <stdio.h>* at the beginning of the program file, use a pointer-to-*FILE* variable instead of a file descriptor, and change a few names. We will come back to the details later, but now let's look at the question of why we have this alternative approach. The answer is that it gives a more efficient, buffered I/O.

The Buffered Approach

Many applications call for examining the contents of a file a character at a time; the *wc* program for counting characters, words, and lines is but one of many examples. But for some storage devices, like hard disks, it is inefficient in time and in device use to read a character at a time. They should be read in blocks of 512 or 1024 bytes. The C standard I/O package meets these conflicting priorities by reading or writing a block at a time and storing it in a temporary storage area (the *buffer*) created by the standard I/O package. The defined constant *BUFSIZE* in *stdio.h* indicates the appropriate block size for a given system. This buffer is in the computer memory (RAM) rather than on disk, so characters in the buffer can be accessed quickly. The input functions of the standard I/O package can then extract data from the temporary buffer a byte at a time, if necessary. When the characters in the buffer are all read, the I/O system automatically fills the buffer with the next block of data. Likewise, during output, bytes accumulate in the buffer until it is full, then the whole block is transferred to the recipient file. When the file is closed or when the *fflush()* function is used to *flush*, or empty, the buffers, partially filled buffers are sent on to the destination file.

Is this buffered approach really more efficient? If the program requires examining each character in a file, the answer is yes. The one test we ran resulted in the buffered method taking one twentieth of the time required by using the system calls with a one-character-at-a-time read. This was on a VAX running under BSD 4.2 UNIX.

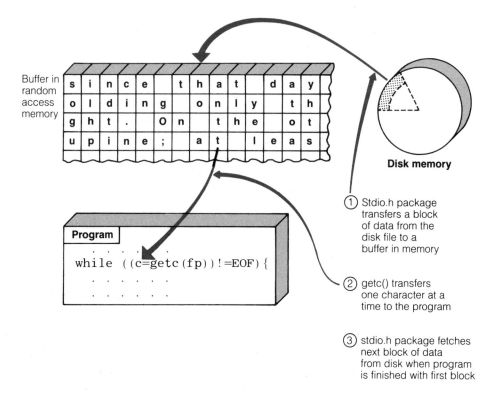

s	i	n	c	e		t	h	a	t		d	a	y
o	l	d	i	n	g		o	n	l	y		t	h
g	h	t	.		O	n		t	h	e		o	t
u	p	i	n	e	;		a	t		l	e	a	s

Buffer in random access memory

Disk memory

Program

```
. . . .  .
while  ((c=getc(fp))!=EOF) {
  . . . . . .
  . . . . . .
```

① Stdio.h package transfers a block of data from the disk file to a buffer in memory

② getc() transfers one character at a time to the program

③ stdio.h package fetches next block of data from disk when program is finished with first block

Figure 7.10
Library I/O Functions Use a Buffer

MIXING READING OR WRITING FUNCTIONS

One convenient aspect of the standard I/O package (STDIO) is that the various input (or output) functions can be interleaved. That is, you can use *getchar()* to get the first character from a file, *scanf()* to get, say, two more characters, and *gets()* to get the rest of a line. This is because they all share the same *FILE* structure and they use the same buffer. Thus when *getchar()* gets a character, it changes the buffer-pointer value of the *FILE* structure, and this lets the next input function know where to start.

However, mixing *read()* calls with the STDIO calls can cause problems. The STDIO calls, remember, read from an intermediate buffer, while *read()* reads directly from the source file. Thus, the STDIO package might be halfway through reading a particular buffer, but a *read()* call would go to the next location in the original file, which would be following the last character that had earlier been read into the buffer.

A similar situation exists for *write()* and the STDIO output functions. The latter write to an intermediate buffer, while the former writes directly to the target file.

The moral is, don't intermix *read( )* and *write( )* with the I/O functions of the standard I/O package.

Standard I/O Functions and *stdio.h*

Creating the buffered approach to I/O requires preliminary work, and that is accomplished in the *stdio.h* file. This file includes definitions that set up the buffers and their use. One of the key provisions is the definition of a C structure to represent a file. This is the *FILE* structure we used in the last example. It ties together information about the temporary buffer with information about the file. The structure has the tag *_iobuf*, and *FILE* is defined to mean a structure of the *_iobuf* type. Here is an annotated excerpt from *stdio.h* to describe the structure. Your UNIX system may use a slightly different definition, but the main ideas are the same.

```
struct_iobuf {
     int    _cnt;     /* bytes left in buffer */
     char   *_ptr;    /* pointer to current buffer position */
     char   *_base;   /* pointer to buffer beginning */
     int    _bufsiz;  /* size of buffer */
     short  _flag;    /* file mode */
     char   _file;    /* file descriptor number */
     };
#define FILE struct _iobuf
```

Figure 7.11 summarizes this structure.

You don't need to memorize this structure; all you need to do is to declare a pointer-to-*FILE* in your program code. But do notice that the structure relates to the buffer and to the file. For example, one member of the structure points to the beginning of the buffer, another member points to the current read/write location in the buffer, and a third member consists of the file descriptor for the opened file. Since functions like *getc( )* use both the file and the buffer, we can see that this structure provides the sort of information the functions need.

As we saw in our example, the standard I/O functions *do not* use the simple file descriptor used by the system calls to identify a file. Instead, they use a pointer to the corresponding file structure. This enables the functions to know about the file *and* the buffer. Let's examine this approach in more detail.

To see the role the *stdio.h* file plays, let's look at the manual synopses of *fopen( )* and *fclose( )*, the standard I/O package functions for opening and closing files:

```
FILE *fopen (filename, type )
char *filename, *type;
```

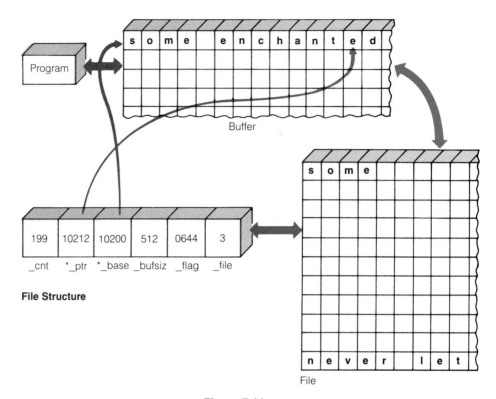

File Structure

Figure 7.11
The FILE Structure

```
int fclose (stream)
FILE *stream;
```

First, note that *fopen()* returns a pointer to type *FILE*. *FILE*, as we just saw, is just a shorthand notation for the file structure we described in *stdio.h*. Thus *fopen()* returns a pointer to the file structure describing the file just opened and describing the buffer created to handle the I/O. *To use the standard I/O library with a file, you must use* **fopen()** *and* **not open()** to open a file. If you were to use *open()*, the buffer and file structure used by the functions would not have been created. The *stdio.h* file also contains the declaration

```
FILE *fopen ()
```

This means we can use the *fopen()* function in a program without declaring it, since it is already declared in that header file.

Next, notice, from the argument declaration, that *fclose()* takes a pointer to type *FILE* as an argument; it would use the value returned by *fopen()*. The term *stream* denotes a file with associated buffering; in particular, it is applied to the *FILE* pointer associated with the file.

The skeleton of a program that opens and closes a file would look like this:

```
#include <stdio.h>
 main()
{
FILE *fp;       /* declare pointer-to-FILE file identifier */

fp = fopen(..., ...);
/*  rest of program goes here */
fclose(fp);
}
```

We would say that *fp* is the stream opened and closed here.

The setup is much the same as for *open()* and *close()*, except that a *FILE* pointer is used instead of a file descriptor.

There are further dependencies on the *stdio.h*. First, *fopen()* returns a *NULL* pointer on failure, and *fclose()* returns *EOF* on failure. These two symbolic constants are defined in *stdio.h*. Also defined there are *stdin*, *stdout*, and *stderr*; these terms symbolically represent *FILE* pointers that point to the standard input, standard output, and standard error respectively.

Obviously, the *FILE* type and pointers to that type are important to the package. Let's run through another example using them.

Using the Standard I/O Package

We mentioned before that when a UNIX program (shell script or C) is run, three files (the standard input, the standard output, and the standard error) are opened automatically. They are, we said, assigned the file descriptors 0, 1, and 2. When we include *stdio.h*, that file sets up pointer-to-*FILE* identifiers for these same three files; they are *stdin*, *stdout*, and *stderr*. The STDIO functions then can use these identifiers when they wish to use those files.

When *fopen()* opens a file, it returns a pointer-to-*FILE*. This pointer then serves to identify the opened file for the rest of the program. If we wish to read the file, we refer to it by that pointer. When we close the file with *fclose()*, we refer to it by that pointer. To illustrate the usage, here is a C program that uses the standard I/O package to count the number of times a given character occurs in a file; it takes the filename and the character as command-line arguments.

```
/* chcnt.c  -- count the occurrences of a given character */
/* Usage: chcnt filename character  */
#include <stdio.h>
```

243

```
main(argc, argv)
int argc;
char *argv[];
{
int ch;                /* holds the read-in character */
int nc = 0;            /*  character counter */
FILE *fp;              /* file identifier    */

if (argc != 3)   {       /* quit if wrong character count */
    fprintf(stderr,"Usage: %s filename character\n", argv[0] );
    exit (1);
    }
if ( (fp = fopen (argv[1], "r") ) == NULL) {
    fprintf(stderr,"%s: cannot open %s\n", argv[0], argv[1]);
    exit (2);
    }
while ( (ch = getc (fp)) != EOF)
    if ( ch == argv[2][0] )   /* compare ch to 2nd argument */
        nc++;      /* increment count by 1 */
printf("%d\n", nc);
if ( fclose(fp) == EOF ) {
    fprintf(stderr,"%s cannot close %s\n", argv[0], argv[1]);
    exit (3) ;
    }
exit (0);
}
```

In this program, we've used the library functions *fopen()*, *fclose()*, *getc()*, *printf()*, and *fprintf()*.

Like *open()*, *fopen()* takes two arguments: a pointer to the name of the file to be opened, and a mode. For *fopen()*, the mode is a character string, with "*r*" indicating *read*, "w" indicating *write*, and "a" indicating *append*. System V allows three additional "update" modes, including "r+" for read and write. Using these update modes is somewhat more involved than using the standard modes. The *fopen()* function returns a pointer to *FILE* if successful, and a pointer to *NULL* if not. In this example the returned value is assigned to the pointer *fp*. Henceforth in this program *fp* is used to identify the file when necessary. Unlike *open()*, *fopen()* will create the named file if it does not already exist.

The *fclose()* function works like *close()*, except it uses a *FILE* pointer instead of a file descriptor as its argument. Also, *fclose()* empties any related buffers and frees them.

The *fprintf()* function works like *printf()* except that the first argument for *fprintf()* should be a *FILE* pointer indicating which file should be written to. Here we made use of the fact that *stdio.h* defines *stderr* as a pointer to the standard error. Thus, using *fprint( )* with *stderr* is analogous to using *echo* with *1>&2* redirection in a shell script. It ensures that error messages don't get diverted down a pipe.

Similarly, *getc( )* is like *getchar( )* except that it takes a *FILE* pointer as argument to indicate which file is being read. In actuality, of course, *getc( )* reads the temporary buffer which, in turn, gets its input from the file. If you read the *stdio.h* file, you will find this line:

```
#define getchar()  getc(stdin)
```

Thus *getchar( )* is just a special case of *getc( )*.

There is one programming point we wish to note, and that is the line

```
if (ch == argv[2][0])
```

Here *argv[2]* is a pointer to the character string representing the second argument. The notation *argv[2][0]* then refers to the first character in the string. (C arrays start counting at 0.) Thus, this expression tests if the character just read is the same as the character on the command line. If it is, the character count is increased by one.

Now that we have discussed it, let's use it to find how many ''c'''s are in the program itself (including the comments).

```
$ cc -o chcnt chcnt.c
$ chcnt chcnt.c c
29
$
```

Running the program on the first draft of this chapter up to this point (right here → ←) finds 941 ''c'''s. Don't bother counting to check, however, for the count is bound to be modified before the chapter reaches print. (Or perhaps you would like to count letters to see how much the chapter was modified.)

Other Members of the Standard I/O Package

In our sample program we used *fopen( )*, *fclose( )*, *getc( )*, *fprintf( )*, and *printf( )* from the standard I/O package, and we mentioned *getchar( )*. Table 7.2 provides a list of all the members of the standard I/O package. Many of these are defined as macros, using preprocessor *#define* directives, in *stdio.h*. Some are grouped together under one description; the last four, for instance, are all described under the *ferror( )* heading.

We'll have occasion to use several of these functions later. For now, however, let's turn to the math library.

Table 7.2 Members of the Standard I/O Family

Function	Action
fopen()	Open a file
fclose()	Close a file
getc(), getchar()	Read a chararacter
putc(), putchar()	Write a character
fgets(), gets()	Read a string
fgetw(), getw()	Read a *word* in the memory size sense
putw()	Write a *word*
fputs(), puts()	Write a string
fprintf(), printf()	Formatted write
fscanf(), scanf()	Formatted read
fread()	Buffered binary input
fwrite()	Buffered binary output
fflush()	Writes buffered data immediately
ungetc()	Puts read character back in input stream
setbuf()	Assign buffering to a stream (overrides the automatic default)
popen()	Opens pipe between a shell command and the program
pclose()	Closes pipe
feof()	Found end of file
ferror()	Found an error
clearerr()	Clears error and EOF indicators
fileno()	Returns file descriptor for a *FILE* pointer

THE UNIX MATH LIBRARY

The math library contains several mathematical functions commonly used in scientific and engineering calculations. First there are the trig functions for sine, cosine, arcsine, arccosine, and arctangent. To this list, System V adds the tangent function. They are described under *TRIG(3M)* in the System V manual and under *SIN(3M)* in the Version 7 manual. Then, under *EXP(3M)* are listed exponential, logarithmic, power law, and square root functions. The hyperbolic functions are listed under *SINH(3M)*, and the Bessel functions are described under *J0(3M)*. The list doesn't end here (although our list does), and it is still being added to. (The listing of library functions in the appendix identifies math functions by using the *M* label.) Incidentally, the random number function *rand()* is sufficiently popular that it is part of the standard C library and not the math library.

When using functions from the math library, remember to include the *math.h* header file and to use the *-lm* option when compiling.

Half-lives — Using the Math Library

Our next example involves half-lives, so it seems appropriate to first explain what a half-life is.

Many phenomena, most notably radioactive decay, are describable in terms of half-lives. The half-life of, say, a radioactive element, is the time it takes half of the material to decay into some other form. You might think the sensible thing to do is to double the time and talk about a whole-life, but nature doesn't agree. If half of the material decays the first half-life, then half of what is left decays the next half-life, and so on. Thus a quarter is left after two half-lives, an eighth after three half-lives, and so on. One important consequence is that it can take many half-lives before a batch of radioactive waste becomes relatively inert.

The half-life rule lets us calculate how much material is left in whole multiples of the half-life, but if we need to know how much is left in, say, 1.6 half-lives, we need to use the exponential function. (The half-life behavior is characteristic of exponential decay.) The formula is this:

amount left $=$ (starting amount) x $e^{(time \ x \ ln \ 2)/halflife}$

The *e* is the base for natural logarithms (value 2.7183...), and the expression *ln 2* is the natural logarithm of 2.

Here is a short program that takes as command-line input the original amount, the half-life, and the time period in question. It then outputs the amount left after that time period.

```
/* halflife.c -- minimal error checking */
#include <math.h>
#define LN2 .6931472   /* natural log of 2 */
main (argc, argv)
int argc;
char *argv[];
{
double num, thalf, time;
double atof();
float ans;

if (argc != 4)   /* quit if argc is not 4 */
    {
    fprintf(stderr,"Usage: %s amount halflife time\n",
            argv[0]);
    exit (1);
    }
```

```
num = atof (argv[1] ) ;   /* converts string to number */
thalf = atof (argv[2]);
time = atof (argv[3]);
ans = num * exp ( -LN2 * time / thalf );
printf("%10.5g\n", ans);
}
```

Incidentally, we are not promoting minimal error checking as an especially desirable feature; we merely wish to concentrate on other features. Now we can compile and run the program:

```
$ cc halflife.c -lm
$ a.out 2000 24300  1000    ← Amount, half-life, elapsed time
1943.8                      ← Amount left
$ a.out 2000 28 1000        ← Amount, half-life, elapsed time
3.547e-08                   ← Amount left
$
```

The first run represents how much Plutonium 239 (a nuclear reactor by-product) would remain after 1000 years, starting with one ton (2000 pounds). As you can see, most of it will still be here. The second run applies to a ton of Strontium 90 for the same time period; the amount left is negligible, less than 4 one-hundred millionths of a pound. (In computer notation *e-08* stands for 10 to the negative 8th power). Clearly, the half-life of a radioactive element is an extremely important factor in the decision of how to dispose of nuclear waste.

Now look at the program. First, note that we remembered to include the *math.h* file. Second, we had to declare the *exp()* function because it is type *double*. Only functions that return type *int* can be used without declaring them.

Third, we have used the library function *atof()*, which converts character strings to floating-point numbers. This is necessary because the command-line arguments are read as character strings. The *2000*, for example, occupies five memory cells, one byte for each character and one additional byte for the null character that C uses to mark the end of a string. The *atof()* function converts this string to a single floating-point value occupying one memory unit. The memory unit for floating-point numbers is larger than the memory unit for characters, but that is another matter. Note that we also had to declare the *atof()* function. It is part of the standard C library on most UNIX systems, and it doesn't require including any special files or using any special compiling instructions. C also has an *atoi()* function that converts strings to integer values.

Finally, note that we used the *-lm* option when compiling this C program. Actually, the *cc* compiler (the UNIX C compiler) does not use this option itself. Instead, it passes it on to the *ld* command, which finishes the work of putting the final program together. The *ld* command is the UNIX *link editor*, and its job includes the searching of libraries for routines to be included in a program. The *ld* command then *links* these functions with the object code the compiler produces from our C program. The *ld* command has to search our program first to find what library functions are needed, and that is why the *-lm* option comes after the filename.

Question 7.9

Write a program that takes a number (x) as command-line input and prints the value of the natural logarithm of x.

PROGRAM TYPES

Let's turn our attention now to a more general matter of program design.

When you design a program, you have to decide on the general form, that is, on how the program will be used. One possibility is a stand-alone program that gets information from its command line. That is the approach we've used, one typical of UNIX commands. A second possibility is an interactive stand-alone program that prompts the user for information. A third possibility is a combination of the two. And a fourth possibility is to create a function that can be used in other programs. The choice depends on the circumstances, but there is room for maneuvering, since some forms are easily adapted to other forms. One method is to blend a C program into a shell script.

Integrating C Programs with Shell Scripts

Suppose, for example, we want an interactive version of our character-counting program. It is not necessary to rewrite it. Instead, we can create a shell script to provide the interaction. Here is a simple version, one devoid of error checking:

```
# charct -- interactive character counter
echo This program counts how often a given character occurs
echo in a file.  Please enter the name of file to be searched:
read file
echo Now enter the name of the character you wish counted:
read char
number=`chcnt $file $char`
echo The $char appeared $number times in $file
```

Here we use the shell's backquote command substitution mechanism to assign the output of the *chcnt* command to the variable called *number*. This script assumes either that you invoke it in the same directory containing the *chcnt* program or that *chcnt* has been placed in your *PATH*.

The basic *chcnt* tool can be incorporated into a variety of shell scripts. For instance, you could write a script that checks to see if the number of left parentheses equals the number of right parentheses. Or you could have it loop through several files, perhaps keeping a cumulative total. One of the beauties of the UNIX system is that once we have developed a basic tool, like *chcnt*, we can use shell scripts to multiply its uses.

Question 7.10

Write an interactive shell script incorporating our *halflife* program, prompting the user for input. Assume the executable C program is in the file *halflife.x*.

What if we want a subroutine, that is, a function we can use in other C programs? Again, it is not necessary to rewrite the program. As we will see in the next chapter, any command file can be run from within a C program.

But suppose we really do want, say, a function version of *chcnt*. That is, suppose we have a program written in C and that we want to use something like *chcnt* as a function call in the program. It is not difficult to convert the stand-alone *chcnt* program to a callable C function. Mainly we need to switch from the *argc* and *argv* arguments to something more specific. Also, we may wish to replace the *exit*s with *return*s. Here we convert our *chcnt* stand-alone program to a called function.

```
/* chrnt.c  -- count the occurrences of a given character */
/* this version is usable as a function call */
/* Usage: chcnt (filename, character)   */
#include <stdio.h>
chrct(file,chr)
char *file;
char chr;
{
int ch;
int nc = 0;
FILE *fp;
```

```
    if ( (fp = fopen (file, "r") ) == NULL) {
        fprintf(stderr,"chrct: cannot open %s\n", file);
        return (-1);    /* replace exit(2) with return(-1) */
        }
    while ( (ch = getc (fp)) != EOF)
        if ( ch == chr )
            nc++;
    if ( fclose(fp)) == EOF ) {
        fprintf(stderr,"chrct cannot close %s\n", file);
        return (-2) ;   /* replace exit(3) with return (-2) */
        }
    return (nc); /* replace printf() with return (nc)  */
    }
```

We replaced the *printf()* statement with a *return(nc)* and relocated it. (Since a function terminates when it encounters a *return*, leaving it in the former position would terminate the function before it closed the file.) The *return* statement then provides the character count *nc* to the calling program.

We also replaced the *exit* statements with *return* statements. Why did we do that? A *return* statement terminates the called function and returns control (and a value) *to the calling function*. An *exit* statement terminates the called function and returns control (and a value) *to the operating system*. Thus an *exit* call terminates the entire program. If that is what we want, then we could leave the *exits* unaltered. By using *return*, however, we can have the calling program decide if it wishes to continue, to try something else, or to exit itself. In this case we used return values (-1 and –2) that would not show up for a valid functioning of *chrct()*.

CONCLUSION

The UNIX system supports a large number of system calls and library routines. These are available as C functions to the C programmer. Sections 2 and 3 of the UNIX manual describe these functions. In particular, they show the function type, the function arguments and argument types, and the value returned by a function. Some functions require that certain files be included via the preprocessor *#include* directive, and this, too, is pointed out. In addition, some library functions, such as the math functions, require special instructions to be given to the compiler.

We have looked at some examples illustrating the use of the manual and the system and library functions. We paid particular attention to the standard I/O package. The vast number of system and library functions, however, precludes comprehensive coverage of them all.

There are still some major areas to look at, and we will take them up in the next chapter.

ANSWERS TO QUESTIONS IN CHAPTER 7

7.1 **a.** One argument

b. *double*

c. *int* (Note: a relational expression like $x > 0$ has the value 1 if true and the value 0 if false; these are *int* values, even if x is *double*.)

7.2 A system call is part of the programming for the kernel. A library function is a program that is not part of the kernel but which is available to users of the system. (Library functions may use system calls.) Neither is a stand-alone program; instead, system calls and library functions must be used as part of some other program. The UNIX commands, however, are stand-alone programs; they may incorporate both system calls and library functions in their programming.

7.3 **a.** 2

b. *int*

c. *int*

d. *kill(1)* is a UNIX command. You use it by typing it on a shell command line. *kill(2)* is a C function. You use it inside a C program. The programming for *kill(1)* includes a call to *kill(2)*.

7.4 The printout would have been

```
oh no!: No such file or directory
```

The advantage of the second form is that it informs us which particular function had a problem.

7.5 Since your program can access *sys_errlist[]*, the array of error messages, it also can redefine this array. You could say, for instance,

```
*sys_errlist[1] = "It's not yours!";
```

You could collect several such redefinitions in a header file and include that file when desired.

7.6 **a.** 4

b. It points to the string ''look''

c. 'i'

7.7 *read(0,buff,1)*, where *buff* is the name of the destination buffer.

7.8 By saying *getc(stdin)*

7.9 (With no error checking)

```
#include <math.h>
main(argc,argv)
int argc;
char *argv[];
{
double x;

  x = atof(argv[1]);
  printf("%g\n", log(x));
}
```

7.10 (With no error checking)

```
# halflife script
echo This program calculates the amount of radioactive substance
echo left after a period of time. You need to provide three
echo quantities: the initial amount, the halflife, and the time
echo Please enter the initial amount as a number (no units)
read amount
echo Now enter the halflife
read halflife
echo Now enter the time period
read period
answer=`halflife.x $amount $halflife $period`
echo The amount left would be $answer
```

EXERCISES

1. Find out what header files are in the */usr/include* directory of your system.
2. Use *ermesg.c* to find the error messages on your system.
3. Write a simple copy function that takes two command-line arguments: the file to be copied, and the name of the target file. Use the system calls; read the manual on *creat( )*.
4. Repeat 3, but use the library functions.
5. Rewrite our *chcnt.c* program using system calls instead of library functions. Run the two versions on a large file, using the UNIX *time* command to gauge the relative speeds of the two versions.
6. Create the parentheses-checking script described just after the *charct* example.

8

THE UNIX-C INTERFACE

In this chapter you will find:

The UNIX-C Interface

Now that we have seen how to find out about UNIX C functions and how to incorporate them into C programs, let's see how to coordinate C programs with the UNIX operating system. One aspect of this coordination is writing programs that blend with the standard UNIX commands. This often means designing a program to be a filter so that it can take input from the redirected output of other programs and so that its output can be channeled to yet other programs. For convenience, we often want programs that can take input from the standard input or from one or more files given as command-line arguments. Another UNIX-like feature is to have programs accept command-line options. In this chapter we will illustrate the programming techniques used to reach these goals.

The second major aspect of program-UNIX coordination we will cover is how to have programs obtain various sorts of information from the operating system. What's the time? Can a certain file be read? Just who is using the program? Is the program being told to quit? Both aspects deal with the information flow between program, operating system, and user. We've dealt with many of these matters for shell scripts; now we'll see how to handle them in a C program.

In this chapter we'll develop the necessary ideas by developing specific examples. The techniques, however, are quite general, and using them will let you take full advantage of the UNIX system. We'll begin with a program that accepts data from either the standard input or else from a filename provided on the command line.

HOW TO ACCESS BOTH STANDARD INPUT AND OPENED FILES

Programs that use standard input get their information (by default) from the keyboard, and programs using standard output send their results (by default) to the terminal. Other programs (such as the *cp* command) get filenames from the command line and use those files for reading and writing. Both approaches have advantages. Let's see what they are.

One advantage of standard input is that is easy to write C programs that use it. The standard input, along with the standard output and the standard error, are opened automatically when a C program is run. The C I/O functions (*getchar()*, *putchar()*, *printf()*, *scanf()*) that you probably used when learning C, use the standard input and output; thus a program using those I/O functions automatically uses standard input and output.

A second advantage of using the standard input and output is that programs of this sort can be used with redirection and pipes to connect the program to other files or programs. As we have seen, if a UNIX program *goop* normally takes its input from the keyboard, it can also get input from a file or from another program:

```
goop < goopinfo
sort goopnik | goop
```

Thus UNIX features greatly enhance the applicability of programs using standard input.

But using redirection is not the same as having the program itself open the file. For one thing, with redirection and pipes, it is the shell and kernel, not the program, that makes the connections. For another, redirection connects just one input and/ or one output file, while a program can open several files using *open()* or *fopen()*.

Which is better: designing a program to use standard input and output, or designing it to open and close files? The first lets us use pipes and redirection, and the second lets us open more files and is slightly more convenient to use. Fortunately, in UNIX we don't have to choose, since we can do both. The trick is to use the *argc* variable, which tells the program how many arguments are on the command line. If there are no command-line arguments (meaning that *argc* is 1), then we have the program read from the standard input, thus giving it the option to take redirected input. If there is a command-line argument (*argc* is 2), then use it for a filename and try to open the file and read it for input.

To illustrate this approach, here is another character-counting program. Last time we counted how often a single character appeared. Now we flex our muscles (or is it just a twitch?) and count the number of times each and every individual alphabetic character appears in its input. This will let you analyze various texts for letter frequencies. In addition, the program will accept standard input (keyboard entry or a redirected file or output from a pipe) or open a file itself, depending on the absence or presence of a command-line filename argument.

We really have two separate problems here. The first is arranging that the program handles its choice of input correctly (using standard input or else opening a file itself), and the second is that it performs its counting and reporting task properly. We have followed this conceptual division of labor by using two functions. The first one (*main()*) sorts out the input, and the second one (*ctch()*) does the desired labor. Here is the complete program.

```
/* charct -- version 1.0 */
/* counts occurrences of each letter in text */
/* can use either standard input or opened file for input */
/* Usage: charct [filename] */
#include <stdio.h>
main(argc,argv)
int argc;           /* argument count */
char *argv[];    /* the command line arguments */
{
FILE *fp;

if (argc == 1)          /* no arguments */
    ctch(stdin);        /* so use standard input */
else {                  /* else try to open named file */
    if ( (fp=fopen(argv[1], "r") ) == NULL ) {
        perror(argv[0]);
        exit (1);       /* exit if can't open file */
        }
    else {
        ctch (fp) ;         /* use named file for input */
        fclose (fp);
        }
    }
}

/* ctch() -- count chars: does the counting and reporting */
#include <ctype.h>      /* system file of character "macros" */
#define ASIZE 26        /* current number of letters in alpabet */
ctch (fp )
FILE *fp;
{
int index;          /* a loop counter */
int cnum[ASIZE];    /* array to hold character counts */
int ch;             /* the read-in character */

for (index = 0; index < ASIZE ; index++)
    cnum[index] = 0;    /* set char. counts to 0 */
while ( (ch = getc(fp) ) != EOF) {
    if ( isalpha (ch) ) {       /* alphabetic character? */
        ch = isupper (ch) ? tolower (ch) : ch; /* to lower case */
        cnum[ch - 'a']++;
        }
    }
for ( index = 0; index < ASIZE ; index++)
    printf("%c %6d\n", 'a' + index, cnum[index] );
}
```

Explaining the Program

First, look at *main()*. If *argc* is 1 (no command-line arguments), it calls up *ctch()* with the standard input (defined as *stdin* in *<stdio.h>*); otherwise, after some checking, it calls up *ctch()* with *fp*, the identifier for the file whose name is given in the command line. Additional filenames on the command line, if any, are ignored. Later, we will modify the program to take more than one file for input.

Next, look at *ctch()*. It uses the argument passed to it to determine which file *getc()* reads. That is the only information it needs from the calling program. Now let's see how the *ctch()* function goes about its job. First, an array of 26 elements (*cnum[]*) is created to keep track of the number of each of the 26 characters. By using the symbolic constant *ASIZE* we render ourselves able to easily alter the program should the number of letters in the alphabet change, as it may for a foreign language, or if we decide to count additional characters, such as punctuation marks. The program first assigns 0 to each element of the array, and then it begins reading the file one character at a time. The *ctch()* function makes use of some *macros* defined in the file *<ctype.h>*; that's why we *#include*d that file. The *isalpha()* macro, for example, is true (nonzero) if the argument is an alphabetic character and false (zero) otherwise. We use *isalpha()* to ensure that only alpabetic characters get passed on to the counting process. Next we use a conditional statement to render all the characters lowercase:

```
ch = isupper (ch) ? tolower (ch) : ch; /* to lower case */
```

This C *conditional* statement asks the question, is *ch* uppercase? If it is, *ch* is converted to lowercase by the *tolower()* macro. Otherwise it is assigned its original value. Now comes a mildly tricky part:

```
cnum[ch - 'a']++;
```

This statement does two things. It sets a value for the array index (*ch − 'a'*) and it increases the value of that array element by one. The index assignment depends on the ASCII representation of the alphabet, in which the alphabet is stored using a numerical code. The constant *'a'*, for example, prints as *a* if you use the *%c* format, but as *97* using the *%d* format and ASCII code. If *ch* is, for example, the character *b*, then the expression becomes

```
cnum['b' -'a']++;
```

or

```
cnum[98 -97]++;
```

or

cnum[1]++;

The ++ operator increments its operand by 1, so in this example, the appearance of a "b" causes the second element of the array to increase by 1. (Remember that 0 is the index of the first element of a C array.) In the same manner, every "a" that shows up increases the first element by 1, and every "z" that shows up increases the last array element by 1. In essence, we are using the letter itself as the index for the array element that counts that letter. This method doesn't work for the EBCDIC code used on IBM® mainframes; in that code there is a numerical gap between the letters "i" and "j".

Question 8.1

What is the difference between *cnum[index++]* and *cnum[index]++* ? Would the expression *cnum[index++]++* have any meaning?

All that remains to do is to print out the results, and a final *for* loop takes care of that. This time the expression *'a' + index* is converted to the equivalent character, and the count stored in *cnum[index]* is shown.

Here is a sample run, piped through the UNIX *pr* command to make the output more easily viewable. (The *-t* option of *pr* suppresses the usual header and trailer. The *-3* option gives three columns, and the *-l1* option produces one-line pages, since the default 66-line page would overflow the screen.) The compiled version of *charct.c* was placed in the file *charct*.

```
$ charct ch8 | pr -t -3 -l1
a    166    b     19     c      63
d     41    e    158     f      32
g     37    h     96     i     152
j      3    k      2     l      66
m     39    n    144     o     150
p     81    q      0     r     136
s     87    t    184     u      68
v     15    w     29     x       4
y     13    z      0
```

We could, of course, have formatted the original output in this compact form, but there are advantages to having one letter per line. The most important is that one data set per line makes it simple to use *charct*'s output as input to other programs, such as *sort*.

Question 8.2

Given *charct*, how could we easily produce a frequency count for *ch8* that was in order of increasing frequency?

THE MACROS OF *<ctype.h>*

Macros are preprocessor *#define* directives that act like functions. For example, suppose we make this definition:

```
#define  sqr(X)    ((X) * (X))
```

Then we can use *sqr()* much like a function in a program:

sqr(2) becomes *((2)*(2))*
sqr(x-3) becomes *((x-3)*(x-3))*
12.0/sqr(y) becomes *12.0/((y)*(y))*

These changes take place when the program is compiled; the end result is as if you typed the final expression instead of using *sqr*.

We had to use all those parentheses to ensure that the result is used correctly. Suppose we had made this naive definition:

```
#define sqr(X)  X*X
```

Then

sqr(x-3) becomes *x-3*x -3*
12.0/sqr(y) becomes *12.0/y*y*

Because of the priority of the C operators, neither would be what was intended.

Table 8.1 Common *ctype.h* Macros*

Macro	True if
isalpha(c)	*c* is a letter
isupper(c)	*c* is an uppercase letter
islower (c)	*c* is a lowercase letter
isdigit(c)	*c* is a digit, i.e, 0-9
isalnum(c)	*c* is alphanumeric (letter or digit)
isspace(c)	*c* is a space, tab, carriage return, newline, vertical tab, or form-feed
ispunct(c)	*c* is a punctuation character
isprint(c)	*c* is a printing character
iscntrl(c)	*c* is a control or a delete character
isascii(c)	*c* is an ASCII character

*Each returns "true" (non-zero) if the character is of the indicated type, and "false" (zero) otherwise.

Question 8.3

Given the definition

```
#define PR(X)  printf("The value of X is %d\n", X)
```

what would this program line become?

```
PR(gross - tax);
```

The header file *<ctype.h>* contains several macros relating to character types. Table 8.1 shows the more common macros. Each returns *true* (nonzero) if the character is of the indicated type, and *false* (zero) otherwise. These macros are quite useful for text-handling tasks. You can check the *ctype.h* (normally found in the */usr/include* directory) to see what *ctype* macros your system keeps in stock.

HOW TO ADD AN OPTION TO A C PROGRAM

An option is a command-line argument that affects the running of a program. For example, if we say

```
sort -r file
```

the *-r* option causes *sort* to sort in reverse order. Suppose that we want our C program to have options, too. How is that done?

To add options we use a technique parallel to the one we used to provide options for shell scripts. The key with scripts was to label options with an initial hyphen and to place the options before other arguments in the command line. Before we implement this approach in our *charct* program, we need to decide which option we would like. What about adding an option for a compact form of printout? It would be simple to do, but it is already simple to pipe the output through *pr*. If the form on page 263 is the one you like, you can make a shell script to reproduce the piping instructions:

```
charct $1 | pr -t -3 -l1
```

Similarly, another option might be to provide the output sorted by frequency of appearance. Again, this is a feature we can provide with existing UNIX tools:

```
charct $1 | sort -n -r +1
```

This example provides reverse (option *-r*) numerical (option *-n*) sorting according to the second data field, which is the count in this case. The *+1* means *skip the first field*.

Another option might be to provide a third column giving the frequency of each letter as a percentage of the total number of letters. This can be done using the *awk* utility, but not too efficiently. So let's incorporate this option into *charct.c*.

Once again, the work falls into two main areas: identifying the presence of the option and executing its intent. The first task belongs to the *main()* portion of the program, and the second task belongs to *ctch()*. Since the job is split between the two functions, *main()* must communicate its findings to the *ctch()* function.

How can *main()* tell *ctch()* that an option has been set? One approach is to let the calling program set a *flag* if it finds the option. The flag is just a variable that gets assigned one of two values: yes or no, on or off, 1 or 0 — some such pairing. How can a flag be set to *yes?* By defining *yes* to be the more computerlike value of 1. See the next program for an example. There are two ways to get this variable to the called program. One is to make it an argument of the called function, and the second is to make the flag an external variable shared by both functions. We'll use the second approach here. This avoids the necessity of changing the function call and the function heading every time we decide to add a new option.

This listing shows our new revised version:

```
/* charct -- version 1.1 */
/* counts occurrences of each letter in text */
/* -p option prints out relative frequencies as percents */
/* Usage: charct [-p] [filename] */
```

```
#include <stdio.h>
#define YES 1   /* symbolic values to be used by option flag */
#define NO 0
int percent;    /* defined externally so that it can be shared */

main(argc,argv)
int argc;
char *argv[];
{
FILE *fp;
char *prog;
extern int percent;

prog = argv[0];   /* let prog point to program name */
percent = NO;     /* don't calculate percent */
while ( argc > 1  && argv[1][0] == '-' ) { /* look for option */
    if ( argv[1][1] == 'p' )
          percent = YES;    /* calculate percent */
    else {
        fprintf(stderr,"%s: Unknown option %s\n", prog, argv[1]);
        exit (1);
        }
    argc--;    /* check one argument off list */
    argv++;    /* go to next argument  */
    }
if (argc == 1)
    ctch(stdin);
else {
    if ( (fp=fopen(argv[1], "r") ) == NULL ) {
        perror(argv[0]);
        exit (1);
        }
    else {
        ctch (fp) ;
        fclose (fp);
        }
    }
}

/* ctch() -- does the counting and printing */
#include <ctype.h>
#define ASIZE 26
ctch (fp )
FILE *fp;
{
int index, pc;
```

```
int sum, cnum[ASIZE];
extern int percent;
int ch;

for (index = 0; index < ASIZE ; index++)
    cnum[index] = 0;
while ( (ch = getc(fp) ) != EOF) {
    if ( isalpha (ch) ) {
      ch = isupper (ch) ? tolower (ch) : ch ;
      cnum[ch - 'a']++;
      }
    }
if (percent == NO ) {
    for ( index = 0; index < ASIZE ; index++)
        printf("%c %6d\n", 'a' + index, cnum[index] );
        }
else {            /* calculate percent if flag is YES */
    for ( sum = 0, index = 0; index < ASIZE; index++)
      sum += cnum[index];
    for ( index = 0; index < ASIZE; index++ ) {
      if (sum != 0) {
          pc = (100 * cnum[index])/sum;
          printf("%c %6d %4d%%\n", 'a' + index, cnum[index], pc);
          }
      else      /* special format if no characters are found */
          printf("%c %6d %4c%%\n", 'a' + index, cnum[index],'*');
      }
    }
}
```

Explaining the Program

Here we have defined *YES* and *NO* as symbolic constants to be used to indicate if the *-p* option is present or not in the command line. We use *percent* as the external variable that is to act as a flag. Once *main()* gets underway, we initialize *percent* to *NO*, since that is to be the default case. We also initialize the character pointer *prog* to point at the program name. This is done to save the name, for the *argv++* operation in the program will change the value of *argv[0]*.

To detect the presence of the option, we use a *while* loop to search for arguments beginning with hyphens:

```
while ( argc > 1  && argv[1][0] == '-')
```

This loop cycles through the arguments until it runs out of arguments (*argc* becomes 1) or until it finds an argument without an initial hyphen. Thus, if the program is inside the loop, it is processing an argument having an initial hyphen. To accomplish this selection, the *while* test condition looks at *argc* and at *argv[1][0]*. Let's see how each of these quantities is handled.

First, the loop checks to see if *argc* is greater than 1, that is, if there are any arguments. At the end of the loop we have the operation *argc* -- . This decreases the value of *argc* by 1. Thus, if we start with one argument (an option, say), then *argc* is 2, and the loop is traversed. At the end of the loop, *argc* becomes 1, and the loop ends. Thus the *argc* part of the test provides an argument countdown and brings the loop to an end if all the arguments have been looked at.

The loop also ends if it encounters an argument not beginning with a hyphen; *argv[1]* is a pointer to the first argument, and *argv[1][0]* is the first character in that argument. (Recall the box on *argc* and *argv* in Chapter 7.) For the loop to work properly, *argv[1]* must point to the *second* argument for each new cycle of the loop; this is accomplished by the operation *argv++* , which makes *argv[1]* move to point to the next argument. If the workings of pointers and arrays are not fresh in your mind, this may seem a bit obscure. If so, check the next section.

Within the loop, we know that the first character of *argv[1]* is a hyphen (that being the condition for entering the loop), so we then check to see if the second character is a *p*, our one allowed option. If it is, we set *percent* to *YES*. Otherwise, we protest the use of an unknown option and exit. Note that this format can easily be extended to include a list of options, each with its own flag to set. In the case of several options, programs usually use C's *switch* statement instead of the *if...else* approach. (The *switch* is similar to the shell *case*.) In Chapter 10 we will show an example using *switch* with multiple options.

Let's review the action of this option-seeking loop. If there is no argument (*argc* = = *1*) or if the first argument does not begin with a hyphen, the loop is skipped, and the program runs in the same manner as the optionless version. If there is at least one argument, and the first argument is -*p*, then the *percent* flag is set to *YES*. If there is a second argument, and it begins with a hyphen, the program exits. Otherwise the loop ends, and the second argument becomes the prospective filename.

The calculations of the percentages takes place in the large *else* section added to *ctch.c*. It is executed only if *percent* is *YES*. There a *for* loop sums up the character counts:

```
for ( sum = 0, index = 0;  index < ASIZE;  index++)
       sum += cnum[index];
```

Then the sum is used to calculate percentages. (We could use floating-point instead of integer calculations if we needed fractional percentages.) Note that it's possible that a file might contain no alphabetic characters; in that case we avoid the embarrassing business of trying to divide by 0 and settle for printing an asterisk instead of a percentage.

Here is a sample run using *charct* with the new *p* option; once again we pipe the output through *pr*:

```
$ charct -p ch8 | pr -t -3 -l1
a  166   9%     b   19   1%     c   63   3%
d   41   2%     e  158   8%     f   32   1%
g   37   2%     h   96   5%     i  152   8%
j    3   0%     k    2   0%     l   66   3%
m   39   2%     n  144   8%     o  150   8%
p   81   4%     q    0   0%     r  136   7%
s   87   4%     t  184  10%     u   68   3%
v   15   0%     w   29   1%     x    4   0%
y   13   0%     z    0   0%
```

MARCHING THROUGH *argv*

The *argc* -- , *argv* ++ mechanism is a common one for examining a series of command-line arguments. To understand how this method works, we need to recall the intimate connection between pointers and arrays in C. The key point is that *the name of an array is a pointer to the first element of an array*. This applies on two levels for the declaration

```
char *argv[];
```

First, this declaration states that *argv* is the name of an array of pointers to type *char*. This means that the name *argv* by itself points to the first member of the array, and that is *argv[0]*. Secondly, each array member itself is a pointer to a character string, which is a form of array. Just as *argv* points to *argv[0]*, so *argv[0]* points to *argv[0][0]*, the first character in the command name. So *argv* really is a pointer to a pointer (as well as an array of arrays), and some programmers use the following declaration instead of the one we used:

```
char **argv;
```

Let's use a concrete example to clarify matters. Suppose our command line looks like this:

```
mix cement gravel
```

Here the command name (argument 0) is *mix*, argument 1 is *cement*, and argument 2 is *gravel*. In this case, *argv* is a pointer to the array *argv[0]*, *argv[0]* is a pointer

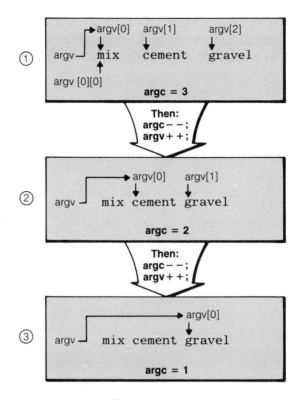

Figure 8.1
***argv* ++ Moves Through Command-Line Arguments**

to the *m* in the string *mix*, and *argv[0][0]* is the character *'m'*. Consider this statement:

```
printf("%u %u %c\n", argv, argv[0], argv[0][0]);
```

It would print, in order, the address of *argv[0]*, the address of *argv[0][0]*, and the contents of *argv[0][0]*, the character *'m'*. Remember, the value of a pointer is the address of what it points to.

Okay, then what does the operation *argv* ++ do? It makes *argv* point to the next member of the array, that which we called *argv[1]*. That is, *argv* now points to a pointer to *cement*.

But once we perform the operation *argv* ++, we can't call *argv[1]* by the name *argv[1]* any more! The reason is that *argv[1]* is interpreted to mean *argv* + *1*; that is, *argv[1]* is the array element that comes immediately after what *argv* itself points to. Thus, after the *argv* ++ operation, *argv[1]* now points to *gravel*, and we must use *argv[0]* if we want to refer to *cement*. That is, the new *argv[0]* is the old *argv[1]*, the new *argv[1]* is the old *argv[2]*, and so on.

Putting the matter more succinctly, the combination of *argc* -- and *argv*++ works very much like the *shift* command in shell scripts; the second argument becomes the first argument, the third argument becomes the second argument, and so on.

Question 8.4

Start with the following command-line:

```
marx harpo zeppo
```

a. What is the value of *argv[1]*?
b. What is the value of *argv[1][2]*?
c. After the operation *argv*++ , what is the value of *argv[1][2]*?
d. What does the operation *argv[1]*++ accomplish?

There are two common ways of putting this argument-shifting approach to use in selecting options. The first is the one we have shown, a *while* loop of this form:

```
while (argc > 1 && argv[1][0] == '-' ) {
    . . .
    argc--;
    argv++;
}
```

This means as long as there is an argument, and as long as the first character of the argument is a hyphen, continue looping. At the end of each loop, decrement the argument count by one and shift to the next argument.

The second form is to use a *for* loop:

```
for( ; argc > 1 && argv[1][0]=='-'; argc--, argv++) {
    . . .
}
```

This collects the test condition and the condition-changing expression on the same line. Since nothing needs to be initialized, that field in the *for* specification is left blank, and the initial semicolon acts as a place holder.

HOW TO PROCESS MULTIPLE FILES
WITH C PROGRAMS

Our program is still limited to processing one command-line file, so let's see next how to remove that restriction.

To process several files, we need to place the file-opening and file-closing part of the program in a loop that cycles through all the argument names. That is, if we give the command

```
charct twain melville
```

we want the program to open the *twain* file, process it, close it, and then repeat that sequence for the *melville* file.

We have already developed a mechanism to cycle through an argument list, namely, a *while* loop using *argc* -- and *argv* ++ . Let's install that mechanism, this time to cycle through files. Since we aren't changing the *ctch()* part of the program, we'll just show the new *main()*.

```c
/* charct -- version 1.3 */
/* counts occurrences of each letter in text */
/* Usage: charct [-p] [filename...]  */
#include <stdio.h>
#include <ctype.h>
#define YES 1
#define NO 0
int percent;

main(argc, argv)
int argc;
char *argv[];
{
FILE *fp;
char *prog;
int header = NO;

prog = argv[0];
percent = NO;
while ( argc > 1  && argv[1][0] == '-' ) {
    if ( argv[1][1] == 'p' )
        percent = YES;
    else {
        fprintf(stderr,"%s: Unknown option %s\n", prog, argv[1]);
        exit (1);
        }
```

```
            argc--;
            argv++;
            }
    if (argc == 1)
        ctch(stdin);
    else {
      if (argc > 2)
          header = YES;   /* set header flag if more than 1 argument */
      while ( argc > 1) {   /* open files until list is used up */
        if ( (fp=fopen(argv[1], "r") ) == NULL ) {
            perror (argv[0]);
            exit (1);
            }
        else {
            if (header == YES)
                printf("\n%s:\n", argv[1]); /* print filename */
            ctch (fp) ;
            fclose (fp);
            argc--;   /* one less file */
            argv++;   /* set argv[1] to next filename */
            }
        }
      }
    }
```

We have a new *while* loop:

```
while ( argc > 1) {   /* open files until list is used up */
```

It steps through each argument until the argument count drops to 1 (no arguments). We added a new flag (*header*) that controls the printing of the filename to precede the output for each file. This is done only if there are two or more files.

Question 8.5

What is the difference between the two *while* loops in *charct*?

We made (through omission) a design decision here. The question is this: when processing several files, do we want a separate output for each file, or just a cumulative total, or both? We opted for separate output for each file, since it is easier to implement. Also, we can get the cumulative total for several files by combining them first and using a pipe:

```
cat file1 file2 file3 | charct
```

Here the *cat* command combines the files into a single data stream that becomes the standard input for *charct*. (It is convenient to have programs that read standard input.) In Chapter 10 we will develop an example that offers a choice of separate totals or else both separate and cumulative totals.

Summing up, we have developed several ways to enhance a C program. We have seen how to allow a program to take input either from standard input or a named file. We have seen how to add options, and how to extend a program to handle more than one file. Let's turn now from program modifications of this sort to the subject of getting information from the UNIX system to a C program.

HOW TO GET SYSTEM INFORMATION TO A PROGRAM

The UNIX system knows many things that might be useful to a program: what the time is, the user's identity and group membership, the shell environment (*HOME*, *PATH*, and so on), the permissions for various files, and the like. The system also provides methods for letting programs easily tap this knowledge. To illustrate a few possibilities, the next listing shows a function called *monit()* that keeps a record of who used the program containing the function and when. You might use it to find if a particular program is proving to be useful. It uses the *getenv(3)* function to get the user's home directory, the *getlogin(3)* function to get the login name, and the *time(2)* and *ctime(3)* functions to get the date and time. It also uses some of the library string manipulation functions, which we will discuss presently.

```
/* monit -- monitors use of a program */
/* usage: monit(programname) */
#include <stdio.h>
monit(cmd)
char *cmd;                    /* takes a command name as argument */
{
  FILE *fp;
  char  *home, *date, *lognm;  /* pointers to strings */
  char file [30];
  char *getenv(), *ctime(), *getlogin();
  long time();
  long tm;

  strcpy(file,"/usr/nosey/acct/");    /*  create a  */
  strncat(file,cmd,10);               /*  name for  */
  strcat(file,"A");                   /*  a file    */
```

```
        home = getenv ("HOME");              /* get home directory */
        lognm = getlogin();                  /* get user's login name */
        time (&tm);                          /* get time in seconds    */
        date = ctime (&tm);                  /* convert to readable form */
        if ( (fp = fopen (file,  "a") ) == NULL) {   /* open acct. file */
            perror ("monit");
            exit (1);
            }
        else {
          fprintf (fp, "%s of %s used %s on %s\n",
                      lognm,  home,   cmd,  date);    /* report use */
          fclose (fp);
          }
}
```

Place the function in a short program in order to test it:

```
/* testout -- testing the monit() function */
main()
{
monit (testout);
}
```

Now suppose a user called *nosey* compiles and runs the program:

```
$ cc -o testout testout.c monit.c
$ testout
$
```

Then he can check the *acct* directory:

```
$ ls acct
testoutA
$ cat acct/testoutA
nosey of /usr/nosey used testout on Tue Jul 24  15:43:41 PDT

$
```

See how the *acct/testoutA* file records the login name and the home directory of the user along with the command name and time of use. Of course, the *acct* directory has to be created before this program can be used successfully. To record other users, the *testoutA* file must be accessible to them, so *nosey* could do this:

```
$ chmod go+w acct/testoutA
$
```

Then, when others use his *testout* program, information about them is added to *nosey*'s *testoutA* file. Another possibility is to use the *set user ID* option that we will discuss in Chapter 9. That approach gives the user of a program (temporarily) the same permissions as the owner of the program, so that the permission for the data file need not be changed.

The *monit()* Function Explained

So the program does what it is supposed to do; now let's see how the different parts of this program work. The simplest of the new functions is *getlogin()*; it returns a *char* pointer to the user's login name. Note that we have to declare this function since its return value is other than *int*.

The *getenv()* needs an argument, a pointer to the name of the environmental variable whose value you wish to obtain. Recall that a quoted string is a pointer, so *"HOME"* serves as a suitable argument. The *getenv()* function then searches the environment for a variable of that name. If it finds one, it returns a pointer to the value of the variable; otherwise it returns *NULL*. Since shell variables are strings, *getenv()* is of type pointer-to-*char*.

Question 8.6

What call would obtain the value of the current value of the *PATH* environmental shell variable?

Getting the date is more complicated. The system call *time()* returns the time in the form of a *long* integer representing the number of seconds from 00:00:00 GMT January 1, 1970 to the time of the call. The library function *ctime()* converts this to the same form used in the *date* command, which is a character string of 26 characters giving the date and time. The details warrant some discussion, and you will find that in the next section.

A Timely Digression

The *ctime()* and *time()* functions are used together, with the latter providing the argument for the former. The *ctime()* function takes as an argument a pointer to the memory location holding the number of seconds since 1970. One way to get

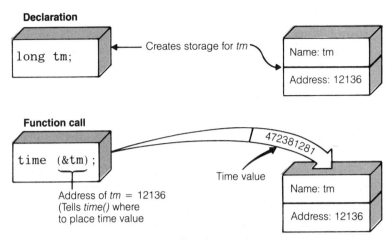

Figure 8.2
The Argument of Time

such a pointer is to take the address (via the address operator &) of the variable holding the time value, and that is what we did by using &*tm* as an argument for *ctime()*.

The second part of the job is for *time()* to provide the time value; the *time()* function has two ways to fetch that value. One is to provide as an argument for the *time()* function the address of the variable that will receive the value. We did it with this statement:

```
time(&tm);
```

Here *tm* is a *long* variable, and the address operator (&) yields its address. Thus &*tm* is a pointer to *long*. Using this sort of call is analogous to a statement like

```
scanf("%d", &number);
```

In both cases, an address is passed to a function, and that function then places a value in that address. In the call *time(&tm)*, the &*tm* provides a location for *time()* to place a time. In the call *ctime(&tm)*, the &*tm* provides a location for *ctime()* to find a time.

The *time()* function also uses the function return mechanism to provide a value, so a second way to use *time()* is like this:

```
tm = time(0);
```

Here *time()* is furnished a null address, which causes it to forgo using the address method of passing a value. But *time()* still uses the *return* statement to provide a value. Indeed, one could pass the time to two variables with a call like this:

```
tm = time(&tim);
```

This assumes that both *tm* and *tim* are type *long*.

We've spent some time on *time()* because the synopsis may be a bit misleading. In part, it reads like this:

```
long time(tloc)
long *tloc;
```

This might lead us to include these declarations in a program and to use the pointer-to-*long tloc* instead of the address *&tm*:

```
time(tloc);
ctime(tloc);
```

The problem with this is that the declaration

```
long *tloc;
```

creates storage for the pointer variable *tloc* (which supposedly will hold the address of the time) but fails to create storage for the time value itself. That is, we haven't provided anything for the pointer to point to. But by declaring

```
long tm;
```

we do create a storage location, and *&tm* is a pointer to it. We could also do this:

```
tloc = &tm;
ctime(tloc);
```

but that uses an unnecessary variable.

The moral here (and hardly a new one) is that the user must use care in interpreting a UNIX manual synopsis.

C Library String Functions

The other new element in the *monit()* function is that we have used some string functions from the C library. In particular, we used *strcpy()* to copy a string and *strcat()* to combine two strings. Let's look at those functions.

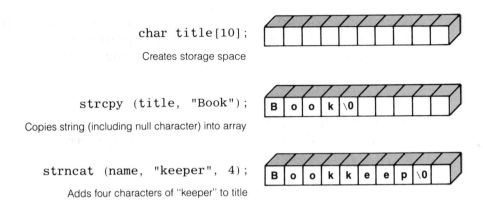

```
char title[10];
```
Creates storage space

```
strcpy (title, "Book");
```
Copies string (including null character) into array

```
strncat (name, "keeper", 4);
```
Adds four characters of "keeper" to title

Figure 8.3
String Functions

First, the *strcpy()* function copies its second argument into the first argument. Each argument is a pointer to *char*, and the first argument should point to the beginning of a storage block large enough to hold the copied string. The simplest way to do this is to have the first argument be the name of a sufficiently large array. Something like this is fine:

```
char name[20];
strcpy(name,"phyllis");
```

The string *"phyllis"* gets copied into the array *name*. But something like this is no good:

```
char *name;
strcpy(name,"phillip");
```

Declaring something to be a pointer to *char* creates storage to hold the pointer but *does not* create storage to hold the string itself.

The *strncat()* function takes two character pointers and a number as arguments. The second string is added to the end of the first string, with the proviso that no more than the specified number of characters (the third argument) are added. Again, the first argument must have sufficient storage allotted for it. If the second string is shorter than the specified number of characters, then just the characters present are added. The *strcat()* function is like *strncat()*, but it doesn't count characters.

In our program, right after the *strcpy()* call, *file* is the string *"/usr/nosey/acct/"*. After the *strncat()* call, it has become *"/usr/nosey/acct/testout"*, and after the *strcat()* call it is *"/usr/nosey/acct/testoutA"*. The string functions are often used for tasks such as constructing complete pathnames from smaller parts. Table 8.2 lists the common string functions.

Table 8.2 String Functions*

Function	Action
strcat(s1,s2)	Adds string s2 to the end of string s1
strncat(s1,s2,n)	Adds at most n characters of s2 to s1
strcmp(s1,s2)	Compares s1 to s2, returning 0 for equality
strncmp(s1,s2,n)	Compares at most n characters of s1 and s2
strcpy(s1,s2)	Copies string s2 to s1
strncpy(s1,s2,n)	Copies at most n characters of s2 to s1
strlen(s)	Returns the number of non-null characters in s
strchr(s,c)	Returns a pointer to the first occurrence of the character c in the string s; returns a pointer to NULL if c not found; formerly called index(s,r)
strrchr(s,c)	Returns a pointer to the last occurrence of the character c in the string s; returns a pointer to NULL if c not found; formerly called rindex(s,r)

*s, s1, and s2 are pointers to *char* and represent strings.

Question 8.7

Suppose we have these declarations:

```
char scratch[40], *ps;
```

Construct program fragments to accomplish the following tasks.

a. Copy the first command-line argument into *scratch*.
b. Add the string "floppy" to the end of whatever is in *scratch*.
c. Print "HO" if the second command-line argument is *HI*.
d. Find the first occurrence of "q" in *scratch*.

Now that we have seen how to obtain login names, environmental values, and the date and time, let's see how to get information about files.

INODE INFO: *stat()* AND *fstat()*

In Chapter 2 we discussed how file information is kept in three places: the file itself, the inode entry, and the directory. The inode contains the greatest variety of information: file type, size, time of last use, various permissions, and the like. The *access()* system call told us about file permissions and types, but the *stat()* (for *status*) and *fstat()* functions give access to the full fund of inode information.

Each of these two new functions works by filling an appropriate C structure with the proper inode information. The difference is that *stat()* refers to a file by its name, and *fstat()* refers to a file by its file descriptor. Here is the synopsis for this pair of functions:

```
#include <sys/types.h>
#include <sys/stat.h>

int stat(path, buf)
char *path;
struct stat *buf;

int fstat(fildes, buf)
int fildes;
struct stat *buf;
```

The *struct stat* type is a structure type defined in the *<sys/stat.h>* file, and that definition uses some special types defined in the *<sys/types.h>* file. Hence both of these files must be included when you use *stat()* or *fstat()*.

The second argument of either function is a pointer to a *struct stat* type. In practice, a program usually defines a structure of *struct stat* type and then uses the address of the structure as an argument to *stat()* or *fstat()*. That is, the basic usage looks like this (assuming the *#include* directives have been given):

```
struct stat nfile;

stat(argv[1], &nfile);   /* argv[1] refers to a filename */
```

This use of *stat()* results in the defined structure (*nfile*) being filled with the appropriate information about whatever file is named by *argv[1]*, a command-line argument.

Both functions return a value of 0 if successful and −1 if not.

To use the information provided by these functions, we need to know about the *stat* structure they use. The exact definition of *struct stat* depends on the UNIX version. The System V version includes the following structure members:

```
ushort    st_mode;   /* File mode */
ino_t     st_ino;    /* Inode number */
dev_t     st_dev;    /* ID of device containing a */
                     /* directory entry for this file */
short     st_nlink;  /* Number of links */
ushort    st_uid;    /* User ID of file's owner */
```

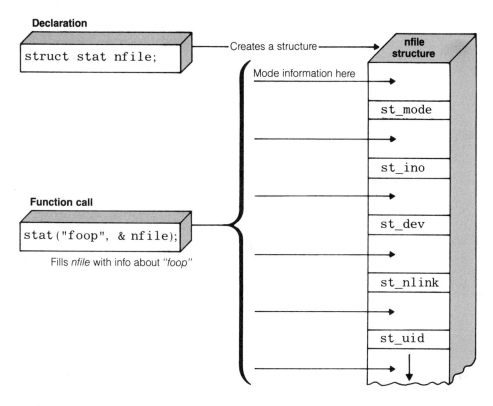

Figure 8.4
Using *stat()*

```
ushort    st_gid;   /* Group ID of file's owner */
off_t     st_size;  /* File size in bytes */
time_t    st_atime; /* Time of last access */
time_t    st_mtime; /* Time of last data modification */
time_t    st_ctime; /* Time of last file status change */
```

Times are measured in seconds from January 1, 1970.

The new types here, such as *ushort* and *ino_t*, are defined in the *<sys/type.h>* file, and we need not worry about them much as long as we remember to include that header file. The one occasion on which you would need to know the type is if you wish to print out a value; then you can check the *TYPES(5)* entry in the manual.

Using Structures

We do need to know how to use the structure members. In C this is done using the membership, or dot (.) operator. The structure name is followed by a dot and then by the member name. For instance, using the *nfile* structure we defined earlier, the *st_nlink* member of the structure holds the number of links to the file, and it is accessed this way:

```
nfile.st_nlink
```

Structure members are used the same as any other value of the same type. Here is a quick example:

```
/* cntln.c -- counts the links a file has */
#include <sys/types.h>
#include <sys/stat.h>
main(argc,argv)
int argc;
char *argv[];
{
struct stat nfile;        /*  creates structure storage */

stat(argv[1],&nfile);     /* fills up nfile struct. with info */
printf("%s has %d link(s).\n", argv[1], nfile.st_nlink);
                          /* accesses st_nlink member */
}
```

After compiling it and placing the executable version in *cntln*, we get this:

```
$ cntln cntln.c
cntln.c has 1 link(s)
$ cntln diverse
diverse has 5 link(s)
$
```

The *cntln.c* file has just one link, but the *diverse* file has five.

This program is totally devoid of error-checking, but all we wanted to do was show the basic manner in which *stat()* and the *stat* structure are used.

Question 8.8

Given the proper header files and the declaration

```
struct stat toad;
```

how could you obtain the size of the file *farm*?

Typically, structure members are compared with corresponding structure members of another file, so even if we are not sure exactly what a *time_t* type is, we can still compare two values of that type. For example, if we need to test which of two files was accessed last, we can use a construction like the following:

```
if (nfile.st_atime > mfile.st_atime)
    dosomething();
```

The File Mode: *st_mode*

The most information-packed member of the *stat* structure is the *st_mode* member. Although just a two-byte integer, the *st_mode* member tells whether the file is a regular file, a directory, or one of two kinds of special files. The mode also reveals the read, write, and execute permissions for user, group members, and others. Those are the items that interest us most, but other information is there, too. Before developing a full-fledged example using *stat()* or *fstat()*, we will have to learn how to use *st_mode*. So let's see how so much information can be stored in such a modest-sized space, and let's find out how to access that information.

Binary Coding and *st_mode*

To squeeze so much information into only two bytes of storage, a form of binary coding is used in the *st_mode* member. A two-byte integer corresponds to 16 bits on most machines. Since each bit can be set to "1" or "0", this gives us, in essence, 16 toggle switches that can set to on (1) or off (0). In *st_mode*, then, each bit position has a meaning. The final bit, for example, is set to 1 if the file has execute permission for others, and is set to 0 otherwise. The next figure illustrates how the bits in *st_mode* are organized. We didn't specify the details of the file-type portion because in some cases combinations of two bit positions are used.

The binary patterns stored in *st_mode* can be expressed conveniently in octal. Consider, for example, the three bits devoted to describing the access permissions for others. Any possible combination of permissions is represented by a three-digit binary number, such as 100 or 111 or 101. But any three-digit binary number corresponds to a one-digit octal number. For example, 100 (*read only*) is 04 and 111 (*read, write,* and *execute*) is 07. We follow the C convention of writing octal numbers with a leading 0.

Furthermore, the next *three* binary digits (group permissions) are represented by *one* additional octal digit. Thus 101000 (*read and execute* permission for group members) is 060 in octal. Similarly, the next three bit positions (user permissions) can be represented by an additional octal digit. For example, 0400 is the same as

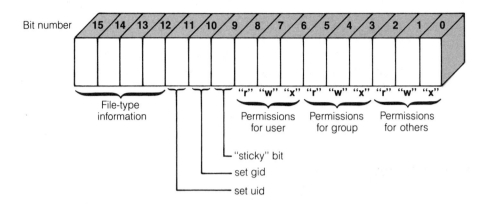

Figure 8.5
Bit Allotment in *st_mode*

010000000 (*read only* for user). In this manner, a three-digit octal number represents the nine binary digits needed to describe the full set of permissions. For instance, the octal number 0644 signifies read and write permission for the user, and read permission for group members and others. Each digit in the octal number represents one particular group: *user*, *group*, or *other*. See Figure 8.6.

This scheme of octal representations of binary numbers can be extended to the whole *st_mode* member. Indeed, the <*sys/stat.h*> file defines several octal constants that can be used with *st_mode*. The following table shows some of them.

SYMBOLIC BIT DEFINITIONS FOR *st_mode*

```
#define S_IEXEC     0000100     /* owner execute permission */
#define S_IWRITE    0000200     /* owner write permission */
#define S_IREAD     0000400     /* owner read permission */
#define S_IFDCHR    0020000     /* character special file */
#define S_IFDIR     0040000     /* directory */
#define S_IFBLK     0060000     /* block special file */
#define S_IFREG     0100000     /* regular file */
#define S_IFMT      0170000     /* file type mask */
```

The symbolic representations are used in tests to determine various aspects of the mode. You could just use the numbers themselves, but the symbolic forms are intended to be more mnemonic.

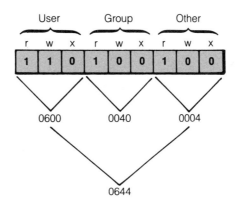

Figure 8.6
File Access Permissions in Octal

Let's take a particular case. Suppose we want to find if the file described by the structure *nfile* is a regular file. Can we do this?

```
if (nfile.st_mode == S_IFREG)   /* don't try it */
```

As the warning suggests, we can, but it won't work. The reason is that the actual mode number (in octal) might be something like *0100644*. That would be a regular file with read and write permissions for the user and read permissions for group members and others. The *010* part indicates that we have a regular file, but the *0644* part messes up the comparision.

What is needed is a way to compare just the *010* part of *st_mode*, and this is done using a *mask*. The correct comparison looks like this:

```
if (nfile.st_mode & S_IFMT == S_IFREG)
```

The *S_IFMT* constant is a mask that hides the irrelevant bits of *st_mode*. This time & is not the address operator but the *bitwise and* operator. Using the *stat()* or *fstat()* system calls often requires using the & operator as well as other bitwise operators, so let's turn to that subject for a bit.

BIT OPERATIONS IN C

The C language offers several *bitwise* operators; we will look at three: & (and), | (or), and ~ (*one's complement*). They are called bitwise operators because they operate on the individual bits within a number.

Let's start with &. It is a *binary operator*, meaning that it takes two operands. Don't confuse this operator with the *unary* (one operand) address operator. Both

A	B	A & B
0	0	0
0	1	0
1	0	0
1	1	1

Figure 8.7
The Bitwise & (AND) Operator

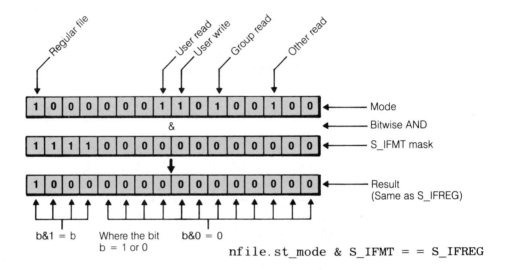

Figure 8.8
ANDing *nfile.st_mode* and *S_IFMT*

use the same symbol (&); the context determines how the symbol is interpreted. The address operator is followed by the name of a variable of some sort, while the *and* operator is placed between two values. The result of applying this operator to two binary numbers is to produce a binary number in which each bit is a 1 only if both corresponding bits of the original numbers are 1. Figure 8.7 illustrates the value of *A & B* for the various possible combinations of values for bits A and B. Note that 0 *and* any bit is 0 and that 1 *and* any bit is the value of that bit.

When the & operator is applied to a binary number with several bits, the operator is applied to each bit position separately. That is, if we have *C & D*, then the first bit of the result corresponds to *and*ing the first bit of *C* with the first bit of *D*, the second bit of the result comes from *and*ing the second bit of *C* with the second bit of *D*, and so on.

Now let's see how the & operator is combined with *S_IFMT* to produce a mask. First, look at the value of *S_IFMT*. Translating from octal to binary, this number becomes 1111000000000000. If we *and S_IFMT* (that is, use the & operator) with a second 16-bit number, the result has the same 4 left-most bits as the second number, since 1 *and* any bit is just that bit. Furthermore, the remaining 12 bits are set to zero, since 0 *and* any bit is 0. Figure 8.8 illustrates the process for *nfile.st_mode & S_IFMT*. The resulting number can be compared to, say *S_IFREG*, to see if the file is a regular file.

Question 8.9

Suppose we wanted a mask that would isolate just the *other* permission bits, that is, the right-most three bits of *st_mode*. What should the mask be?

The & operator, when used with a mask, is useful for *testing* the value of certain bits within *st_mode*. What if we wish to *set* certain bits within *st_mode*? Then we can use the | and ~ operators. Let's see what these operators do. Then, to take a definite example, we'll see how to use them to turn the user *execute* permission bit *on* and *off*.

The | (or) operator, like &, compares two numbers a bit-position at a time. If *A* and *B* are two bits, then *A* | *B* has the value 1 if *A* or *B* is 1 (or if both are 1). Figure 8.9 shows the possible combinations. Note that *or*ing 1 with any bit yields a 1, while *or*ing 0 with any bit yields that bit.

Suppose we are dealing with a type *stat* structure called *nfile*. Then the mode information is in the *nfile.st_mode* member. Now suppose we want to set the user *execute* flag to *on*. Then we can perform this operation:

```
nfile.st_mode = nfile.st_mode | S_IEXEC;
```

The *S_IEXEC* symbolic constant corresponds to a bit string with the user execute bit set to 1 and all other bits set to 0. We see that user execute bit in *nfile.st_mode* is *or*ed with 1, so it gets set to 1, since 1 *or* any bit is 1. All the remaining bits are *or*ed with 0, so they remain unchanged, since 0 or any bit is just that bit. Figure 8.10 illustrates this process.

Incidentally, we can also use the expression

```
nfile.st_mode |= S_IEXEC;
```

The |= operator is analogous to operators like + =; the quantity on the right is *or*ed with the left-hand variable, and the result is stored in the left-hand variable.

A	B	A|B
0	0	0
0	1	1
1	0	1
1	1	1

Figure 8.9
The Bitwise | (OR) Operator

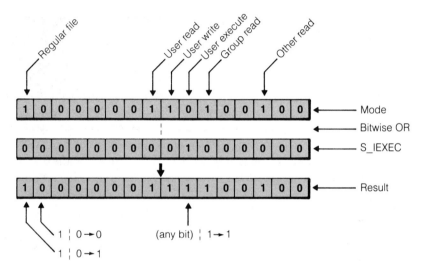

Figure 8.10
nfile.st_mode | S_IEXEC

One particular point to note about using the *or* operator this way is that if the target bit already is *on*, it gets left *on*.

To turn more than one bit *on* we can just *or* several bits together. For instance, the combination

```
S_IREAD  |  S_IWRITE
```

is just the bit pattern 0000000000110000 and can be used to turn both the user read and the user write bits *on*.

Okay, we can turn a bit *on*. What do we do if we want to turn the user execute bit *off*, that is, set it to 0? Then we can say

```
nfile.st_mode = nfile.st_mode & ~S_IEXEC;
```

$$
\begin{array}{c|c}
\textbf{A} & \textbf{\~A} \\
\hline
0 & 1 \\
1 & 0
\end{array}
$$

Figure 8.11
The Bitwise ~ (One's Complement) Operator

or, more succinctly,

```
nfile.st_mode &= ~S_IEXEC;
```

We have used the ~ (*one's complement*) operator, which changes every 1 to a 0 in a binary number and vice versa. Figure 8.11 shows its effect on a single bit *A*.

When applied to a number with several bits, each bit is affected individually. Thus, while *S_IEXEC* is 0000000001000000 ~*S_IEXEC* is 1111111110111111.

Recall that 1 *and* any bit is just that bit, while 0 *and* any bit is 0. Thus, *and*ing ~*S_IEXEC* with the mode forces the user execute bit to be 0 and leaves the other bits unchanged.

In short, if *SYMBIT* is a symbolic bit pattern, we can use

```
variable |= SYMBIT
```

to turn the corresponding bits in *variable* to *on*, and we can use

```
variable &= ~SYMBIT
```

to turn those bits to *off*. Both expressions work regardless of the original settings in *variable*.

Now that we have seen how to check and set modes, let's use those skills in a program utilizing *stat()* and *fstat()*.

A MODEST, CAUTIOUS COPY PROGRAM

UNIX already has its own copy program, *cp*, and it works well. However, now we will produce another copy program to illustrate the use of *fstat()* and *stat()*. This version will be more limited than *cp* in that it will only copy one file to another; it will forgo the variant of copying one or more files to a directory. However, it will retain the feature of not allowing you to copy a file to itself. Our version will add one nonstandard feature: if the target name is already a file, the program will ask if you wish to copy over it or not. These criteria demand that the program know intimate details about the concerned files, and that is where the *stat()* and *fstat()* system calls prove invaluable.

Even with such limited objectives, all the checking makes this a longish program. As you read through it, note that in many cases the error message explains what a particular test was about.

```
/* copy.c -- copies a file, checks target for existence */
/* Usage: copy file1 file2  */
#include <stdio.h>
#include <sys/types.h>
#include <sys/stat.h>
main(argc, argv)
int argc;
char *argv[];
{
struct stat stold, stnew;   /* info on old and new files */
int old, new, n;
char response(), buf[BUFSIZ];

if (argc != 3) {    /* quit if wrong number of arguments */
    fprintf(stderr, "Usage: copy file1 file2\n ");
    exit(1);
    }
if ( (old = open(argv[1],0)) < 0 ) {
    perror("copy");
    exit(1);             /* can't open file, so exit */
    }
if (fstat(old, &stold) < 0 ) {
    fprintf(stderr, "copy cannot find %s\n", argv[1]);
    exit(1);             /* exit if fstat() fails */
    }
if (stold.st_mode & S_IFMT != S_IFREG) {
    fprintf(stderr, "copy: %s not a regular file\n", argv[1]);
    exit(1);
    }
if (stat(argv[2], &stnew) >= 0 ) {
    if ( stnew.st_mode & S_IFMT != S_IFREG) {
        fprintf(stderr, "copy: %s exists, is not a file\n",
                    argv[2]);
        exit(1);
        }
    else {
        if (stnew.st_ino == stold.st_ino  &&
          stnew.st_dev == stold.st_dev      ) {
            fprintf(stderr, "copy won't copy file to itself\n");
            exit(1);
            }
```

```
            fprintf (stderr, "copy: %s is an existing file\n", argv[2]);
            fprintf (stderr, "Do you wish to overwrite it? y/n\n");
            if (response() != 'y')
                exit (1);
            }
        }
    if ( (new = creat(argv[2], stold.st_mode)) < 0 ) {
        perror ("copy");
        exit (1);
        }
    /* now we are ready to copy ! */
    while ( (n = read(old, buf, BUFSIZ)) > 0 )
        if (write(new, buf, n) !=n) {
            perror ("copy");    /* in case of write error */
            exit (2);
            }
    if (n < 0 ) {           /* in case of read error */
        perror ("copy");
        exit (2);
        }
    exit (0);
    }

char response ()
{
FILE *term;
char ch;

if ( (term = fopen("/dev/tty", "r")) == NULL ) {
    perror ("response");
    exit (1);
    }
if ( (ch = getc(term) ) != EOF ) {
    close (term);
    ch = isupper(ch)? tolower(ch) : ch ;
    return (ch);
    }
else
    exit (0);
}
```

Explaining the *copy.c* Program

Let's examine what the program does. First, it checks to see that there are exactly
two arguments (*argc* should be 3) and quits if this is not the case (*argc != 3*).

Then it attempts to open the presumed file named by the first argument; failure here halts the program. Otherwise the program then attempts to acquire the inode information with the call

```
fstat(old, &stold)
```

This is embedded in an *if* statement that halts the proceedings in case the *fstat()* function fails to work. Otherwise, the status information about the file is copied into the *stold* structure. Note that the *fstat()* function requires that we refer to the file by its file descriptor number, *old*.

Next the program uses the status information now in the structure *stold* to check if the opened file is indeed a regular file and not, say, a directory. (The *open()* function can also open directories for reading.) The mechanics of the comparison are as we described earlier.

Now we advance to the part of the program dealing with the target name for the copy. Again the program attempts to gather inode information, this time about the target file:

```
stat(argv[2], &stnew)
```

Now, because we use the actual filename, we use *stat()* instead of *fstat()*. In this case failure implies that there is no such file, and the program skips down to creating the new file. Before looking at that step, let's check what happens if the file already exists.

First, if the file exists, the program checks to see if it is other than a regular file; if so, goodbye. If it is a regular file, the program checks to see if it is the same as the original file. Here it is *not* sufficient to check if the second name is the same as the first, for the *ln* command makes it possible to assign multiple names to the same file. Instead, we check to see if the two files have the same inode number (stored in the *st_ino* structure member). In addition we check to see if the two files are also in the same file system (using *st_dev*). Some systems, as you may recall from many chapters ago, have more than one file system, each with its own inode setup. Thus the second part of the comparison screens out files of the same inode number but, say, stored on different hard disks. The program takes a firm stand against copying a file to itself.

The case that is left (after throwing out nonregular files and screening against copying a file to itself) is that the target name belongs to another file. Here the program asks the user if she or he wishes to overwrite the existing file. If the user responds with a *y* or *Y*, the program continues; otherwise it ends. (We'll discuss the *response()* function soon.)

Now we come to the act of creating the target file. The *creat()* function takes two arguments: the filename and a mode. The mode is typically an octal number (such as 0644) describing the permissions to be given to the new file; *creat()* uses the same system we described for *st_mode*. The program simply passes on to the new file the mode settings (*stold.st_mode*) of the old file. One reason for using *open()* and *creat()* instead of *fopen()* is to allow this passing of mode settings. See, however, the following section on *creat()*, *umask()*, and *chmod()*. Note that one property of the *creat()* function is that if the target file already exists, *creat()* arranges for it to be rewritten with the new material.

Finally, the program copies one file to the other, using the system buffer size (*BUFSIZ*) for maximum efficiency. The program checks for read and write errors.

The *copy.c* program has relied upon the fact that the *exit()* function closes any open files, hence we did not use *close()* explicitly.

There is one loose end to describe, the *response()* function. We used this:

```
if (response () != 'y');
    exit (1);
```

We could have said

```
if ( getchar () != 'y')
    exit (1);
```

The potential problem with the second approach is that *getchar()* reads the standard input. While it would be bizarre to try to use *copy* itself with redirected standard input, it is possible that *copy* could be used in a shell script that uses redirected input for a legitimate reason. If this happened, then the user's response would *not* be read by *getchar()*. So the *response()* function opens the user's terminal as input, ensuring the user's response is read whether or not the standard input has been redirected.

FILE PERMISSIONS: *creat()*, *chmod()*, AND *umask()*

On UNIX systems, new files are created using the *creat()* system call. This is even true of files created using *fopen()*, for the library function *fopen()* includes calls to *creat()*. The synopsis for *creat()* is this:

```
int creat(filename, mode)
char *filename;
int mode;
```

The mode describes the read, write, and execute permissions, using the bit-scheme we discussed for *st_mode*. The mode, when supplied literally, is usually represented as an octal number, again, as we discussed for *st_mode*. Thus read and write permission for everyone would be represented by a mode of 0666, which, in binary, is 110110110.

The mode provided to *creat()*, however, is first combined with a quantity called *the file creation mask*. Normally, the value of this mask is 0022 (octal) or 000010010 (binary). This mask is used to turn the two concerned bits (the group write permission bit and the others write permission bit) off. The final permission mode for a file, then, is this:

```
mode & ~0022
```

Recall we use the *and* and the *one's complement* operators to turn bits off.

The value of the file creation mask can be altered by using the *umask()* system call:

```
int umask(cmask)
int cmask;
```

This function sets the file creation mask to the value *cmask*, and it returns the previous value of the creation mask. You could use the call

```
umask(0000);
```

just before a *creat()* call to avoid any masking of the *creat()* mode.

The creation mask also can be set from the shell by using the shell command *umask*. For example,

```
umask 0000
```

sets the mask to 0000, so that the mask does not alter the *creat()* mode at all.

The *chmod* command, of course, can be used to change the mode of a file. We have used the symbolic form, as in

```
chmod u+x superduper
```

However, as we saw in Chapter 2, *chmod* also accepts mode assignments using the octal code we have discussed. For instance, the shell command

```
chmod 0644 goss
```

sets the user read and write bits and the group and others read bits to *on*.

There is also a system call *chmod()*; it can be used to set permissions from within a C program. It has this synopsis:

```
int chmod(filename, mode)
char *filename;
int mode;
```

Suppose, for example, you have a file called *private* that you normally maintain in the user read-only mode (0400). In a C program designed to work with that file, you can use the system call

```
chmod("private",0600);
```

to make the file read and write so that the program can modify the file. Then, at the end of the program, you can reset the more restricted mode with

```
chmod("private", 0400);
```

USING COMMAND FILES

We have investigated several aspects of getting information from the system; now let's see how to use command files in a C program.

A UNIX command file is a file containing an executable program. The regular UNIX commands are examples of command files, as are any executable programs you produce, including shell scripts. UNIX offers the means to run such programs from within a C program. We'll go through the rudiments now, using very simple examples to show the mechanics.

The *system()* Library Function

The simplest method to run a command from within a C program is to use the *system()* library function. It takes as an argument a character string representing a command. The command is run, and when it finishes, the program resumes with the next statement. Here is a very simple example:

```
/* date0.c -- runs the date command */
main()
{
    printf("Here comes the date.\n");
    system("date");
    printf("That was the date.\n");
}
```

Compile and run it:

```
$ cc -o date0 date0.c
$ date0
Here comes the date.
Thu Jul 26 10:23:55 PDT 1984
That was the date.
$
```

The argument string can include options and arguments for the command:

```
system("sort -r -o /tmp/faff.2321");
```

The *-r* option causes the sort to be in reverse order, and the *-o* option causes the sorted material to be placed in the original file.

In this case we wrote out the command string explicitly, but the command string can be constructed within the program by using string functions. Here is an example that constructs a command string using information from the program and from the program command line:

```
char command[BUFSIZ];
    . . .
strcpy(command, "sort");
if (rflag == YES)
    strcat(command, " -r ");
strcat(command, "-o ");
strcat(command, argv[1]);
system(command);
    . . .
```

Note that the filename comes from a command-line argument and that the *-r* option gets set only if the C program read in a *-r* option from its command line.

The *system()* function passes on the same file connections (including standard input and output) that the calling function has. This means that if the calling program is used with redirection, then any standard input and output used by a command summoned by *system()* will use the calling program's versions instead of using the terminal.

The *system()* function is a library function. It, in turn, is constructed from the system calls *execl()*, *fork()*, and *wait()*. Studying them offers much more insight into how UNIX works, so let's move on to them.

The System Function *execl()*

Under the *exec(2)* entry in the manual are listed four closely related functions which differ slightly from one another in the arguments they use. All serve to run a command file from a C program. First on the list is *execl()*, which has this synopsis:

```
int execl(path, arg0, arg1,...,argn, 0)
char *path, *arg0, *arg1,..., *argn;
```

The *path* argument is the name of the file holding the command we wish to run, *arg0* is the name of the command, and the other *arg*s are arguments for that particular command. The 0 is used to mark the end of the list. Rather than giving away what this function does, let's replace *system()* with *execl()* in our example and see what happens:

```
/* date1.c -- runs the date command */
main()
{
    printf("Here comes the date.\n");
    execl("/bin/date", "date", 0);
    printf("That was the date.\n");
}
```

Now compile and run it:

```
$ cc -o date1 date1.c
$ date1.c
Here comes the date.
Thu Jul 26 10:39:21 PDT 1984
$
```

The key difference in behavior between *system()* and *execl()*, as you can see, is that once *execl()* is called, it does not return to the calling program. The final print statement in *date1* was never executed. What happens is that when *execl()* acts, it replaces, or *overlays* the original program with the called program, and the called program becomes the program of record. In terms of processes, the summoned command has the same PID that the calling program had before it was overlaid. In other words, the process remains the same, but the program instructions in the process are replaced. The original code is lost.

Note that in the call, we had to use the full pathname (*/bin/date*) for the filename; the *execl()* command does not expand partial pathnames for you. However, the *execle()* version does.

What if you want to run a command like

```
cat fil[1-9].* > newf
```

Will *execl()* recognize the shell metacharacters? No. But the shell program (*sh*) does, so the trick is to use *execl()* to run *sh* to run the final command. This, in fact, is what the *system()* function does. The form is this:

```
execl("/bin/sh", "sh", "-c", command, 0);
```

Here *command* represents the desired command string, and *-c* is a shell option that tells the shell to interpret the following string as a list of arguments rather than as a single one. This is analogous to the shell symbolism *$@*. Thus, for the following command

```
execl("/bin/sh", "sh", "-c", "cat file1 file2", 0);
```

we have *sh* as the 0 argument, *-c* as argument 1, *cat* as argument 2, *file1*, as argument 3, and so on.

Starting a New Process: *fork*

The *execl()* command, as we have seen, does not start a new process; it just continues the original process by overlaying memory with a new set of instructions. As this occurs, the old program is replaced, so there is no way to return to the old program. To create a library function like *system()*, on the other hand, it is necessary to start a new process, leaving the old process unaltered. This is done with the help of the *fork()* function.

Let's take an empirical approach by putting a *fork()* into our program and seeing what happens:

```
/* date3.c-- date2.c with a fork */
main()
{
    printf("Here comes the date.\n");
    fork();
    execl("/bin/date", "date", 0);
    printf("That was the date.\n");
}
```

Compile and run it:

```
$ cc -o date3 date3.c
$ date3
Here comes the date.
Thu Jul 26 11:02:34 PDT 1984
Thu Jul 26 11:02:34 PDT 1984
$
```

The date gets printed twice! Why? Because *fork()* causes the process to split (''fork'') into two identical processes. One (the original) retains the original process identification number (PID) and is called the parent. The other, called the child,

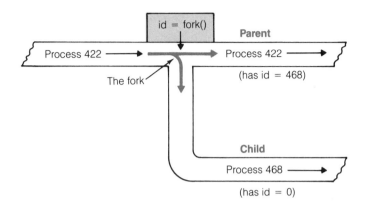

Figure 8.12
fork() **Creates Two Nearly Identical Processes**

gets a new PID. The child process inherits the same environment, the same open files, and the same file descriptors that the parent process had. Both programs run simultaneously; more precisely, both processes are part of the time-sharing scheme, so that they (and other current processes) take turns being run.

This may sound interesting but useless. Why have two identical programs running simultaneously? The trick is to get one of them (the child) to run the *execl()* command and the other one (the parent) not to. Then the child process gets overlaid by the command run by *execl()*. Meanwhile, we arrange for the parent to wait until the child dies, then resume its course. This is the basic structure of *system()*. The original process forks, the child runs *exec()* and eventually terminates, and the original resumes its way.

But how do we get just one of two identical programs to run a command? (If an exact duplicate is created of you with your exact memories, how can you tell which of you is the duplicate?) Well, there is a small difference between the two programs, and it has to do with the value returned by *fork()*. For the parent process, *fork()* returns the PID of the child. For the child, *fork()* returns the value 0.

Let's check out this aspect of *fork()* by looking at the return values. For comparison, we'll use the *getpid()* function, which returns the PID of the calling program. In the following program, *ID* refers to value returned by the *fork()* call, and *PID* refers to the *PID* returned by the *getpid()* call:

```
/* date4.c -- fork study */
main()
{
    int id;
```

```
        printf("Here comes the date.\n");
        id = fork();
        printf("PID is %d and ID is %d\n", getpid(), id);
        execl("/bin/date", "date", 0);
        printf("That was the date.\n");
}
```

Compile and run:

```
$ cc -o date4 date4.c
$ date4
Here comes the date.
PID is 1919 and ID is 1923   ← From the parent
PID is 1923 and ID is 0      ← From the child
Thu Jul 26 11:27:14 1984 PDT
Thu Jul 26 11:27:14 1984 PDT
$
```

The first print message is printed but once, since it comes before the fork. After the fork, the program is duplicated, so each print statement thereafter is printed twice, once by the parent, and once by the child. Here the parent process prints its PID and the ID value returned by *fork()*. Then the time-sharing system gave the child process its turn. We can tell which is which, because the parent prints the child's PID (1923) for its *fork()* return value (ID), while the child prints 0 for its ID. First one, and then the other, prints its date message. That the parent went first is a case of happenstance; running this program a few times, I noted that there seems to be about a 50-50 chance of either one running first.

Now we have a way to make just the child run *execl()*: use an *if* statement that looks at the value returned by *fork()*. Let's try that out:

```
/* date5.c -- committing a fork child to action */
main()
{
    int id;

    printf("Here comes the date.\n");
    if ( (id = fork() ) == 0) {  /* select child process */
        printf("PID is %d and ID is %d\n", getpid(), id);
        execl("/bin/date", "date", 0);
        }
    printf("That was the date.\n");
}
```

Compile and run it:

```
$ cc -o date5 date5.c
$ date5
Here comes the date.
PID is 2232 and ID is 0
That was the date.
Thu Jul 26 11:34:17 1984 PDT
$
```

Success! Almost! The process forked into two parts. Only the child printed the PID information (as the ID of 0 reveals). And the parent, having avoided the *exec1()* statement, was able to continue to its final print statement. But it didn't wait for the child to finish. With time sharing, the two processes took turns, and the parent finished before the child did. The one missing ingredient is something to make the parent wait until the child is finished. That ingredient is the appropriately named *wait()* function.

The *wait()* System Function

The *wait()* function causes a parent to stop running and await the termination of a child process. The *wait()* function feeds back two numbers to its calling function. First, it returns the PID of the defunct child. Second, using a pointer argument, *wait()* provides the exit status of the completed child process. Here is an example:

```
/* date6.c -- fork and wait */
main()
{
    int id, wid, status;

    printf("Here comes the date.\n");
    if ( (id = fork() ) == 0) {    /* select child process */
        printf("PID is %d and ID is %d\n", getpid(), id);
        execl("/bin/date", "date", 0);
        }
    wid = wait(&status);          /* wait for child to finish */
    printf("That was the date.\n");    /* parent continues */
    printf("wid = %d and status = %d\n", wid, status);
}
```

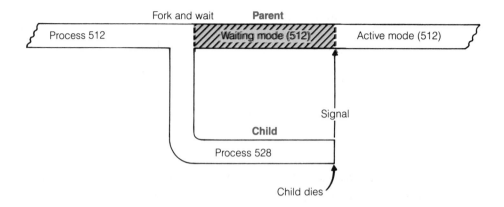

Figure 8.13
The Fork and Wait Method

Compile and run:

```
$ cc -o date6 date6.c
$ date6
Here comes the date.
PID is 2482 and ID is 0
Thu Jul 26 11:54:37 1984 PDT
That was the date.
wid is 2482 and status is 0
$
```

A program that generates several children needs a wait for each child; a wait with no child to wait for returns a value of -1. In a situation with several children, the return value of *wait()* (the PID or else -1) can be used to specify which child is being waited for. This is a typical statement used in such programs:

```
while ((pid = wait(&status)) != id && pid != -1) ;
```

We use the same notation as in the sample program, so *id* is the PID value returned by *fork()*, and *pid* is the PID value returned by *wait()*. This loop ends when the proper child is detected (the correct PID is returned) or if there are no children left (-1 returned). Then the program can go on to process the next statement.

Summarizing, if you want a C program to run a UNIX command file and then resume running, you can use the library function *system()* or you can use a combination of the *fork()*, *execl()*, and *wait()* system calls (which, basically, is how *system()* is put together). Usually *system()* is adequate, but certain redirected or interactive programs may require a customized job using the system calls.

Table 8.3 Common Interrupts

Symbolic Name	Signal Number	Description
SIGHUP	1	Hangup (sent when phone is hung up)
SIGINT	2	Interrupt (typically [CTRL] C key)
SIGQUIT	3	Quit (typically [CTRL] \)
SIGILL	4	Illegal instruction
SIGFPE	8	Floating-point exception
SIGKILL	9	Kill
SIGSYS	12	Bad argument to system call

HOW TO TRAP SIGNALS: *signal()*

There is one feature of shell scripts that we have not yet duplicated for C programs, and that is signal trapping. Let's take a quick look at that.

Most programs are terminated if you type the interrupt key (usually [Control] C or [Break]) while they are running. This key sends a particular signal, the *interrupt* signal, to the process, causing it to terminate, or *die*. A process notices when this or any of several other signals is sent, and the default response to these signals is to terminate the program. The *signal()* function, however, allows you to specify an alternative response to the reception of a signal.

First, what are the signals? The exact number will depend on the system, but there are several standard signals. The signals are designated by number, and the file *<signal.h>* provides symbolic names for them. Table 8.3 provides a list of symbolic names, signal numbers, and brief descriptions for the most common interrupts.

The *kill* signal is special in that a program is *not* allowed to ignore it. Some signals, like 1, 2, 3, and 9, are initiated by the user. Some, like 4, 8, and 12, are generated by the system.

Suppose we want a program to ignore telephone hangups. Then we would use *signal()* this way:

```
signal(SIGHUP, SIG_IGN);
```

The function takes two arguments. The first signifies the signal to be *caught* (here *SIGHUP*), and the second indicates the action to be taken (here *SIG_IGN*). The first argument could be expressed as a number (1, in this case) but the symbolic representation is more mnemonic. It is also more likely to be independent of the particular UNIX system. The second argument is a pointer to a function. Two special pointers to function are defined for this purpose in the *<signal.h>* file. They are *SIG_IGN*, which causes the process to ignore the signal, and *SIG_DFL*, which indicates taking the system default action of terminating the process. Otherwise, you can use a pointer to the function that *you* wish to be executed; in this case the function should be declared at the beginning of the program. And how do you get a pointer to a function in C? If the function you want is, for instance, *bailout()*, then the name *bailout* without the parentheses is a pointer to that function, just as *name* would be a pointer to the array *name[]*.

Let's see a few examples using signals. First,

```
#include <signal.h>
    . . .
signal (SIGHUP, SIG_IGN) ;
signal (SIGINT, SIG_IGN) ;
```

is the equivalent of the shell script command

```
trap ' ' 1 2
```

Both cause the program to ignore signals 1 and 2. If we wanted the C program to stop ignoring these two signals later on, we could use

```
signal (SIGHUP,  SIG_DFL) ;
signal (SIGINT,  SIG_DFL) ;
```

Only the portion of the program between this pair and the earlier pair of *signal()* calls would be immune to the two signals.

Now let's supply our own response to a signal:

```
/* trapper.c -- traps a signal    version 1.0 */
#include <signal.h>
main ()
{
   int i;
   void alter () ;     /* declare function used by signal () */

   signal (SIGINT, alter) ;
   for (i = 0;  i < 50;  i++)  {
     printf ("ho ho ho ho\n") ;
     sleep (2) ;           /* pauses for 2 seconds */
     }
}
void alter ()   /* the alternative response to SIGINT */
{
   printf ("I can't stop! \n") ;
}
```

Recall that *void* is a new C-type used for functions that don't return a value. If your system doesn't support that type, use *int* or else *#define void* as *int*. Compile and run the program:

```
$ cc trapper.c
$ a.out
ho ho ho ho
ho ho ho ho
ho ho ho ho Control C
I can't stop!
ho ho ho ho
ho ho ho ho Control C
$
```

Hmm! It worked, but it only worked once. The second interrupt signal stopped it. The reason for this behavior is that when *signal()* catches a signal (but not when it ignores one), it gets reset to its default value. If we don't want this to happen, then we have to reset *signal()* after it catches a signal. Since the first thing it does after catching an interrupt is go to the function *alter()*, we should reset *signal()* there:

```
/* trapper.c -- traps a signal repeatedly  version 1.1 */
#include <signal.h>
main()
{
    int i;
    void alter();

    signal(SIGINT,alter);
    for (i = 0; i < 50; i++) {
        printf("ho ho ho ho\n");
        sleep(2);
        }
}
void alter()
{
    signal(SIGINT, alter);    /* reset signal() */
    printf("I won't quit!\n");
}
```

Try it again:

```
$ cc trapper.c
$ a.out
ho ho ho ho
```

```
ho ho ho ho [Control] C
I can't stop!
ho ho ho ho [Control] C
I can't stop!
ho ho ho ho [Control] C
I can't stop!
ho ho ho ho [Control] \
Quit (core dump)
$
```

This time all the interrupts were caught and diverted. Fortunately we had another signal available to halt the program. The quit signal ([Control] \) is similar to the interrupt signal ([Control] C), except that it also saves a copy of the part of memory that held the instructions for the process being run. The copy is placed in a file called *core*, and it can be used for debugging purposes.

If we try running *trapper* in background, we find another problem:

```
$ a.out &
4218
$ ho ho ho ho [Control] \
ho ho ho ho [Control] C
I can't stop!
ho ho ho ho  kill 4218
$
```

Background jobs are supposed to ignore interrupt and quit signals. The quit signal is ignored here, but the interrupt signal somehow is getting through, causing the "I can't stop!" line to be printed. The reason is that the *signal()* statement in the program supercedes the *signal()* condition set up by the background command. UNIX programmers have developed a gambit to deal with this problem. It is based on the fact that *signal()* has a return value, and this return value is the previous (or initial) value of *signal()*'s second argument. Thus, when we use *signal()* in a program, we can check to see if it has already been set to *SIG_IGN*. If it has, then we can keep it that way. The actual form looks a bit peculiar. In our program, we would replace the first occurrence of

```
signal(SIGINT, alter);
```

with

```
if ( signal(SIGINT,SIG_IGN) != SIG_IGN)
    signal(SIGINT,alter);
```

The best way to see how this works is to run through two cases. First, suppose the *SIG_IGN* condition had been previously set. Then the returned value is *SIG_IGN* and the *if* comparison becomes

```
if ( SIG_IGN != SIG_IGN)
```

This comparison is false, so the action part of the *if* statement is skipped; the signal is ignored. If you send a second interrupt, the situation is the same, for the call *signal(SIGINT,SIG_IGN)* reset *signal()* to *SIG_IGN* in addition to returning the previous value. Thus if *SIG_IGN* is set initially (by, say, the background command), then all interrupts wind up ignored.

On the other hand, suppose the *SIG_IGN* condition was not set. Then the line

```
if ( signal(SIGINT,SIG_IGN) != SIG_IGN)
```

has two effects. First, it sets the condition to *SIG_IGN*. But, since the previous value was not *SIG_IGN*, the *if* inequality becomes true, and the next line is executed. This resets the condition to *alter*, and that function gets run.

A slightly more typical use than our example would have the called function do something like remove temporary files, much as we did with shell scripts. However, we decided to use an example that made the workings of *signal()* more easily visible. We'll show a more typical use in Chapter 9.

CONCLUSION

In this chapter we have discussed the following points: how to have programs choose between reading standard input and reading a file, how to add options to a program, how to have a program read several files, how to get information from the system, how to run command files and create new processes, and how to catch system signals.

ANSWERS TO QUESTIONS IN CHAPTER 8

8.1 *cnum[index++]* increases the array index by one, while *cnum[index]++* increases the value of the array element by one. *cnum[index++]++* does both operations.

8.2 `charct ch8 | sort +1n` (The *+1n* means skip the first field (the character name) and sort numerically.)

8.3 `printf("The value of gross - tax is %d\n", gross - tax);`

8.4 a. *argv[1]* is a pointer to the string *harpo*, and its value is the address of the beginning of the string, the memory location holding the ''h''.

b. *argv[1][2]* is the third element of the string, the letter ''r''.

c. *argv[1]* now points to the next string (*zeppo*), so *argv[1][2]* is the third element of that string, the letter ''p''.

d. *argv[1]* (at the end of c.) pointed to the "z" in *zeppo*. Incrementing a pointer by one makes it point to the next address, the one holding "e". Thus *argv[1][0]* would now be "e", not "z".

8.5 The first loop processes only arguments with initial hyphens, while the second loop processes any argument. However, because it follows the first loop, only arguments without initial hyphens ever reach it.

8.6 `char *path, *getenv();`
      `path = getenv("PATH");`

8.7 a. `strcpy(scratch, argv[1]);`
b. `strcat(scratch, "floppy");`
c. `if (strcmp("HI", argv[2]) == 0)`
            `printf("HO");`
d. `ps = strchr(scratch, 'q');`

8.8 `stat("farm", &toad);`
`printf("%ld\n", toad.st_size);`
(The *TYPES(5)* entry reveals that *off_t* means type *long* for the system described by the manual.)

8.9 We want to leave the last three bits unaltered and to turn the rest off. Hence the last three bits of the mask should be *1*s and the rest *0*s. So the mask would be 0000000000000111 in binary, or *07* in octal.

EXERCISES

1. Modify our *show* program of Chapter 7 so that it will read either standard input or else one or more files named in the command line. Have it skip unreadable files.

2. Modify Exercise 1 so that the *show* program will interpret a lone hyphen as designating the standard input. Thus a command like

   `grep fowl will | show farm -`

   would output first the contents of *farm* and then the output from the *grep* command.

3. Modify the ever-burgeoning *show* program so that it has a -*h* option that, when activated, causes the program to precede each file with the filename sandwiched between two blank lines. For standard input, have it print *standard input* in lieu of a filename.

4. Write a program that takes one or more file or directory names as command-line input and reports the following information on the file:
   a. File type
   b. Read, write, and execute permissions (use the rwx format)
   c. Number of links
   d. Time of last access
      (Note: the *st_atime* structure element holds the time in the same form that the *time(2)* system call provides. Use *ctime(3)* to place this in a more readable form.)

5. Write a program that takes a UNIX command as a command-line argument and that then runs that command.

9

WORKING WITH UNIX C FILES AND GRAPHICS

In this chapter you will find:

9

Working with UNIX C Files and Graphics

In this chapter we will look at several interesting and useful topics concerning UNIX C. First, we will investigate dynamic memory allocation, whereby a program can request additional memory as it needs it. We'll develop an instructional example illustrating its use, and this example will involve structures and pointers. These are heavily used features in C programming, but many new C programmers find them a bit obscure at first. Working with them helps breed familiarity (but not, we hope, contempt).

Memory allocation deals with program memory, typically CPU memory. When a program ends, so does the associated memory. To preserve the results of a program, we can place them in a file, which can be stored in a more permanent form of memory, such as a hard disk, magnetic tape, or floppy disk. Often the most efficent way to do this is to use binary files, which store data in the same binary format used in program memory. Again, we will develop a simple, instructional program to illustrate the basics.

Once we create a file, we should worry about controlling access to it. We will look at two aspects of that problem. The first is arranging it so that the file can be altered only by using the associated program and not, say, by someone using a system editor. The second is file locking — that is, allowing only one user at a time to work on a file.

Finally, for a complete change of pace, we will look at the standard UNIX graphics package.

For each of these topics, we will develop examples that bridge the gap between simplified introductions and full-blown developments. Thus we will skimp on such matters as error checking and options in order to concentrate on the new ideas.

DYNAMIC MEMORY ALLOCATION

One purpose of declarations in C is to inform the compiler how much memory need be allotted for data. For instance, the declaration

```
int foxholes[20];
```

informs the compiler that it should set aside storage for 20 adjacent *int*-sized memory units. In many kinds of programs, however, we do not know in advance how much memory will be needed. For example, a program might read in data up to an end-of-file and then sort or otherwise process the data. In a case like that, one could set aside an array of, say, 1000 elements, and terminate input if this value is reached before end-of-file. A better approach, however, is to use dynamic memory allotment. This means obtaining and assigning new memory as needed. If the user inputs only a few items, then only a little memory need be allocated. If, however, the user needs to enter many items, she doesn't run into an arbitrary 1000-item limit. The UNIX C library offers several memory-management functions dealing with memory allotment, and we will look at them next.

Memory Allocation with *malloc()*

The most basic memory function in the C library is *malloc()* (for memory allocation). Its declaration looks like this:

```
char *malloc(size)
unsigned size;
```

Its argument (*size*) indicates the amount of memory, in bytes, that you require. *Malloc()* finds a block of memory of at least the requested size and returns a pointer to the first byte of the block. The calling program then makes use of this pointer value to find the memory location. Dynamically allocated memory has no name or label in the sense that a declared variable does. It can be accessed only though using a pointer.

Here is a simple program that illustrates how *malloc()* can be used:

```
/* name.c -- a simple use of malloc()   */
#include <stdio.h>
main()
{
  char temp[40];              /* temporary storage  */
  char *fname, *lname;        /* pointers to storage */
  char *malloc();             /* declare the type for malloc() */

  puts("What's your first name?");
  scanf("%39s", temp);                /* read into temp storage */
  fname = malloc(strlen(temp) + 1); /* allot storage */
  strcpy(fname, temp);                /* copy into allotted storage */
  puts("What's your last name?");
  scanf("%39s", temp);                /* reuse temp storage  */
```

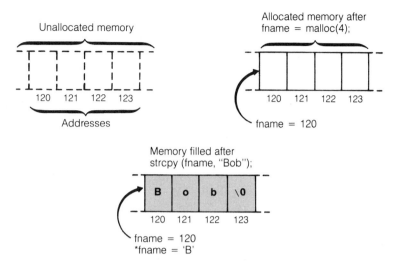

Figure 9.1
Using *malloc()*

```
    lname = malloc(strlen(temp) + 1);
    strcpy(lname,temp);
    printf("Hello, %s %s\n", fname, lname);
}
```

Note that we did have to declare some temporary storage (*temp[]*) in order to have a location in memory into which we could read input. This we made large enough to handle most instances of input. Suppose, then, that the user responds to the first question with *Bob*. This uses only 4 bytes out of the 40 in the *temp* array. (Remember, strings need one extra byte for the terminal '\0'.) Then *malloc()* obtains 4 bytes of memory. The address of this location is assigned to the pointer variable *fname*. Then the program copies *Bob* from *temp* to the location pointed to by *fname*. Thus, *fname* now points to where *Bob* is stored. Figure 9.1 illustrates this process. The whole process is repeated for the last name, reusing *temp* for temporary storage.

Question 9.1

Why do we have to declare *malloc()* in *main()*?

It is vital that the program keep track of where the new memory locations are. The pointers *fname* and *lname* are the only means that this program has of finding the stored names. Suppose, however, we wished to read in many names, not just two. How do we keep track of all the names? It would be awkward if we needed to declare separate pointers for each name. Fortunately, that isn't necessary. We will look at two approaches for keeping track of the new names. The first is to use contiguous, equally sized memory units. Then, knowing the beginning location of the memory block, we can use pointer arithmetic to move from name to name. The second approach is to create storage not only for the name (or whatever) but also for a pointer that will point to the next storage item. Although more complex than the first approach, this eliminates the requirement for contiguous, equally sized memory units. Let's examine these approaches in detail.

Extending a Memory Block with *realloc()*

One way to keep track of new memory is by making sure that it is tacked on to the end of old memory. We can do this by using the *realloc()* (for reallocation) function. This function is described in Section 3 of the manual under the *malloc()* heading. Here is its declaration:

```
char *realloc(ptr,size)
char *ptr;
unsigned size;
```

This function takes as arguments a pointer (*ptr*) to an existing memory block and a size in bytes. It then changes the size of the block to *size* and returns a pointer to the beginning of the block. It can happen that changing the size of a block requires moving it to a different location in memory, so the returned pointer value may be different from the original value passed to the function. The contents of the new block are unchanged up to the lesser of the new and old sizes. Figure 9.2 shows *realloc()* at work.

The important fact for us about *realloc()* is that if we use successive calls requesting additional memory, the new memory will be contiguous with the (possibly moved) old. This is not necessarily the case with *malloc()*. Note, however, that *realloc()* doesn't start from scratch; it needs an existing memory location to start with.

Here is a sample program using *realloc()*. This program prompts the user to enter a list of movie titles. Input continues until end-of-file or until the user hits ⌈Return⌉ at the beginning of a line. Then the program reprints each movie title, asking the user to enter the number of times he has seen it. (This gives us an

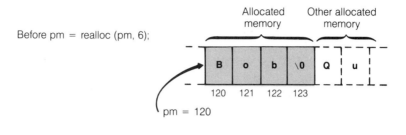

Before pm = realloc (pm, 6);

pm = 120

After pm = realloc (pm, 6);

pm = 152   Memory block is expanded
            and relocated

Figure 9.2
Using *realloc()*

opportunity to show how to access the stored data.) A structure of fixed size is used to store each title and the number of times viewed. Finally, the program prints out its results: movie names and times seen.

The main intent of this program is to show how *realloc()* can be used to create memory and to demonstrate methods for accessing that memory. The secondary intent is to illustrate the use of structures and pointers-to-structures. Note those points as you read through the program. We'll discuss them in detail next.

```
/* movies1.c -- using realloc()   */
#include <stdio.h>
#define MLINE 81
struct movie { char title[MLINE];    /* movie title */
               int times;            /* times viewed */
             };
main()
{
    char temp[MLINE];                    /* temporary storage */
    int num = 0;                         /* number of movies   */
    int  index;
    char *malloc(), *realloc(), *gets();
    struct movie *ps, *pm;           /* pointers to memory */

    ps = NULL;                           /* initialize pointer */
    puts("Please enter a list of movie titles; a [return] at");
```

```
            puts("the beginning of a line terminates input.");
            while (gets(temp) != NULL && temp[0] != '\0')
                {
                if ( ps == NULL )                        /*  first pass */
                        ps = (struct movie *) malloc(sizeof (struct movie));
                else                                     /* later passes */
                        ps = (struct movie *) realloc(ps,
                            (num + 1 ) * sizeof (struct movie) );
                strcpy((ps + num)->title, temp);
                num++;                                   /* one more movie */
                }
        if (ps == NULL)
            {
            puts("No input: Bye!");
            exit(0);
            }
        printf("Now enter the times seen for each title as it is shown.\n");
        for ( index = 0; index < num; index++ )
            {                                        /* looping by count */
            puts( (ps + index)->title);
            scanf("%d", &(ps + index)->times);
            }
        for ( pm = ps; (pm -ps) < num; pm++ )    /* pointer looping */
            printf("%s: %d\n", pm->title, pm->times);
    }
```

First, see how the memory functions are used. The first pass through the read-in loop, the *malloc()* function is used to create memory for one *movie*-sized structure. The structure has two components: a character array to hold the movie title, and an integer to hold the times viewed. Subsequent passes use *realloc()* to add to (and possibly move) the memory block. Each time, one more *movie* structure's worth of memory is added. Note that the *realloc()* argument is the total size, not the added size, of memory.

Second, note that we use a type cast on the return values of *malloc()* and *realloc()*. These functions return pointers to type *char*, while the program requires pointers to type *struct movie*. The type cast makes this conversion. Thus the statement

```
ps = (struct movie *) malloc(sizeof (struct movie));
```

takes the pointer returned by *malloc()* and converts its type to *(struct movie *)*, that is, a pointer to a *movie* structure.

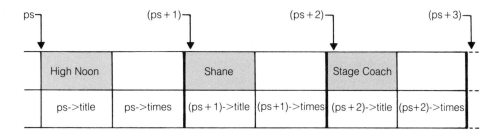

Figure 9.3
Pointers and Structure in Memory

Next, notice how pointers are used to refer to structure locations in memory. First, if *ps* is a pointer to a particular structure, then *ps->title* is the title component and *ps->times* is the times component of the structure. In this program *ps* always is a pointer to the beginning of the memory block. Hence it points to the first structure in memory. To find the second structure, we need only to add 1 to *ps*. This is a consequence of defining *ps* as a pointer to type *struct movie*. Adding 1 to a C pointer corresponds, in bytes, to adding a number of bytes equal to the size of the pointed-to object. So the sequence *(ps + 0), (ps + 1), (ps + 2)* would point to the first, second, and third structures in the memory block. It follows then, that *(ps +2)->title* refers to the title stored in the third structure in the block. Thus, we use *(ps + num)->title* to access the structures created in the first loop. See Figure 9.3.

The next two loops in the program illustrate two methods for cycling through the structures stored in memory. The first of the two *for* loops duplicates the method of the opening *while* loop: *(ps + num)* is used to access each structure in turn as *num* increases from 0 to its final value.

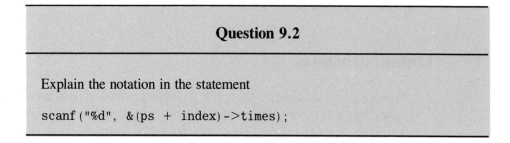

Question 9.2

Explain the notation in the statement

```
scanf ("%d", & (ps + index) ->times);
```

In the second *for* loop, we initialize a pointer *pm* to the beginning of the block *(ps)*, then use pointer incrementation *(pm ++)* to march through the block, structure by structure.

Those are the main points. The rest of the program is fairly rudimentary. For instance, we don't guard against movie titles longer than *MLINE* in length, and we don't check input for errors. One point we should note, however, is the control statement for the *while* loop:

```
while (gets(temp) != NULL && temp[0] != '\0')
```

The *gets()* function returns a pointer to the read-in string if successful, and returns the *NULL* pointer if it encounters *EOF*. Thus, the first comparision in the loop test terminates the loop if *EOF* is encountered. The second test (*temp[0] != '\0'*) terminates the loop if the user hits ⌈Return⌉ at the beginning of a line; in that case, *temp* is assigned the empty string, which this test detects. Here is a sample run of the program after it has been compiled:

```
$ a.out
Please enter a list of movie titles; a [return] at
the beginning of a line terminates input.
Mrs. Blicket's Holiday
Star Chores
Kung-Fu Rascals
⌈Return⌉
Now enter the times seen for each title as it is shown.
Mrs. Blicket's Holiday
3
Star Chores
5
Kung-Fu Rascals
2
Mrs. Blicket's Holiday: 3
Star Chores: 5
Kung-Fu Rascals: 2
$
```

Using Linked Structures

Now let's look at another approach to keeping track of dynamically allocated memory. We will modify the *movie* structure so that it has one more member, a pointer that points to the next structure. With this approach, there is no necessity that the structures be stored adjacently, for we rely upon the stored pointer to link one structure to the next. (This is an example of a linked list, one of many data structures that can be easily implemented using C structures.) We'll illustrate this approach with a modification of the preceding program.

```
/* movies2.c  -- using linked structures  */
#include <stdio.h>
#define MLINE 81
typedef struct movie {
                    char title[MLINE];   /* movie title */
                    int times;           /* times viewed */
                    struct movie *pnext; /* ptr to next strct */
                    } *MOVPTR;
main()
{
   char temp[MLINE];
   char *malloc(), *gets();
   MOVPTR ps, ps0, pprev; /* ptrs to current structure, first
                              structure, and preceding structure */

   ps0  = NULL;              /* no structures yet */
   puts("Please enter a list of movie titles; a [return] at");
   puts("the beginning of a line terminates input.");
   while (gets(temp) != NULL && temp[0] != '\0')
       {
       ps = (MOVPTR) malloc(sizeof (struct movie));
       if (ps0 == NULL)     /* first pass */
           ps0 = ps;            /* store initial pointer */
       else                 /* later passes */
           pprev->pnext = ps; /* store ps in previous structure */
       strcpy(ps->title, temp);   /* copy title */
       ps->pnext = NULL;          /* set pnext to NULL */
       pprev = ps;                /* save ps value */
       }
   if (ps0 == NULL) {        /* no data read in */
       puts("No input! Bye");
       exit(0);
       }
   puts("Now enter the times seen for each title as it is shown.");
   ps = ps0;                      /* set ps to first structure */
   do  {
       puts( ps->title);
       scanf("%d", &ps->times);
       ps = ps->pnext;            /* advance to next structure */
       } while ( ps != NULL);
   ps = ps0;
   do  {
       printf("%s: %d\n", ps->title, ps->times);
       ps = ps->pnext;
       } while (ps != NULL);
}
```

319

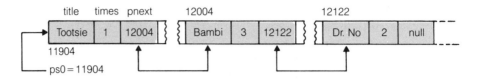

Figure 9.4
Linked Structures

What are the changes? First, as promised, we added a new member to the *movie* structure. This new member is a pointer to type *struct movie*, giving the structure the ability to hold a pointer to another structure of the same type. This is the most significant change to the program. We also used the *typedef* statement to establish *MOVPTR* as a synonym for "pointer to type *struct movie*". This is merely a cosmetic change that simplifies the declarations and type cast in the main program. These could have been left as they were in the preceding program.

The remaining changes are accommodations to the linked structure approach. When a title is read, the location of a memory block is assigned to the pointer *ps*. Thus, in this version, *ps* points to the current structure being filled. In the preceding version, *ps* always pointed to the first structure. Since *ps* changes each loop, we use *ps0* the first time through the loop to save the address of the very first structure. Since *ps0* is preset to *NULL* before the loop is entered, the program can use the value of *ps0* to identify the first passage through the loop:

```
if (ps0 == NULL)    /* first pass */
    ps0 = ps;       /* store initial pointer */
  else              /* later passes */
    prev->pnext = ps; /* store ps in previous structure */
```

On each subsequent pass through the loop, the *pnext* component of the previous structure is set to the current *ps* value. Thus each structure contains a pointer to the next structure. See Figure 9.4. Of course, the final structure has no following structure to point to, so we set its *pnext* component to *NULL*. Subsequently, we use the *NULL* value to mark the end of the list of linked structures.

To cycle through the list of structures, we set *ps* equal to *ps0*, thus having it point to the first structure. We process the structure, then have *ps* point to the next structure:

```
ps = ps->pnext;
```

This structure is processed, and so on, until the *NULL* pointer shows up, marking the final structure.

Question 9.3

Since the control test for a *do...while* loop is not examined until the *end* of each loop, a *do...while* loop always attempts to execute its instructions at least once. Does that pose problems with the *movies2.c* program?

Using Unequally Sized Memory Units

One extravagance of the *movies2.c* program is that we are still allotting 81 bytes for the title member of the structure, even though the actual title may not require that much space. We can be more frugal with memory by using *malloc()* again in the program, this time to find just enough storage to hold each movie title. The key is to redefine the *movie* structure. Let's define it this way:

```
struct movie {
            char *title;   /* pointer to title */
            int times;     /* times viewed */
            struct movie *pnext; /* ptr to next strct */
            };
```

Now the structure is much smaller than before, for a pointer requires much less storage than an 81-byte array. The *title* member will be used to hold an address returned by *malloc()* for movie title storage. Figure 9.5 illustrates the differences between the old and new structure definitions.

Let's check the mechanics of using the new structure. Suppose we have read a value into *temp*. First, as before, we allot space for the *movie* structure:

```
ps = (MOVPTR) malloc(sizeof (struct movie) );
```

Then we create enough storage to hold the movie title, placing the address in the *title* member of the structure:

```
ps->title = malloc( strlen(temp) + 1);
```

Then we copy the title into this storage area:

```
strcpy(ps->title, temp);
```

321

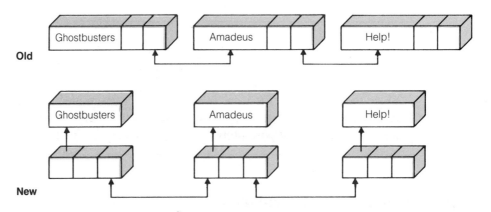

Old

New

Figure 9.5
The Old and New Structures

Those of you that favor the compact, obscure C style may wish to combine the last two statements into one:

```
strcpy(ps->title = malloc(strlen(temp)+1), temp);
```

Question 9.4

a. How does this combined statement work?
b. How must we modify *movies2.c* to utilize this new approach?

Other Memory Allocation Functions: *calloc()* and *free()*

Two other memory functions are listed under the *malloc()* heading. The *calloc()* function assigns memory and initializes it to zero. The *free()* function frees memory previously allocated by *malloc()*. Let's take a brief look at each.

Here is the declaration for the *calloc()* function:

```
char *calloc(nelem, elsize)
unsigned nelem, elsize;
```

The *nelem* argument specifies the number of elements desired, and the *elsize* argument gives the size of each element. The elements are initialized to zero, and *calloc( )* returns a pointer to the beginning of the memory block. This is a convenient function for creating and initializing an array, for example.

The *free( )* declaration looks like this:

```
free(ptr)
char *ptr;
```

Here *ptr* should be a pointer to a block previously allocated by *malloc( )*. The function call *free(ptr)* then frees that block of memory for future memory allocation calls. The contents of the block are left undisturbed by the *free( )* call.

The memory functions we have discussed are part of the C library. They are based on the system calls *brk( )* and *sbrk( )*, discussed in Section 2 of the manual. The library calls, however, are more convenient to work with.

BINARY FILES AND TEXT FILES

The memory functions we have been discussing allocate random access memory while a program is running. When the program ends, so do the memory assignments. The variables we have so carefully declared, the values we so cunningly calculated, the data we so diligently acquired — all vanish to make room for the next program, testifying to the ephemeral nature of existence. But don't despair. If we want to preserve data from one running of a program to the next, we can save the data in permanent memory, typically on a hard disk. That is, we can create a file and store the data there. Next time the program is run, it can retrieve the data from the file and add more data. Such a file is a simple example of a database. A sophisticated program would be able to add to, subtract from, alter, and operate upon a database. That is beyond the scope of this book, but there are several basic matters we can go into. In particular, we will look into how to transfer data between linked structures and files, how to *lock* a file while it is being used, and how to give a program read and write permissions that the user lacks. First, though, let's look into the types of files available.

When you wish to copy information from program memory into a file, you have a choice of two basic file types: binary files and text files. In a binary file, data are stored in the same form in which they are stored in program memory. If the system uses a two-byte *int*, then an integer is stored as a binary number in two bytes of file space. In a text file, however, numerical data is converted to characters and stored as a sequence of characters, one character to a byte. Thus the integer 2 would be stored as the character '2' (one byte), while the integer 31051 would be stored as the 5 characters '3', '1', '0', '5', '1' (five bytes).

One advantage of a text file is that we can inspect its contents easily, using, for example, *cat* or an editor. A binary file, however, typically would be accessed through a program or set of programs designed to be used with that particular file.

The advantages of the binary file are compactness (perhaps), speed, and integrity. Let's look at each point briefly.

Whether or not a binary file is more compact than a text file depends on the nature of the data. Character data are stored in the same fashion in both files, a character to a byte, typically using ASCII code. An integer, regardless of size, occupies a fixed amount of binary storage. This may be two bytes for one machine (such as a PDP™ 11) or four bytes for another (such as a VAX™) or some other size, but for a given machine, the size is constant. Storage in a text file, however, takes up a number of bytes equal to the number of digits in the number. Thus, storing a set of two- and three-digit integers as a text file on a VAX will take less space than storing them in a binary file using four bytes per integer. But storing a set of six-to-eight digit integers will take less space in a binary file than in a text file for the same system.

The speed advantage for binary files comes from the fact that numerical data is copied directly to and from binary files without the need to convert back and forth between binary forms and character forms.

It is this lack of data conversion that makes binary files more reliable, too. The chief problem facing text files is the handling of floating-point numbers. There may not be an exact correspondence of value between the binary form and decimal representation used by the text form. Round-off errors can occur. In short, a number converted from binary to text and back to binary may not have the same value it began with. (It's a bit like the apocryphal story about an English-to-Russian-to-English computer translation that converts ''hydraulic ram'' to ''water sheep.'').

Next, we will look at how I/O can be handled for text files and for binary files.

TEXT FILE I/O

Text file I/O is accomplished through the familiar I/O functions of the *stdio.h* package, such as *fprintf()*, *fscanf()*, *getc()*, *putc()*, *fgets()*, and *fputs()*. To handle numerical I/O, we use the *%d*, *%f*, and related format specifiers for *fscanf()* and *fprintf()*. Suppose, for example, we are using the linked structures of *movies2.c*. Then we have these declarations:

```
#define MLINE 81
typedef struct movie {
                char title[MLINE];    /* movie title */
                int times;            /* times viewed */
                struct movie *pnext; /* ptr to next strct */
                } *MOVPTR;

MOVPTR ps, ps0, pprev; /* ptrs to current structure, first
                            structure, and preceding structure */
```

Suppose, too, that *fp* is a pointer-to-*FILE* identifying the target file:

```
FILE *fp;   /* pointer to data file */
```

Then we can copy the contents of the structures into the opened file with a loop like this:

```
ps = ps0;
do {
    fprintf(fp, "%s\n%d\n", ps->title, ps->times);
    ps = ps->next;
    }  while (ps != NULL);
```

Note that we don't copy the *pnext* member of the structure into the file. It represents a location in program memory and has no connection with where things are stored in a file.

Each cycle of the loop writes the information from one structure. The combined information about one movie constitutes a *record*, and the individual items within the record are termed *fields*. In this example, we have a two-field record. When writing records, it is important to have some method of retrieving them. That is why we inserted newlines in the format statement. Certainly, the format ''%s%d'' would have been more compact, but a program trying to read a file would have a difficult time with the following:

```
Amarcord3Samurai Part 35The Gods Must Be Crazy4
```

Where does one record end and another begin? One solution is to use a *record separator*, a special symbol to separate one record from the next. Within a record, we can use a *field separator* to separate one field from the next. In our example, we used the newline (*'\n'*) for both purposes. It produces the following format:

```
Amarcord
3
Samurai Part 3
5
The Gods Must Be Crazy
4
```

This format makes it much simpler to implement the reverse process, reading from the file to the program. Let's see how that can be done. You might be inclined to use *fscanf()*, since it is more or less the inverse of *fprintf()*. Unfortunately, although the *%s* format for *fprintf()* prints an entire string, the same format for *fscanf()* just reads in a single word. However, since we have terminated the title string with a newline, we can use *fgets()*, since it reads input up to a newline. One problem with *fgets()*, however, is that it includes the newline character as part of the returned string. We can use the *strchr()* function of the C library string functions to locate the newline in the string and replace it with a '\0'. (Many UNIX systems use the older name *index()* instead of *strchr()*.) Then we still need *fscanf()* to read in the numerical portion. Here is one approach to reading the contents of a file into a set of linked structures. In it we assume the same declarations as before, along with a temporary storage array, a character pointer, and the string function *strchr()*:

```
char temp[MLINE];
char *pnl, *strchr();

pprev = NULL;
while ( fgets(temp, MLINE, fp) != EOF)
    {
    ps = (MOVPTR) malloc( sizeof (struct movie));
    if (pprev == NULL)
        ps0 = ps;
    else
        pprev->pnext = ps;
    if ( (pnl = strchr(temp, '\n')) != NULL)
        *pnl = '0';     /* find and replace \n with \0 */
    strcpy(ps->title, temp);
    fscanf(fp,"%d", &ps->times);
    getchar();     /* get rid of newline after times value */
    ps->next = NULL;
    }
```

This fragment reads the data file up to EOF, placing the results in linked structures created by *malloc()*. There are two complications to explain. First, as we indicated, we need to remove the newline character that *fgets()* leaves in the string. The *strchr()* function takes two arguments: a pointer to a string and a character. It returns a pointer to the first occurrence of the character in the string. We use the function to find the terminal '\n' in *temp[]*, and we replace it with a null character ('\0'). See Figure 9.6. The *strchr()* function returns a pointer to *NULL* if it fails to find the character.

Question 9.5

The program checks to see if *strchr()* does, indeed, find a newline character. Is it possible that *temp[]* will not contain a newline character?

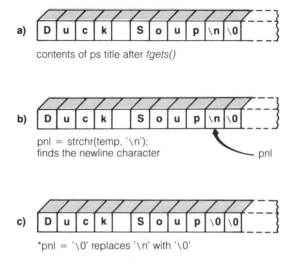

a) contents of ps title after *fgets()*

b) pnl = strchr(temp, '\n');
finds the newline character
pnl

c) *pnl = '\0' replaces '\n' with '\0'

Figure 9.6
Replacing the Newline Character

The second complication is that we need to clear the newline after reading the *times* member. The *%d* mode of *fscanf()* leaves the input file pointer pointing to the next character after the integer, in this case, a newline character. If this character is left unread, then the next call to *fgets()* would read the newline character as an empty line. A single call to *getchar()* clears the newline character, allowing *fgets()* on the following loop to start at the beginning of the next line.

Question 9.6

This problem of clearing a line of input before a call to *fgets()* or *gets()* is a common one, particularly in interactive programs. How could we generalize our solution so that it would handle not only a solitary newline character but also any intervening characters between the last character read and the newline character?

Instead of developing a complete program using a text file for storage, let's consider a drawback. Suppose we decide to expand the information held in the *movie* structure. We could add, say, the producer, the director, the studio, a viewing rating, a critical rating, and the year released. Extending the technique we have been using would require a separate *fgets()* or *fscanf()* statement for each of these members. It would be much more convenient if we could read in and read out all the structure information *as a single unit*; that is, read and write information a record at a time. This becomes possible when we use a binary file. We will look at how to handle binary I/O and then develop a complete program using that approach.

BINARY I/O

The system calls *read()* and *write()* read and write data as bytes, thus performing binary I/O. Suppose, for instance, we have a structure we wish to copy into a file:

```
#define MLINE 81
struct movinfo {
                char title[MLINE];
                int times;
                } sample;
```

Then, if *fd* is a file descriptor, the system call

```
write(fd, &sample, sizeof (struct movinfo));
```

copies the contents of the structure *sample* into the file specified by *fd*. The synopsis for *write()*, recall, (from Chapter 7) is

```
int write(fildes, buffer, nbytes)
int fildes;
char *buffer;
int nbytes;
```

Here, *fildes* is a file descriptor, and *buffer* is the address of the *nbytes* of contiguous memory we wish to copy. In our example, the address operator (&) supplies the address of the *sample* structure, and *sizeof (struct movinfo)* is the size of the structure in bytes. Thus our example copies one structure's worth of data into a file.

Similarly, the system call

```
read(fd, &sample, sizeof (struct movinfo));
```

copies one structure's worth of data from a file into the structure beginning at the address *&sample*.

However, as we discussed in Chapter 7, it is usually more convenient and efficient to use the standard I/O package. The members of this package that accomplish binary I/O are called *fread()* and *fwrite()*. Here are the synopses of these two functions:

```
#include <stdio.h>

int fread(ptr, nbytes, nitems, stream)
char *ptr;
int nbytes;
int nitems;
FILE *stream;

int fwrite(ptr, nbytes, nitems, stream)
char *ptr;
int nbytes;
int nitems;
FILE *stream;
```

The *ptr* argument is the beginning address of the location in program memory from which (*fwrite()*) or into which (*fread()*) data is to be taken or placed. The *nbytes* argument specifies, in bytes, the size of the memory chunks. The *nitems* argument specifies how many memory chunks, and *stream* is a pointer-to-*FILE* identifying which file is to be used. For example, to copy our *sample* stucture into a file identified by *fp*, we would use this call:

```
fwrite(&sample, sizeof (struct movinfo), 1, fp);
```

If we wished to copy an array of 10 such structures, we would use an *nitems* value of 10. The total number of bytes written is *nbytes* * *nitems*.

To read information from a file back into the *sample* structure, use this call:

```
fread(&sample, sizeof (struct movinfo), 1, fp);
```

Now that we've seen the basics of binary I/O, let's use them in a program.

USING A BINARY FILE

Since we have already developed a program (*movies2.c*) that collects and saves input data in structures, let's modify it so that it maintains a binary file for more permanent storage of movie data. There are many possible extensions we could make, such as recalling data from a file, merging it with new data, deleting or modifying data, sorting it alphabetically or by times viewed or length of title, counting the total number of titles, calculating the average times viewed, extending the structure to include year of release, director, dollars grossed, and so forth. But since our chief purpose is to illustrate access to and from a binary file, we'll leave most of those other possibilities as exercises for the interested reader. Instead, we will concentrate on the most basic operations.

Outlining the Program

A sensible first step is to decide what we would like the program to do. The central idea is that it should let us use a binary file to store movie data. The first time the program is run, the file will be created and will be filled with the initial input from the user. Subsequent uses will allow the user to add to that database. To let the user see what is happening, the program should print out the file contents, if any, and also should show the user what will be in the file after a session with the program.

We can outline the program this way:

```
if the data file exists
    open it
    read its contents into program memory
    show the user the data
get new data from user, adding it to old list, if any
show the revised data
save the revised data in the file
```

This bare-bones plan suggests some obvious program modules, which we will implement as separate functions. We'll create functions to do the following:

- Load the contents of a file into program memory. Call this function *getfile()*.
- Load user input into program memory. Call this function *getdata()*.
- Load the contents of program memory into a file. Call this function *storedata()*.
- Print the contents of program memory on the screen. Call this function *showdata()*.

Before designing the program, including these functions, we need to decide on what data form to use for the information we will acquire and save. The implementation of the various functions will depend on that choice. Because *fwrite()* can be used to transfer a whole structure as a unit, a structure is the obvious choice. However, the *movie* structure we used earlier contains some information (the pointer to the next structure) that is pointless to store in a file. Let's modify our original structure to something more suitable, then design the appropriate functions.

Representing the Data

Our original *movie* structure contained three items: the movie title, the times viewed, and a pointer to the next structure. Viewed another way, it contains two classes of data: information about movies, and information about another structure. This suggests reorganizing the *movie* structure so that it has two items: a structure containing movie information, and a pointer to the next structure. We can do that with this set of definitions:

```
#define MLINE 81
struct movinfo {
            char title[MLINE];
            int times;
            };
  struct movie {
            struct movinfo data;    /* collected movie data*/
            struct movie *pnext;    /* ptr to next strct   */
            };
```

Adding new kinds of data, such as running time for the movie, can be done by redefining *movinfo*.

Now, when we go to place information in a file, we can use the *data* member of a *movie* structure as the structure that is to be copied. The *data* member is the program structure corresponding to the file record.

Accessing a Structure Within a Structure

How do we access data in a structure within a structure? Suppose, for instance, we have these declarations:

```
struct movie sample, *ps;
```

That is, *sample* is the *name* of a *movie* structure and *ps* is a *pointer* to a *movie* structure. Suppose, too, that *ps* is set to point to *sample*, that is, it is assigned *sample*'s address:

```
ps = &sample;
```

Then the name of the *data* component of the *movie* structure can be expressed as

```
sample.data
```

or as

```
ps->data
```

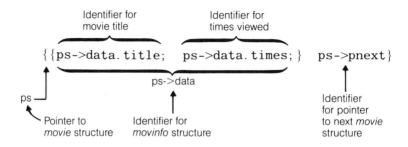

Figure 9.7
Identifiers for a *movie* Structure

Either represents a *movinfo* type of structure. (Remember, the dot (.) membership operator is used with structure names to yield a member, and the indirect membership operator (->) is used with pointer-to-structures to yield a member.)

The *times* component of the *data* structure then would be called

```
sample.data.times
```

or

```
ps->data.times
```

Here we just use the membership operator again. One important point to note is that although *ps* is a *pointer*, the combination *ps->data* is *not* a pointer. Its type is the type declared for *data*, which is *struct movinfo*. Similarly, *ps->data.times* is of type *int*, for that is the declared type for *times*. Keep in mind that the rightmost name in a structure member name identifies the type for the whole expression. Figure 9.7 summarizes the identification scheme.

Tracking the Data

Now that we have an appropriate data structure, let's outline a first draft for the program.

One problem we face is how do we keep track of where the data (old and new) are stored. Each structure, of course, points to the next one. But we need to keep track of the address of the first structure. Its contents will lead to the next structure, and so on. We'll use the same method as before, having the program assign the first address to a pointer variable called *ps0*. This assignment may take place in *getfile()* or in *getdata()*, depending on where the first data appear. Also, when the program goes to add new data to the list, it needs to know the address of the previous structure. This we will assign to the variable *pprev*. We mention these two pointers now, for the functions we discussed will need to use one or both of these pointers, as well as a file identifier, *fp*. These requirements will be reflected in the arguments and return values associated with the functions.

Here is an implementation of the outline. We show the main program first in the following listing. It uses the functions *getfile( )* to get information from the file, *showdata( )* to show the data, *getdata( )* to get user input, and *storedata( )* to place the results back in the binary file, which we've called *data.b*. We'll look at those functions after we examine the main program.

```
 /*  movies3.c -- uses a binary file */
#include <stdio.h>
#define MLINE 81
#define DATA "/usr/lucas/movie/data.b"
#define ENDLINE()   while ( getchar() != '\n')
struct movinfo    {
                     char title[MLINE];   /* movie title */
                     int times;           /* times viewed */
                   };

typedef struct movie {
                     struct movinfo data; /* collected info */
                     struct movie *pnext; /* ptr to next strct */
                     } *MOVPTR;
main()
{
    char temp[MLINE];
    char *malloc(), *gets();
    MOVPTR ps, ps0, pprev; /* ptrs to current structure, first
                              structure, and preceding structure */
    FILE *fp;        /* FILE pointer for data.b */
    void cpymem(), showdata(), storedata();
    MOVPTR getfile(), getdata();

    ps0 = pprev = NULL;   /* initialize structure pointers */
    if ( access(DATA,0) == 0)   /* does the file exist? */
        {        /* open file, exiting if attempt fails */
        if (( fp = fopen(DATA, "r")) == NULL) {
            perror(DATA);
            exit(1);
            }
        ps0 = getfile(fp, ps0, &pprev); /* get data from file */
```

```
            if  (ps0  ==  NULL)
                    puts ("The data file is empty");
            else  {
                    puts ("Here are the current file contents:");
                    showdata (ps0);        /* show the data */
                    }
            }
       ps0 = getdata (ps0, pprev);   /* get user input */
       if  (ps0 == NULL)  {
            puts ("No input! Bye");
            exit (0);
            }
       puts ("Here are the current movie data:");
       showdata (ps0);
       /* open file for writing, exiting if attempt fails */
       if  ((fp = fopen (DATA, "w"))  == NULL)  {
            perror (DATA);
            exit (1);
            }
       storedata (fp, ps0);   /* store data in file */
       fclose (fp);
    }
```

The comments in the listing explain several points about the program; here are
some additional points to note.

We used a *#define* statement to create an abbreviation for the data file. We used
a full (but hypothetical) pathname to identify the file. If we had just said

```
#define DATA "data.b"
```

then the system would assume the file is in your current working directory. Giving
the full pathname removes that possible source of confusion.

The program flow goes like this. Set the *ps0* and *pprev* pointers to *NULL*. Later,
we can compare their values to *NULL* in order to see if they have been assigned
new values or not. Use the *access()* function (see Chapter 7) to see if the file exists.
If it does, try to open it in the "read" mode. If that succeeds, have the *getfile()*
function load the file into program memory. Use the value returned to *ps0* to see
if the file was empty or not. If not empty, use *showdata()* to print out the list. Then
solicit new data, using *getdata()* to place the input into program memory. Again
check to see if *ps0* is *NULL* (no data) and quit if it is. Otherwise, show the
combined list of data with *showdata()*, open *data.b* for writing, and use *storedata()*
to place the information into the file. Note that the *fopen()* function creates the
data.b file if it did not exist prior to the call, and clears the file if it did exist.

Looking at the Functions

The choice of arguments and return values for the functions may seem strange, but they are dictated by the information flow in the program. Let's consider what information each function needs to know to do its task and what information it needs to pass back to the program.

First, consider the *getfile()* function, which has the most complex set of arguments. It needs to know what file to work with, so we provide it with *fp* as an argument. If it finds data in the file, it creates memory to hold it. It needs to let the rest of the program know the location of the first of the linked structures. To do this, it returns that address to the main program, in which the address is assigned to *ps0*. We also provide *ps0* as an argument to the function so that it can use an *if (ps0 = = NULL)* expression internally to test if it is on the first cycle of data read-in. (The code will make this point clearer.)

When *getfile()* finishes, it also has to let the main program know the location of the last structure filled so that *getdata()* can tack on the new data to the same list of linked structures. (Actually, it is not absolutely necessary for *getfile()* to do this, for *getdata()* could start at the first structure in the list and look through it until finding the last one. But it is friendlier to save *getdata()* the work.) How can *getfile()* transmit this data back to the main program? We've already used the function return value for *ps0*, so that avenue is closed. We could make *pprev* a global variable for *getdata()*. That is, we could include this declaration in the function:

```
extern MOVPRT pprev;
```

However, we got pointer happy and passed the *address* of *pprev* to *getfile()*. Then, *getfile()* can place the proper *pprev* value in that address, making it available to the main program.

The next listing shows the implementation of this scheme. The function itself follows the same pattern we used in *movies2.c*, except it takes input from the *data.b* file instead of the keyboard. Note that the *fread()* statement reads an entire record (title and times) into the temporary storage structure *movbuf*. We could have used

```
fread (&ps->data, sizeof (struct movinfo),1,fp)
```

to read directly into the *data* component of the *movie* structure, but this would require allocating memory for the structure before knowing for sure if there were any data to put into it.

We also defined a *cpymem()* function to copy the contents of the temporary location into the appropriate *movie* structure.

One point to notice in both *getfile()* and *cpymem()* is the use of pointers. We pass to *getfile()* the address of *pprev*. This address is a pointer to *pprev*, so we declare the formal argument *pptr* as a pointer-to-*MOVPTR*, since *MOVPTR* is *pprev*'s type. Within the function, we use the value of *pprev*, not its address, so we use the value operator (*) with the pointer. That is, since *pptr* points to *pprev*, then **pptr* is the value of *pprev*.

One final point to note is that if nothing is found in the file, then *ps0* is left with the *NULL* value.

```
/*  gets movie data from file --uses cpymem() function */
MOVPTR getfile(fp, ps0, pptr)
FILE *fp;
MOVPTR ps0, *pptr;
{
    MOVPTR ps;
    struct movinfo movbuf;   /* temporary storage */

    while ( fread (&movbuf, sizeof (movbuf),1,fp) != 0) {
        ps = (MOVPTR) malloc(sizeof (struct movie));
        if (ps0 == NULL)
                ps0 = ps;    /* save initial pointer value */
        else
                (*pptr)->pnext = ps; /* put ps in preceding strt */
        cpymem(&ps->data, &movbuf, sizeof(movbuf));
                        /* copy temp into movie structure */
        ps->pnext = NULL;
        *pptr = ps;
        }
    return (ps0);   /* return location of 1st strct */
}


/* copies n bytes of memory from one location to another */
void cpymem(ptarg, porig, nbytes)
char *ptarg, *porig;   /* ptrs to 2 locations */
unsigned nbytes;
{
    int count;

    for ( count = 0; count < nbytes; count++)
        *ptarg++ = *porig++;
}
```

Next, let's turn to *getdata()*. This function needs to know if *ps0* is *NULL* or not. If it is *NULL*, that means that either the *data.b* file has not been created yet or that it exists but is empty. If this is the case, it is up to *getdata()* to create the first memory block and to assign a value to *ps0*. For this reason, *ps0* is an argument to *getdata()*, and it is also the return value for the function. If the *getfile()* function already has set a value for *ps0*, then *getdata()* should leave it unaltered.

Second, if there is already a sequence of linked structures, *getdata()* should know the address of the last one so that it can tack on new structures to the old list. For this purpose, *getdata()* has *pprev* as an argument. The following listing presents this function.

```
/* gets keyboard input     */
MOVPTR getdata(pstart, pprev )
MOVPTR pstart, pprev;   /* ptrs to first, last structures */
{
    MOVPTR ps,ps0;
    char temp[MLINE];

    ps0 = pstart;
    printf("Please enter a movie title; a lone return terminates.\n");
    while (gets(temp) != NULL && temp[0] != '\0')
        {
        ps = (MOVPTR) malloc(sizeof (struct movie));
        if (pprev == NULL)   /* if no previous structures */
            ps0 = ps;          /* save address of first    */
        else                    /* later passes */
            pprev->pnext = ps; /* store ps in previous structure */
        strcpy(ps->data.title, temp);    /* copy title */
        puts("How many times have you viewed that picture?");
        scanf("%d", &ps->data.times);   /* get viewing times */
        ENDLINE();                       /* clear line -- a macro*/
        ps->pnext = NULL;         /* set pnext to NULL */
        pprev = ps;                /* save ps value */
        puts("Next movie? A lone return terminates.");
        }
    return(ps0);
}
```

Note that *getdata()* uses the *ENDLINE()* macro defined at the beginning of the main program. It clears the line so that the next *gets()* starts on the next line. See Question 9.6.

Question 9.7

One problem with *getdata()* is that it is conceivable (if unlikely) that the length of the title obtained by *gets()* is larger than the 80 characters (plus one null character) provided by the *movie* structure. How could this be remedied?

Table 9.1 Information Flow Between Functions

Function	Values from *main()*	*Values to main()*
getfile()	*fp,ps0*	*ps0,pprev*
getdata()	*ps0, pprev*	*ps0*
storedata()	*fp,ps0*	
showdata()	*ps0*	

The remaining two functions, *showdata()* and *storedata()*, are much simpler. They just need to know the location of the first structure and, for *storedata()*, what file to use. The next listing presents these two functions.

```
/* send data to terminal */
void showdata(ps)
MOVPTR ps;
{
    do  {
        printf("%s: %d\n", ps->data.title, ps->data.times);
        ps = ps->pnext;
        } while (ps != NULL);
}

/* store data in file */
void storedata(fp,ps)
FILE *fp;
MOVPTR ps;
{
    do  {
        fwrite(&ps->data, sizeof (struct movinfo), 1, fp);
        ps = ps->pnext;
        } while (ps != NULL);
}
```

The two functions are quite similar. The difference is that *showdata()* outputs the data in text form to the screen, while *storedata()* outputs the data in binary form to a file.

Table 9.1 summarizes the information flow between the main program and the other functions.

FILE ACCESS

The program we just finished is simple example of a database program in which a program maintains and modifies data stored in a file. Programs of this sort require some thought about controlling access to the data file. Ideally, access should be allowed only through the program. The *movies3.c* program, for example, assumes the data in *data.b* is stored in a particular format. If someone used the *ed* or *vi* editor to modify the *data.b* file, this format could be disrupted, causing the file-reading part of the program to crash.

A second problem of access is that we shouldn't allow two people to work on the same file at once. Whoever finished first would have his changes wiped out by the second user, since the final call to *fopen()* wipes the file clean before the program writes back the new data. What is needed is *file-locking*, which means closing a file to use by others while someone is using it.

Let's see how to meet these two problems.

Protecting the Data File with the "Set User ID" Command

The obvious thing to do to protect a file from unwanted changes is to use the *chmod* command (see Chapter 2) to change the permissions to the *data.b* file. Thus either

```
chmod go-rw data.b
```

or

```
chmod 600 data.b
```

would serve to keep other users from fiddling with the file. However, this change presents a problem if you want them to be able to use the *movies3.c* program, for the program's abilities to use *data.b* are the same as the user's — zilch in this case.

This is the same type of problem that the UNIX *passwd* command faces. It is supposed to let a user change her password, but the password is stored in a file (*/etc/passwd*) that ordinary users are not allowed to modify. The solution is to use the "set user ID" *chmod* command. This command causes the program *user* to assume the effective identity of the program *owner* while the program is running. That is, someone using your program will temporarily have the same file permissions you do. To set this permission using *chmod*'s symbolic mode, give the following command:

```
chmod u+s movies
```

Here *movies* is the name of the file containing the executable program. Note that we are altering the program permissions, not the data file permissions. To use the absolute mode of *chmod*, make the fourth digit from the right a "4". The next three digits represent the usual permission setting. The following command sets the user ID bit, gives the user read, write, and execute permissions, and gives everyone else execute permission:

```
chmod 4711 movies
```

When you try an *ls –l* listing, an *s* will show up where the user *x* normally appears in the mode string. That is, the mode for the last example would look like this:

```
-rws--x--x
```

In short, to protect the data file, we take two steps. First, use *chmod* with the data file to deny everyone else its use:

```
chmod go-rw data.b
```

Retain, however, your permissions to use the file. Second, use *chmod* with the executable program file to set the user ID bit:

```
chmod u+s movies
```

Now someone else using the *movies* program will temporarily have your permissions and be able to use the *data.b* file.

Another possibility is to grant the user the same permissions possessed by members of the program owner's group. The symbolic form for this is as follows:

```
chmod g+s movies
```

In the absolute mode, use a "2" instead of a "4":

```
chmod 2711 movies
```

Of course, this serves a purpose only if other group members have read and write permission for *data.b*.

File Locking

UNIX solved one problem for us. Now what about file locking? Is there a UNIX command that limits access to a file to one customer at a time? For most UNIX systems, the answer is no. System V provides for file locking, but that provision was not yet implemented at this writing. Pre-System V systems lack it anyway. Berkeley 4.2 UNIX also instituted a form of file locking, but older Berkeley versions lack it. However, we can produce the desired effect through programming.

The method is simple. Have the program begin by checking if there is a file called, for example, *lock* in the same directory as *data.b*. If there is such a file, have the program report that the data file is busy and then quit. If there is not such a file, have the program make one. Then, if other people try to use the program, *they* find a *lock* file and get dumped. Of course, the program should remove *lock* when it finishes, for no one can use the program until *lock* is gone.

The chief difficulty with this approach is making sure the *lock* file gets removed. The *unlink()* system call can be used to remove the file. Just provide it with the name of the *lock* file as argument. But we must make sure that *unlink()* is invoked under all the circumstances under which the program may end. For instance, the *movies* program has several exit points: if *data.b* can't be opened for reading, if there is no data, if *data.b* can't be opened for writing, and if the program terminates normally. The *unlink()* function must be called in each of these eventualities. That is accomplished by placing an *unlink()* call at the appropriate locations in the program.

And what if the user terminates the program in mid-run by striking the interrupt key? The *unlink()* function should be called then, too. To do this, we can use the *signal()* function in the manner discussed in Chapter 8. We set up the *signal()* calls so that upon receiving one of the interrupt signals, the program invokes a closing-up function that we've called *unlock()*. This function, defined at the end of the program, removes the *lock* file, then calls exit.

The following listing shows the *movies3.c* program modified to include file locking.

```
/* movies4.c -- includes file locking */
#include <stdio.h>
#include <signal.h>
#define MLINE 81
#define DATA "/usr/lucas/movie/data.b"
#define LOCK "/usr/lucas/movie/lock"
#define ENDLINE()  while ( getchar() != '\n')
struct movinfo    {
                    char title[MLINE];  /* movie title */
                    int times;          /* times viewed */
                  };

typedef struct movie {
                    struct movinfo data; /* collected info */
                    struct movie *pnext; /* ptr to next strct */
                  } *MOVPTR;
```

341

```
main()
{
    char temp[MLINE];
    char *malloc(), *gets();
    MOVPTR ps, ps0, pprev; /* ptrs to current structure, first
                              structure, and preceding structure */
    FILE *fp, *fl;     /* ptrs to data file, lock file */
    void cpymem(), showdata(), storedata(), out();
    MOVPTR getfile(), getdata();

    /* go to unlock() function on program interrupt */
    if (signal(SIGINT, SIG_IGN) == SIG_DFL) signal(SIGINT, unlock);
    if (signal(SIGQUIT, SIG_IGN) == SIG_DFL) signal(SIGQUIT, unlock);
    if (signal(SIGHUP, SIG_IGN) == SIG_DFL) signal(SIGHUP, unlock);
    if (signal(SIGTERM, SIG_IGN) == SIG_DFL) signal(SIGTERM, unlock);

    if ( access(LOCK,0) == 0) {   /* is there a lock? */
        puts("The file is busy; try again later.");
        exit(2);
        }
    else if (( fl = fopen(LOCK,"w")) == NULL) { /* set lock */
        perror(LOCK);
        exit(1);
        }
    ps0 = pprev = NULL;
    if ( access(DATA,0) == 0)
        {
        if (( fp = fopen(DATA, "r")) == NULL) {
                perror(DATA);
                unlink(LOCK);
                exit(1);
                }
        ps0 = getfile(fp, ps0, &pprev);
        if (ps0 == NULL)
            puts("The data file is empty");
        else {
            puts("Here are the current file contents:");
            showdata(ps0);
            }
        }
```

```
    ps0 = getdata(ps0, pprev);
    if (ps0 == NULL) {
        puts("No input! Bye");
        unlink(LOCK);
        exit(0);
        }
    puts("Here are the current movie data:");
    showdata(ps0);
    if ((fp = fopen(DATA, "w")) == NULL) {
        perror(DATA);
        unlink(LOCK);
        exit(1);
        }
    storedata(fp,ps0);
    fclose(fp);
    fclose(LOCK);
    unlink(LOCK);
}

void showdata(ps)
MOVPTR ps;
{
    do  {
        printf("%s: %d\n", ps->data.title, ps->data.times);
        ps = ps->pnext;
        } while (ps != NULL);
}

 void storedata(fp,ps)
FILE *fp;
MOVPTR ps;
 {
    do  {
        fwrite(&ps->data, sizeof (struct movinfo), 1, fp);
        ps = ps->pnext;
        } while (ps != NULL);
}


MOVPTR getfile(fp, ps0, pptr)
FILE *fp;
MOVPTR ps0, *pptr;
{
    MOVPTR ps;
    struct movinfo movbuf;
```

```
        while ( fread (&movbuf, sizeof (movbuf),1,fp) != 0) {
            ps = (MOVPTR) malloc(sizeof (struct movie));
            if (ps0 == NULL)
                    ps0 = ps;
            else
                    (*pptr)->pnext = ps;
            cpymem(&ps->data, &movbuf, sizeof(movbuf));
            ps->pnext = NULL;
            *pptr = ps;
            }
        return (ps0);
}

void cpymem(ptarg, porig, bytes)
char *ptarg, *porig;
unsigned  bytes;
{
    int count;

    for ( count = 0; count < bytes; count++)
        *ptarg++ = *porig++;
}

MOVPTR getdata(pstart, pprev )
MOVPTR pstart, pprev;
{
    MOVPTR ps,ps0;
    char temp[MLINE];

    ps0 = pstart;
    printf("Please enter a movie title; a lone return terminates.\n");
    while (gets(temp) != NULL && temp[0] != '\0')
        {
        ps = (MOVPTR) malloc(sizeof (struct movie));
        if (pprev == NULL)
            ps0 = ps;
        else                    /* later passes */
            pprev->pnext = ps;/* store ps in previous structure */
        strcpy(ps->data.title, temp);   /* copy title */
        puts("How many times have you viewed that picture?");
        scanf("%d", &ps->data.times);   /* get viewing times */
        ENDLINE();                      /* clear line */
        ps->pnext = NULL;               /* set pnext to NULL */
        pprev = ps;                     /* save ps value */
        puts("Next movie? A lone return terminates.");
        }
```

Figure 9.8
Simple Graphics

```
    return(ps0);
}
void unlock()
{
  /* ignore all further interrupts */
signal(SIGINT, SIG_IGN);
signal(SIGQUIT, SIG_IGN);
signal(SIGHUP, SIG_IGN);
signal(SIGTERM, SIG_IGN);

unlink(LOCK);   /* remove lock */
exit(0);
}
```

And now for something completely different.

UNIX GRAPHICS

Computer graphics is the use of a computer to generate visual images. These may
be simple figures, such as lines, boxes, or circles (see Figure 9.8), or they may be

rotatable projections of three-dimensional objects in full color (check out many contempory advertisements and futuristic movies). UNIX comes with a standard graphics package able to produce images of the first sort. This package can be accessed at two levels. First, the C library includes several plotting routines for producing lines, arcs, and the like. We can incorporate these functions into C programs. Second, the standard UNIX plotting command (known as *plot* in Version 7 and as *tplot* in System V) lets us use these same routines at the UNIX command level.

Overview of the UNIX Plot Package Philosophy

One problem faced by graphics developers is that different graphics devices have different capabilities and instruction sets. Thus the instructions needed to produce graphics, for example, on a DASI™ 450 terminal (a daisy-wheel printer) differ from those needed for a Tektronix™ 4014 terminal (a storage-scope screen); and many terminals have no graphics capabilities at all. UNIX meets this diversity in a limited fashion by offering the plotting routines in multiple flavors. One version will work with a DASI 450, one with a Tektronix 4014, and so on. You can specify the particular target device when you compile a C program. Let's see how that works.

Suppose you wish to write a program that draws a circle inscribed in a box or, as an exciting variant, a box in a circle. You can do this using the *circle()*, *line()*, and *move()* functions we describe later. Whether you intend the output to be for, say, a Tektronix 4014 or a DASI 450 terminal, you would use these same function names. However, when you compile the function, you specify which terminal by using a loader option. For example, to run the program on a DASI 450, you could compile it this way:

```
cc circbox.c -l450 -lm
```

UNIX has several versions of each graphics function. The DASI 450 versions are stored in one library, the Tektronix versions in a second library, and so on. Here the *-l450* option tells the loader to look in the DASI 450 library for the appropriate functions. Table 9.3 lists the available libraries.

The *-lm* tells the loader to use the math library. We need this because some of the graphics functions use the *sqrt()* function, which is in the math library. Note that the *-lm* option is listed after the *-l450* option. The reason for this is that the loader doesn't learn that it needs the *sqrt()* function until after it has loaded in the *l450* library.

Table 9.2 C Plotting Functions

Function	Action
openpl( )	Prepares the target device for writing
erase( )	Erases the screen,starts a new page
label(str)	Prints a label
line(x1,y1,x2,y2)	Draws a line between two given points
circle(x,y,r)	Draws a circle of specified size and center
arc(x,y,x1,y1,x2,y2)	Draws an arc of a circle
move(x,y)	Moves to a point
cont(x,y)	Draws a line from the current point to a new point
point(x,y)	Puts a point at the specified location
linemod(str)	Specifies kind of line
space(x1,y1,x2,y2)	Defines the plotting area
closepl( )	Flushes the graphic output

However, you don't necessarily have to commit yourself to a particular terminal at this point. Instead, you can use the *device-independent* choice for library by using the *-lplot* option:

```
cc circbox -lplot -lm
```

Don't get too excited by the *device-independent* label. This option does not produce output that works for all devices. Actually, the output of a program compiled in this manner doesn't work with any device, at least not directly. Instead, the program produces output designed to act as input for the UNIX filter commands (*tplot* or *plot*.) Then, when *tplot* or *plot* is invoked, you specify the device. This two-step approach lets you defer device-selection until run time, allowing one compiled program to be used with several different devices. The UNIX *graph* command, for example, uses the *lplot* library; and *graph*'s output is used as input to *tplot*.

Let's look at details now, beginning with the C library.

The C Graphics Library

We'll start by taking an overview of the library contents. The various C plotting functions are listed under the heading *PLOT(3X)* in the C library section of the UNIX manual. As an added inconvenience, the effects of these functions are described in a different section *(PLOT(5)* in Version 7 and *PLOT(4)* in System V). Table 9.2 contains a list of these functions along with a brief explanation of what they do.

Table 9.3 PLOT (3X) Device Options

Option	Device
-lplot	Device-independent graphics stream for *plot* or *tplot*
-l300	GSI or DASI 300 terminal
-l300s	GSI or DASI 300S terminal
-l450	DASI 450 terminal
-l4014	Tektronix 4014

As we said earlier, the same function names are used regardless of the target terminal. The distinction comes during compilation, at which time you indicate which terminal will be used. Table 9.3 lists the various standard library choices that are available. Don't forget that the library options come after the filename of the C program:

```
cc goofy.c -l4014 -lm
```

To see how to use the graphics functions, let's put together a simple graphics program. After that we can take a more detailed look at the function calls.

```
\*  boxo.c -- draws boxes *\
main()
{
    int x1,y1,x2,y2;
    void box();

    while (scanf("%d", &x1) == 1 && x1 >= 0)
            {
            scanf("%d %d %d", &y1, &x2, &y2);
            openpl();
            box(x1,y1,x2,y2);
            closepl();
            }
}

void box(llx,lly,urx,ury)
int llx,lly, urx,ury;
{
    line(llx, lly, urx, lly);
    cont(urx,ury);
    cont(llx,ury);
    cont(llx,lly);
}
```

This program, of course, draws boxes. It has a *while* loop that reads in four numbers. The first two numbers represent the location of the lower left-hand corner of the proposed box, and the next two numbers represent the upper right-hand corner. These values are passed to the *box()* function, which then uses the plotting functions to produce the box. Before looking at these functions, however, let's examine the input scheme.

In particular, consider the line

```
while (scanf("%d", &x1) == 1 && x1 >= 0)
```

It attempts to read the first coordinate and to make two tests. First, did *scanf()* succeed in reading in a number? The *scanf()* function returns the number of items read, so a successful read returns a value of 1. Second, is the number equal to or greater than 0? The practical import of these tests is that they offer several ways to terminate input. One, we can end input with an end-of-file, since that results in *scanf()* returning a value of -1. Two, we can terminate input with a non-numeric entry for *x1*, such as *!* or *stop*; in these cases, *scanf()* returns a value of 0. Three, we can halt input by using a negative number. Once a viable *x1* value is read, the program reads the other 3 values.

Question 9.8

Is this input process completely safe?

Now let's get graphic and look at the plotting commands used in this program.

Preparing the Device: *openpl()*

This command prepares the device to accept graphics instructions. (Not all devices require this command, but using it preserves the generality of the program.) The place to use this command, of course, is before any other plot functions are called.

Flushing the Output: *closepl()*

Normally, output is saved in a temporary buffer, and the contents of the buffer are sent on whenever the buffer gets full. The *closepl()* function *flushes* any output that remains in a buffer. That is, it sends the output on whether or not the buffer is full.

Drawing a Straight Line Between Two Points: *line()*

Here is the declaration for the *line()* function:

```
line (x1,y1,x2,y2)
int x1,y1,x2,y2;
```

This function draws a line between two points. The coordinates x1 and y1 are the x (horizontal) and y (vertical) locations of the starting point, and x2 and y2 are the coordinates of the end point. The range of allowable coordinates depends on the device. In all cases, the coordinates of the lower left corner are (0,0). The upper right-hand corner coordinates for the largest square are (3120,3120) for the Tektronix 4014 and (4096,4096) for the DASI and GSI terminals. If the terminal display area is not a square, points beyond the square may be displayable.

In our program we start the box drawing by using the *line()* function.

Drawing a Straight Line to a Point: *cont()*

This function draws a straight line from the current position (which is wherever the previous command left it) to an indicated point. Here is the function declaration:

```
cont (x,y)
int x,y;
```

Here *x* and *y* are the coordinates of the target point. In our program, once we have the first side drawn, each new line starts at the end of the preceding line, so we can use the *cont()* function instead of *line()* to draw all but the first side.

Using the Program

We can key in input from the keyboard, but then we clutter the screen or paper with the input. A cleaner approach is to place the input data in a data file and to use UNIX redirection to feed the data to the program. Here, for example, is a representative datafile:

```
1700 2500 2300 3000
1850 2800 1900 2850
2100 2800 2150 2850
1975 2650 2025 2800
1850 2570 2150 2600
1650 2700 1700 2800
2300 2700 2350 2800
1900 2400 2100 2500
1200 1200 2800 2400
```

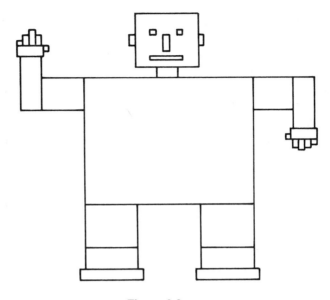

Figure 9.9
Not a Self-Portrait

```
800 2100 1200 2400
600 2100 800 2600
575 2600 825 2700
575 2700 635 2750
635 2700 695 2800
695 2700 755 2850
755 2700 815 2800
825 2650 875 2700
2800 2100 3200 2400
3200 1900 3400 2400
3175 1800 3425 1900
3125 1800 3175 1850
3365 1750 3425 1800
3305 1725 3365 1800
3245 1700 3305 1800
3185 1725 3245 1800
1200 800 1700 1200
2300 800 2800 1200
1200 600 1700 800
2300 600 2800 800
1150 500 1750 600
2250 500 2850 600
```

The Figure 9.9 shows the result of processing these data with our program.

Stick Figures

Let's look at a few more graphics functions. The program in the next listing introduces the *move()*, *point()*, *circle()*, and *arc()* functions. This program draws simple stick figures, such as those in Figure 9.8. The *stickman()* function does the actual plotting. It takes as arguments the *x* and *y* coordinates of the center of the figure's head and a scale factor for setting the size of the figure. The main program fetches values for these arguments from the user or, through redirection, from a file.

```
/*  stick.c -- slightly sophisticated stick figures */
#include <stdio.h>
main()
{
    int posx,posy,scale;
    void stickman();

    while ( scanf("%d", &posx) == 1 &&  posx >= 0 )
        {
        scanf("%d %d", &posy, &scale);
        stickman(posx,posy, scale);
        }
}

void stickman(x,y,scale)
{
    openpl();
    circle(x,y, 10 * scale);
    point (x - 3 * scale, y);
    point (x + 3 * scale, y);
    arc (x, y + 2 * scale, x - 3 * scale, y - 6 * scale,
         x + 3 * scale, y - 6 * scale);
    y = y - 10 * scale;
    move (x, y);
    y = y - 10 * scale;
    cont (x, y);
    cont (x - 30 * scale, y + 10 * scale);
    move (x, y);
    cont (x + 25 * scale, y + 20 * scale);
    move (x, y);
    y = y - 30 * scale;
    cont (x,y);
```

```
        cont (x - 10 * scale, y - 40 * scale);
        move (x, y);
        cont (x + 15 * scale, y - 38 * scale);
        closepl();
}
```

Let's look at the new plotting functions.

Moving Without Drawing: *move()*

The *move()* function lets you move the plotting position from one location to another without drawing a line. Here is its declaration:

```
move (x, y)
int x, y;
```

The function moves the plotting position from its current position to the point with coordinates *x,y*.

Making a Point: *point()*

The *point()* function draws a point at the coordinates given by its two arguments:

```
point (x, y)
int x, y;
```

Drawing a Circle: *circle()*

To draw a circle, use the *circle()* function. Here is its declaration:

```
circle (x, y, r)
int x, y, r;
```

The first two arguments are the *x* and *y* coordinates of the circle center, and the third argument is the circle radius. You should check that the extreme limits of the circle remain within the boundaries of the display. For instance, the call

```
circle (100, 100, 200);
```

is no good, since it would try to plot below and to the left of the lower left corner.

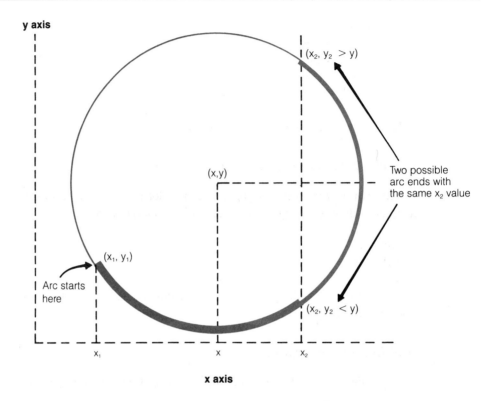

Figure 9.10
Specifying the End of an Arc

Drawing an Arc: *arc()*

The *arc()* function draws an arc, or portion of a circle. Here is its declaration:

```
arc(x,y,x1,y1,x2,y2)
int x,  y,  x1,  y1,  x2,  y2;
```

The arguments *x* and *y* specify the center of the circle of which the arc is a part. The *x1* and the *y2* specify the point from which the arc starts, and *x2* and *y1* specify the end of the arc. The *y2* coordinate is different from the others in that it need not be the actual coordinate; it merely determines in which quadrant the arc ends. The reason for this peculiar usage lies in geometry. Look at Figure 9.10. Once the first five arguments are given, there are only two possible values for *y2*. Rather than make you calculate what those two values are, the *arc()* function lets you specify your choice by giving a *y2* value larger or smaller than *y*, and that tells it which arc you want.

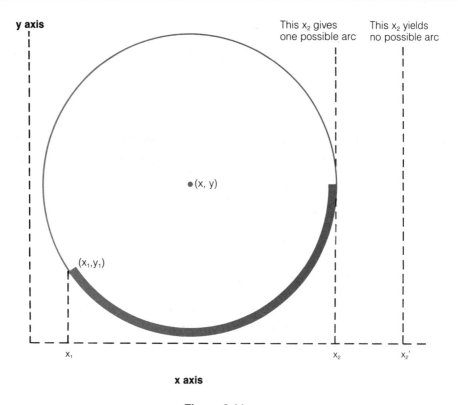

Figure 9.11
Limitations on X_2

We've said that there are two possible *y2* values; this assumes that *x2* was chosen so that it lies within the x-range of the circle. It is possible to choose an *x2* that results in one or even no real *y2* values. See Figure 9.11.

Other Graphics Functions

We haven't used all the functions in our examples. Here are short descriptions of the ones we didn't use.

Clearing the Screen: *erase()*

The *erase()* function clears the screen or starts a new page. It takes no argument, so it has a rather simple synopsis:

```
erase()
```

Labeling: *label()*

The *label()* function lets you place labels in the drawings. Here is the declaration:

```
label(s)
char *s;
```

Here *s* represents the character string you wish to have written. It is written with the first character positioned at the current graphics cursor position. Remember, a quoted string is a string pointer, so calls such as

```
label("Teacher");
```

are fine.

Setting Line Style: *linemod()*

The Tektronix 4014 allows a choice of line styles for plotting. The *linemod()* function lets you specify which one to use. Here is its synopsis:

```
linemod(s)
char *s;
```

Here are the choices for the string *s*:

```
"dotted"
"solid"
"longdashed"
"shortdashed"
"dotdashed"
```

Defining the Plot Area: *space()*

The *space()* command defines the plotting area. Here is its declaration:

```
space(x0,y0,x1,y1)
int x0, y0, x1, y1;
```

The *x0,y0* pair are the coordinates of the lower left corner of the plotting area, and the *x1,y1* pair specify the upper right corner.

Other Terminals

Suppose your system has a graphics device other than one of the supported ones. Can you use these graphics functions with it? Perhaps. For instance, I often use an ADM™ 5 terminal retrofitted with a graphics board that emulates a Tektronix 4010. A Tektronix 4010 is not a Tektronix 4014, but most of the 4014 library work with the 4010, too. Just the *label()* and *linemod()* functions fail. I have also used the 4014 library on a Tektronix 4012 with similar results.

Similarly, the DASI 450 library works for the Diablo 1620 and Xerox 1700 terminals, which are functionally equivalent.

The best approach for using another terminal would be to find documentation for its graphics code and to prepare a library of functions to fit.

USING THE UNIX COMMANDS *tplot* AND *plot*

As we mentioned before, *tplot* and *plot* are two names for the same command. For simplicity, we will stick to the System V monicker, *tplot*. In the grand tradition of UNIX commands, *tplot* is a filter. It takes as input a stream of graphics commands, and it converts that stream into its output, a graphics figure. And whence do we get the stream of graphic commands? They come from programs using the *lplot* library versions of the C plotting functions. Let's look at a particular example.

We produced Figure 9.9 with this sequence of commands:

```
cc boxo.c -14014 -lm
a.out < boxdata
```

Here *boxdata* contained the set of numbers we displayed previously. We could have produced the same figure with this sequence of commands:

```
cc boxo.c -lplot -lm
a.out < boxdata | tplot -T4014
```

The *-T4014* option to *tplot* tells it to convert its input to instructions for the Tektronix 4014. If, instead, we wished to use a DASI 300, we could then use the same *a.out* program this way:

```
a.out < boxdata | tplot -T300
```

Another possibility would be to save the output from *a.out*:

```
a.out < boxdata > plotdata
```

357

Table 9.4 *tplot* Device Options

Label	Device
300	DASI 300
300S	DASI 300s
450	DASI 450
4014	Tektronix 4014
ver	Versatec D1200A

Then, later, we could send the contents of *plotdata* to *tplot*, using whichever terminal option we desired:

```
tplot -T450 < plotdata
```

The number of options available are fairly small: just the terminals recognized by the C plotting functions plus the Versatec D1200A printer-plotter. To specify the device, append the appropriate label from Table 9.4 to *-T*, as in the preceding examples.

One example of a program that uses the *-lplot* library is the UNIX *graph* command. This command takes a stream of number pairs as input, interprets them as x-y coordinates, and produces a set of plotting commands as output. These can be used as input for *plot*. For instance, suppose the file *calories* contains the following data:

```
1 2100 2 2300 3 1800 4 1700 5 2500 6 2300 7 2200
```

Then the following command will produce Figure 9.12, providing you have the right sort of terminal:

```
graph -s -y 0 < calories | plot -T4014
```

The *-s* option suppresses some text output that gets garbled by our not-quite-right sort of terminal, and the *-y 0* option has the vertical axis start at 0. (By default, the axis will start at the lowest y-value in the data).

More UNIX Graphics

The standard plotting package has a limited graphics vocabulary. For instance, it doesn't have any commands dealing with color, with the shading of figures, or

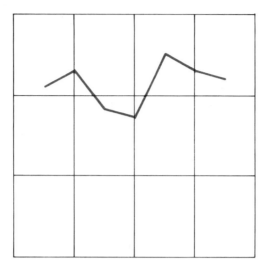

Figure 9.12
Weekly Calorie Intake as Shown by Graph and Plot

with the rotation or translation of figures. System V extends the graphics vocabulary somewhat with the inclusion of a graphics subshell, which is invoked by the new UNIX command *graphics*. Once there, you can use the *ged* command, which starts up an interactive graphics editor. Its commands can create the basic geometrical forms of the C library. It can also move, rotate, copy, and rescale graphical constructs. The editor is designed to work with a Tektronix 4010 terminal. The file of commands produced by the editor, however, can be processed by the *gdev* command to produce instructions for the Hewlett-Packard™ 7221A Graphics Plotter.

As UNIX becomes more involved with commercial applications, it most likely will continue to expand its graphics capabilities.

CONCLUSION

As promised, we've looked into several topics in this chapter. Using the C memory allocation functions such as *malloc()*, we can expand program memory as needed to accomodate new input data. Linked structures offer a convenient way to store the data. The C binary I/O functions–*read()*, *write()*, *fread()*, and *fwrite()*–let us copy a structure as a unit to and from permanent files. Using *chmod* and the *lock-file* concept, we can limit access to such a data file so that it can only be modified through the concerned program. Finally, we investigated the use of UNIX's facilities for graphics.

ANSWERS TO QUESTIONS IN CHAPTER 9

9.1 Undeclared functions are assumed to return type *int*. *Malloc()*, however, returns type pointer-to-*char*.

9.2 The *scanf()* function requires as an argument the address of the location in which the read value is to be placed. This address can be specified by using the address operator (&) before the name of a variable, or by using a pointer variable containing the address of the destination. Since *ps* is a pointer, it might seem that we don't need the address operator. However, the combination *ps->times*, or, more generally, *(ps + index)->times*, is not a pointer. It is the identifying name of a particular variable, and its type is the type declared for the *times* member of the structure, *int*, in this case. So just as we would use

```
scanf("%d", &num);
```

to read in the value of a simple *int* variable *num*, we use

```
scanf("%d", &(ps + index)->times);
```

to read in the value of the structure member *int* variable called *(ps + index)->times*.

9.3 It would pose problems if *ps0* were *NULL*, for then it wouldn't point to an actual structure. Fortunately, the program quits before reaching the *do...while* loops if *ps0* is *NULL*.

9.4 a. In C, the value of an assignment expression, such as

```
ps->title = malloc(strln(temp)+1
```

is just the value of the left-hand member. So, once this expression is evaluated, *ps->title* acquires a value, and

```
strcpy(ps->title = malloc(strlen(temp)+1), temp);
```

becomes

```
strcpy(ps->title, temp);
```

b. Simply replace the line

```
strcpy(ps->title, temp);
```

with the two lines

```
ps->title = malloc(strln(temp)+1;
strcpy(ps->title, temp);
```

or with the single line

```
strcpy(ps->title = malloc(strlen(temp)+1), temp);
```

9.5 Yes, *temp[]* may lack a newline. The reason is the writing format (%s\n) tags one more character (the newline) to the end of the string. Suppose that the original title were a full *MLINE – 1* characters long (not counting the terminating \0). The *fgets(fp,MLINE,temp)* call reads up to *MLINE –1* characters or up to a newline, whichever comes first. In the hypothesized situation, the *MLINE – 1* characters come first. They are placed into *temp[]*, and the newline character is left in the input queue. This, incidentally, would pose a problem if the next input call was to *fgets()*, for that call would interpret the remaining newline character as an empty line. However, our program's next input call uses the %d mode of *fscanf()*, which skips over spaces and newlines.

9.6
```
while( getchar() != '\n')   ;
```
(This loop reads characters up through the first newline, discarding them.)

9.7 Use *fgets()* instead of *gets()*. The call

`fgets(temp,MLINE,stdin)`

will fetch from the standard input a string up to the first *MLINE - 1* character or to the first newline, whichever comes first. Unfortunately, the newline character, if present, also is placed in *temp*. (The *gets()* function replaces it with a null character.) Thus you need to add programming to replace the newline character, if present, with a null character. See the discussion in the Text File I/O section of this chapter.

9.8 No. The program doesn't check to see if attempted input values for the last three variables are numeric and non-negative.

EXERCISES

1. Write a function that looks through a list of linked structures of the *movie* type for a certain title. As arguments, provide a pointer to the first structure to be searched and a pointer to the string to be matched. Have the function return a pointer to the first matching string or to *NULL* if none is found.

2. Write a function that sorts a list of linked *movie* structures by number of times viewed.

3. Redefine the *movie* structure so that it contains a pointer to the preceding structure as well as to the following structure. Modify *movies3.c* to use this form of structure.

4. Add to *movies3.c*, as modified in Exercise 3, a function that lets you modify a specified (by title) structure from the list.

5. Add to *movies3.c*, as modified in Exercise 3, a function that deletes a specified structure from the list. Note that it should link the preceding structure to the following structure.

6. Produce a program that draws snowmen or houses or other figures of your choice.

10

UNIX PROGRAM DEVELOPMENT: cc, *make*, AND APPLICATIONS

In this chapter you will find:

10

UNIX Program Development: *cc*, *make*, and Applications

In Chapters 8 and 9 we viewed several programming techniques for expanding the flexibility of C programs and for developing the interface between C programs and the UNIX operating system. In this chapter we will put some of these techniques to work to develop programs of considerable value (if you need them) and of general interest (even if you don't need them). The UNIX system offers many useful resources to aid program development, and in this chapter we will describe two of them. The one essential resource for C program development is a C compiler. UNIX uses a C compiler called *cc*. We have used it all along, but in this chapter we will discuss its workings and its options more fully. The second useful program on our agenda is *make*, which helps you develop and maintain programs. As we examine these features, we will develop some programs that are designed to fit the UNIX philosophy and thereby make use of other aspects of the UNIX system. Finally, we will return to the topic of integrating C programs and shell scripts into an effective, effort-saving blend.

The focal point for the first part of this chapter will be the development of a program to find some useful statistical properties of a set of numbers. As we work through the program, we will discuss *cc* and *make*, and we will develop two input functions of more general interest.

The second part of the chapter features a word-frequency counting program; it illustrates the integration of the shell-script and the C programming approaches.

SIMPLE STATISTICS: THE MEAN AND THE STANDARD DEVIATION

Most of the examples in this book have concerned text processing, file manipulation, and the like. There are, however, people who still use computers for numerical calculations, so we thought a quantitative example would be in order, especially since the standard UNIX package of commands is relatively weak in this area. Our goal is to create a new command in the UNIX style, one that complies with UNIX conventions and meshes with the UNIX environment. That aspect of the problem should be of interest even to those of you who find deviations (even standard ones) offensive. First, let's explain what the program is supposed to do.

One of the most common of tasks facing educators, scientists, engineers, pollsters, baseball statisticians, MBAs and other fans of statistics is finding the mean and the standard deviation of a set of numbers. The mean is just the average value of a set of numbers. You get it by adding up the numbers and dividing by the number of items in the list. This part of the problem is simple conceptually and simple to program.

The standard deviation is a little more devious. It is an indication of how closely clustered the numbers are around the average value; it is a weighted average of how far an individual number is from the average. Suppose, for instance, we have the list of measurements 96, 100, 104, 98, 100, 102, 101, 99, 99, 100, 101. The average for this list turns out to be 100. The standard deviation, using the formula we will give later, is 2.1. If you look at the list of numbers, you will see that some are more than 2.1 from the average of 100, while some numbers are closer. But the 2.1 gives a fair description of how far any one measurement is likely to deviate from the average. On seeing this data, a scientist might conclude that we should write the individual measurements as 100 ± 2 (*100 plus or minus 2*) in order to indicate the precision of these measurements. A large standard deviation means the numbers are all scattered about, while a small standard deviation means the numbers are close to one another. For example, suppose we found the mean and standard deviation for the batting averages over ten years for two baseball players. The mean (or average) would tell us who was, on the average, the better batter. The standard deviation tells who was the more consistent batter. The guy who batted .280 to .300 every year would have a smaller standard deviation than the guy whose average varied between .230 and .350, even though both might have the same overall average.

Question 10.1

a. What is the mean of the following numbers?

100 120 110 80 90 100 110 90 100 100

b. Give an eyeball estimate of the standard deviation for those numbers.

The mean, then, is the average of a set of numbers, and the standard deviation represents a measure of how far individual numbers in the set may vary from the mean. In a large sample of measurements, such as 100 I.Q. tests, normally about

68 percent of the individual numbers will be within one standard deviation of the average value, and about 95 percent will be within two standard deviations. Like many measurements, I.Q. tests fit the so-called "normal" or "bell-shaped" curve, with results clumped around the average rather than spread uniformly.

There is one more statistical value of interest. It is called the *standard deviation of the mean*, and it indicates how precise the average itself is. This discussion may take you further into statistics than you wish to go, so, if you like, you can just take our word that the standard deviation of the mean is of interest to some people. But if you wish to know more, here is the scoop. Suppose, for example, you undertake to measure the speed of light. One of the facts of scientific life is that there is no such thing as an exact measurement, so you make 100 measurements to get a better handle on the value. The mean gives you your estimate for the speed of light. The standard deviation gives you your estimate for how precise any one measurement is. And the standard deviation of the mean gives you your estimate for how precise the average of all 100 values is. That is, the standard deviation tells how big a plus or minus value we apply to one measurement, and the standard deviation of the mean tells how big a plus or minus value we apply to the overall average. Since you took many measurements, you would expect the average to provide a more precise measurement than just one measurement, and, indeed, the standard deviation of the mean is smaller than the ordinary standard deviation. For instance, in our example with the mean of 100 and the standard deviation of 2.1, the standard deviation of the mean is 0.6.

Formulas

Whence did we obtain these values we have been flinging about? We used some standard formulas. Suppose we have a list of N numbers: x[1], x[2], ..., x[N]. Let's call the mean (or average) value X. Then we have this formula for the mean:

$$X = \frac{SUM(\ x[i]\ )}{N}$$

Here SUM(x[i]) means add together x[1], x[2], ..., x[n].
Now call the standard deviation SD. Then we have

SD = SQRT((SUM(x[i]*x[i]) − N*X*X)/(N − 1))

where SQRT stands for square root.
Finally, let SDM represent the standard deviation of the mean. Then we have

SDM = SD / SQRT(N)

These are the formulas we will have to incorporate into our program.

To be meaningful, such statistical estimates should be used with fairly large samples of numbers, at least 30, and more comfortably, at least 100 or so. But to show how the formulas are used, let's try them on a small sample. The following table shows five measurements, their squares, and the corresponding sums. It also shows calculations for the various quantities. Rounding the values off, we would say that each individual measurement was no more precise than plus or minus 1 (that is, 8±1), and that the mean was 10.0±0.6.

STATISTICS FOR A SMALL SAMPLE

I	$X[I]$	$X[I]*X[I]$
1	10	100
2	11	121
3	8	64
4	10	100
5	11	121
Sums	50	506

N = 5
Mean = X = 50/5 = 10.0
Standard Deviation = SD = SQRT((506 – 5*10*10)/ (5-1)) =
   SD = SQRT (6/4) = 1.22
Standard Deviation of the Mean = SDM = 1.22/ SQRT(5) = 0.55

Design Philosophy

There is no great problem in writing a C program to calculate the average and the standard deviation of a set of numbers. The real problem is deciding on which of many approaches to use. How will the program get its input data? What will it do with the answers?

On a UNIX system, the best answer is to design the program as a filter. This way it can take input from the terminal, from a redirected file, or from a pipe. And the output can be passed on to the screen, to a file, or to another program. Such a program could also be easily incorporated into shell scripts. The filter approach gives us the flexibility to use the same program in dozens of different ways.

Input and Output

Let's think about input some more. Certainly, if the program is to be a filter, it should read the standard input. But it would also be convenient if we could give it

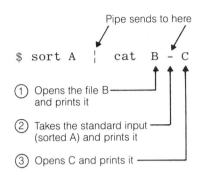

Figure 10.1
***cat* Blends Standard Input with File Input**

a list of filenames as arguments for it to process. The files would contain the data we wish to process. It would be nice, too, if we could intermix standard input and filename arguments, the way we can with *cat*, by using a - (hyphen) to signify the standard input. See Figure 10.1 for a representation of *cat*'s abilities. Our goal will be to incorporate all those features.

What about output? We can model it along the lines of *wc*, giving a line consisting of the data followed by the filename:

```
$ wc flerd dorkimer
     202     789    4528 flerd
     135     611    3822 dorkimer
     337    1400    8350 total
$
```

Placing all the information for each file on one line without, say, having a separate line for a heading, provides an output that can easily be processed by other filters. For instance, the output of *wc* can be piped to *sort*.

Options

Any options? Sometimes it would be useful to echo the input data as it is read; we can make that an option. Another useful option would be to find the collective statistics for the combined input from several files, much the way *wc* prints total counts when two or more files are read. We won't make it the default, for in practice the files might be unrelated. If the first file is of baby elephant weights and the second of elephant peanut consumption, we don't really want to know what the combined average is.

One more point: we need a name for the program. We'll use *stdev*.

FIRST DRAFT OF *stdev*

Designing the program falls into two main parts. The first is arranging for the program to handle all the choices of input and of options. The second part is performing the calculations. This conceptual division suggests using an actual division, with *main()* attending to making the proper input and option arrangements and a second function doing the calculations. To make sure we do have a working concept, we will develop a simple version first, one without options or choice of input. That way we can check to see if the calculation portion is correct before getting fancy. Then we can go back and modify the program to include the other features.

One key decision to make is whether the main program or the calculating function print out the results. Since *main()* eventually will have a better idea of the names and numbers of files, we choose to let *main()* handle the printing. That means that the results of the calculation have to be communicated back to *main()*. Since more than one value is calculated, a simple C function return won't do. Also, we would like to reserve the return value for indicating if the function ran into trouble.

Just what values should be provided as output? Of course, we want the mean, the standard deviation, and the standard deviation of the mean, since that is the point of the program. But it is also good to know how many items were read, so let's provide that. That makes four values. One solution is to provide four addresses as arguments, with the called function using four pointers to access the values. One address can indicate where the mean is to be stored, one can show where the standard deviation is to be stored, and so on. A more elegant solution is to create a C structure that holds all four values and to use just the address of the structure. This also gives us a chance to practice using structures.

The next listing presents a first draft; at this point, the options are still missing, and the program only reads standard input.

```
/* stdev.c -- mean, st.dev, st.dev of the mean   version 1.0 */
#include <stdio.h>
#include <math.h>
#define FORMAT "%5d %8.4g %8.4g %8.4g  %s: n,mean,stdv,stdvm\n"
#define STLIST(X) X.num, X.mean, X.stdv, X.stdvm
struct stats {
            int num;       /* number of items read */
            float mean;    /* mean of the numbers */
            float stdv;    /* standard deviation  */
            float stdvm;   /* standard dev. of the mean */
            };

main()                     /* arranges for input and output */
{
struct stats data;    /* structure to hold individual results */
```

```
    if (calstdev(stdin, &data) == 0) {       /* use standard input */
        printf( FORMAT, STLIST(data), "standard input");
        exit (0) ;
        }
    else
        exit (1);
}

calstdev( fp, statp)
FILE *fp;               /* pointer to file to be read */
struct stats *statp; /* pointer to structure to store results */
{
int n = 0;        /* number of items */
double num;        /* input item */
double sum = 0;    /* sum of items */
double sum2 = 0;   /* sum of the squares */
double mean, stdev, stdevm;

while ( fscanf(fp,"%lf",&num) != EOF ) {
    sum += num;
    sum2 += num * num;
    n++;
    }
if ( n < 2 ) {
    fprintf(stderr,
      "stdev: at least two data values required for stdev\n");
    return (1);
    }
mean = sum / (double) n; /* famous way to find average */
stdev = sqrt ( ( sum2 - n * mean * mean)/( double)(n - 1) );
            /* less famous way to find std. dev */
stdevm = stdev/sqrt( (double)n);
statp->num = n;
statp->mean = mean;
statp->stdv = stdev;
statp->stdvm = stdevm;
return (0);
}
```

First we have some preprocessor statements. We need to include the *math.h* file because we use the *sqrt()* function from the math library. We used *#define* statements to make the actual *printf()* statement more compact. Note that the format provides for printing out the four members of a structure. Also, we anticipate that the final version will use the *printf()* statement more than once, so we are saving retyping it later.

Next, we present the template for the *stats* structure used in the program. We do this externally (outside of any function definition) to make the template global, known to all the functions in the file.

The *main()* function is pretty simple. It defines a structure *data* of the *struct stats* type. Then *main()* calls up *calstdev()* to make the calculations:

```
if (calsdev(stdin, &data) == 0) {
```

We provide for the standard input explicitly by using *stdin* as an argument. In later versions, by using a *FILE* pointer as an argument, we can have *calsdev()* operate on other files, too. We have the *calsdev()* function return zero if all goes well. In that case, *main()* goes on to print the results, which *calsdev()* has placed in the structure *data*. Otherwise, the program exits immediately.

Note that the *calstdev()* function quits if not enough values ($n < 2$) are provided. Instead of calling *exit()*, however, it uses *return(1)* and lets the main program exit. Again, we are anticipating. Once we modify the program to read several files, we will want it to simply skip over bad files rather than stopping.

What are those arrows (->) in *calstdev()*? Remember that the dot operator is used to specify a member of a structure when we are given a structure name, but the arrow operator is used when we use a pointer-to-structure (a la *statp*). Thus *statp->mean* means the *mean* member of the structure pointed to by *statp*. In this program, *statp* is just the address of the *data* structure in *main*, that is, *&data*. So

```
statp->mean = mean;
```

means put the value of *mean* into the storage location *data.mean*. (See Figure 10.2).

Question 10.2

Suppose we have the following statements:

```
struct stats data, *ps;
ps = &data;
```

Give two ways to refer to the *num* member of the structure.

The calculations in *calstdev()* encode the formulas we gave earlier. They find the mean, standard deviation, and standard deviation of the mean. The function also keeps track of the total number of input values read.

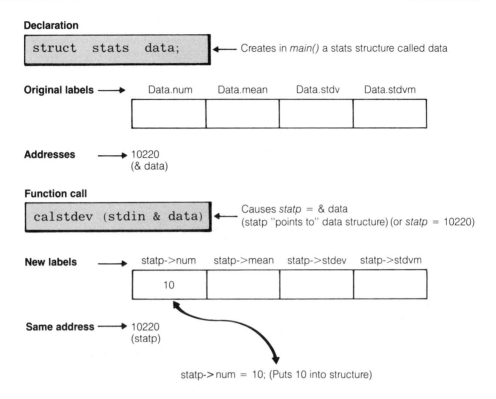

Declaration

```
struct  stats  data;
```
◄ —— Creates in *main()* a stats structure called data

Original labels ——► Data.num   Data.mean   Data.stdv   Data.stdvm

Addresses ———► 10220
(& data)

Function call

```
calstdev (stdin & data)
```
◄ —— Causes *statp* = & data
(statp "points to" data structure) (or *statp* = 10220)

New labels ——► statp->num   statp->mean   statp->stdev   statp->stdvm

| 10 | | | |

Same address ——► 10220
(statp)

statp-> num = 10; (Puts 10 into structure)

Figure 10.2
***statp* — A Pointer to a Structure**

We've mentioned several anticipated improvements in the program, but first we should check to see if it works as is. That means using the compiler.

THE *cc* COMPILER

To compile the program in the *stdev.c* file, we try typing

```
cc stdev.c
```

where *stdev.c* is the filename. If all goes well, this produces an executable file called *a.out*. This is the basic *cc* usage we have followed so far, but there is more to *cc* than that. That there is more is shown by the fact that this command fails:

```
$ cc stdev.c
Undefined:
_sqrt
$
```

Table 10.1 *cc* Options

cc Option	Description
-c	Suppresses link phase, forces production of object file
-g	Generate information used by the symbolic debugger *sdb*
-O	Invokes object code optimizer
-S	Place assembler-language version in file with a *.s* suffix

We get a complaint indicating that the *sqrt()* function is undefined. That function is part of the math library, so the proper command is this:

```
cc stdev.c -lm
```

As we discussed in Chapter 7, most math functions are in the math library portion of the system library. That portion is not searched unless we explicitly ask by providing the *-lm* option.

To understand what is happening, we need to realize that the *cc* command evokes a command package consisting of a preprocessor, a compiler, and a linker.

Here are the main steps. First, the preprocessor handles the preprocessor directives, getting those files we ask to be *#include*d and substituting the true values for the symbolic representations we have *#define*d. Next comes the compilation process. If it succeeds, a new file of *object code* is produced. It has the same name as the source file, but with the *.c* replaced by a *.o*. For our example, the name would be *stdev.o*. The object file contains the machine code for the program code we wrote.

The object code file *stdev.o* is not, however, a complete program. Missing, for example, would be the code for any library functions we used, such as *scanf()* or *sqrt()*. The code for these functions must be sought in the system libraries and combined with our code. The compiler passes this problem, along with the object code, to the *ld* command. The *ld* program is the system *linker*; it ties the various pieces together and produces the executable file. In the example above, the *-lm* option is passed on to the *ld* linker, which uses it to see which library to search. The *cc* command automatically has *ld* search the standard C library, which is why *scanf()* was not reported missing. Once the executable file (*a.out*) is put together, the object code file (*stdev.o*, in this case) is removed.

You can provide two or more files as arguments for *cc*; in that case the object code files *are not* removed. One reason for this is that *cc* accepts both *.c* files and *.o* files as arguments. If you just change one file, you can compile it along with the object code of the other files, and save the compiler some work. We'll return to this point later.

The *cc* compiler has several options. Tables 10.1 and 10.2 describe some of them.

Table 10.2 *ld* Options

ld Option	Description
-lm	Search the system math library for math functions
-o name	Place the executable program in a file called *name* instead of in *a.out*

Note that the *-lm* option is not part of the list of *cc* options. That is because it is an option for the *ld* command rather than for the compiler proper. The *cc* command kindly passes linker options (like *-ld*) on to *ld*. The option should be placed following the files that use the math library. This ensures that the library is searched after the file is read. Another useful option that gets passed on by *cc* to *ld* is the *-o* option for changing the name of the executable file. To use it, follow the option with the chosen name. For instance, in our example we could use the following command to make the executable file be called *stdev* instead of *a.out*:

```
cc stdev.c -lm -o stdev
```

Let's try that command and see if our program works. We will provide input from the keyboard, the default standard input.

```
$ cc stdev.c -lm -o stdev
$ stdev
1 2 3 4 5
6 7 8 9 10
Control  D
    10   5.5   3.0277   0.9574   standard input: n,mean,stdv,stdvm
$
```

Yes, it works, so let's go expand it now.

SECOND DRAFT OF *stdev*

Our goal is to add two options (echo input and calculate combined totals), to add filename arguments, and to have the hyphen (-) accepted as a filename argument for the standard input. Let's begin with the options.

In Chapter 8 we saw how to add a command-line option to the *charct* program. We'll use the same technique here. The method, as you may recall, consists of tagging options with an initial hyphen and requiring that options be given before filename arguments. A loop inspects the arguments for those beginning with hyphens and sets a *flag* for each option it finds. We'll use *-p* for the printing-the-input option, and *-t* for the totals option. Here's the programming we can add to the beginning of *main()* to do that:

```
prog = argv[0];
while ( argc > 1 && argv[1][0] == '-' && argv[1][1] != '\0') {
    switch( argv[1][1] ) {
        case 'p' :  prinput = YES; break;
        case 't' :  totals = YES; break;
        default  :  fprintf(stderr,
                    "Usage: %s [-p,-t] [-] [file(s)]\n", prog);
                    exit (1);
    }
    argc--;
    argv++;
}
```

Here *prinput* and *totals* are the flag names; of course, they will have to be declared elsewhere in the program. The one new element we have added to the loop (compared to our example of Chapter 8) is the test condition

```
argv[1][1] != '\0'
```

The purpose of this test is to stop the loop if a lone hyphen is encountered, for a lone hyphen will indicate standard input instead of an option. In C, the null character (\0) marks the end of a character string, so the combined test

```
argv[1][0] == '-' && argv[1][1] != '\0'
```

looks for strings starting with a hyphen and having at least one additional character. In C, logical tests are performed from left to right, halting when a false statement is reached. Therefore the final expression is reached only if the preceding one is true.

We will also follow the *charct* example of Chapter 8 in adding filename arguments. That is, we will have something of the form

```
if (argc < 2 )
    use standard input;
else
    use files;
```

Again we add one new feature. The program must be on the lookout for a file called – (a hyphen), and it must open the standard input when encountering that name.

We have also come up with means of implementing the options. Since *calstdev( )* reads the input, it is natural to assign the input echoing to it. We can make *prinput* an external variable so that the flag status is communicated to the function. To handle the totaling option, we will use a new function *total( )*, which is called from *main( )*. Adding all these features makes the program quite a bit longer; the next listing shows the new package:

```
/* stdev.c -- mean, st.dev. and st.dev of mean  Version 1.1 */
/* includes options, multiple file and st. input capabilities */
#include <stdio.h>
#include <math.h>
#define YES 1
#define NO 0
#define FORMAT "%5d %8.4g %8.4g %8.4g  %s: n,mean,stdv,stdvm\n"
#define STLIST(X) X.num, X.mean, X.stdv, X.stdvm
struct stats {
            int num;      /* number of items read */
            float mean;   /* mean of the numbers */
            float stdv;   /* standard deviation  */
            float stdvm;  /* standard dev. of the mean */
            };
int prinput = NO;    /* print input? */
char *prog;          /* program name  */

main(argc,argv)
int argc;
char *argv[];
{
FILE *fp;            /* file pointer */
int totals = NO;     /* find stats for combined input? */
extern int printput;
struct stats data;   /* structure to hold individual results */
struct stats tot;    /* strt. for holding totals */

prog = argv[0];
while ( argc > 1 && argv[1][0] == '-' && argv[1][1] != '\0') {
   switch( argv[1][1] ) {        /* detect the options */
      case 'p' :  prinput = YES; break;
      case 't' :  totals = YES; break;
      default   :  fprintf(stderr,
                   "Usage: %s [-p,-t] [-] [file(s)]\n", prog);
                   exit (1);

   }
```

```
        argc--;
        argv++;
        }
    if ( argc < 2 ) {          /* use the standard input */
        if (calstdev(stdin, &data) == 0) {
            printf ( FORMAT, STLIST(data), "standard input");
            exit (0) ;
            }
        else
            exit (1);
        }
    else {                      /* open a file */
        while ( argc-- > 1 ) {
            if ( strcmp(argv[1],"-") == 0)
                fp = stdin;        /* special case--open std. input */
            else
                if ( (fp = fopen(argv[1],"r")) == NULL) {
                    perror(prog);
                    exit (1);
                    }
            if (calstdev( fp, &data) == 0 ) {
                if (totals == YES)
                    total (&data, &tot);
                printf (FORMAT, STLIST(data), argv[1]);
                }
            argv++;
            }
        }
    if (totals == YES)
        printf (FORMAT, STLIST(tot), "combined input");
    exit (0);
    }

calstdev( fp, statp)
FILE *fp;
struct stats *statp;
{
extern int prinput;
int n = 0;       /* number of items */
double num;       /* input item */
double sum = 0;    /* sum of items */
double sum2 = 0;   /* sum of the squares */
double mean, stdev, stdevm;
while ( fscanf(fp,"%lf",&num) != EOF ) {
```

```
       if (prinput == YES )
           printf("%8.4g\n", num);
       sum += num;
       sum2 += num * num;
       n++;
       }
  if ( n < 2 ) {
     fprintf(stderr,
        "%s: at least two data values required for stdev\n",prog);
     return (1);
     }
  mean = sum / n;
  stdev = sqrt ( ( sum2 - n * mean * mean)/( double)(n - 1) );
  stdevm = stdev/sqrt( (double)n);
  statp->num = n;
  statp->mean = mean;
  statp->stdv = stdev;
  statp->stdvm = stdevm;
  return (0);
  }


  total( one, tot)          /* find cumulative totals */
  struct stats *one, *tot;
  {
  static double sum = 0;
  static double sum2 = 0;
  static int n = 0;

  n += one->num;
  sum += one->num * one->mean;
  sum2 += one->stdv * one->stdv * (one->num -1) +
             one->num * one->mean * one->mean;
  tot->num = n;
  tot->mean = sum / n;
  tot->stdv = sqrt( (sum2 - n * tot->mean * tot->mean)/ (n - 1));
  tot->stdvm = tot->stdv / sqrt((double)n);
  return (0);
  }
```

The new function *total()* keeps a cumulative total of the statistical quantities; this allows the program to find the mean, standard deviation, and standard deviation of the mean for the combined data from all sources of input. One important element in the design of *total()* is the use of *static* storage class variables. These are variables that retain their value between calls to the function; that's what makes them able to keep a cumulative total. The default storage class for a variable

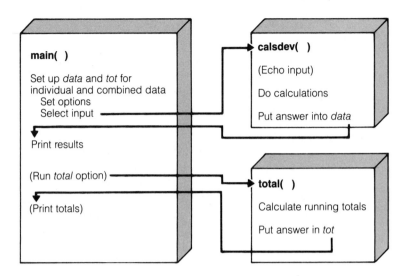

Figure 10.3
Organization of *stdev* Version 1.1

(storage class *auto*) provides for the variable to be cleared each time the function is called, so that class is useless for keeping running totals between calls. The *total()* function is invoked only if the *totals* flag is set. Once all the files have been processed, the results are printed, again, only if the *totals* flag is set.

Let's see how the new *stdev* works. First, we try it on a file containing test grades:

```
$ stdev grades1
    16   80.6875   10.4033    2.6008   grades1: n,mean,stdv,stdvm
$
```

The file had 16 scores that average to 80.6875, and the individual scores are within about 10 of the mean on the average (that is, the standard deviation is about 10). That looks good. Now let's try the *-t* (totaling) option. Also, let's use a somewhat artificial example to test the use of the hyphen to represent standard input. We will process three files of grades, using *cat* and a pipe to send the contents of one file to *stdev*'s standard input:

```
$ cat grades2 | stdev -t grades1 - grades3
    16   80.6875   10.4033    2.6008   grades1: n,mean,stdv,stdvm
     7   83.1429    8.8775    3.3554   -: n,mean,stdv,stdvm
    19   76.4737   11.9693    2.7459   grades3: n,mean,stdv,stdvm
    42   79.1905   10.9995    1.6973   combined input: n,mean,stdv,stdvm
$
```

Ah! Just what we asked for. The lone – (hyphen) is the second *filename* in the argument list, and the piped-in data is processed second. All 42 scores from the three sources are combined in the final output line.

Question 10.3

Do the results for the combined input look plausible?

Are we done, then, with this program? Not really, for there are other possible refinements. Let's discuss four.

Further Thoughts on *stdev*

One area deserving further thought is that of options. Should there be any more? One approach is to see how much you use the program and what features you find yourself wanting. One useful addition would be an option changing the number of significant figures reported. It doesn't make a lot of sense to report test score averages to six figures, but other kinds of data may require even more figures.

Another useful feature would be if *stdev* could be applied just to specified *fields* in a file. For example, if the file contains a table with several columns (or fields) of data, you might just want to process, say, the third column of numbers. Rather than monkey with *stdev*, however, it is simpler to construct a shell script using *stdev* along with *awk* to select the columns. We'll work out a version of this later. If the standard UNIX commands can handle a job, let them.

Another possible option is one that sorts the results for multiple files in order of increasing mean values. But to us it makes more sense to pipe the output of *stdev* to a sorting filter. We could, for example, pipe the output to

```
sort -n -1
```

which uses numeric sorting starting with the second field (the mean field). Unfortunately, the *-n* option does integer sorting and does not handle floating-point representations like 1.3e08 correctly. So there is a need for a floating-point sort program. It makes more sense to develop a separate floating-point sort program than to incorporate sorting into *stdev*. For one thing, it gives you a tool that can be used with other numerically oriented programs.

There is a second area in which we may wish to improve *stdev*, and that is in how it handles input. The *fscanf()* function behaves well when fed what it is told to expect, but our program balks when one gives it alphabetic characters, for example, instead of the expected floating-point numbers. One way to fix this problem is to reprogram the input part of *calsdev()*, making more intelligent use of *fscanf()*. A second solution is to replace *fscanf()* with a function particularly designed to read numbers. Either approach would make *stdev* more *robust* — that is, more resistant to input errors.

The simpler way is to work with *fscanf()*, so let's see how that can be done.

Making *stdev* Input More Robust

The key to improving the handling of bad input is to use *fscanf()*'s return value. We have already made use of the fact that it returns *EOF* upon reaching the end of file. To refresh your memory, here is the old code from *calsdev()*:

```
while ( fscanf(fp,"%lf",&num) != EOF ) {
    if (prinput == YES )
        printf("%8.4g\n", num);
    sum += num;
    sum2 += num * num;
    n++;
    }
```

But what does *fscanf()* return otherwise? It returns the number of items it read successfully. In our case, since we read one number at a time, it returns the value of 1. And what if it encounters bad input, say, the character string "bad"? Then *fscanf()* returns the value 0. Also, and this is important, the buffer pointer used by *fscanf()* remains pointing at the beginning of the bad input.

This suggests the following scheme. When we use *fscanf()* save the return value in a variable called, say, *status*. If we haven't reached *EOF*, then check to see if the return value (*status*) is 1. If so, proceed as usual. If not, skip over the bad input so that the next read will start at the next input item. Here is the new code:

```
while ( (status = fscan(fp,"%lf", &num) ) != EOF ) {
    if (status == 1) {    /* was a number read? */
        if (prinput == YES)
            printf("%8.4g\n", num);
        sum += num;
        sum2 += num * num;
        n++;
        }
    else
        fscanf(fp,"%*s");   /* skips over bad input item */
    }
```

The "*%*s*" specification in *fscanf( )* instructs it to skip over the next string, which, in this case, would be the bad input.

Question 10.4

What happens if we omit the *else* part of the *if...else* statement in the revised *fscanf( )* loop?

For reference, the following listing presents the revised version of the complete *stdev*:

```
/* stdev.c -- mean, st.dv., and st.dv. of mean   Version 1.2 */
#include <stdio.h>
#include <math.h>
#define YES 1
#define NO 0
#define FORMAT "%5d %8.4g %8.4g %8.4g  %s: n,mean,stdv,stdvm\n"
#define STLIST(X) X.num, X.mean, X.stdv, X.stdvm
struct stats {
            int num;      /* number of items read */
            float mean;   /* mean of the numbers */
            float stdv;   /* standard deviation  */
            float stdvm;  /* standard dev. of the mean */
            };
int prinput = NO;    /* print input? */
char *prog;          /* program name   */

main(argc,argv)
int argc;
char *argv[];
{
FILE *fp;            /* file pointer */
int totals = NO;     /* find stats for combined input? */
extern int printput;
struct stats data;   /* structure to hold individual results */
struct stats tot;    /* strt. for holding totals */

prog = argv[0];
while ( argc > 1 && argv[1][0] == '-' && argv[1][1] != '\0') {
   switch( argv[1][1] ) {
```

```
            case 'p'  :   prinput = YES; break;
            case 't'  :   totals = YES; break;
            default   :   fprintf(stderr,
                            "Usage: %s [-p,-t] [-] [file(s)]\n", prog);
                          exit (1);
          }
      argc--;
      argv++;
      }
  if ( argc < 2 ) {
      if (calstdev(stdin, &data) == 0) {
          printf( FORMAT, STLIST(data), "standard input");
          exit (0) ;
          }
      else
          exit (1);
      }
  else {
      while ( argc-- > 1 ) {
          if ( strcmp(argv[1],"-") == 0)
              fp = stdin;
          else
              if ( (fp = fopen(argv[1],"r")) == NULL) {
                  perror(prog);
                  exit (1);
                  }
          if (calstdev( fp, &data) == 0 ) {
              if (totals == YES)
                  total (&data, &tot);
              printf(FORMAT, STLIST(data), argv[1]);
              }
            argv++;
            }
      }
  if (totals == YES)
      printf(FORMAT, STLIST(tot), "combined input");
  exit (0);
  }

#define YESNUM 0
#define NONUM 1
calstdev( fp, statp)
FILE *fp;
struct stats *statp;
{
```

```
    extern int prinput;
    int n = 0;        /* number of items */
    double num;       /* input item */
    double sum = 0;    /* sum of items */
    double sum2 = 0;   /* sum of the squares */
    double mean, stdev, stdevm;
    int status;        /* number found? */

    while ( (status =fscanf(fp,"%lf",&num)) != EOF) {
       if (status == YESNUM) {
          if (prinput == YES )
             printf("%8.4g\n", num);
          sum += num;
          sum2 += num * num;
          n++;
          }
       else
          fscanf(fp,"%*s");
       }
    if ( n < 2 ) {
       fprintf(stderr,
         "%s: at least two data values required for stdev\n",prog);
       return (1);
       }
    mean = sum / n;
    stdev = sqrt ( ( sum2 - n * mean * mean)/( double)(n - 1) );
    stdevm = stdev/sqrt( (double)n);
    statp->num = n;
    statp->mean = mean;
    statp->stdv = stdev;
    statp->stdvm = stdevm;
    return (0);
    }


    total( one, tot)
    struct stats *one, *tot;
    {
    static double sum = 0;
    static double sum2 = 0;
    static int n = 0;

    n += one->num;
    sum += one->num * one->mean;
    sum2 += one->stdv * one->stdv * (one->num -1) +
            one->num * one->mean * one->mean;
```

```
tot->num = n;
tot->mean = sum / n;
tot->stdv = sqrt( (sum2 - n * tot->mean * tot->mean)/ (n - 1));
tot->stdvm = tot->stdv / sqrt((double)n);
return (0);
}
```

Let's try this latest version out:

```
$ stdev -p
2 eggs 4 legs 6  8 10
2
4
6
8
10
Control  D
      5   6      3.1623   1.4142  standard input: n, mean, stdv, stdvm
$
```

Just the numbers got read and echoed, and the words were ignored. This feature is handy, for instance, if a table of data includes a heading. The heading will be ignored as long as it doesn't contain numbers. If you need numbers in the heading, put them in quotes or preface them with some nonnumerical symbol; as long as the first character is not a digit, a plus sign, or a minus sign, the string will be ignored.

Notes on *fscanf()*

We should note here exactly what *fscanf()* does recognize as numbers when the *%ld* format is used. First, it recognizes ordinary integers, such as 3 or –4. Second, it recognizes decimal point notation, such as 3.14 or –0.003 or +1.2. Third, it recognizes exponential notation, such as 6.0E+24 or 2.24e6 or 1.6e-19. Here the number after the *E* or the *e* indicates the power of ten by which the rest of the number is multiplied.

What if one of these forms is part of a word? If a number is embedded in a word, as in *im4u*, it is ignored. So you can include numbers in a table heading if you precede them with some other character, as in */1984 Results* or *"1984" Results*. If, however, a number starts off a word, as in *3rd*, the numerical part is processed and the rest is rejected. Thus, *3rd* is read as *3*.

On the systems we have tried, there is a bug, or perhaps just a peculiarity, about *fscanf()* when using the *"%lf"* format. It reads a lone period or a period beginning a nonnumeric string (as in *".profile"*) as a zero instead of rejecting it as nonnumeric.

The Other Way

We mentioned that a second approach to making input more robust would be to write our own input function. What advantages might that approach have? The *fscanf( )* function is a general purpose input function; it can read integer input, floating-point input, character input, and string input. If we construct a more specialized function that concentrates exclusively on floating-point input, the chances are that the new function will be more compact and faster than *fscanf( )*. Also, we can avoid the *fscanf( )* bug we just mentioned. Finally, we would learn more about programming and program development. A floating-point input function would be useful for many numerically oriented programs, so let's make the development of such a function our next project.

A FUNCTION FOR READING FLOATING-POINT NUMBERS: *getn()*

Our first project in this chapter was designing a program along the lines of a UNIX command. Our next project is to design a function along the lines of a UNIX C library function. The C library already includes a *getchar( )* function to get a character and a *gets( )* function to get a string, so *getn( )* seems like a suitable name for a function designed to get a number.

Design Goals

First, we need to decide what we want the *getn( )* function to do. What should it do if it encounters numerical input, such as *22* or *52.1*? Clearly, we want the function to provide that number to the calling program. But what if it encounters nonnumeric input, such as *peanut* or *.profile*? Here there are two choices to consider. We could have *getn( )* skip on and read the next input, or we can have *getn( )* report its discovery to the calling program, and let the calling program decide what to do next. The second choice seems to offer greater flexibility, so let's take it. Finally, what if *getn( )* encounters end-of-file? We can have it inform the calling program of the fact.

Note that we want *getn( )* to provide *two* kinds of data to the calling program. First, we want the value of a number provided. Secondly, we want a *status report*: is the input item a number, a nonnumber, or the end-of-file signal? This two-fold requirement suggests following the *fscanf( )* plan: use the *return* statement to provide the status, and use an address (or pointer) argument to *getn( )* to tell the function where to place the number it finds. Thus a use of *getn( )* would look like this:

```
status = getn(fp,&number)
```

Here *fp* is a *FILE* pointer to the file to be read, *number* is a *double* variable that receives the input value, and *status* is an *int* variable to receive the "status" report. Let's have *getn()* return *0* if it finds a number, *1* if it finds a nonnumber, and *EOF* if it finds the end-of-file.

We're making progress. We know exactly what we want *getn()* to do. Now all we have to do is figure out how it will do it.

Implementation Strategy

The key point to implementing *getn()* is to have it read input as a *string*. Then the program can examine the string to see if it is, indeed, a number and then act accordingly. Here are the three main elements of a workable strategy:

- Read an input item as a character string
- Determine if the string is a number
- If so, convert the string to a numerical value

Let's look at each element in turn.

Reading in an Input Item: *getword()*

What should an *input item* be? The usual answer is a single *word*, where a word is a string with no white space (spaces, tabs, newlines) in it. Thus we need a *getword* function. There is a *getw()* in the standard C library, but the word it gets is the unit of memory. (A 16-bit processor, for example, uses a 16-bit, or 2-byte, *word* as a standard storage unit.) What we want for a word is a string of characters without spaces, tabs, or newline characters in it. In other words, we want the same sort of word that the UNIX *wc* command recognizes in counting words. Here is one possible version of a *getword()* function that gets that kind of word:

```
/*getword.c -- gets a word */
#include <stdio.h>
#include <ctype.h>
getword(fp,word,limit)
FILE *fp;        /* pointer to file to be read */
char word[];     /* pointer to array to store word */
int limit;       /* limit to the length of word */
{
    int ch;
    int cnt = 0;
```

```
    while ( (ch = getc(fp)) != EOF && isspace (ch))
            ;  /* skip leading spaces, etc. */
    if (ch == EOF)
       return (EOF);
    do
      {
      if (cnt < limit -1)   /* truncate word if too long */
         word[cnt++] = ch;
      }
         while ( (ch = getc(fp)) != EOF && !isspace (ch) );
    word[cnt] = '\0'; /* terminate character string */
    ungetc(ch,fp); /* put EOF or space back into input stream  */
    return (cnt);
  }
```

First the program wades through spaces looking for a nonspace. The *isspace()* macro function of the *ctype.h* file is "true" if its argument is a space, a tab, a newline, a carriage return, a vertical tab, or a form-feed character. If the first nonspace character is *EOF*, the function terminates and returns *EOF*. Otherwise, it starts collecting characters until it reaches one less than the maximum number of characters or else finds a space-type character or *EOF*. It adds a null character to terminate the string. Then it puts the *EOF* or a space-like character back in the input string so that this character will start off the next call to *getword()*. This ensures that the current word gets processed before an *EOF* gets reported back. The *ungetc()* function is one of the luxuries allowed by the buffered approach of the standard I/O package; *ungetc()* just has to replace the character in an array, not in the original file.

This design truncates strings that are too long. For instance, if the input string is "enormous word" and if *limit* is set to 5, then the first call to *getword()* would return "enor" (the fifth character is the null character that terminates a string) and the second call would return "word". The rest of "enormous" would be skipped over. Another way to design *getword()* would be so that the second call would pick up where the first left off. That way, the second call would return "mous". We leave that version as an exercise for the interested reader.

Because *getword()* might be useful in other programs, we will keep it in its own file, *getword.c*. It can be combined with the rest of the program during compile time. We'll return to that topic later.

Our *getn()* program, then, will use *getword()* to fetch the next word from input. The next step is to decide if this word is a number.

Is the Input Word a Number?

How can we (or *getn()*) tell if the string of characters comprising the input word is a number? We can simplify matters by emulating *fscanf()* and recognizing any string that starts as a number to be a number. Later, any nonnumerical part can be truncated. Thus we just have to worry about the beginning of a string. This leaves three classes of number beginnings.

1. The string can start with a digit, as in 3 or 39 or 22.1.
2. The string can start with plus sign, minus sign, or decimal point and have the next character be a digit. Examples include +83, −16.83, and .35.
3. The string can start with a plus or minus sign followed by a decimal point followed by a digit: −.422 or +.91, for instance.

We can define some macros to make the testing easier. First, here is a macro that tests if its argument is a plus sign or a minus sign:

```
#define ISSIGN(X)  (((X) == '+' || (X) == '-') ? 1 : 0 )
```

Here the conditional operator (?:) sets the value to 1 (true) if X is a sign and to 0 (false) otherwise.

The next macro tests to see if its argument is a decimal point:

```
#define ISDPNT(X)  ((X) == '.' ? 1 : 0 )
```

Finally, this macro tests if its argument is a plus sign, minus sign, or decimal point; it combines the other two tests:

```
#define ISNPRF(X)   (ISSIGN(X) || ISDPNT(X) ? 1 : 0 )
```

(The name *ISNPRF* is supposed to suggest *is number prefix*.)

Combining these macros with the *isdigit()* macro from the *ctype.h* file, we can test for the three forms of number beginnings we gave above. Suppose that the prospective number is in the string array *temp*. Here, then, are the tests:

1. Is the first character a digit?

   ```
   isdigit(temp[0])
   ```

2. Is the first character a plus sign, minus sign, or decimal point, and the second character a digit?

   ```
   ISNRPF(temp[0]) && isdigit(temp[1])
   ```

3. Is the first character a plus or minus sign, the second character a decimal point, and the third character a digit?

   ```
   ISSIGN(temp[0]) && ISDPNT(temp[1]) && isdigit(temp[3])
   ```

Combining these tests with an *if* statement will let the function decide if the input word is a number or not. If it is, we have to convert it.

Converting a String to a Numerical Value: *atof()*

This part is easy. The UNIX C library contains a function called *atof()* (for "ASCII-to-float") designed to convert strings to numerical values. It takes the address of the string as an argument, converts it to a type *double* number, and returns that value. Thus, *atof()* itself is of type *double*. Strings like *4ever* result in the value 4 being returned; that's why our *getn()* only has to check to see if the string starts out as a number. The *atof()* function correctly handles exponential notation, so *getn()* needn't worry about that. If a purely nonnumeric string (like "fashion") is provided to *atof()*, it returns the value zero. However, our programming prevents such strings from reaching *atof()* in the first place. Thus, if *getn()* provides a zero value as the value read, we know that a zero in some form (0 or 0.0 or -0.0e22, for example) was really read.

Putting It All Together

The next listing shows the programming to unite the fragments we have developed:

```
/* getn.c -- get a number */
#include <stdio.h>
#include <ctype.h>
#define MAXWD 20    /* maximum word size */
#define ISSIGN(X)   ( ((X) == '+' || (X) == '-') ? 1 : 0 )
                        /* a plus or minus sign? */
#define ISDPNT(X)   ( (X) == '.' ? 1 : 0 )    /* a decimal point? */
#define ISNPRF(X)   ( ISSIGN(X) || ISDPNT(X) )
                        /* a sign or a decimal point? */
#define YESNUM 0    /* the word's a number */
#define NONUM  1    /* the word's not a number */
getn(fp,np)
FILE *fp;
double *np;
{
    char temp[MAXWD];
    double atof();

    if ( getword(fp,temp,MAXWD) != EOF )
        {
        if ( isdigit(temp[0]) ||
                 (ISNPRF(temp[0]) && isdigit(temp[1])) ||
```

```
                (ISSIGN(temp[0]) && ISDPNT(temp[1]) && isdigit(temp[2])))
                    {
                    *np = atof(temp);
                    return(YESNUM);
                    }
            else
                    return(NONUM);
            }
        else
            return(EOF);
}
```

Note that we declare *atof( )* as type *double*. As you can see, the program starts with *getword( )* fetching the next input item. If it is *EOF*, the *getn( )* function returns that value and quits. Otherwise the input is placed in the array *temp*. Then the *if* statement makes all the tests we described earlier and determines if *temp* is a number or not. If it is, *atof( )* makes the conversion, and the value is placed in the location indicated by the argument to *getn( )*; a value of 0 is returned. Otherwise, if *temp* is not a number, *getn( )* returns the value 1.

If we were preparing a standard UNIX-style manual description for *getn( )*, we could include these entries:

SYNOPSIS
    #include <stdio.h>
    int getn(fp,np)
    FILE *fp;
    double *np;

RETURN VALUE

Upon successful reading of a number, a value of 0 is returned. Upon reading a nonnumber, 1 is returned, and *EOF* is returned on end-of-file.

Using *getn( )* and *getword( )*

Suppose we want to use *getn( )* in *stdev*. How do we go about it? First, we have to change the programming in the *calsdev( )* function. Then we have to include *getn( )* and *getword( )* in the compiling process.

First, change the program. What we had, in part, was this:

```
while ( (status =fscanf(fp, "%lf", &num)) != EOF) {
    if (status == YESNUM) {
```

```
        if  (prinput == YES )
            printf("%8.4g\n",  num);
        sum += num;
        sum2 += num * num;
        n++;
        }
    else
        fscanf(fp, "%*s");
    }
```

Replace it with this:

```
while ( (status =getn(fp, &num)) != EOF) {
    if (status == YESNUM){
        if  (prinput == YES )
            printf("%8.4g\n",  num);
        sum += num;
        sum2 += num * num;
        n++;
        }
    }
```

The main difference in usage is that *getn()* automatically advances to the next input item after reading a word, so it doesn't have to use *fscanf(fp, "%*s")* to move ahead if nonnumeric input is met.

What about compilation? We could just add *getn()* and *getword()* to the end of the *stdev.c* file. However, both of these new functions can be used by other programs, so it makes more sense to maintain them in separate files, say *getn.c* and *getword.c*. To compile the final program, then, we would use this command:

```
cc stdev.c getn.c getword.c -lm -o stdev
```

PROGRAM MAINTENANCE: *make*

When we develop a program with several files, as with our *stdev* program, we would often go through the compilation step several times as we made corrections and revisions to the various functions. At the end of a long work session, typing such a long command line repeatedly can get tiring and frustrating. The UNIX *make* command, however, eliminates those difficulties. Let's see what it does.

Suppose we revise the *getword.c* file. We could give this command to recompile the program:

```
cc stdev.o getn.o getword.c -lm -o stdev
```

Since the other two files are unchanged, we use the object code versions of them. If, however, we had implemented the *make* facility, all we would have to do is to type this:

```
make
```

And how do we implement the *make* facility? We create a file called *makefile* and place these lines in it:

```
stdev :   stdev.o getn.o getword.o
          cc stdev.o getn.o getword.o -lm -o stdev
```

As you can see, this file contains instructions for creating the complete *stdev* program. Clearly, if we wish to save ourselves needless effort, the *make* program warrants a closer look.

The *make* program lets you specify what needs to be done to put a program together, and then it takes care of the details itself. If you update one of the files that form part of the program, *make* attends to the updating of the whole package, recompiling only those parts that have been changed. The instructions describing the program are placed in a file called the makefile. The default choice for the name of this file is, naturally enough, *makefile* or *Makefile*. (We'll use the second choice.) Typing the command *make* then causes the program to follow the directives in *Makefile*. This may sound a bit like a shell script, and it is a bit like a shell script. But, as we will see, the *make* command adds quite a bit of cleverness.

Setting up a Makefile: Dependencies and Commands

Let's look at the example we gave for our *stdev* program:

```
stdev :   stdev.o getn.o getword.o
          cc stdev.o getn.o getword.o -lm -o stdev
```

The first line is a *dependency* description. The entry before the colon (*stdev*) is termed the *target*; it is the program or file that *make* aims to produce. The entries after the colon consist of the files that *stdev* depends on.

The second line provides the executable command needed to obtain *stdev* from the files it depends on. The line itself begins with a tab character. Lines beginning with tabs are interpreted as shell commands. The list of commands continues until the first line that doesn't begin with a tab or to a #. The # is used to mark lines that are comments. Using spaces instead of a tab to start the line will confuse *make*.

Using *make*

What happens if we have a file *Makefile* with these lines and we type *make*? The end result is to produce the *stdev* file, but the route depends on the circumstances. Let's consider particular examples. Suppose the first time you use it, you have the three object files (*stdev.o*, etc.) and no C-code files or target file in the directory. Then the shell command instruction (line 2) is executed, and *stdev* is produced.

Now suppose you have C files (*stdev.c*, etc.) but no object files or target file. Then *make* uses *cc* to *produce* the missing object files so that it can then move on and make *stdev*. Moving up in complexity, suppose that both C files and object files are present. Then *make* checks to see if the C file has been updated since the corresponding object file was produced. For instance, is *getn.c* newer than *getn.o*? If so, *make* recompiles *getn.c*, producing a new object file; if not, it uses the old one.

Suppose the target file (*stdev*) does exist. Then its time of creation is compared to those of the files it depends on. If one or more of these files is newer, then the target file is updated. Thus *make* attends to keeping the entire *stdev* program system updated.

The practical significance of this is if, say, we revise the *getn.c* file, we don't have to type

```
cc stdev.o getn.c getword.o -lm -o stdev
```

Instead, we just type

```
make
```

and anything that needs to be updated gets updated.

The *make* command is most useful for more complex examples than ours, but even in the *stdev* case it is helpful.

Elaborations on *make*

There is more to *make* than we have said. For example, you don't have to rely upon a default name for the makefile. If, for example, you want instructions kept in a file called *makestdev*, you can use the *-f* option to specify that file:

```
make -f makestdev
```

Then, too, the files themselves can contain more information than we have shown. For example, here is a slight extension in complexity. In *stdev*, both *stdev.c* and *getn.c* made use of the preprocessor definitions *YESNUM* and *NONUM*. Instead of repeating these definitions twice, as we did, we could have placed the following line in each file:

```
#include "numdef.h"
```

Here *numdef.h* would be a header file containing those definitions. This brings a new file into the program and creates new dependencies. We would then change the makefile to reflect this:

```
stdev :  stdev.o getn.o getword.o
         cc stdev.o getn.o getword.o -lm -o stdev

stdev.o getn.o : numdef.h
```

With this additional dependency line, *make* knows that if the *numdef.h* file has been changed, then it is necessary to update *stdev.o* and *getn.o*. The *make* command realizes that it needs to use the *stdev.c* and *getn.c* files to do the updating. Then, once the object files are updated, it becomes necessary to update *stdev* itself.

Note how two or more files separated by blanks can be used to the left of the colon if they depend on the same files.

Besides dependency lines and executable command lines, *macro definitions* can be included in the makefile. These are much like shell variables. One difference is that quotes are not needed for value strings containing blanks. That is, both these definitions are valid:

```
LIB = -lm
OBJECTS = stdev.c getn.c getword.c
```

The value of a macro is given by enclosing the name in braces and preceding this concoction with a dollar sign. The braces can be omitted for one-character names. Our current makefile can be rewritten this way:

```
# makefile for stdev
LIB = -lm
OBJECTS = stdev.c getn.c getword.c

stdev : ${OBJECTS}
        cc ${OBJECTS} ${LIB} -o stdev

stdev.o getn.o : numdef.h
```

This is useful, for example, if you add more object files to a program. Then you need only redefine *OBJECTS* in makefile.

We have seen a simple use of *make*, but it does illustrate the basic features. Now let's turn to another topic, the co-opting of *stdev* into a shell script.

SHELL SCRIPTS USING *stdev*

Since we designed *stdev* as a filter, it can easily be incorporated into shell scripts. Suppose we want a program that calculates statistics for one column of a file. That is, suppose we have a file that looks like this:

```
farm        dogs    cats    horses
Pighaven    2       3       1
Tinkey's    5       8       2
Foghole     14      5       8
Bugstone    3       3       3
```

Suppose, too, we just want the statistics for cats. We need a filter that will pass along only the cat column. To be more precise, we should use the word *field* instead of column, for *column* implies a single character width.

The *awk* command fits the bill. It recognizes fields in a line by looking for the blank spaces. A field is a sequence of nonblanks separated by blanks from other fields. Thus, in the file above, the cat stats constitute the third field of each line. (System V also provides a *cut* command specifically designed to extract selected fields from a file. However, since it is not generally available, we'll stick with *awk*.) The *awk* command (see Appendix A) uses *$1* to stand for the first field, *$2* to stand for the second field, and so on. Here is a script using *awk* and *stdev*:

```
# statfield -- finds stats for a field in a file
case $# in
  2) ;;
  *) echo Usage: $0 filename fieldnumber 1>&2 ; exit 1
esac
echo standard input is field $2 of the file $1
awk '{print $'$2} $1 | stdev
```

Let's try it out:

```
$ statfield farmpets 3
standard input is field 3 of the file farmpets
    4    4.7500    2.3629    1.1815    standard input: n,mean,stdv,stdvm
$
```

Well, 4.75 is the average of the cat numbers, so we trust the rest is okay. There are a few points worth mentioning about the script. One is that field 3 included the word *cat*. But our final design of *stdev* conveniently ignores words, so the presence of a heading did not botch up the program.

Secondly, there is some odd punctuation in the *awk* line. A normal *awk* command asking for a field to be printed would look like this:

```
awk '{print $3}'
```

Here the quotes make the whole print instruction into one argument. But we don't want to use a fixed integer like *3*. We want to use a positional parameter *$2*. Now we have warring dollar signs. One belongs to *awk* and should be quoted to protect it from the shell; that means using single quotes. The other, the one in *$2*, belongs to the shell and should be interpreted by it. So we put it out of the quotes. Since the one space in the instruction is still in quotes, the whole string appears as a single argument to the shell:

```
awk '{print $'$2}
```

If there were any further spaces in the instruction, we could use double quotes for that part, since double quotes still let the shell interpret *$*:

```
awk '{print $'"$2 }"
```

There are many possibilities for using *stdev* in scripts. One could create an interactive program that prompts the user for input. Or one could expand *statfield* to accept multiple fields. These are all examples of integrating C programs with shell scripts. But, as the last application in this chapter, we look at an example that carries that integration of C programs and shell scripts one step further.

Question 10.5

Make *statfield* into an interactive script.

A WORD-FREQUENCY COUNTER: AN INTEGRATED APPROACH

Some tasks are done most easily using UNIX commands and shell scripts. Others are better done using a C program. Here we will develop an example that draws upon both approaches. It differs from our *stdev*-using shell script in that we will develop a C program to be used as part of a specific shell script rather than to be used as a general-purpose program.

The vehicle for this study is a word-frequency program. It looks at a file and counts how often each individual word appears in it. For output, it will produce a list of the words and corresponding frequencies sorted in order of decreasing frequency.

If we want to do the whole project as a C program, we would have a lot of programming to do. We would need to identify words in the input with more precision than *getword( )* does. That function accepts any character sequence without spaces as a word, but our new program needs to do things like toss out numbers and strip away punctuation. It should also convert everything to lower case, so that *The* and *the* will be counted as the same word. Then we would need to develop an algorithm for determining whether each new input word has been seen yet and for keeping count. And we would have to write a sorting routine.

To avoid this work, let's see how far we can get just using UNIX commands. First, we need a general plan. Here is one approach.

1. Start by converting the file into a list of lower-case words, one word per line.
2. Sort the list. This will place multiple occurrences of a word one after the other, making them easy to count.
3. Count the occurrences of each word.
4. Sort the result by frequency.

How much of this can we do using UNIX filters? Quite a bit, as we shall see.

Getting a List of Words and Converting to Lower Case

We could use *sed* to filter the input into a list of words. For example, we could use the *s* command to replace punctuation with null strings, and we could substitute newlines for spaces and tabs. But there is an easier way, and that is to use *tr*. The *tr* command (see Appendix A) lets us replace specified characters with other characters. It lets us do two things. First, we can use it to replace all capital letters with lowercase letters. The command for this is as follows:

```
tr A-Z a-z
```

The letters in the first range are replaced by the corresponding letters in the second range (''A'' by ''a'', ''B'' by ''b'', and so on). Then we can use *tr* to replace every character that is not a letter with a newline; that gets rid of spaces, punctuation, numbers, and the like. This could produce multiple newline characters (the pattern of a comma followed by a space becomes two newlines, for example), but an option lets us collapse multiple newlines into single newlines. What is even more marvelous is that the one example given in the UNIX manual tells how to accomplish this precise task! Here is the second *tr* command:

```
tr -cs a-z '\012'
```

(We describe both of these *tr* examples in Appendix A).

We need to connect these commands with each other and with the input. Here's how:

```
# wordfreq -- initial steps
cat $* |              ← Gather input
tr A-Z a-z |          ← Decapitalize it
tr -cs a-z '\012'     ← Convert to a word list
```

Since *tr* only reads standard input, we use *cat* to gather input and pipe it to *tr*. Since *cat* accepts standard input and file input, we can use *wordfreq* with either, too.

Sorting the Word List

Now we have a list of words, one per line, and it is simple to get the list sorted; just use the UNIX *sort* command:

```
# wordfreq -- a step further
cat $* |
tr A-Z a-z |
tr -cs a-z '\012' |
sort                        ← Sort the word list alphabetically
```

Counting Word Frequencies

These beginning steps are quite similar to what the UNIX *spell* command uses to get started. Now we need a program that will take the sorted output and count how many times each separate word occurs in it. Can this be done using a UNIX command? The task involves comparing each line to the preceding one to see if the new word is the same as the last one. It also involves keeping a running total for each word. These tasks involve programming: comparisons, decisions, numerical calculations. There is one UNIX command that offers such features, and that is the filter *awk*. Of course, the C language also offers those features. We (the author and his computer) produced a C program before it occurred to one of us that the same programming approach could be done with *awk*. So the answer is, yes, it is possible to do this step using a UNIX command. However, the C version turns out to be about 5 to 20 times faster for the various combinations of systems and files we tried, so let's use it. (Is the time savings important? We'll return to that question later.) We'll see the *awk* version in Appendix A; here is the C version now (we decided to add a word-length parameter to the output):

```
/* wdfreq.c -- word frequencies for a sorted list */
#include <stdio.h>
#define WSIZE 30 /* limit word size to 29 characters */
main()
{
char last[WSIZE];          /* last word read */
char word[WSIZE];          /* latest word read */
int length;                /* length of word */
int count;                 /* number of occurrences */
int n = 0;                 /* number of distinct words */

while ( getword(stdin,word,WSIZE) != EOF ) {
    if (n == 0) {              /* first word */
        strcpy(last,word);     /* copy and save it */
        count = 1;
        length = strlen(word);
        n++;
        }
    else {
        if ( strcmp(word, last) != 0) {   /* new word found */
            printf("%s %d %d\n",last, length, count);
            strcpy(last,word);
            count = 1;
            length = strlen(word);
            n++;
            }
        else               /* word same as preceding word */
            count++;       /* update count */
        }
    }
if ( n > 0)
    printf("%s %d %d\n",last, length, count);
}
```

Note that we used *getword( )*, so that function would be included in the compilation. Since there is just one word per line, we also could have used the library function *fgets( )*, which reads one line at a time.

The logic is straightforward. When the first word is read, the count is set to 1, and *last* is set to the first word. From then on, each new word is compared to *last*. If it is different, then *last* is printed along with its length and number of occurrences.

Then *last* is reset to the new word, and the count and word length are reset. If the new word is the same as *last*, then the count is incremented. Once *EOF* is detected, the information on the final word is printed, providing at least one word was found.

Call the compiled version *wdfreq*. We can use *sort* to sort the output by frequency, and our final shell script is this:

```
# wordfreq -- finds word frequencies for files or stdin
cat $* |
tr A-Z a-z |
tr -cs a-z '\012' |
sort |
wdfreq |
sort +2nr
```

The *+2nr* means skip the first two fields and sort in reverse numerical order. We could also sort by frequency and then by word length by using this option:

```
sort +2nr +1nr
```

Or we could sort by word length then frequency with this option:

```
sort +1nr
```

You might want to think about how to make these choices options for the *wordfreq* program. Meanwhile, let's apply it to a file.

First, we show the file, then we apply the shell script:

```
$ cat bigtext
The big train trundled down the Big Pine track; a big man
waved a big hand at the big dog by the track.
$ wordfreq bigtext
big 3 5
the 3 4
a 1 2
track 5 2
at 2 1
by 2 1
dog 3 1
down 4 1
hand 4 1
man 3 1
pine 4 1
train 5 1
trundled 8 1
waved 5 1
```

Now we can check word frequencies and examine the hypothesis that Francis Bacon wrote Shakespeare's plays. Of course, we first need to get someone to put Bacon's works and Shakespeare's works on the computer.

Second Thoughts

What have we gained with this hybrid program? First, we avoided having to learn how to use *awk* (but only for one chapter). Secondly, by using a C program, we speeded up part of the program. Let's further examine this point.

The C version, we said, is about 5 to 20 times faster than the *awk* version, so using it results in a great reduction in running time for that part of the program. But that segment is not the only time consumer in the program. Other slow spots are the two sorting segments. If the *awk* part were fast compared to the sorting, then replacing *awk* wouldn't speed up the program as a whole very much. The real question becomes, how much does using the C program instead of the *awk* program speed up the program as a whole. Tests on a couple of systems using files ranging in size from about 1000 words to 60,000 words showed running time reductions for the whole program ranging from 30 percent to 80 percent. That is quite a worthwhile improvement for a modest effort.

What did we gain by not doing the whole program in C? By letting UNIX commands do most of the work, we saved a lot of programming effort. For example, since we don't know in advance how many words will be read, we should provide for expanding the storage space for new words as needed. With our approach, we let *sort* worry about that. Can we cut down the running time by writing our own sorting programs? That's not too likely; *sort* is an effective, efficient program. To cut the running time further would involve changing the word-counting algorithm and writing a program that processes unsorted input, storing away new words as they show up, and matching and counting repeated words. Doing that efficiently could involve using *trees* or some other advanced data structure. See, for example, the recursive, binary-tree word-counting program in *The C Programming Language* by Kernighan and Ritchie (Englewood Cliffs: Prentice-Hall, 1978). In short, we would have to be knowledgeable and highly motivated to really do the program right. Even then, the time reductions might not prove to be dramatic.

A reasonable approach to UNIX programming, then, is to see how much of the problem can be solved using UNIX commands alone. This may provide an excellent solution. Even if it is only a so-so solution, it can be adequate if you need only to use the program occasionally. If you find that the speed of the program is a concern, then use the *time* command on the various segments of the program to see which are the time-eaters. If a major offender is something you can easily reprogram in C, go for it. Likely candidates would be segments applying *awk*, or perhaps *sed*, to large files. In any case, the all-UNIX-command version can be a testing ground for different approaches; if a method turns out not worth doing, then it is not worth doing well.

CONCLUSION

The UNIX system embodies the programming philosophy of creating small, well-focused programs that do particular tasks well. The philosophy also provides for an environment that makes it possible to tie these programs together into larger efforts. When using the system, we should take advantage of facilities it provides. And if we need something that the system lacks, we would do well to design new programs or functions that fit in with the rest. Our *stdev* program, for example, can be used at either end of a pipe, so it can be easily linked with other UNIX commands.

Another point to keep in mind when solving a programming problem is that you need not think in terms of shell scripts versus C programs. The most convenient route may be to integrate the two routes, using each for what it does best. Your ability to combine both approaches depends, in part, on your familiarity with basic UNIX commands. In Appendix A we summarize some of the commands that are most useful in shell scripts.

BOOKEND

The main point of this book is that UNIX is designed to let you solve problems. The exact approach you should take depends on the nature of the problem. We have seen four major approaches. First, see if an existing UNIX command can solve the problem. This approach can yield results as simple as typing a single command name or as complex as a long *awk* program. Second, if one command won't do the job, perhaps a pipe of two or more commands will. In this chapter, for example, we put together a string of UNIX commands that produces an alphabetized word list from a text file. Third, you can use a shell script. Such scripts essentially are programs in which UNIX commands form the elements of the language. Since the scope of UNIX commands is great, and since scripts offer programming features such as I/O control and flow control, the shell script approach is very powerful. Fourth, some applications need the fine control of a C program; here, system calls and the C library place the resources of the system at the program's disposal.

Often, even complex problems can be solved using either a script or a C program. The advantages of the script are that it is easier to create, it is easier to modify (it doesn't need recompilation), and it uses much less space sincc it uses existing programs. The C program, on the other hand, offers more control over input and output, and it may run quite a bit faster.

Sometimes the best course is to combine the shell script and C programming approaches. In handling a large problem, use whatever approach is best for each subtask, and use a script to coordinate the result.

Indeed, program coordination is one of UNIX's most important features. The UNIX commands are designed to work with one another. It is for this reason that so many UNIX commands are filters. By writing scripts and programs that follow UNIX conventions and philosophy, you work with this cooperative effort. We hope this book provides you with the incentive and the means to follow that approach.

ANSWERS TO QUESTIONS IN CHAPTER 10

10.1 a. Mean = 100

b. Numbers vary from the average value to 10 to 20 off the average value, so estimate std.dev = 10 to 15. (The actual value is 11.6.)

10.2 *data.num* and *ps->num*. Just use the dot with structure names and the arrow with structure pointers. One other possibility is *(*ps).num*, since the value that *ps* points to (**ps*) is *data*.

10.3 Yes, they do. The only number that is easy to check is the total of number scores, and 16 + 7 + 19 is, indeed, 42. The overall average looks plausible, for it is larger than the smallest, and smaller than the largest contribution. The standard deviations are all roughly the same, which is okay, since that says the scores had roughly the same distribution for the three sets of scores. Finally, the standard deviation of the mean is smaller, with makes sense because that is the usual consequence of a larger sample size.

10.4 If we omit the *else* section, the next *fscanf( )* call will read the same bad input that the preceding call read, and the program gets caught in an endless loop.

10.5 (Without error checking)

```
# statfield -- finds stats for a field in a file
echo This command finds the mean, the standard deviation,
echo and the standard deviation of the mean for a column of
echo figures from a file.
echo Which file do you want\?
read file
echo Which column do you want\?
read column
echo standard input is field $column of the file $file
awk '{print $'$column} $file | stdev
```

EXERCISES

1. Add a formatting option to the *stdev* program.
2. Write a floating-point sort program. Design it as a UNIX filter that can also take filenames from command-line arguments.

3. The *stdev* program can be used as a stand-alone command or as part of a pipe or a shell script. Write a version of *stdev* that can be used as a function call by other C programs.

4. Our version of *getword( )* reads up to a specified number of characters in an input word and skips over the rest of the word. Devise a version that picks up on the next input cyle where it left off last time, so that extra-long words get read in parts.

5. Our *getn( )* picks up a number embedded in a string if that string starts with the number. Devise a version that picks up only those numbers not embedded in a string.

6. Write a filter that passes on to output the numbers in its input.

7. Expand the *statfield* script so that it can accept multiple fields, each to be processed as a separate file.

A

UNIX Tools: *grep, sed, tr,* and *awk*

The shell script is a potent programming technique in part because it can draw upon potent UNIX commands. Four commands often drafted into script service are *grep* (a pattern-searching utility), *sed* (a *stream* editor), *tr* (a character transliteration program), and *awk* (a pattern-scanning and processing language); they are the subjects of this appendix. This discussion provides the background necessary for using these commands elsewhere in this book, but the material also provides a stand-alone discussion of the commands. What makes these commands useful is that they can search through and modify their input; they can be used to find information and to transform data.

These four UNIX commands are all filters. They receive input from the standard input or (except for *tr*) from named files, and they send their output to the standard output. They all scan a file for patterns or specific characters and perform some sort of action when they find a match. They differ, however, in what they can do once they find a matching pattern.

The *grep* command is the least versatile. It simply prints any line it finds that matches the pattern. The *sed* command goes further; it can perform editing changes on matching lines. And *awk* goes further yet; it breaks a matching line into separate *fields* and lets you process them in various ways, including rearranging the order or performing arithmetic operations. The *tr* command transliterates; that is, it replaces specified characters by other specified characters.

The *grep* command and the *sed* command are closely related. True, they perform different functions, but both are based on the old UNIX *ed* editor and use its pattern-matching scheme. Thus, a major aspect of learning *grep* or *sed* is learning that scheme. We will begin by discussing *grep* and showing its method of representing patterns.

SEARCHING FOR A PATTERN: *grep*

The name *grep* stands for *g*lobal *r*egular *e*xpession *p*rinter. The term *regular expression* refers to the generalized search patterns that *grep* accepts. As the name suggests, *grep* searches out these patterns globally (for an entire file, not just a single line) and prints out the lines containing them.

The most basic form of *grep* is this:

```
grep pattern filename
```

Here *grep* searches the named file (*filename*) for the pattern (*pattern*) and prints out the lines containing the pattern. For instance,

```
grep post inventory
```

searches the file *inventory* for the string of characters *post*. It is important to realize that *grep* seaches for the string *post* and not the word *post*. By this, we mean it searches for the consecutive characters "p", "o", "s", and "t" (the string) without caring whether they form a word or just part of a word. Thus output produced by the preceding command could look like this:

```
fence posts      423
compost pails    19
posterior hooks  3
```

Each line contains the string *post*.

This basic *grep* usage can be altered or embellished in several ways. First, one can take input for *grep* from several files or from standard input. Second, *grep* has some options available. Finally, the pattern portion can be made more complex. Let's look at each in turn.

Input for *grep*

If no filename is given after the pattern, *grep* takes its input from the standard input. This means, for instance, that you can use the keyboard to create text; but that is not the reason *grep* was designed to accept the standard input. (If you do try using keyboard input, however, remember that a [Control] D at the beginning of a line closes keyboard input to the program.) The reason for providing for standard input is that this allows *grep* to receive input from a pipe. If, for example, you wanted to know if *basil* was logged in and didn't wish to read through the whole *who* output yourself, you could type

```
who | grep basil
```

Table A.1 Common Options for *grep*

Option	Result
-v	Prints those lines that *do not* match
-c	Prints only a count of the number of matching lines
-l	Prints only the names of files with matching lines
-n	Prints the line number with each output line
-s	Prints no output, just return status (In System V, just error messages are suppressed)

and the output of the *who* command would become the input to *grep*.

Besides accepting no filename and one filename, *grep* also accepts multiple filenames. In this case, each file is searched in succession. When matching lines are printed, they are preceded with the filename, so that you can tell which file contains which lines:

```
$ grep execrable ch1 ch2 ch3
ch1: a more execrable example of expurgation would be
ch3: An execrable version is placed in throw.out and
$
```

Here examples were found in *ch1* and *ch3*, but none in *ch2*.

Question A.1

How could you find all uses of *putchar()* in all the C program source code listings in a directory?

Now let's look at options.

Options for *grep*

These options follow the usual UNIX pattern; that is, they begin with a hyphen and immediately follow the command name. The choice of options varies from UNIX system to UNIX system, so you will have to check the documentation for your own system. Table A.1 shows some common ones found in most versions.

For example, if we want to know how many times the string *aspirations* occurred in a document, we could do this:

```
$ grep -c aspirations speech
22
$
```

At this point the speech writer might decide that 22 usages were not enough.

The *-s* option description refers to *status*. Each UNIX command, when run, produces a status number to indicate failure or success. This is the value that is represented by *$?* in shell scripts. For *grep*, a status of *0* means success, a status of *1* means no matches were found, and a status of *2* indicates something went wrong: a syntax error, perhaps, or specifying an inaccessible file. The status value is returned whether or not the *-s* option is invoked; the purpose of this option is to suppress other output when only the status is needed. (An example would be if *grep* were used as a test condition for an *if* or *while* statement.)

Question A.2

How would you find the names of all the C program listings in a directory using the *ctype.h* header file?

Pattern Specification in *grep*

Now let's look at the patterns *grep* recognizes. We'll look at two matters here. The first is how to search for a phrase containing spaces, and the second is how to use *grep*'s pattern-matching scheme.

The *grep* search pattern is the first argument following the command name and possible options. If the pattern contains a space or a tab character in it, it's necessary to put the pattern in single or double quotes. That is, a command like

```
grep San Francisco hotels
```

would cause *grep* to seek the pattern *San* in the files *Francisco* and *hotels*. To seek the pattern *San Francisco*, use

```
grep 'San Francisco' hotels
```

or

```
grep "San Francisco" hotels
```

The quotes identify the whole phrase as a single argument. Note, however, that *grep* does not provide for finding phrases spread over more than one line. The whole phrase must be on one line for *grep* to find the match. That is, if *San* came at the end of one line, while the next line began with *Francisco*, that instance of *San Francisco* would not be caught.

Now let's look at the pattern-matching scheme for *grep*. The key is to use metacharacters to represent general patterns. For instance, in *grep*, a period represents any one character, just as the question mark represents any one character in a shell command line. Here is an example using both *grep*'s pattern-matching and the shell's pattern matching:

```
grep 'sp.t'  ch?
```

The shell, of course, matches up *ch?* to any three-character filename beginning with *ch*. If the directory contains files *cha*, *ch1*, *ch2*, *ch3*, and *chap*, all but the last fit this pattern, and all but the last get searched by the *grep* command.

And what does *grep* look for? Any line containing a four-character string beginning with *sp* and ending with *t*. Here are examples of matching patterns:

```
spate
spot
respite
sputter
the asp took
```

We've underlined the matching part. Note that a space, too, is a character. Similarly, *sp..t* would match any 5-character string beginning with *sp* and ending with *t*. One example would be *sport*. Note that the second period is not required to match the same character that the first period matches.

Now that we have seen a representative example, let's take a more systematic look at the various special symbolisms used in *grep*. Table A.2, on page 413, summarizes these symbolisms.

To see how these rules work, let's look at a few short examples.

h.t	Matches *hot, hit, hst, h8t, h&t,* and so on. Note that the period matches any character, not just alphabetic characters.
h[ea]t	Matches *het* and *hat*, but not *hit*. Only one character is matched by a bracket pair, so *heat* is not matched.

[A-Z][^A-Z]	Matches any two-character string in which the first character is a capital letter and the second is not. Matches include *B4*, *Me*, and *I!*.
^The	Matches any line beginning with *The*. Note that this use of the caret is quite different from its use inside a bracket pair.
\.$	Matches any line ending with a period. Note the use of the backslash to show we mean a period and not the special symbol for any character.
ho*t	Matches *ht* (zero occurrences of the preceding pattern), *hot*, *hoot*, *hooot*, and so on.

Note the final example carefully. Even zero occurrences of *o* are matched; *grep* uses the asterisk quite differently from the shell. If you wanted to match one or more *o*s in that pattern, you would use

    hoo*t

Question A.3

Devise *grep* patterns to match the following:

a. Swine or swine
b. 3-character strings starting with ''b'' and ending with ''t''
c. All lines beginning with BEGIN
d. All lines in which the first nonspace character is a C

Now let's get some practice by solving some typical pattern-matching problems.

Problem 1: Counting Blank Lines

You want to count the number of blank lines in a file. First, we will use *grep*'s -c option, which counts the number of matches. Second, we need a pattern to match a blank line. A true blank line, one with no characters, is matched by this *grep* pattern:

    ^$ ← Matches an empty line

Table A.2 Pattern-Matching Metacharacters for *sed*

Pattern	Meaning
.	A period matches any one character.
\	A backslash despecializes special characters. For instance, to explicitly match a period, use \.
[...]	Matches any one character from the enclosed list. Thus [af2] matches an *a*, an *f* or a *2*. A hyphen can be used to match a range of characters: *[n-z]* matches any one character in the range *n* through *z*. To include a right bracket in the list, make it the first character: *[]()#]*
[^...]	Matches any one character not in the enclosed list. Thus *[^aeo]* matches any one character except an *a*, *e*, or *o*
*	An asterisk matches 0 or more occurrences of the preceding character.
^	Matches the beginning of a line.
$	Matches the end of a line.

This represents the beginning and end of a line with no characters in between. Very simple! However, there are other ways to get a blank-looking line, and we have to find ways to catch them, too.

For example, when writing the file, you may have started a new line, hit the space bar a few times, then hit the return key. In this case there would be something between the beginning and end of the line: space characters. They would be present, but invisible. So we need to indicate that there could be zero or more spaces between the ends of the line, and that is a job for the * special character:

   ^ *$ ← Matches blank line with any number of spaces

We follow the caret with a space, and we follow the space with an * to show we can have zero or more of them.

But a blank-looking line can also contain a tab character, the character produced when you hit the tab key. The space character tells the computer to skip one space when printing it; the tab character tells the computer to skip to the next tab position. Typically, the tab positions are set to columns 9, 17, 25, and so on. To look for lines containing just tabs, we could use this pattern:

   *$ ← Matches blank line with any number of tabs

Here we didn't hit the space key seven times, we just hit the tab key once. Since that is not at all obvious, let's use \t to represent a tab character in our text representation here. (This is the representation used in C programs.) That is, to indicate the previous example, we will use

```
^\t*$
```

How can we combine these patterns to catch lines that may have blanks, tabs, or both? The key is that the asterisk can be used with a character or anything that represents a character, such as a bracket pattern indicating a list of possible characters. Thus we can use this pattern:

```
^[ \t]*$   ← Matches any number of tabs and spaces
```

It stands for a line with zero or more occurrences of spaces and tabs in any combination. That is, this single pattern matches all of the following (and more):

```
^$
^[ \t]$
^[ \t][ \t]$
^[ \t][ \t][ \t]$
```

Our final command, then, if we wish to count the blank lines (with or without spaces or tabs) in the file *text*, is

```
grep -c '^[ \t]*$' text
```

(Again, if you were actually using this command, you would use the tab key where we used the \t symbol.) Now on to another problem.

Problem 2: Finding Two Patterns in Proper Sequence

Suppose we want to find all lines that contain *Mickey* and *Donald* in that order, but which may have additional characters in between them. An example would be, "Then Mickey tossed the gem to Donald." If we are searching the *hero* file, this can be our command:

```
grep 'Mickey.*Donald' hero
```

Here the pattern .* stands for zero or more occurrences of any character. Just as the second period in .. need not stand for the same character as the first period, the .* pattern does not mean that the matched characters have to be identical. Thus the pattern matches the following line:

```
"Hey, Mickey," said Donald, "get a look at this!"
```

Incidentally, if we *didn't* care about which order the two words came in, we could do this:

```
grep Mickey hero | grep Donald
```

The first pass through *grep* produces only lines containing *Mickey*. The pipe makes the list of lines containing *Mickey* into input for the second pass through *grep*, and the only lines making it through both passes are the ones containing both *Mickey* and *Donald*.

Problem 3: Finding a Word

As we have noted, *grep* finds strings; it doesn't care whether the string forms a complete word or just part of one. Thus

```
grep cat text
```

will turn up lines containing *cat*, *cattle*, and *scatter*. Suppose, though, you want just the word *cat*. On some systems, *grep* has a *-w* option to do just that. Lacking this option, we must concoct a suitable pattern. (This is the problem we faced in designing *speller* in Chapter 6.)

The obvious choice is to surround the word with space:

```
grep ' cat ' text
```

This will catch most instances, but several loopholes in this pattern may let a *cat* sneak through undetected. First, there may be some punctuation adjacent to the word:

```
cat. cat; {cat  cat! cat, cat? cat] "cat (cat
```

One way to plug this loophole is to include all the possibilities:

```
grep '[ ({['\''"]cat[])} ,.?;:'\''"*]' text
```

Here we have preceded and followed *cat* with bracketed lists of possible adjoining punctuation. (The sequence '\'' is used to include a single quote in the list of possibilities. The first single quote acts as a metacharacter, terminating the preceding quoted string, the backslash-quote combination adds a nonmetacharacter quote to the list, and the third quote is a metacharacter again, starting a new quoted string.) But are these all the possibilities? Might the text have something like /cat/ in it? A different approach is to specify which characters *don't* come before or after the word:

```
grep '[^A-Za-z]cat[^A-Za-z]' text
```

This says we don't want any letters of the alphabet before or after the string *cat*. This formulation screens out *scat* and catches *cat!*. It also catches *cat22*, but such combinations are rare.

There is still one more problem. The word might come at the beginning or end of the line. These two patterns catch those possibilities:

```
grep '^cat[^A-Za-z]' text
grep '[^A-Za-z]cat$' text
```

In our example in Chapter 6, we run all three of these *grep* commands to catch a word.

Is it possible to combine these three tests into one? No, at least not for *grep*. But the *grep* variant known as *egrep*, found on many UNIX systems, can combine them. Let's take a quick look at the rest of the *grep* family.

THE REST OF THE *grep* FAMILY: *fgrep* AND *egrep*

The *fgrep* and *egrep* commands differ from *grep* in the pattern-recognition schemes they use. The *fgrep* command doesn't use any special characters (like * or $); it just uses pure strings (no metacharacters) for its search patterns. In compensation for this limitation, *fgrep* is a faster, more compact program than the others. Also, *fgrep* can search for several strings simultaneously. The *egrep* command can also search for several strings simultaneously. In addition, it extends *grep*'s pattern-matching powers. Both commands offer a *-f* option that lets them take the search pattern from a file instead of the command line.

Suppose you wished to search the */etc/passwd* file for *Roosevelt*, *Eisenhower*, and *Truman*. You can do it with one pass of *fgrep* by using one string per line in the search pattern:

```
fgrep 'Roosevelt    ← Return key is struck to continue the line
       Eisenhower
       Truman'    /etc/passwd
```

Note that we used a pair of single quotes to mark the three names as one argument.

The *egrep* command will accept the same kind of instruction, but it also accepts extended pattern matching. One of the chief extensions is that *egrep* offers an *or* operator in the form of the | symbol. For instance, we can also do the presidential search with this command:

```
egrep 'Roosevelt|Eisenhower|Truman' /etc/passwd
```

This looks for lines containing *Roosevelt* or *Eisenhower* or *Truman*. This is more compact than the split-line form we used with *fgrep*, and it is also more versatile.

The versatility of the | (or) form arises from how patterns can be grouped. What does this pattern mean?

```
Marilyn|James Monroe
```

Does this mean *Marilyn Monroe* or *James Monroe*, or does it mean *Marilyn* or *James Monroe*? The answer is the latter. Everything to the left of the | is one pattern, and everything to the right is the second pattern. But parentheses can be used to change the grouping. Thus

```
(Marilyn|James) Monroe
```

matches both *Marilyn Monroe* and *James Monroe*.

Two other additions to *egrep* are the special characters + and *?*. Both are similar to *, which stood for zero or more occurrences of the preceding character. The + stands for 1 or more occurrences, and the *?* stands for zero or one occurrence. Thus we have the following:

*ho*t* matches *ht, hot, hoot, hooot,* etc.

ho + t matches *hot, hoot, hooot,* etc.

ho?t matches *ht* and *hot*

Parentheses can be used with *, +, and *?*; this means they can be applied to whole expressions, not just single characters. Hence this:

*(ho)*t* matches *t, hot, hohot, hohohot,* etc.

Patterns using the *egrep* scheme of special characters are known as *full regular expressions*. This distinguishes them from the ordinary *regular expressions* of *grep*. Later, we will see that *awk* also uses full regular expressions. Meanwhile, let's move on to *grep*'s relative, *sed*.

Question A.4

Devise *egrep* patterns to match

a. *Twain* or *Clemens*

b. Dave Parker or Dorothy Parker or Parallel Parker

THE STREAM EDITOR: *sed*

To place *sed* (for *stream ed*itor) in perspective, first consider what a typical text editor (such as *ed*, *ex*, or *vi*) does. Suppose you go to edit a file called *homilies*. You type

```
ed homilies
```

The editor then creates a temporary copy of *homilies* in the */tmp* directory. All the editing changes you make are made to the copy. Then, when you give the *w* command, the temporary file is copied into the original. The net result is that a regular editor alters the original file.

The *sed* editor, however, is a UNIX filter. It can take input from a file, but its output is sent to the standard output; the original file is not altered. The output from *sed* can be redirected to a new file if you wish to save it. Or it can be piped along to some other program as input. This makes it an easy matter to make *sed* part of a chain of UNIX tools.

That may sound interesting, but what exactly does *sed* do? It takes a line from input, applies an editing command to it, and prints the result. Then it takes the next line and repeats the process until the whole file has flowed through *sed*. The basic usage looks like this:

```
sed 'editing-command' filename
```

If no filename is given, then *sed* reads the standard input; this means it can receive input from a pipe. If more than one filename is given, then they are processed in turn.

The editing commands of *sed* basically are those of *ed*. If the command contains no spaces and no characters special to the shell (such as *?* or *[*), it doesn't have to be in single quotes, but it's easiest to always use them and not worry about what the shell might think. Let's look at the editing commands now.

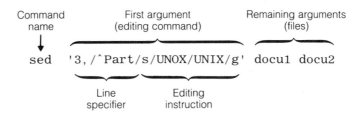

Figure A.1 A *sed* Command Line

Editing Commands for *sed*

A typical editing command has two parts: a line-specifier and an editing instruction. If there is no line-specifier, then the command is applied to every line. There are two approaches to specifying lines, so let's look at them first.

Line Specifiers

One way to specify a line is to give a line a number or a range of line numbers. As with *ed*, the symbol $ stands for the last line. Here are some examples:

```
3          ← The third line
5, 8       ← Lines 5 through 8
10, $      ← Lines 10 through the last line
```

Because the input flows through a line at a time, *sed* doesn't know in advance when the last line will show up. Only when it reaches the end does it find where the end is. Thus *sed* won't recognize such *ed* address patterns as

```
$-9, $     ← Last 10 lines for ed, nonsense for sed
```

The second way to specify a line for *sed* is to provide a matching pattern enclosed in slashes. The patterns are the same as those used by *grep*. Here are some examples:

```
/huge/       ← All lines containing the string huge
/[Dd]o/      ← All lines containing strings Do or do
/^[ \t]*$/   ← All blank lines  (see the section on grep)
```

In the last example we use the symbol \t to represent the tab character; if the pattern seems obscure, see the section on *grep* for a discussion of it.

The *sed* command augments *grep*'s arsenal slightly. In particular, we can use the notation \\n to stand for a newline character.

The two forms of line identification (line numbering and pattern-matching) can be combined:

```
1,/gossip/      ← From line 1 to the first mention of gossip
```

Finally, you can use an *!* to indicate the command is to be applied to lines that *don't* match the line specifier; it is placed between the line specifier and the command. There's an example in the next section.

Question A.5

How would you specify the lines running from the first mention of *dodo* or *Dodo* to the end of a file?

The line specifier in a complete command is followed by an editing instruction, so let's check those out next.

Editing Instructions for *sed*

The *ed* instructions most often used with *sed* are *s* (substitute), *p* (print), *d* (delete), and *q* (quit). The editing instruction immediately follows the line specifier. Here are some short examples:

```
sed '10q' text    ← Quit after reading line 10
```

Since *sed* prints each line as it is processed, this command prints the first 10 lines of a file.

```
sed '$p' text    ← Print the last line
```

Since each line is printed anyway, this results in the last line being printed twice. More typically, the *p* instruction is used with the *-n* option to suppress printing of all lines except those covered by the *p* instruction. The *-n* option is explained more fully in a few pages.

```
sed '/^[ \t]*$/d' text    ← Delete all blank lines from text
```

The matching lines get deleted and so are not printed.

```
sed '/value/!d' portfolio    ← Delete every line in portfolio not
**                           ← containing the string value
```

Here we use the *!* command (the NOT command) to reverse the usual sense of a command.

The *sed* substitution command (*s*) is more involved, since we need to indicate what is to be replaced and what the replacement is. The general form is

```
s/oldstring/newstring/
```

This replaces the first occurrence of *oldstring* on a line with *newstring*. If we want to replace all occurrences on a given line, we tack on a *g* (for global) at the end of the command. Thus a simple command might look like this:

```
sed 's/Michael/Michele/g' text
```

This replaces each occurrence of *Michael* with *Michele*. Since *sed* automatically examines each line of input, we don't have to specify an address range for a substitution unless we want only part of a file affected. Thus

```
sed '1,/Jessup/s/Michael/Michele/g' text
```

replaces *Michael* with *Michele* up through the first line containing *Jessup*.

Since the substitution command is more involved than the others, let's take a closer look.

A Closer Look at Substitution

The general form is, as we've said,

```
/oldstring/newstring/
```

The old and new patterns can be simple strings, but they can also include special characters. The pattern for oldstring can include all the special characters that *grep* does. In addition, *sed* offers a way to *tag* part of a pattern, and we will come to that in a moment.

The *newstring* portion also allows some special characters. One useful one is *&*, which stands for the entire *oldstring*. For example, suppose we want to place all occurrences of UNIX in quotes. We can do this:

```
sed 's/UNIX/"UNIX"/g' adcopy
```

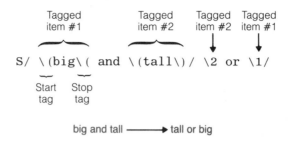

Figure A.2 Using *sed* Tags

Or we can do this:

```
sed 's/UNIX/"&"/g' adcopy
```

Here, & stands in for *UNIX*.

If you are writing a Broadway musical about UNIX and want to add pizazz to the working title of *UNIX*, you can do this:

```
sed 's/UNIX/&! &!/g' promo
```

This converts all mention of *UNIX* to *UNIX! UNIX!*

The second special notation used in the *newstring* portion is part of the *tag* mechanism we mentioned earlier. This is how it works. You can enclose part of *oldstring* between \(and \); the enclosed part is said to be *tagged*. You can then refer in *newstring* to the tagged part as *1*. If you tag more than one part in *oldstring*, you can call the second tagged part *2*, and so on. For instance,

```
s/\(incredible\) and \(amazing\)/\2 and \1/
```

replaces the phrase *incredible and amazing* with *amazing and incredible*. Here, *1* stands for the first tagged string, *incredible*, and *2* stands for *amazing*. Remember, however, that a phrase has to be on one line for a substitution command to spot it.

By using this mechanism, you can save some typing. You can also use it to represent pattern-matching formations. To see what this means, let's consider a simple example.

Suppose you want to change all occurrences of *occurence* and *Occurence* to *occurrence* and *Occurrence*. Can we use this command?

```
s/[Oo]ccurence/[Oo]ccurrence/g
```

No, we can't; the pattern *[Oo]* can only be used in the left-hand pattern (*oldstring*); the only special symbols usable on the right side (*newstring*) are & and the *1* family. So patterns using *[]*, ., and * can't be used on the right side. But we can do this:

```
s/\([Oo]ccur\)ence/\1rence/g
```

If the original is *Occurence*, then *1* is *Occur*; and if the original is *occurence*, then *1* is *occur*. The tag mechanism lets us refer to complex patterns on the right side of a substitution command. We made use of this feature in our substitution commands in *speller* in Chapter 6.

Question A.6

Devise editing commands to do the following:

a. Change all occurrences of "Grissmuttle" to "Barney Grissmuttle".
b. Replace all occurrences of *foregoon* and *Foregoon* with *foregone* and *Foregone*, respectively.
c. Replace all occurrences of *Brenda Gempsoth* with *Brenda Jean Gempsoth*.

The *sed* command does not limit us to one editing command per line of text. We can give a series of commands, and they will act upon each line of input text in turn. The method for giving multiple commands is to give one per line, enclosing the whole set in a pair of single quotes:

```
sed 's/Michael/Michele/g
     s/Joanie/Johnie/g
     s/Potatohead/Spudmug/g' chapter1
```

As each line comes up, first the first command is performed on it, then the second, and so on. Thus the later commands work on material that may already have been altered by the first command. For instance,

```
sed 's/Dodger/Giant/g
     s/Giant/Cub/g' teambio
```

changes all *Giants* to *Cubs*, including those which had been *Dodgers* but moments before.

The spreading of commands over several lines works differently with the Berkeley *csh* shell. If you are using *csh*, you need to end each to-be-continued line with a backslash. Or you can just type *sh* to use the regular Bourne shell. Type a [Control] D to return to the *csh* shell. Or you can use the *-f* option. Yes, *sed* does have options. Let's look at them now.

Options for *sed*

The *sed* command has three options: *-n*, *-f*, and *-e*. The *-n* option suppresses the automatic printing of each processed line. When it is in effect, only those lines affected by a *p* command get printed. For instance, consider this command:

```
sed -n '$p' list
```

It prints just the last line of the file *list*.

The *-f* option is followed by a space, then a filename. This option causes *sed* to take its editing commands from the named file. Thus

```
sed -f edit sermon
```

would cause *sed* to look in the file *edit* for commands to apply to the file *sermon*.
You can use the *-f* option more than once:

```
sed -f namech -f form  memo
```

This command first uses the editing commands from *namech*, then those from *form* on each line from *memo*. All the editing commands from both files are applied to one input line before the next line is read.

The *-e* option lets you mix a command-line editing command with commands in a file:

```
sed -e 's/Boston/Wasco/g' -f form trav.broch
```

This causes the Boston substitution to be attempted on a line, then the editing commands in *form* to be applied, and then on to the next input line.

Several *-e* and *-f* options can be intermingled; the editing commands are executed in the order in which they occur in the command line.

Uses of *sed*

One use of *sed* is to produce global editing changes in a large file. For example, you can develop a set of abbreviations and keep them in a file of editing instructions.

That is, you can have a file called *abbr* with entries like these:

```
s/GPI/Global Products Incorporated/g
s/DRD/Department of Research and Development/g
s/OGL/our glorious leader/g
```

Then you can use the abbreviations in the original and use *sed* as a prefilter for, say, the *nroff* formatter:

```
sed -f abbr report85 | nroff
```

This would replace each abbreviation in the *report85* document with the corresponding phrase, and the *nroff* command would reformat the text. Of course, you should avoid abbreviations that might pop up as part of words.

Another use is as a quick formatter:

```
sed 's/$/\
/' letter
```

This inserts a newline character (produced by hitting ⎡Return⎤ at the end of the first line) at the end of each text line, thus producing double spacing. (The *csh* shell requires a double backslash at the end of the first line.)

The *sed* instruction is often used in shell scripts. Sometimes the essence of the script is editing. For instance, if you double space a lot, you can convert the preceding command into a shell script:

```
# dblsp -- double-spaces text
sed 's/$/\
/' $*
```

Other times, *sed* is used as a tool to modify a stream or other text as part of a larger program. Suppose, for example, that a command within a script requires input of one word per line. Then a sequence like this can start the script off:

```
cat $* | sed 's/[ \t][ \t]*/\
/g' |
```

The *cat* command gathers input, which is piped to *sed*. There, any sequence of one or more spaces and tabs is replaced by a newline character, and the output is piped on to whatever command line follows.

CHARACTER TRANSLITERATION: *tr*

There is another UNIX command that can do the last task a bit more efficiently. It is *tr*, which transliterates characters. Let's look at it now.

In its simplest form, *tr* replaces characters in one list with the corresponding characters in a second list. The *tr* command is not as versatile as *sed*, but within its realm it is quite effective. Here is an example; first we use *cat* to show what is in a file, then we show the effects of *tr*:

```
$ cat philosophy
I compute, therefore I am.
$ tr eiou ~#$% < philosophy
I c$mp%t~, th~r~f$r~ I am.
$
```

Note that *tr* is a pure filter. It takes input from the standard input, so we need to use redirection to access a file. Note, too, how each character in the first list following *tr* is replaced by the corresponding character in the second list. The command pays attention to upper and lower case; thus the *I* is not affected, even though *i* is in the list.

What happens if the second list is shorter than the first?

```
$ tr eiou EU < philosophy
I cUmpUtE, thErEfUrE I am.
$
```

The last character from the second list is used for all the leftover characters from the first list.

Special Notations

You can indicate ranges with *tr* by using a hyphen. A very common usage is this:

```
tr A-Z a-z
```

It converts upper case to lower case. Some versions require that ranges be enclosed in *escaped* brackets:

```
tr \[0-9\] 9876543210
```

or

```
tr "[a-z]" "[A-Z]"
```

You can use C code for ASCII representation of characters. That is, the ASCII octal code for a newline character is 012. To indicate that character, precede the octal number (including a leading 0) with a backslash:

```
$ tr '\012' # < philosophy
I compute, therefore I am.#$
```

Here we replace the newline character at the end of the text with a #. That is why the *$* prompt appears at the end of the line instead of at the beginning of the next. The quotes protect the pattern from shell meddling.

Options

The *tr* command has three options. The first, *-d*, uses just one list of characters, and it causes them to be deleted.

Returning to *philosophy*, we find this:

```
$ tr -d eiou < philosophy
I cmpt, thrfr I am.
$
```

The *-c* option causes the substitutions to affect every character *but* those in the first list. Using it is the same as dropping the *-c* option but typing the entire ASCII sequence minus the original list. Here is an example without and with the option:

```
$ tr eiou "*" < philosophy
I c*mp*t*, th*r*f*r* I am.
$ tr -c eiou "*" < philosophy
***o**u*e****e*e*u*e*******$
```

In the second example, everything but the four letters in the list was replaced with an *, even the spaces, punctuation, and the newline character at the end of the line. The * is in quotes to protect it from being interpreted by the shell.

Finally, the *-s* option compresses strings of repeated output characters into a single character. That is, strings like **** become *. *Output* characters are those that have been produced by the substitution process. Double letters that weren't substituted are not affected. Let's try a little more philosophy:

```
$ tr -cs eiou "*" < philosophy
*o*u*e*e*e*e*e*$
```

This takes us to a point where we can interpret the example in the UNIX manual. The example is this:

```
tr -cs A-Za-z '\012' < file1 > file2
```

The first string consists of all the alphabetic characters. The *-c* option says the substitution affects all characters but those alphabetic characters. The second string says all affected characters are to be replaced with a newline. And the *-s* option says that multiple newlines are to be replaced by a single newline. The net result is to produce one word per line, where a word is a string of alphabetic characters. Spaces, commas, numbers, and the like become newlines.

Question A.7

a. Devise a doubt-provoking command that replaces periods and exclamation marks with question marks.
b. Devise a command to delete everything but the digits 0-9 from a file.
c. Devise a command that reverses the case; that is, that changes uppercase to lowercase and vice versa.

The *tr* is a very specialized command; its sole function is to replace characters with other characters. Our next command, *awk*, while still a filter, is general enough to be termed a language.

A PATTERN-SCANNING AND PROCESSING LANGUAGE: *awk*

The *awk* command (named after and by its creators: Aho, Weinberger, and Kernighan) is one of the more unusual UNIX commands. It combines pattern matching, comparison making, line decomposition, numerical operations, and C-like programming features into one program. It offers much to the user, and it is going to take time to present all its features.

We can start by noting that the *awk* command resembles *sed* in that it operates on its input line by line. A basic command line looks like this:

```
awk awk-command filename
```

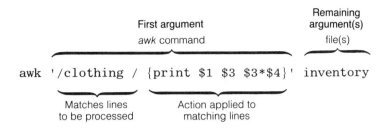

Figure A.3 An *awk* Command

Each *awk command*, like a *sed command*, in general has a line-specifier (a *pattern*) part followed by an instruction (an *action*). What distinguishes *awk* from *sed* are the scopes of its patterns and actions. For instance, *awk* lets you identify particular fields within a line. By default, a field is a sequence of characters containing no blanks and separated by blanks from other fields. For example, each word on this line is a separate field. Its actions provide for numerical operations, for creating variables, and for providing programming flow control statements.

Here is a simple example of an *awk* command line:

```
awk '/poultry/ { print $1, $3, $6}' supplies
```

In this case, the pattern part is */poultry/*. As in *sed*, this matches those lines containing the string *poultry*. The action part is enclosed in braces; it requests that the first, third, and sixth fields of the matching line be printed. The *$1* stands for the first field, the *$3* stands for the third field, and so on. The first field might name an item, the third give an amount, and the sixth provide a cost. So this command could extract relevant information about poultry supplies from a large file.

If there is no pattern portion, the action is applied to *every* line of input. Thus the following prints the first and second fields of the file *table2* in reversed order:

```
awk '{print $2, $1}' table2
```

If there is no action portion, the default action is to print the entire line. Thus the following prints all lines of the file *nat.enq* containing the string *scandal*:

```
awk '/scandal/' nat.enq
```

More than one command can be included by starting a new line for each command:

```
$ awk '/scandal/ {print $0}
       /rumor/ {print $0} ' rag
```

Field $1	$2	$3	$4	4 fields (NF = 4)
corn	300	pounds	$100	record 1 (NR = 1)
beans	400	pounds	$200	record 2 (NR = 2)
okra	10	pounds	$5	record 3 (NR = 3)
milk	100	gallons	$200	record 4 (NR = 4)
eggs	10	dozen	$10	record 5 (NR = 5)

$0

Figure A.4 Fields and Records

The *$0* stands for the entire line. Since the entire line gets printed if no action is specified, we could have omitted the action part entirely, but we wished to show that each action normally is kept on the same line as the corresponding pattern.

If you have many commands, it is usually more convenient to place them in a file and have *awk* get its commands from the file. This is done by using the *-f* option:

```
awk -f cawk rag
```

This command tells *awk* to apply the command in the *cawk* file to the input from the *rag* file.

To learn more about *awk*, we need to learn more about its patterns and its actions. But first we need to learn a bit more about fields and records.

Fields and Records

An *awk* program processes its input a *record* at a time. By default, a record is just a line. The newline character is the default *record separator*, the character that separates one record from the next. Whenever *awk* encounters a newline character (and hence a new line) it starts a new record.

Within a record, the input is divided into fields. A field is a series of characters delineated by a *field separator*. By default, the field separator is a blank, that is, a space or a tab. Suppose we have the following input:

```
He marshalled his faculties, such as they were,
and attempted to explain his presence in the tub.
```

In this example, *were* is the eighth field in the first record, and *to* is the third field in the second record.

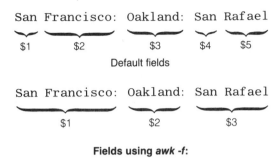

Fields using *awk -f:*

Figure A.5 Changing the Field Separator

Awk has some built-in variables dealing with fields and records. First, *NR* represents the current record number. *NF* represents the number of fields in the current record. Thus, after reading the first line above, *NR* has the value *1* and *NF* has the value *8*. Both of these variables can be incorporated into *awk* programs, and we will show some examples soon.

Question A.8

What are the values of *NR* and *NF* after the second line of the example is read?

The variable *FS* stands for the field separator. By default, this is a blank, or, to be more precise, a space character or a tab character. But it can be reset to another value. This can be done as an *awk* action (more on that later) or by using the *-F* option. To use this option, follow the *-F* immediately by the desired field separator:

```
awk -F: '{print $1, $2}' /etc/passwd
```

This prints the first two fields of the */etc/passwd* file, using a colon as a field separator for the input. In that file, the various entries are separated by colons, so the colon is the obvious choice for a field separator.

Finally, the variable *RS* represents the record separator; it, too, can be redefined in the action part of an *awk* program.

Let's move on to the patterns and actions of *awk* now.

Table A.3 Pattern-Matching Metacharacters for *awk*

Pattern	Meaning
\	Match following character literally
^	The beginning of a line
$	The end of a line
.	Any one character
[*list*]	Any one character in *list*
[^ *list*]	Any one character not in *list*
*	Zero or more occurrences of the preceding character or group
+	One or more occurrences of the preceding character or group
?	Zero or one occurrence of the preceding character or group
(*exp*)	Is *exp*
exp1 | *exp2*	Means *exp1* or *exp2*

Patterns in *awk*

The *awk* command accepts several forms of pattern-matching, including the regular expressions of *egrep* and numerical comparisons. Let's look at the various forms in turn.

Full Regular Expressions

First, *awk* recognizes the same full regular expressions that *egrep* does. Thus it recognizes the special symbols shown in Table A.3.

For examples and further discussion of these expressions, please check the sections on *grep* and *egrep*.

Regular Expressions and Fields

We can apply these pattern specifiers to individual fields. The first field, recall, is termed *$1*, the second *$2*, and so on. The entire line is called *$0*. The ~ and !~ symbolisms are used to indicate a match and no match respectively. Thus, if we want to find all lines in which the second field matches *Flubbo*, we could use

```
$2 ~ /Flubbo/
```

This also matches lines in which *Flubbo* is just part of the second field; for example, *Flubboson* would be matched. In this context (matching a field), we can use ^ and $ to indicate the beginning and end of the field, not of the line. Thus the pattern

```
$2 ~ /^Flubbo$/
```

matches only those lines in which the second field in its entirety is *Flubbo*. Similarly, the pattern

```
$2 !~ /^Noxin$/
```

matches all lines for which the second field is not *Noxin*.

Question A.9

Devise patterns to match the following:

a. The third field contains Paddy or Mickey
b. The third field consists of Paddy or Mickey
c. The first field consists of Paddy and Mickey separated by one or more spaces.
d. The line contains one or more occurrences of Kitty, with each separated from the following by one or more spaces, and with the final Kitty followed by an exclamation mark. That is, match lines like

```
Kitty!
Kitty Kitty    Kitty!
```

Relational Expressions

Relational expressions compare two expressions. Are they the same? Is one bigger? The *awk* command recognizes the same relational operators that C does. They are listed in Table A.4.

If, for example, field 2 of a file contains 1983 sales data and field 3 contains 1984 sales data, then the following command prints those lines for which 1983 sales exceeded 1984 sales:

```
awk '$2 > $3' salesreport
```

Remember that the default action is to print the matching line.

Awk also recognizes the arithmetic operators $+$, $-$, $*$, $/$, and $\%$. The last is the *modulus* operator and yields the remainder produced when the number preceding it is divided by the number after it. Thus *7 % 3* is *1*. These arithmetic operators can be used in the relational expressions. For example, if we want to print those

Table A.4 Relational Operators for *awk*

Operator	Meaning
<	Less than
<=	Less than or equal to
==	Equal to
!=	Not equal to
>=	Greater than or equal to
>	Greater than

lines for which 1984 sales are four times or more greater than 1983's, we can use this command:

```
awk '$3 >= 4 * $2' salesreport
```

These relational tests can also be performed with strings. The test

```
$1 == "Flubbo"
```

is the same as our earlier

```
$1 ~ /^Flubbo$/
```

The test

```
$1 > "q"
```

selects lines beginning with letters after *q* in the alphabet.

Awk attempts to tell from context whether it should be doing a numerical or a string comparision. If both operands are numeric, then a numerical comparison is made; otherwise a string comparison is made. Thus, if *$1* is *3*, the test

```
$1 > "q"
```

asks if *3* comes after *q* in the ASCII collating sequence.

Question A.10

How could we specify those lines in which the sum of the third and fourth fields exceeds the fifth field?

Table A.5 Logical Operators for *awk*

Operator	Meaning
&&	and
||	or
!	not

Logical Operators: Combinations

We have not reached the end of *awk*'s pattern-matching abilities. It also provides the logical operators of C so that we can combine relational expressions. Table A.5 shows these operators.

For example, the pattern

```
$3 > $2 && $3 > $4
```

selects records for which the third field is larger than the second field *and* larger than the fourth field. On the other hand, the pattern

```
! ($3 > $2 && $3 >$4)
```

selects records for which the previous condition is not true; that is, it selects records which do not have field three larger than fields two and four.

Question A.11

a. How could we specify a line in which the first field is Cygnus and for which the third field is greater than 12?

b. How could we specify a line in which the first field is Leo or in which the fourth field is not cluster?

Ranges

Like *sed*, *awk* allows you to specify a range of lines. Just separate two patterns by a comma. Here are two examples:

```
NR = = 20,  NR = = 40     ← The records 20 through 40
NR = = 1,  /[D]ismay/     ← Record 1 through the first appearance of Dismay or dismay
```

Note that patterns of the regular expression type can be mixed with patterns of the relational expression type.

Special Patterns

Awk has two special patterns: *BEGIN* and *END*. *BEGIN* is used to label actions to be done before any records are read. For example, the command

```
BEGIN {RS = ":";   FS = "/"}
```

establishes that the colon, not the newline, will be used as the record separator. It also sets up the slash as the field separator.

The *END* label is used to identify actions that are done after all the input has been read. We will see samples soon.

All these possibilities give *awk* awesome (if you are awe-prone) line-matching capabilities. Now let's look at what actions can be performed.

Actions

The *awk* actions take it into the realm of a programming language. It can print, of course. It also has built-in functions, the ability to create variables and even arrays, arithmetic operations, and flow control statements. It is a form of simplified C, slower-running, but easier to use. Let's examine this range of actions.

Printing

The simplest way to print is to use the *print* statement. As with arguments, it usually takes a field designator or some combination of designators. Suppose the file consists of the following single line:

```
Bertram Crewham  23 45 192
```

Then here are some examples of *print* statements and their effects:

```
{print $2, $1}
Crewham Bertram

{print $2 $1}
CrewhamBertram
```

```
{print $3 + $4}
68

{print}
Bertram Crewham 23 45 192

{print $0, "total:", $3 + $4 + $5}
Bertram Crewham 23 45 192 total: 260
```

These examples point out several aspects of *print*. First, the arguments are typically fields, combinations of fields, or strings. No argument results in the whole record being printed. Separating arguments with a comma results in the output being separated by a space. Omitting a comma causes the output to be run together. You can do arithmetical operations on the fields.

If you want more control over the appearance of the output, you can use the *printf* statement from C. The only difference is that in *awk* you omit the enclosing parentheses and closing semicolon. That is, if a C statement looks like this:

```
printf("quantity: %6d  cost: $%d\n", q, c);
```

then the corresponding *awk* statement would have this appearance:

```
{printf "quantity: %6d  cost: $%d\n", $3, $5 }
```

Question A.12

Suppose you have a file with lines like these:

```
Daniel Boone
Davy Crockett
etc.
```

How could you get the contents reprinted as

```
Boone, Daniel
Crockett, Davy
etc.?
```

Print Redirection

One sneaky aspect of *awk* is that *print* output can be redirected to other files. Suppose we want to convert a file with three fields into three files with one field each. Then we can do this:

```
{print $1 >> "col1"; print $2 >> "col2"; print $3 >> "col3"}
```

Here we have used UNIX redirection with each field. The statement *print $1 >>* *"col1"* causes the first field in each line to be appended to the file *col1*. If the file doesn't exist, it gets created. We place the filename in quotes to identify it as a string. If we left the quotes off, *awk* would think *col1* was the name of an *awk* variable. (Read about that later.) You also can use > and | in similar fashion. Note that we can include more than one action within the action braces; we just have to separate them by semicolons.

Variables

Awk lets us create a variable by using it. The value of a variable can be numeric or a string. The regular C operations can be performed on numerical variables. For example, suppose we want to count the number of lines that begin with *Tuffy* or with *Buffy*. We can use this command:

```
$1 == "Tuffy" || $1 == "Buffy" { count = count + 1}
END { print count, "lines"}
```

First, the pattern identifies lines beginning in the desired fashion. Each time one is found, the variable *count* is increased by one. Very conveniently, *awk* variables are initialized to 0, so *count* starts with that value and then keeps a running total. After all the lines are read, the instruction following *END* is executed, and we get the total.

Incidentally, the various C assignment and increment operators are available, so we could have used either of the following actions:

```
{ count += 1}
{ count++ }
```

The += operator adds whatever is to its right to whatever variable is to its left. The ++ operator increments its variable by 1.

Suppose you have a table of numbers and wish to total the third column. This command will do it:

```
{sum += $3}
END { print sum}
```

Now suppose you have a table of numbers like this:

```
District1    300        0.30
District2    200        0.25
District3    250        0.33
```

Here the second column is the number of Gollywups sold and the third column is the price each sold for. The boss wants a new table in which the fourth column represents the total cost. He also wants the total number of units sold and the total cash value. Here are the rudiments of a program to do that:

```
{ sum1 += $2; value = $2 *$3; sum2 += value; print $0, value}
END { print "totals      ",sum1, sum2}
```

Suppose this is in the file *bawk*. Then we can run it thus:

```
$ awk -f bawk  distdata
District1    300        0.30 90
District2    200        0.25 50
District3    250        0.33 82.5
totals       750 222.5
$
```

To line up the output better, you can use quotes to print blank spaces between *sum1* and *sum2*, or you can use *printf* instead of *print*.

What happens if we run this program on a file with column headings, like the following:

```
District   items    unit price
District1    300        0.30
District2    200        0.25
District3    250        0.33
```

What, for example, is *items * unit*? The output would look like this:

```
District   items    unit price 0
District1    300        0.30 90
District2    200        0.25 50
District3    250        0.33 82.5
totals       750 222.5
```

When *awk* encounters strings in arithmetic operations, it treats them as having the value 0, so *items * unit* becomes *0*. This won't affect the sums, but it could mess up some arithmetic operations, such as finding the average. It is better to clean up the input before submitting it to such a program. Or you can use the pattern-recognition abilities of *awk*. For example, you could apply the summing instructions only to those lines for which the second field begins with a digit:

```
$2 ~ /^[0-9]/
```

If the field doesn't begin with a digit, just print the line. To identify those lines, we can use

```
$2 !~ /^[0-9]/
```

Or we can use the *if...else* structure that we will discuss soon.

Question A.13

Implement the suggestion we just made for the *awk* script.

Arrays

Arrays are created just like ordinary variables; just mention one and voila! it exists. For instance, if we wish to find the sum of three separate fields, we can do this:

```
{ sum[1] += $1; sum[2] += $2; sum[3] += $3}
END {print sum[1], sum[2], sum[3]}
```

This creates an array *sum* with three elements: *sum[1]*, *sum[2]*, and *sum[3]*. Each element is used to store a number.

Of course we could have used three distinct variables instead, but the loop structures we discuss soon will make the array form simpler.

The array index (or subscript) can be any non-null value, including a string; we could have used *"tom"*, *"dick"*, and *"harry"* instead of *1, 2,* and *3*. This non-numeric choice is convenient for certain uses; after all, why include a feature unless it is useful (or perhaps beautiful)? For example, suppose we have a file of words, one per line (in Chapter 9 we saw how to produce such a file from a regular file), and we want to know how often the words *philodox* (a lover of one's own opinions) and *snoach* (to speak through the nose) occur in it. We can do this:

```
/philodox/ { count[philodox]++}
/snoach/ { count[snoach]++}
END {print count[philodox], count[snoach]}
```

Again, *awk* offers a loop mechanism to make this more convenient. We'll take a look at the *awk* control statements next.

Flow Control

Awk uses the *if*, *if-else*, *for*, and *while* loops of C. If you know C, you are home free. Otherwise, please feel free to learn from the following examples.

The *if* Statement

The *if* statement performs an action if a given condition is true. The *if...else* statement performs one action if a given condition is true and an alternative action if the condition is false. Here is an example of *if...else*:

```
{  if ( $1 < $2 )
       print $1, $2
   else
       print $2, $1 }
```

The condition to be tested follows the *if* and is enclosed in parentheses. In this case we test to see if *$1* is less than *$2*; if so, we print the fields in that order; otherwise print them in the opposite order.

Suppose we apply this action to the following file:

```
3 5
4 2
10 8
```

Then we would get

```
3 5
2 4
8 10
```

The test condition should be a relational expression, an arithmetic expression, or a combination of such using the logical operators. What does that all mean? A relational expression is one using one of the relational operators we discussed or else using one of the matching operators (~ or !~). We can think of such expressions as having a value of true or false. An arithmetic expression is something like *3 + 5* or *count --*. An arithmetic expression (as in C) with a zero value counts as false and with a nonzero value counts as true.

Question A.14

How would you print field four of records containing *Smith* and field five otherwise?

The *else* part can be omitted if it is not needed in an *if* statement. Additional braces can be used if there is more than one command associated with the *if* or the *else*. Let's look at an example that uses additional braces. In Chapter 10, as part of a word frequency program, we developed a C program to count the number of times each word occurs in a sorted list containing one word per line. Here is the equivalent *awk* program:

```
NR == 1 { oldw = $1; ct = 1}
NR != 1 { if (oldw != $1) {
            print  oldw, length(oldw), ct
            oldw = $1
            ct = 1
        } else
            ct++ }
END {print oldw, length(oldw), ct}
```

It follows the same logic as the C program. The first word (which occurs on the first line, with *NR* equaling 1), is stored, and a count is set to 1. The next word is checked to see if it is different from the last word. If so, information about the last word is printed, and *oldw* and *ct* are reset. Otherwise the count is increased by one. After the last word is read, information is printed about the final word. We have used the built-in *awk* function *length*, which returns the length, in characters, of its argument.

Question A.15

Redo Question A.13 using *if...else*.

For comparison, here is the original C program:

```
#include <stdio.h>
#define WSIZE 20
```

```
main()
{
char last[WSIZE];
char word[WSIZE];
int length;
int count;
int n = 0;

while ( getword(stdin,word,WSIZE) != EOF ) {
   if (n == 0) {
       strcpy(last,word);
       count = 1;
       length = strlen(word);
       n++;
       }
   else {
       if ( strcmp(word, last) != 0) {
           printf("%s %d %d\n",last, length, count);
           strcpy(last,word);
           count = 1;
           length = strlen(word);
           n++;
           }
       else
           count++;
       }
   }
printf("%s %d %d\n",last, length, count);
}
```

Obviously, the *awk* version is simpler to set up, even though both use the same logic. In *awk* we don't have to declare variables, and string comparisons are more easily expressed than in C. Also, the *awk* version doesn't have to provide the programming for reading the input. The main disadvantage of *awk* is its lack of speed; whether that is an important disadvantage depends on the circumstances, as we discussed in Chapter 10.

The *for* Statement

The *for* statement has this form:

```
for( initialize; test; update)
    command
```

The *initialize* expression is performed once, when the loop starts up. Then the *test* expression is examined. If it is true, the command is executed; if it is false, the loop is terminated. Each time the loop is executed, the *update* statement gets executed. For example, suppose we want a program that sums each field of a file, even if we don't know in advance how many fields there will be. We can use the variable *NF* (the number of fields) along with a *for* loop to take care of the matter:

```
NR = = 1 { nf = NF}
{for ( i =1; i <= NF; i++ )
        sum[i] += $i}
END { for (i = 1; i <= nf; i++)
        printf "%g ", sum[i]
      printf "\n" }
```

Put it in a file *sawk* and try it out:

```
$ cat nums
1 2.2 3.33
2 3.3 4.44
3 2.2 1.11
$ awk -f sawk nums
6 7.7 8.88
$
```

There are a few points to note. First, only the command immediately following the *for* is part of the loop. If you want to include more commands, bracket them in braces, as we did for the *if* command. Second, for the *END* address, there are no fields, so we couldn't use *NF* there. Instead, we saved the *NF* value as *nf* so that we could use it with *END*. Third, the *for* loop and the array go together beautifully. The loop gives a simple way to step through each array member. Fourth, we used *printf* instead of *print* so that all the sums would appear on the same line; *print* automatically advances one line each use. The *printf* ''\n'' statement prints a newline, that is, advances one line, after all the sums are printed; it is outside the *for* loop. Finally, the program assumes all the lines have the same number of fields; for instance, a blank first line would mess up the assignment of *nf*.

Awk offers a second, non-C form of *for* loop. It has the form

```
for (i in array)
        command
```

Here *array* is an array name. The *command* is performed for each array element. This form is quite handy when you use nonnumerical subscripts.

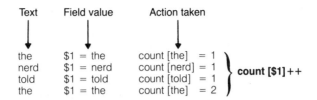

Figure A.6 What *count [$1]* ++ Does

Going back to our word frequency program, here is another approach. Again, we assume we are starting with a list having one word per line. However, in this case, it is not necessary to use an alphabetically sorted list:

```
{ count[$1]++}
END { for (word in count)
        print word, length(word), count[word] }
```

How does this work? Suppose the first word in the list is *nerd*. Then the first action becomes *count[nerd]* + +. Here *nerd* becomes the subscript of the array, and the array element *count[nerd]* becomes 1. Whenever another *nerd* appears, the count for that element increases by 1 again. When a new word shows up, *preppy*, say, then a new array element (*count[preppy]*) is created and set to 1.

At the end, for each array element we print the subscript (which is the word itself), the length of the word, and the value of the array element (the number of occurrences of the word).

This form is even more concise than our earlier *awk* version, and it avoids the necessity of sorting the list first. The hard part of the programming (keeping track of previous words and checking to see if the next word is new or not) is done for us by *awk*. The overall speed is about the same as that of the other *awk* version, much slower than the C version. On the other hand, this program is much more compact than the C version.

The *while* Loop

The *while* loop has this form:

```
while ( test )
    command
```

The *command* gets executed as long as the *test* is true. Again, braces can be used to include more than one command. Here is a command that prints out the fields in a line until it hits the end of the line or the word *private*:

```
{  field = 1
   while ( field <= NF && $field != "private" ) {
          printf "%s ", $field
          field++
          }
   printf "\n"}
```

Place this in the file *pawk* and try it:

```
$ cat sample
Jackie's hobbies are swimming skating bicycling reading
Ben's hobbies are fishing private sewing toe-picking
Jillian's hobbies are philately poker volleyball
$ awk -f pawk sample
Jackie's hobbies are swimming skating bicycling reading
Ben's hobbies are fishing
Jillian's hobbies are philately poker volleyball
$
```

The program uses the variable *field* to keep track of the field number. The *while* loop ends when it reaches the last field number (at which point *field* $= =$ *NF*) or when the value of the field (*$field*) is *private*.

Awk offers some auxiliary commands useful with control-flow statements. We look at them next.

Jumps: *continue, break, next,* and *exit*

The *break* and *continue* statements work just as they do in C and in UNIX shell scripts. The *break* statement causes the loop to break off and terminate. The *continue* statement causes a loop to skip to the beginning of the next iteration.

The *next* statement causes *awk* to skip to the next record, restarting the action there. And *exit* takes you to the end of input, but does not skip over an *END* statement.

Suppose, for example, you have a table of daily rainfall figures, and you wish to find by which day, if any, the total rainfall exceeds a certain number, say 10 inches. Suppose a typical line in the data file has this layout:

```
17 Feb 1.23
```

Then we can try this program:

```
{ sum += $3
  if ( sum >= 10 ) {
     date = $1" "$2
     exit
     } }
END { if (sum < 10)
        print "Total was never reached"
     else
        print date, "sum reached:", sum}
```

Here *sum* keeps track of the cumulative rainfall. Put these *awk* instructions in a file *rawk* and try it:

```
$ awk -f rawk rainfall
19 Mar sum reached: 10.23
$
```

Note how *date* was constructed by combining the three strings *$1, '' '',* and *$2.*

This program just works for 10 inches of rain. Can it be generalized to take other values? Yes, we just have to produce a shell script.

An *awk* Shell Script

Let's devise a shell script that runs an *awk* program like the previous one, taking a rainfall amount and a filename as arguments. Here (without error checking) is how:

```
# raincheck--checks cumulative rainfall
# Usage: raincheck rainlimit filename
awk '{ sum += $3
   if ( sum >= '$1' ) {
      date = $1" "$2
      exit
      } }
END { if ( sum < '$1' )
        print "Total was never reached"
     else
        print date, "sum was", sum }' $2
```

We have replaced *10* with *$1.* The key point is that this *$1* should mean "the first argument of the shell script" and not "the first field of the current record." This

447

was accomplished by leaving it outside the single quotes. Outside of quotes, *$1* is interpreted by the shell, and in running *awk*, this *$1* is replaced by 10 or 12 or whatever first argument we provide the script. Similarly, the final *$2* is outside the quotes, so it is interpreted as the second argument to the script.

Built-In Functions

Awk features several built-in functions. We'll give them a brief rundown. One of the most useful is one we already have seen: *length*. It gives the length of its argument. For example, *length("fish")* is 4, since "fish" is a 4-character string. If no argument is given, *length* refers to the whole record. To find lines longer than 80 characters, for example, we could use this command:

```
length > 80 { print "line", NR, "is too long."}
```

For mathmatical work, *awk* provides *sqrt* (square root), *log* (natural logarithm), *exp* (exponential function), and *int* (the integer part of a number).

There are several string-related functions. The *substr* function produces a substring from an input string. It takes three arguments: the original string, the position at which the substring will start, and the limit for the length of the substring. For instance,

```
{new = substr("throttle",3,4); print new}
```

would assign the value *rott* to *new*. The substring starts at the third character of *throttle* and includes four characters.

The *index* function tells where a substring starts in a string:

```
{print index("throttle", "rot")}
```

would produce the value 3. If the second argument is not found in the first, the value 0 is returned.

The *sprintf* function lets you format various expressions into a string. It uses the formatting conventions of C's *printf()*. Suppose, for example, that *$1* has the value *Dan* and *$3* has the value *65*. Then the expression

```
label = sprintf("%s of the %d kg class", $1 ,$3)
```

results in the variable *label* having the value

```
"Dan of the 65 kg class"
```

The *split* function breaks a string down to fields. The first argument is the string, and the second is an array to hold the individual fields. Carrying on with our variable *label*, we can try this:

```
n = split(label,part)
```

Then we get *part[1]* being *Dan*, *part[2]* being *of*, and so on. The returned value *n* is the number of fields, six in this case. So *part[n]* is the last field, *class*.

The *split* function uses the current value of the field separator (*FS*) to make its divisions, but we can override that by providing a third argument:

```
n=split(label,part,a)
```

would use the character *a* as a separator. In this case, *part[1]* would be *D*, and *part[3]* would be *ss*.

These string functions give *awk* powerful string-processing capabilities.

END *{awk}*

The multitudinous talents of *awk* threaten to overrun the confines of any one appendix, so we will exercise some restraint and conclude matters now. If you need to process fields within a line or perform numerical operations on a file or process strings in a file, think of *awk*.

In some cases, an *awk* program may prove too slow for your needs. In that case, the resemblance of *awk* to the C programming language should help you translate the *awk* approach to a successful C program.

END *{appendix a}*

In this appendix we have studied four diverse programs that illustrate the power of UNIX filters. The *grep* family lets us search files and other input for strings and patterns. *Sed* lets us use editing instructions to modify the data that flow through it. *Tr* lets us make wholesale character substitutions. *Awk* combines pattern recognition with field processing, numerical processing, and programming features. Each can be used individually or in concert with other UNIX facilities.

ANSWERS TO QUESTIONS IN APPENDIX A

A.1 grep putchar *.c
A.2 grep –l ctype.h *.c
A.3 **a.** [Ss]wine
   b. b.t

      c. ˆBEGIN

      d. ˆ *C

A.4 **a.** Twain|Clemens

      b. (Dave|Dorothy|Parallel) Parker

A.5 /[Dd]odo/,$

A.6 **a.** s/Grissmuttle/Barney &/g

      b. s/\([Ff]orego\on)/\1ne/g

      c. s/\(Brenda \)\(Gempsoth\)/\1Jean \2/g

A.7 **a.** tr .! ''?''

      b. tr –cd 0-9

      c. tr a-zA-Z A-Za-z

A.8 *NR* is 2, and *NF* is 9

A.9 **a.** $3 ~ /Paddy|Mickey/

      b. $3 ~ /ˆ(Paddy|Mickey)$/

      c. $1 ~ /ˆPaddy +Mickey$/

      d. /(Kitty +)*Kitty!/

A.10 $3 + $4 > $5

A.11 **a.** $1 == ''Cygnus'' && $3 > 12

      b. $1 == ''Leo'' || $4 != ''cluster'' or $1 == ''Leo'' || !($4 == ''cluster'')

A.12 {*print $2 '','' , $1*} (Print the second field, print a comma, skip a space, print the first field.)

A.13
```
$2 !˜ /ˆ[0-9]/ {print $0}
$2 ˜ /ˆ[0-9]/   { sum1 += $2; value = $2 * $3;
                       sum2 += value; print $0, value}
END { print "totals     ",sum1, sum2}
```

A.14
```
{ if ($0 ˜ /Smith/)
            print $4
       else
            print $5 }
```

A.15
```
{ if ($2 !˜ /ˆ[0-9]/)
            print $0
      else
            { sum1 += $2; value = $2 * $3;
              sum2 += value; print $0, value}
      }
END { print "totals     ",sum1, sum2}
```

EXERCISES

1.   Simplify *wordseek* in Chapter 5 by using *fgrep*.
2.   Devise a script that replaces a tab by 5 spaces. Why can't *tr* be used?
3.   Devise a script that converts multiple adjacent spaces to just one space.
4.   Devise an interactive *grep* script that asks for a word and a filename and then tells you how many lines contain that word.

5. Repeat Exercise 4, but using *awk*. Which version is faster?
6. Devise an interactive script that asks for a word and a filename and then tells you how many times that word occurred in the file. (Note that this is different from asking for the number of lines.)

B

A Survey of the C Shell: *csh*

The C shell is a UNIX command language interpreter developed at the University of California, Berkeley. It is the standard shell provided with BSD 4.1 and 4.2 versions of UNIX; however, these releases can also use the standard Bourne shell. The name of the program for the C shell is *csh*, just as *sh* is the name of the program for the Bourne shell. The two shells have much in common; both, for instance, have such features as redirection, filename expansion, command substitution (the backquote feature), shell variables, and programmability. Some of the details differ however; for example, the shell variables are handled somewhat differently. The C shell also has several major features absent from the Bourne shell. These are a *history* feature that allows rerunning and altering previous commands, a more extensive job control system that allows processes to be moved from background to foreground and vice versa, and an *alias* system for setting up shorthand notations for commands.

All in all, *csh* is more extensive than *sh*, and it would take much more than this appendix to do *csh* justice. Instead, we will concentrate on features that both systems share but handle somewhat differently. If you are interested in features peculiar to the C shell, you will find a discussion in *UNIX Primer Plus*, by Waite, Martin, and Prata (Indianapolis: Howard W. Sams & Co., 1983). Even in this more limited context of examining differences between the two shells, this appendix is not intended to be comprehensive; it merely tries to hit the most important points.

THE LOGIN SHELL AND OTHER SHELLS

When you log on a C shell version of UNIX, a *csh* process (your *login shell*) is created for you to interpret your commands. Typically, the shell uses a % prompt instead of the $ prompt of the Bourne shell. To create a C subshell, you type *csh*. To create a *sh* subshell, type *sh*; you will get a $ prompt in this case to indicate the change in shell type. Either type of subshell is terminated by a ⌐Control⌐ D, but the login shell is typically terminated by the *logout* command.

Usually, you can arrange with the system administrator to have a *sh* login shell instead. Or you can do the job yourself by using the *chsh* (change shell) command. Information about which login shell you use is placed in the */etc/passwd* file. If your login shell is *sh*, you still can invoke the C shell by typing *csh*.

LOGIN FILES

Recall that for Bourne shell users, the system reads the user's *.profile* file and executes the commands found there. C shell users, however, have two files read and executed. One is called *.login* and is read when the user logs in. The second is called *.cshrc* and is read whenever a new C shell is created, including the login shell.

You can also create a *.logout* file. Commands in that file get executed when you log out.

SHELL VARIABLES

In the Bourne shell, a shell variable is local unless it is *export*ed. Even then, a variable can only be exported to a subshell, not to a parent shell.

The C shell maintains two kinds of shell variables: regular variables, which are local, and environment variables, which are global. Both varieties are string variables, just as the Bourne shell variables are.

Regular Variables

Regular variables are set using the *set* command. For instance, to create a variable called *name* and to assign the value *Violet* to it, do this:

```
set name=Violet    ← C shell
set fame = quilting    ← C shell (spaces okay)
```

Note that the form is different from the Bourne equivalent:

```
name=Violet        ← Bourne shell
```

Using a shell variable value is the same as for the Bourne shell; just use a *$* prefix:

```
% echo The name is $name
The name is Violet
%
```

As in the Bourne shell, braces can be used around the variable name to indicate grouping:

```
% set names=Furths
% echo All the ${name}s are not $names
All the Violets are not Furths
%
```

453

To remove the definition of a shell variable, use the *unset* command:

```
unset name
```

There are a couple of ways to assign a string of more than one word to a variable. The first is to enclose the string in single or double quotes, as in the following:

```
% set name='Rufus Dogbane'
% echo $name
Rufus Dogbane
%
```

This is much the same as for the Bourne shell. The second method is to enclose the string in parentheses, as in the following:

```
% set handle=(Polly Dartoff)
% echo $handle
Polly Dartoff
%
```

Using parentheses instead of quotes (single or double), however, lets one access the individual words in a variable string by using an array-like notation:

```
% echo $handle[1]
Polly
% echo ${handle[2]}, $handle[1]
Dartoff, Polly
%
```

The first word is indicated by the index *1*, and so on. This scheme does not work for multiword strings defined using quotes. Such a string is, in effect, just a single "word" that happens to include some space characters.

One can also indicate a range of words by using a hyphen:

```
% set list=(he was a bold chartered accountant)
% echo $list[2-4]
was a bold
%
```

The special notation *$#variable-name* yields the number of words in a string:

```
% echo $#list
6
%
```

If the first member of a range is omitted, it is assumed to be 1. If the last member of a range is omitted, it is assumed to be the total number of words. Thus *echo $list[4-]* would echo from the fourth word to the end of *list*. The notation *$list[*]* would stand for all the words in the variable *list*.

Just as in the Bourne shell, you can type *set* by itself to get a list of all current regular shell variables and their values. Those consisting of multiple words will have the parentheses printed, too.

The C shell has no *export* command, so what do you do to make a variable available to subshells? One approach is to place the variable definition in the *.cshrc* file. Since this file is executed each time a new C shell is created, the variable will be defined for each shell. However, the variable is still local in the sense that changing the value in one shell has no effect on the value of the variable in a different shell. For a global variable, we must use the *setenv* command.

Environment Variables

An "environment" variable is known to all shells. As in the case of the Bourne exported variable, changes made in the value of an environment variable in a child shell are not transmitted back to a parent shell. Changes made in a parent shell, however, are transmitted to a child shell created after that change. To create an environment variable and to assign it a value, use the *setenv* command:

```
% setenv food sarmele
% echo eat some $food
eat some sarmele
% csh                       ← Create a new shell
% echo can I have some $food\?
can I have some sarmele   ← Variable still known
%
```

Note that, unlike the case for *set*, no equals sign is used in the definition.

Here we used *echo* to print out the value of an environment variable. This works only if there is not a regular variable of the same name. We can have a variable of each type and with different values. In any case, we can always use the *printenv* command to print the value of an environment variable.

```
% set food = falafal
% echo $food
falafal                 ← The value of the regular variable
% printenv food
sarmele                 ← The value of the environment variable
%
```

Note that *food* is used without a $ prefix in the *printenv* command. The *printenv* command without arguments prints out all the currently defined environment variables.

To remove a definition, use *unsetenv*:

```
% unsetenv food
%
```

Variable Modifiers

The C shell recognizes several suffixes that modify the interpretation of a regular shell variable (but not of environment variables). Some are particularly useful for working with variables that have been set to filenames. Here they are:

h Remove a trailing pathname component, leaving the head
t Remove all leading pathname components, leaving the tail
r Remove a trailing ''.xxx'' extension, leaving the root
e Remove all but the extension ''.xxx''

They are used by preceding them by a colon (:) and placing them at the end of a variable name. Here are some examples:

```
% set file=/usr/snerd/cwork/wood.c
% echo $file
/usr/snerd/cwork/wood.c
% echo $file:h
/usr/snerd/cwork/
% echo $file:r
/usr/snerd/cwork/wood
% echo $file:t
wood.c
% echo %file:e
c
%
```

There is a facility for doing numerical operations with shell variables. We will return to that topic when we discuss C shell expressions.

SHELL SCRIPTS

You can collect a sequence of commands in a file and have them executed by the shell. For instance, suppose you have a file called *hipat* containing the following commands:

```
echo Hi, Pat. Here is the current date and time.
date
```

Then you can have the script executed as follows:

```
% csh hipat
Hi, Pat. Here is the current date and time.
Mon Jun 24 12:54:39 PDT 1985
%
```

Or you can use *chmod* to make the script executable:

```
% chmod u+x hipat
% hipat
Hi, Pat. Here is the current date and time.
Mon Jun 24 12:54:39 PDT 1985
%
```

Actually, this executable version gets executed by *sh*, not by *csh*! To preserve compatability with the Bourne shell, executable shell scripts in the C shell are run by the *sh* shell *unless* the script begins with a # symbol. Of course, a script run by using *csh* explicitly, as in our first example, is run by the *csh* shell regardless. Thus, we can make the executable script a *csh*-run script by starting it off with a comment:

```
# a simple script
echo Hi, Pat. Here is the current date and time.
date
```

If you have a Bourne shell script with #-marked comments, you will either have to remove the comments or run the script using *sh*, as in

```
% sh oldsh_scpt
```

Like the Bourne shell, the C shell provides command-line substitution and programming constructs such as *while* loops, *for* loops, and *if...else* constructions. The details differ, however, so let's look into that now.

COMMAND-LINE SUBSTITUTION

The command-line arguments to a shell script are assigned to the shell variable *argv*. The separate arguments can then be accessed using the bracket notation we described earlier. Suppose, for instance, that the file *cline* contains these lines:

```
# cline -- shows how to access command-line arguments
echo There are $#argv arguments
echo The first argument is $argv[1]
```

```
echo The last argument is $argv[$#argv]
echo The second through fourth arguments are $argv[2-4]
```

Make the file executable and try it out:

```
% cline Oh beautiful for spacious skies and amber waves
There are 8 arguments
The first argument is Oh
The last argument is waves
The second through fourth arguments are beautiful for spacious
%
```

The C shell also accepts the *$1*, *$2*, etc., notation of the Bourne shell. Thus, *$1* is the same as *$argv[1]*. Also, *$** is the same as *$argv[*]*.

Here are some other useful parameters:

$0	The name of the shell script
$$	The PID of the parent shell
$?name	Equals 1 if the variable *name* is set; equals 0 otherwise
$status	The status returned by the last command

C SHELL LOOPS

The C shell supports three loop structures: the *foreach* loop, the *while* loop, and the *repeat* loop.

The *foreach* Loop

The *foreach* loop structure looks like this:

```
foreach name (wordlist)
    command(s)
end
```

This is pretty much like the following Bourne shell *for* loop:

```
for name in wordlist
do
    command()s
done
```

In each case the shell variable *name* takes on in turn each value from *wordlist*, cycling through the commands until the list is exhausted. For example, here is the C shell equivalent to our first *for* loop in Chapter 5:

```
foreach i (fly spider frog)
    echo I know an old lady who swallowed a $i.
    echo Swallowed a $i\?
    echo Swallowed a $i\!
end
```

Here we escaped the exclamation mark because it is a C shell metacharacter.

The various techniques we used to provide a wordlist for the Bourne *for* carry over to the C shell *for*. In addition to providing an explicit list, as we just did, you can do the following:

1. Take values from the shell script command line: *foreach word ($*)* or *foreach word ($argv)* or *foreach word (argv[2-])*. The first two loop through the entire command-line argument list. The last form skips the first command-line argument and processes the argument list from the second argument through the final argument.

2. Take filenames from a directory as values: *foreach file (*)* or *foreach file (*.c)*. The first processes all files in the current directory; the second processes all files with names ending in .c in the current directory.

3. Take values from a shell variable: *foreach name ($path)*. This would set the *name* variable in turn to each directory name in the *path* shell variable.

4. Take values from the output of a command by using the backquote command-substitution mechanism:

```
foreach beast (`cat animals`)
   echo I never met a $beast I did not like
   end
```

Here *beast* would be set in turn to each word in the file *animal*.

The major difference between the Bourne *for* loop and the C-shell *foreach* loop is that with the former, the output of the whole *for* loop statement can be redirected, while it cannot be for the *foreach* loop. That is, this Bourne shell construct is valid:

```
for beast in `cat animals`.
do
    echo I never met a $beast I did not like
end > newbeast          ← Valid redirection
```

But this C-shell redirection is not valid:

```
foreach beast (`cat animals`)
   echo I never met a $beast I did not like
end > newbeast      ← Invalid redirection
```

However, you can still use redirection for commands within a *foreach* loop:

```
foreach beast (`cat animals`)
   echo I never met a $beast I did not like >> newbeast  ← Okay
end
```

The *while* Loop

The C-shell *while* loop looks like this:

```
while (expression)
     commands
end
```

The *expression* is tested each cycle, and the *commands* are executed for as long as the *expression* tests true. Here there is a significant difference from the Bourne *while*. In the Bourne *while* the *expression* part referred to the success or failure of *commands*. Here the C-shell *expression* more typically is a comparison of values. The syntax is like that of the C language, with some extensions to allow both numerical and string comparisons. Note that the *expression* is enclosed in parentheses, unlike the case for the Bourne shell *while*.

Here is an example that interactively quizzes a user. The C-shell doesn't have a *read* statement to get input. Instead, it uses $< to indicate input from the shell's standard input. That input can then be assigned to a shell variable. The script uses the *!*= operator to test for inequality.

```
echo What is the largest kind of whale\?
set ans=$<       ← Assign keyboard input to ans
while ( "$ans" != "blue whale" )
    echo Wrong\! Guess again.
    set ans=$<
end
```

Here double quotes are used to ensure that $ans and *blue whale* are each interpreted as single strings despite the presence of spaces. The loop repeats until the input (*ans*) matches the answer (*blue whale*).

We'll talk more about C shell *expressions* shortly, for they form the basis for using the C shell *while* and *if then* statements. First, though, let's complete the list of loop structures.

The *repeat* Statement

The format for the *repeat* command is this:

```
repeat count command
```

The *command* is executed *count* times. The *command* must be a simple command. It can have arguments and I/O redirection, but no pipes or lists of command. Here is a simple example:

```
% repeat 4 echo Brother, can you spare a byte\?
Brother, can you spare a byte?
Brother, can you spare a byte?
Brother, can you spare a byte?
Brother, can you spare a byte?
%
```

EXPRESSIONS

As in the C programming language, C shell expressions involve *operators* and *operands*. Table B.1 lists the host of available operators. All but $=\sim$ and $!\sim$ are taken from the C language.

These operators are typically applied to character strings or to strings representing numbers or to other expressions. The value of an expression can be assigned to a shell variable via the @ command. This command works much like *set*, except it assigns the value of an expression rather than a word to a variable. In either case, the variable is stored as a string, but the @ command allows for numerical manipulations in the expression. Let's look at some examples.

First, either @ or *set* can be used to assign a single number to a variable:

```
% set age = 24
% @ toes = 10
% echo $age $toes
24 10
%
```

Table B.1 C Shell Operators in Increasing Precedence

Operators	Meanings
‖ &&	Logical OR and logical AND
	^ &	Bitwise OR, EXCLUSIVE-OR, and AND
= = !=	EQUALS and DOESN'T EQUAL
=~ !~	EQUALS and DOESN'T EQUAL a string pattern
< <=	LESS THAN and LESS THAN OR EQUAL TO
> >=	GREATER THAN and GREATER THAN OR EQUAL TO
<< >>	Bitwise LEFT-SHIFT and RIGHT-SHIFT
+ −	PLUS and MINUS
* % /	MULTIPLY, MODULUS, and DIVIDE
!	Logical NEGATION
~	Bitwise ONE'S COMPLEMENT
()	Grouping

But only the @ command allows you to use expressions with operators on the right-hand side of the equation:

```
% @ sum = 10 + 15
% echo $sum
25
% @ sum = 2 * $age + 5
% echo $sum
53
%
```

The increment (+ +) and decrement (− −) operators of C can be used with shell variables and the @ command to increase or decrease the value of a variable by 1:

```
% @ sum++
% echo $sum
54
% @ sum--
% echo $sum
53
%
```

Even though these examples illustrate numerical operations, the numbers are stored as strings. For example, when *sum* is *53*, it is a string consisting of the *5* character and the *3* character. The @ notation informs the shell to find the numerical value corresponding to the string, do the indicated operations, and convert the result back to a string variable.

Relational Expressions

As in the C language, relational expressions have the value 1 if true and the value 0 if false:

```
% @ isit = $sum > 52
% echo $isit
1
% @ isit = $sum  > ( 30 + 40)
% echo $isit
0
%
```

Here is C-shell countdown script that uses the *greater than* operator along with numerical expressions:

```
# count.csh -- counts down
# Usage:   count.csh number
@ start = $argv[1]
while ( $start > 0)
   echo $start\! ...
   @ start--
end
echo Blast off\!
```

The *expression* part of the *while* and *if* statements is often a relational expression of the sort we just used. Most comparisons are numeric. Thus, expressions like

```
$plant > tree
```

are rejected. However, the equality and inequality comparisons are string comparisons. Thus, we can use *if* statements (discussed a few pages later) that start like the following examples:

```
if ( $argv[1] == stop )...
if ( $deputy != sam) ...
```

Of course, the string can be a number. Note, however, that different strings with the same numeric value, such as *7* and *007* would be considered to be unequal, since they consist of different characters.

Table B.2 C Shell File Enquiries (Form is *-l name*)

Enquiry	Tests for
-r	Read access
-w	Write access
-x	Execute access
-e	Existence
-o	Ownership
-z	Zero size
-f	Plain file
-d	Directory

The $=\sim$ and $!\sim$ forms allow the right-hand side to be a pattern using the *, ?, and *[]* metacharacters of the shell. For example, the following checks to see if a filename (represented by a variable named *file*) is that of an object code file:

```
if ( $file =~ *.o) ...
```

Here is a C-shell script that checks a file for FORTRAN programs and places backup copies in a directory called *Forback*; the *.f* extension is replaced by *.bak*.

```
# fortran backup
foreach file ( * )
    if ( $file =˜ *.f)  cp $file  Forback/${file:r}.bak
end
```

Note that we used the *:r* modifier that we mentioned earlier; it strips off the extension (*.f*, in this case), leaving the root filename.

File-Testing Expressions

The C shell offers a variety of file enquiries. They have the form

-l name

where *l* is one of eight letters. Table B.2 shows the enquiries and what they test for.

For example, the following statement executes the *echo* command only if the variable *file* is set to the name of an executable file:

```
if ( -x $file)  echo $file is an executable file
```

Command Testing

The Bourne shell *while* and *for* statements test for the success or failure of a command, while the C-shell equivalents test for the truth or falsity of an expression. The Bourne shell, in order to test expressions, had to use the *test* command. The C-shell, in turn, needs a special mechanism to test for the success or failure of commands. This is provided by enclosing in braces the command to be tested. For instance, if we want to know if the *grep* command succeeded in finding a word, we can use a statment like this:

```
if ( { grep -s libel trans* } ) echo Found it
```

The braces need room; there should be space between the braces and the enclosed material.

Now that we've had a quick look at C shell expressions, we can look at the C shell *if* structures.

THE *if* STRUCTURES

The C shell offers the simple *if* structure, which we have used without a formal introduction, and a more elaborate *if then ... else ... endif* form.

The simple *if* goes like this:

```
if ( expression ) command
```

If the *expression* is true, the *command* is executed. Otherwise, it isn't. The command must be a simple command. Redirection is allowed, but pipes and compound commands are not. The entire *if* statement is a one-liner. Note that the *expression* is enclosed in parentheses, unlike the case for the Bourne shell *if*.

If you desire to perform several commands upon a successful *if* test, use the *if then ... endif* form. The syntax looks like this:

```
if (expression ) then
    commands
endif
```

Here the *if...then* portion should be on one line, the *endif* on another line, and the *commands* on lines in between those two lines. If the *expression* is true, then all the commands up to the *endif* are executed. Here is an example:

```
if ( $response == yes ) then
    cat $argv[2] $argv[3] > $argv[4]
    rm $argv[2] $argv[3]
endif
```

465

Adding an *else*

The *if...then* form can be extended by adding *else if...then*s and *else*s to offer two or more choices. Here is the general form:

```
if (expression ) then
    commands
else if (expression) then
    commands
  . . .
else
    commands
endif
```

If the first *expression* proves false, then the next *expression* is tested, and so on. If none of the *if* or *else if expressions* is true, then the commands following the final *else*, if present, are executed.

For comparison, we will show a Bourne shell script from Chapter 5 and then the C-shell equivalent. First, here is the Bourne version:

```
echo What is your age\?
read age
if [ $age -le 6 ]
then
    echo What a nice child!
elif [ $age -gt 6 -a $age -le 9 ]
then
    echo That\'s a good age!
elif [ $age -gt 9 -a $age -le 20 ]
then
    echo Ah! In the prime of life!
elif [ $age -gt 20 -a $age -le 30 ]
then
    echo Watch out, the younger ones are gaining on you.
else
    echo Well, have fun, and don\'t look back.
fi
```

Here is the C-shell version. Notice the differing placement of the *then*s.

```
#
echo What is your age\?
set age=$<
if ( $age <= 6 ) then
    echo What a nice child\!
```

```
else if ( $age >  6 && $age <= 9 ) then
   echo That\'s a good age\!
else if ( $age > 9 && $age <= 20 ) then
   echo Ah\! In the prime of life\!
else if ( $age > 20 && $age <= 30 ) then
   echo Watch out, the younger ones are gaining on you.
else
   echo Well, have fun, and don\'t look back.
endif
```

MULTIPLE CHOICE: THE *switch* STRUCTURE

The C-shell *switch* structure plays much the same role as the Bourne shell *case* structure. It offers an efficient way to compare a value to a list of choices and to take the corresponding action. In form, it closely follows the *switch* of the C language. Here is the general form:

```
switch (string)
case string1:
   commands
   breaksw
case string2:
   commands
   breaksw

 ...

default:
   commands
   breaksw
endsw
```

The *string* is compared with successive *case* labels (*string1*, *string2*, etc.) until it finds a match. Then all the commands from that matching label to the next *breaksw* (or to *endsw* if no *breaksw*s are present) are executed. If there is no match, program flow goes to the *default* label. Note that this follows the C model, not the Pascal model emulated in the Bourne shell. That is, the *breaksw* (*break switch*) keyword is needed to keep command execution from continuing through to the following commands in a *switch*.

For example, in Chapter 6, we had this example of a *case*:

```
case $1 in
   -L) flagL='-la'; shift;;
   -I) flagI='-is'; shift;;
   -D) flagD='-dp'; shift;;
    *) break ;;
esac
```

Here is the C-shell equivalent. (Note that we can use *$1* for *$argv[1]* and that the the C-shell uses *shift* the same way that the Bourne shell does.)

```
switch ($1)
    case -L: set flagL='-la ; shift
            breaksw
    case -I: set flagI='-is'; shift
            breaksw
    case -D: set flagD='-dp'; shift
            breaksw
    default:
            breaksw
endsw
```

MISCELLANEOUS

The C-shell has *break* and *continue* statements available for use in *foreach* and *while* loops. The *break* statement causes the loop to be exited, while the *continue* statement causes flow to skip to the next cycle of the loop. The *switch* statement, however, requires the use of *breaksw* rather than of *break*.

The *shift* command shifts command-line argument *argv[2]* to *argv[1]* and so on. It can also be used with other multivalued shell variables. For example, suppose we make the following assignment:

```
set names=(mary gail freiya nadia)
```

Now we have *names[1]* set to *mary*, *names[2]* set to *gail*, and so on. Then the command

```
shift names
```

moves *gail* to *names[1]*, and so on.

The *source* command is the C-shell equivalent of the Bourne dot command; the current shell reads and executes the commands in *file* when the following command is given:

```
source file
```

The *csh(1)* entry in the BSD version of the UNIX manual gives a complete rundown of C shell capabilities.

C

Binary Numbers and Others

BINARY NUMBERS

The way we usually write numbers is based on the number 10. Perhaps you were once told that a number like 3652 has a 3 in the thousand's place, a 6 in the hundred's place, a 5 in the ten's place and a 2 in the one's place. This means we can think of 3652 as being

$$3 \times 1000 + 6 \times 100 + 5 \times 10 + 2 \times 1.$$

But 1000 is 10 cubed, 100 is 10 squared, 10 is 10 to the first power, and, by convention, 1 is 10 (or any positive number) to the zero power. So we also can write 3652 as

$$3 \times 10^3 + 6 \times 10^2 + 5 \times 10^1 + 2 \times 10^0.$$

Because our system of writing numbers is based on powers of ten, we say that 3652 is written in *base 10.*

Presumably, we developed this system because we have 10 fingers. A computer bit, in a sense, only has 2 fingers, for it can be set only to 0 or 1, off or on. This makes a *base 2* system natural for a computer. How does it work? It uses powers of 2 instead of powers of ten. For instance, a binary number such as 1101 would mean

$$1 \times 2^3 + 1 \times 2^2 + 0 \times 2^1 + 1 \times 2^0.$$

In decimal numbers this becomes

$$1 \times 8 + 1 \times 4 + 0 \times 2 + 1 \times 1 = 13.$$

The base 2 (or "binary") system lets one express any number (if you have enough bits) as a combination of 1s and 0s. This is very pleasing to a computer, especially since that is its only option. Let's see how this works for a 1-byte integer.

A byte contains 8 bits. We can think of these 8 bits as being numbered from 7 to 0, left to right. This "bit number" corresponds to an exponent of 2. Imagine the byte as looking like this:

bit number		7	6	5	4	3	2	1	0
		| | | | | | | | |							
value		128	64	32	16	8	4	2	1

Here 128 is 2 to the 7th power, and so on. The largest number this byte can hold is one with all bits set to 1: 11111111. The value of this binary number is

$$128 + 64 + 32 + 16 + 8 + 4 + 2 + 1 = 255.$$

The smallest binary number would be 00000000, or a simple 0. A byte can store numbers from 0 to 255 for a total of 256 possible values.

Binary Floating Point

Floating-point numbers are stored in two parts: a binary fraction and a binary exponent. Let's see how this is done.

Binary Fractions

The ordinary fraction .324 represents

$$3/10 + 2/100 + 4/1000$$

with the denominators representing increasing powers of ten. In a binary fraction, we use powers of two for denominators. Thus the binary fraction .101 represents

$$1/2 + 0/4 + 1/8$$

which in decimal notation is

$$.50 + .00 + .125$$

or .625.

Many fractions, such as 1/3, cannot be represented exactly in decimal notation. Similarly, many fractions cannot be represented exactly in binary notation. Indeed, the only fractions that can be represented exactly are combinations of multiples of powers of 1/2. Thus 3/4 and 7/8 can be represented exactly as binary fractions, but 1/3 and 2/5 cannot be.

Floating-point Representation

To represent a floating-point number in a computer, a certain number (system-dependent) of bits are set aside to hold a binary fraction. Additional bits hold an exponent. In general terms, the actual value of the number consists of the binary fraction times two to the indicated exponent. Thus multiplying a floating-point number by, say, 4, increases the exponent by 2 and leaves the binary fraction unchanged. Multiplying by a number that is not a power of 2 will change the binary fraction and, if necessary, the exponent.

OTHER BASES

Computer workers often use number systems based on 8 and on 16. Since 8 and 16 are powers of 2, these systems are more closely related to a computer's binary system than is the decimal system.

Octal

"Octal" refers to a base 8 system. In this system, the different places in a number represent powers of 8. We use the digits 0 to 7. For example, the octal number 451 (written 0451 in C) represents

$$4 \times 8^2 + 5 \times 8^1 + 1 \times 8^0 = 297 \text{ (base 10)}.$$

Hexadecimal

"Hexadecimal" (or "hex") refers to a base 16 system. Here we use powers of 16 and the digits 0 to 15. But since we don't have single digits to represent the values 10 to 15, we use the letters A to F for that purpose. For instance, the hex number A3F (written·0xA3F in C) represents

$$10 \times 16^2 + 3 \times 16^1 + 15 \times 16^0 = 2623 \text{ (base 10)}.$$

D

ASCII Table

Numerical Conversion

DECIMAL-HEXADECIMAL-OCTAL-BINARY-ASCII NUMERICAL CONVERSIONS

DEX X_{10}	HEX X_{16}	OCT X_8	Binary X_2	ASCII	Key
0	00	00	000 0000	NUL	CTRL/1
1	01	01	000 0001	SOH	CTRL/A
2	02	02	000 0010	STX	CTRL/B
3	03	03	000 0011	ETX	CTRL/C
4	04	04	000 0100	EOT	CTRL/D
5	05	05	000 0101	ENQ	CTRL/E
6	06	06	000 0110	ACK	CTRL/F
7	07	07	000 0111	BEL	CTRL/G
8	08	10	000 1000	BS	CTRL/H, BACKSPACE
9	09	11	000 1001	HT	CTRL/I, TAB
10	0A	12	000 1010	LF	CTRL/J, LINE FEED
11	0B	13	000 1011	VT	CTRL/K
12	0C	14	000 1100	FF	CTRL/L
13	0D	15	000 1101	CR	CTRL/M, RETURN
14	0E	16	000 1110	SO	CTRL/N
15	0F	17	000 1111	SI	CTRL/O
16	10	20	001 0000	DLE	CTRL/P
17	11	21	001 0001	DC1	CTRL/Q
18	12	22	001 0010	DC2	CTRL/R
19	13	23	001 0011	DC3	CTRL/S
20	14	24	001 0100	DC4	CTRL/T
21	15	25	001 0101	NAK	CTRL/U
22	16	26	001 0110	SYN	CTRL/V
23	17	27	001 0111	ETB	CTRL/W
24	18	30	001 1000	CAN	CTRL/X
25	19	31	001 1001	EM	CTRL/Y
26	1A	32	001 1010	SUB	CTRL/Z

27	1B	33	001 1011	ESC	ESC, ESCAPE
28	1C	34	001 1100	FS	CTRL<
29	1D	35	001 1101	GS	CTRL/
30	1E	36	001 1110	RS	CTRL/=
31	1F	37	001 1111	US	CTRL/-
32	20	40	010 0000	SP	SPACEBAR
33	21	41	010 0001	!	!
34	22	42	010 0010	''	''
35	23	43	010 0011	#	#
36	24	44	010 0100	$	$
37	25	45	010 0101	½	½
38	26	46	010 0110	&	&
39	27	47	010 0111	'	'
40	28	50	010 1000	(	(
41	29	51	010 1001	)	)
42	2A	52	010 1010	*	*
43	2B	53	010 1011	+	+
44	2C	54	010 1100	,	,
45	2D	55	010 1101	-	-
46	2E	56	010 1110	.	.
47	2F	57	010 1111	/	/
48	30	60	011 0000	0	0
49	31	61	011 0001	1	1
50	32	62	011 0010	2	2
51	33	63	011 0011	3	3
52	34	64	011 0100	4	4
53	35	65	011 0101	5	5
54	36	66	011 0110	6	6
55	37	67	011 0111	7	7
56	38	70	011 1000	8	8
57	39	71	011 1001	9	9
58	3A	72	011 1010	:	:
59	3B	73	011 1011	;	;
60	3C	74	011 1100	<	<
61	3D	75	011 1101	=	=
62	3E	76	011 1110	>	>
63	3F	77	011 1111	?	?
64	40	100	100 0000	@	@
65	41	101	100 0001	A	A
66	42	102	100 0010	B	B
67	43	103	100 0011	C	C
68	44	104	100 0100	D	D
69	45	105	100 0101	E	E

70	46	106	100 0110	F	F
71	47	107	100 0111	G	G
72	48	110	100 1000	H	H
73	49	111	100 1001	I	I
74	4A	112	100 1010	J	J
75	4B	113	100 1011	K	K
76	4C	114	100 1100	L	L
77	4D	115	100 1101	M	M
78	4E	116	100 1110	N	N
79	4F	117	100 1111	O	O
80	50	120	101 0000	P	P
81	51	121	101 0001	Q	Q
82	52	122	101 0010	R	R
83	53	123	101 0011	S	S
84	53	124	101 0100	T	T
85	55	125	101 0101	U	U
86	56	126	101 0110	V	V
87	57	127	101 0111	W	W
88	58	130	101 1000	X	X
89	59	131	101 1001	Y	Y
90	5A	132	101 1010	Z	Z
91	5B	133	101 1011	[	[
92	5C	134	101 1100	\	\
93	5D	135	101 1101	]	]
94	5E	136	101 1110	^	^
95	5F	137	101 1111	—	—
96	60	140	110 0000	`	`
97	61	141	110 0001	a	a
98	62	142	110 0010	b	b
99	63	143	110 0011	c	c
100	64	144	110 0100	d	d
101	65	145	110 0101	e	e
102	66	146	110 0110	f	f
103	67	147	110 0111	g	g
104	68	150	110 1000	h	h
105	69	151	110 1001	i	i
106	6A	152	110 1010	j	j
107	6B	153	110 1011	k	k
108	6C	154	110 1100	l	l
109	6D	155	110 1101	m	m
110	6E	156	110 1110	n	n
111	6F	157	110 1111	o	o
112	70	160	111 0000	p	p

113	71	161	111 0001	q	q
114	72	162	111 0010	r	r
115	73	163	111 0011	s	s
116	74	164	111 0100	t	t
117	75	165	111 0101	u	u
118	76	166	111 0110	v	v
119	77	167	111 0111	w	w
120	78	170	111 1000	x	x
121	79	171	111 1001	y	y
122	7A	172	111 1010	z	z
123	7B	173	111 1011	{	{
124	7C	174	111 1100	|	|
125	7D	175	111 1101	}	}
126	7E	176	111 1110	~	~
127	7F	177	111 1111	DEL	DEL,RUBOUT

E

UNIX System Calls (System V)

access (2)   Determine accessibility of a file
acct (2)   Enable or disable process accounting
alarm (2)   Set a process's alarm clock
brk (2)   Change data segment space allocation
chdir (2)   Change working directory
chmod (2)   Change mode of file
chown (2)   Change owner and group of a file
chroot (2)   Change root directory
close (2)   Close a file descriptor
creat (2)   Create a new file or rewrite an existing one
dup (2)   Duplicate an open file descriptor
exec (2)   Execute a file
exit (2)   Terminate process
fcntl (2)   File control
fork (2)   Create a new process
getpid (2)   Get process, process group, and parent process IDs
getuid (2)   Get real user, effective user, real group, and effective group IDs
ioctl (2)   Control device
kill (2)   Send a signal to a process or a group of processes
link (2)   Link to a file
lseek (2)   Move read/write file pointer
mknod (2)   Make a directory, or a special or ordinary file
mount (2)   Mount a file system
msgctl (2)   Message control operations
msgget (2)   Get message queue
msgop (2)   Message operations
nice (2)   Change priority of a process
open (2)   Open for reading or writing
pause (2)   Suspend process until signal
pipe (2)   Create an interprocess channel
plock (2)   Lock process, text, or data in memory
profil (2)   Execution time profile
ptrace (2)   Process trace
read (2)   Read from file

semctl (2)	Semaphore control operations
semget (2)	Get set of semaphores
semop (2)	Semaphore operations
setpgrp (2)	Set process group ID
setuid (2)	Set user and group IDs
shmctl (2)	Shared memory control operations
shmget (2)	Get shared memory segment
shmop (2)	Shared memory operations
signal (2)	Specify what to do upon receipt of a signal
stat (2)	Get file status
stime (2)	Set time
sync (2)	Update super-block
time (2)	Get time
times (2)	Get process and child process times
ulimit (2)	Get and set user limits
umask (2)	Set and get file creation mask
umount (2)	Unmount a file system
uname (2)	Get name of current operating system
ulink (2)	Remove directory entry
ustat (2)	Get file system statistics
utime (2)	Set file access and modification times
wait (2)	Wait for child process to stop or terminate
write (2)	Write on a file

F

UNIX Library Functions (System V)

a64l (3c)	Convert between long integers and base-64 ASCII string
abort (3c)	Generate an IOT fault
abort (3f)	Terminate FORTRAN program
abs (3c)	Return integer absolute value
abs (3f)	FORTRAN absolute value
acos (3f)	FORTRAN arccosine intrinsic function
aimag (3f)	FORTRAN imaginary part of complex argument
aint (3f)	FORTRAN integer part intrinsic function
asin (3f)	FORTRAN arcsine intrinsic function
assert (3x)	Verify program assertion
atan (3f)	FORTRAN arctangent intrinsic function
atan2 (3f)	FORTRAN arctangent intrinsic function
atof (3c)	Convert ASCII string to floating-point number
bessel (3m)	Bessel functions
bool (3f)	FORTRAN bitwise Boolean functions
bsearch (3c)	Binary search
clock (3c)	Report CPU time used
conjg (3f)	FORTRAN complex conjugate intrinsic function
conv (3c)	Translate characters
cos (3f)	FORTRAN cosine intrinsic function
cosh (3f)	FORTRAN hyperbolic cosine intrinsic function
crypt (3c)	Generate DES encryption
ctermid (3s)	Generate filename for terminal
ctime (3c)	Convert date and time to string
ctype (3c)	Classify characters
cuserid (3s)	Get character login name of the user
dial (3c)	Establish an outgoing terminal line connection
drand48 (3c)	Generate uniformly distributed pseudo-random numbers
ecvt (3c)	Convert floating-point number to string
end (3c)	Last locations in program
erf (3m)	Error function and complementary error function
exp (3f)	FORTRAN exponential intrinsic function
exp (3m)	Exponential, logarithm, power, square root functions
fclose (3s)	Close or flush a stream
ferror (3s)	Stream status inquiries
floor (3m)	Floor, ceiling, remainder, absolute value functions

fopen (3s)	Open a stream
fread (3s)	Binary input/output
frexp (3c)	Manipulate parts of floating-point numbers
fseek (3s)	Reposition a file pointer in a stream
ftw (3c)	Walk a file tree
ftype (3f)	Explicit FORTRAN type conversion
gamma (3m)	Log gamma function
getarg (3f)	Return FORTRAN command-line argument
getc (3s)	Get character or word from stream
getcwd (3c)	Get pathname of current working directory
getenv (3c)	Return value of environment name
getenv (3f)	Return FORTRAN environment variable
getgrent (3c)	Obtain
getlogin (3c)	Get login name
getopt (3c)	Get option letter from argument vector
getpass (3c)	Read a password
getpw (3c)	Get name from UID
getpwent (3c)	Get password file entry
gets (3s)	Get a string from a stream
getut (3c)	Access utmp file entry
hsearch (3c)	Manage hash search tables
hypot (3m)	Euclidean distance function
index (3f)	Return location of FORTRAN substring
l3tol (3c)	Convert between 3-byte integers and long integers
ldahread (3x)	Read the archive header of a member of an archive file
ldclose (3x)	Close a common object file
ldfhread (3x)	Read the file header of a common object file
ldgetname (3x)	Retrieve symbol name for object file
ldlread (3x)	Manipulate line number entries of a common object file function
ldlseek (3x)	Seek to line number entries of a section of a common object file
ldohseek (3x)	Seek to the optional file header of a common object file
ldopen (3x)	Open a common object file for reading
ldrseek (3x)	Seek to relocation entries of a section of a common object file
ldshread (3x)	Read an indexed/named section header of a common object file
ldsseek (3x)	Seek to an indexed/named section of a common object file
ldtbindex (3x)	Compute the index of a symbol table entry of a common object file
ldtbread (3x)	Read an indexed symbol table entry of a common object file
ldtbseek (3x)	Seek to the symbol table of a common object file
len (3f)	Return length of FORTRAN string
log (3f)	FORTRAN natural logarithm intrinsic function
log10 (3f)	FORTRAN common logarithm intrinsic function
logname (3x)	Return login name of user
lsearch (2c)	Linear search and update
malloc (3c)	Main memory allocator
matherr (3m)	Error-handling function
max (3f)	FORTRAN maximum-value functions
mclock (3f)	Return FORTRAN time accounting

memory (3c)	Memory operations
min (3f)	FORTRAN minimum-value functions
mktemp (3c)	Make a unique filename
mod (3f)	FORTRAN remaindering intrinsic functions
monitor (3c)	Prepare execution profile
nlist (3c)	Get entries from name list
perror (3c)	System error messages
plot (3x)	Graphics interface subroutines
popen (3s)	Initiate pipe to/from a process
printf (3s)	Print formatted output
putc (3s)	Put character or word on a stream
putpwent (3c)	Write password file entry
puts (3s)	Put a string on a stream
qsort (3c)	Quicker sort
rand (3c)	Simple random-number generator
rand (3f)	FORTRAN uniform random-number generator
regcmp (3x)	Compile and execute a regular expression
round (3f)	FORTRAN nearest integer functions
scanf (3s)	Convert formatted input
setbuf (3s)	Assign buffering to a stream
setjmp (3c)	Non-local goto
sign (3f)	FORTRAN transfer-of-sign intrinsic function
signal (3f)	Specify FORTRAN action on receipt of a system signal
sin (3f)	FORTRAN sine intrinsic function
sinh (3f)	FORTRAN hyperbolic sine intrinsic function
sinh (3m)	Hyperbolic functions
sleep (3c)	Suspend execution for interval
sputl (3x)	Access long integer data in a machine independent fashion
sqrt (3f)	FORTRAN square root intrinsic function
ssignal (3c)	Software signals
stdio (3s)	Standard buffered input/output package
stdipc (3c)	Standard interprocess communication package
string (3c)	String operations
strtol (3c)	Convert string to integer
swab (3c)	Swap bytes
system (3f)	Issue a shell command from FORTRAN
system (3s)	Issue a shell command
tan (3c)	FORTRAN tangent intrinsic function
tanh (3f)	FORTRAN hyperbolic tangent intrinsic function
termcap (3x)	Terminal independent operation routines
tmpfile (3s)	Create a temporary file
tmpnam (3s)	Create a name for a temporary file
trig (3m)	Trigonometric functions
tsearch (3c)	Manage binary search trees
ttyname (3c)	Find name of a terminal
ttyslot (3c)	Find the slot in the utmp file of the current user
ungetc (3s)	Push character back into input stream

Index

☐ Computer Dictionary

Contains over 12,000 entries with 1,000 new entries, most of which pertain to Robotics, Artificial Intelligence, and Factory Automation. Includes definitions, acronyms, abbreviations, and extensive cross-referencing. A must for teachers, scientists, computer personnel, engineers, students, and people in business. Charles J. Sippl.
ISBN 0-672-22205-1........................$24.95

☐ Crash Course in Artificial Intelligence

A detailed, self-study course in Artificial Intelligence. Discusses AI principles and methods, and provides introductory applications of AI through sample programs in Prolog and Lisp. An excellent book for programmers, students, and engineers who need a thorough understanding of AI. Louis Frenzel.
ISBN 0-672-22443-7........................$21.95

☐ Mobile Communications Design Fundamentals

Introduces you to mobile communications including cellular radio. This book is based on the physical interpretation of the unique mobile radio environment. It discusses related problems and ways of solving them by choosing properly designed parameters. Practical design method and curves are clearly presented, then followed by illustrations and examples. William C. Y. Lee.
ISBN 0-672-22305-8........................$34.95

☐ Cellular Mobile Telephone Guide

Invest the time to read this book before you invest dollars in a cellular mobile telephone. This book traces the history of mobile telephone systems, and then describes, in non-technical terms, both the pros and cons of this new service.
Andrew M. Seybold.
ISBN 0-672-22416-X $9.95

☐ Mastering Serial Communications

This intermediate/advanced book, is written for technicians and programmers interested in asynchronous serial communications. Part One explains the history and technical details of asynchronous communications, while Part Two addresses the specifics of the technical programmer with an emphasis on popular UARTS and pseudo-assembly language. Joe Campbell.
ISBN 0-672-22450-X $21.95

☐ Computer-Aided Logic Design

An excellent text to introduce you to logic design, using CAD (computer-aided design) programs for logic simulation and logic minimization, compatible with TRS-80®, Commodore 64™, and IBM® PC. Provides hands-on experience with CAD tools and covers combinational logic, sequential logic, finite state machines, and tri-state logic fundamentals using practical design examples.
Robert M. McDermott
ISBN 0-672-22436-4........................$19.95

☐ MS™-DOS Developer's Guide

If you have a working knowledge of 8088 ALC, this book will help you learn the tips and tricks needed to get your software running in the MS-DOS environment. The book offers assembly coding tips, explains the differences between MS-DOS versions, the MS-DOS bios, and higher-level language debuggers and aids.
Angermeyer and Jaeger.
ISBN 0-672-22409-7........................$21.95

☐ Principles of Digital Audio

The first comprehensive description of the fundamentals of digital audio technology. Details the complete audio digitization chain, beginning with the fundamentals of numbers and sampling, plus analysis of storage mediums and error protection. Includes a special chapter on the Compact Disc. For anyone who wants to improve the fidelity of recordings. Kenneth C. Pohlmann.
ISBN 0-672-22388-0........................$19.95

☐ Image Tubes

This ready reference examines the complex subject of image tube technology. A wide range of topics are included, such as electron optics, imaging, electron lenses, low light level intensification, photo-cathodes, secondary electron emitters, phosphor screens, and fiber optic plates.
Illes P. Csorba.
ISBN 0-672-22023-7........................$44.95

☐ Gallium Arsenide Technology

Experts from industry, academia, and government laboratories have joined together to present a composite and comprehensive view of this growing technology. Growth of GaAs, its properties and crystal structure, its use in digital ICs and microwave MESFETs, plus superlattice structures, heterojunction devices, detectors, and optical sources are all covered. David K. Ferry, Editor.
ISBN 0-672-22375-9........................$44.95

More Books from Sams and The Waite Group